SAS/ETS® Softwa
Applications Guide 2

Econometric Modeling, Simulation, and Forecasting

Version 6
First Edition

D. Chen
Nov. 25, 2003

SAS Institute Inc.
SAS Campus Drive
Cary, NC 27513

The correct bibliographic citation for this manual is as follows: SAS Institute Inc., *SAS/ETS® Software: Applications Guide 2, Version 6, First Edition: Econometric Modeling, Simulation, and Forecasting*, Cary, NC: SAS Institute Inc., 1993. 429 pp.

SAS/ETS® Software: Applications Guide 2, Version 6, First Edition

Contents

Part 2 ▪ Simulation   201

Part 3 · Forecasting 301

Reference Aids

Figures

Tables

x

Credits

Documentation

Design, Programming, and Production	Design, Production, and Printing Services
Proofreading	Heather B. Dees, Josephine P. Pope, David A. Teal, John M. West
Technical Review	James J. Ashton, Brent L. Cohen, Mark W. Craver, Anwar H. El-Jawhari, Minbo Kim, Gary S. Klonicki, Tae Yoon Lee, Mark R. Little, David M. Price, Donna E. Woodward
Writing and Editing	Patsy P. Blessis, Gary R. Meek, Patricia Glasgow Moell, James D. Seabolt

Software Development and Support

Complete software development, support, and quality assurance credits for
SAS/ETS software are listed in the reference documentation for this product.

xii

Acknowledgments

Hundreds of people have helped the SAS System in many ways since its inception. The individuals listed below have been especially helpful in the development of the procedures in SAS/ETS software. Acknowledgments for the SAS System generally are in base SAS documentation and SAS/STAT documentation.

A.R. Gallant	North Carolina State University
Marvin Jochimsen	Mississippi R&O Center
Robert Parks	Washington University
George McCollister	San Diego Gas & Electric
Phil Hanser	Sacramento Municipal Utilities District
Wayne Fuller	Iowa State University
Mary Young	Salt River Project
David Dickey	North Carolina State University
William Fortney	Boeing Computer Services
David Amick	Idaho Office of Highway Safety
Gregory Sali	Idaho Office of Highway Safety
Terry Woodfield	Risk Data Corporation

The individuals listed below have reviewed this book or provided examples.

George C. Davis	University of Tennessee at Knoxville
Terry G. Seaks	University of North Carolina at Greensboro

The final responsibility for the SAS System lies with SAS Institute alone. We hope you will always let us know your opinions about the SAS System and its documentation. It is through your participation that the progress of SAS software has been accomplished.

The staff of SAS Institute Inc.

Using This Book

Purpose

SAS/ETS Software: Applications Guide 2, Version 6, First Edition: Econometric Modeling, Simulation, and Forecasting provides applications and examples showing how to use SAS/ETS software for econometric modeling, simulation, and forecasting. This book is a companion volume of *SAS/ETS Software: Applications Guide 1, Version 6, First Edition: Time Series Modeling and Forecasting, Financial Reporting, and Loan Analysis*. This book documents Version 6 SAS/ETS software. It does not attempt to cover all features of the system, all statements for a procedure, or all options for a statement. Instead, this guide focuses on common tasks and explains simple ways of accomplishing them.

"Using This Book" contains important information to assist you as you read this book. This information describes the intended audience, the audience's prerequisite knowledge, and the book's organization and conventions. "Using This Book" also has an "Additional Documentation" section that provides references to other books containing information on related topics.

Audience

SAS/ETS Software: Applications Guide 2 is written for new or experienced users of the SAS System who want to learn how to use SAS/ETS software for econometric modeling, simulation, and forecasting.

Prerequisites

No prior experience with SAS/ETS software is required for you to use this book. The following table summarizes the SAS System concepts you need to understand in order to use *SAS/ETS Software: Applications Guide 2.*

You need to know how to	Refer to
invoke the SAS System at your site	instructions provided by the SAS Software Consultant at your site.
have a basic understanding of SAS System concepts, such as the DATA step	*SAS Language and Procedures: Introduction, Version 6, First Edition* for a brief introduction, or *SAS Language and Procedures: Usage, Version 6, First Edition* for a more thorough introduction.

It is assumed that you have some knowledge of statistical concepts, such as mean and variance. The type of knowledge required is roughly equivalent to that learned in a first course in college-level statistics.

SAS/GRAPH software is also used in some examples, but knowledge of SAS/GRAPH software is not a prerequisite for effective use of this book.

How to Use This Book

This section provides an overview of the organization and contents of this book.

Organization

SAS/ETS Software: Applications Guide 2 is divided in three parts.

Part 1: Econometric Modeling

Part 1 describes economic data and explains how to use SAS/ETS software to model economic data.

Chapter 1, "Background Information"
> contains an overview of the research process, and econometric tasks and goals. Processing economic data and preliminary analyses are also discussed.

Chapter 2, "Fitting OLS Regression Models"
> presents examples of fitting a Capital Asset Pricing Model and a Cobb-Douglas Production Function. The AUTOREG and SYSLIN procedures are used.

Chapter 3, "Using Dummy Variables"
> presents examples of fitting a Keynesian consumption function and a Capital Asset Pricing Model with and without dummy variables. The SYSLIN procedure is used to fit the models and test for significance of dummy variables.

Chapter 4, "Violations of the OLS Error Assumptions"
> presents examples of fitting a Monetarist model of inflation, which is corrected for autocorrelation with the AUTOREG and MODEL procedures. Chapter 4 also presents a model of state and local government expenditures, which is corrected for heteroskedasticity by the MODEL procedure.

Chapter 5, "Fitting Regression Models with Lagged Variables"
> presents examples of fitting a Koyck lag model and correcting for autocorrelation with the AUTOREG procedure. Chapter 5 also presents an example of fitting an Almon polynomial distributed lag model, correcting for autocorrelation, and restricting a lag endpoint using the PDLREG procedure.

Chapter 6, "Fitting Systems of Linear Equations"
> presents examples of fitting a Klein Model 1 (a small, simultaneous model of the United States economy) by seemingly unrelated regressions (SUR) and three-stage least squares (3SLS), as well as correcting the model for autocorrelation using the MODEL procedure. Chapter 6 also presents an example of fitting the United States wholesale market for pork by two-stage least squares (2SLS) using the MODEL procedure, and limited-information maximum likelihood (LIML) using the SYSLIN procedure.

Chapter 7, "Fitting Nonlinear Models"
    presents examples of fitting a logistic growth curve and a Constant Elasticity
    of Substitution production function using the MODEL procedure.

Chapter 8, "Fitting Time Series Cross-Sectional Models"
    presents examples of fitting a model of electricity consumption of three states
    over a 19-year period using the TSCSREG procedure.

Part 2: Simulation

Part 2 explains how to use SAS/ETS procedures to simulate economic data and
perform what-if and goal-seeking analyses. Many of the examples build upon
models fit in Part 1.

Chapter 9, "Introduction to Simulation"
    presents examples of fitting models for general revenue funds for North
    Carolina, comparing the models by goodness-of-fit statistics, then using the
    final fitted model for what-if simulation and goal-seeking analysis with the
    MODEL procedure.

Chapter 10, "Simulating Regression Models with Lagged Variables"
    presents an example of fitting a model for new single-family home sales, then
    using the models for static and dynamic simulation with the MODEL
    procedure. Chapter 10 also presents an example of fitting a Koyck lag model
    of consumer expenditures with the AUTOREG procedure, and then simulating
    the model using the SIMLIN procedure.

Chapter 11, "Simulating Systems of Linear Equations"
    presents an example of using the Klein Model 1 (fit in Chapter 6) for what-if
    simulation and goal-seeking analyses with the MODEL procedure. Chapter 11
    also presents examples of solving a supply-and-demand system and a profit
    model with the MODEL procedure.

Chapter 12, "Simulating Nonlinear Equations"
    presents an example of using the logistic growth-curve model (fit in Chapter 7)
    for historical simulation, Monte Carlo simulation, and goal-seeking analysis
    with the MODEL procedure. Chapter 12 also presents examples of solving a
    cubic polynomial cost function, a present-value model, and an income-growth
    model with the MODEL procedure.

Part 3: Forecasting

Part 3 explains how to use SAS/ETS procedures to forecast economic data. Many
of the examples build upon models fit in Part 1 and simulated in Part 2.

Chapter 13, "Introduction to Forecasting"
    presents an example of using the general revenue-fund model (fit and used for
    simulation in Chapter 9) for scenario forecasting using the AUTOREG
    procedure.

Chapter 14, "Forecasting Regression Models with Lagged Variables"
    presents an example of using the Koyck lag consumption function model (fit in
    Chapter 5 and used for simulation in Chapter 10) and the Keynesian
    consumption function (introduced in Chapter 3) for forecasting and comparing
    forecasts across time using the MODEL procedure. Chapter 14 also presents
    an example using the Almon polynomial distributed lag model (fit in

(Chapter 14, Forecasting Regression Models with Lagged Variables continued)

Chapter 5) for forecasting and examining the impact of polynomially distributed lagged effects across time using the AUTOREG and PDLREG procedures.

Chapter 15, "Forecasting with Linear Systems"
presents an example of using the Klein Model 1 (fit in Chapter 6 and used for simulation in Chapter 11) for scenario forecasting using the MODEL procedure. Chapter 15 also presents an example fitting a model of United States energy consumption with data for eastern states, and then using the model to forecast energy consumption for western states to validate the model, also using the MODEL procedure.

Chapter 16, "Combining Forecasting Methods"
presents an example of using the general revenue fund model (fit and used for simulation in Chapter 9) as a regression model, fitting a time series model and a transfer function model to the general fund revenue data, and then comparing and combining forecasts using the ARIMA and AUTOREG procedures.

Topics of time series modeling and forecasting, financial reporting, and loan analysis are found in *SAS/ETS Software: Applications Guide 1*.

Reference Aids

SAS/ETS Software: Applications Guide 2 contains a variety of reference aids to help you find the information you need.

Table of Contents	lists part and chapter titles and major subheadings with page numbers.
Glossary	provides concise definitions of statistical terms, SAS/ETS software terms, and general SAS software terms you find in this book.
Index	provides page numbers for specific topics and cross-references where appropriate.

Each chapter also contains special reference aids to help you find specific information.

Table of Contents	lists the page numbers of sections within a single chapter.
Learning More	lists SAS publications covering topics discussed within each chapter.
References	lists the full reference information for books and articles cited within each chapter.

Conventions

This section explains the various conventions used in presenting text, examples, and output in this book.

Typographical Conventions

SAS/ETS Software: Applications Guide 2 uses several type styles for presenting information. The following list explains the meaning of the typographical conventions used in this book.

roman	is the standard type style used for most text in this book.
UPPERCASE ROMAN	is used for SAS language elements that appear in text and syntax.
bold	is used for headings, matrices, and vectors.
bold italic	is used for italicized words when they appear in headings.
italic	is used for terms that are defined in text, for emphasis, for user-supplied values (in text or syntax), and for references to publications.
`monospace`	is used to show examples of SAS programs and SAS System titles, labels, and footnotes in text.
`code`	is used to show example code and SAS System messages that are set off from the text. In most cases, this book uses lowercase type for SAS code, with the exception of some title characters. SAS System messages appear in mixed case.
oblique	is used for user-supplied values in example code.

Conventions for Examples and Output

Each of the chapters in this book includes examples you can work through, showing some of the features of SAS/ETS software. Most examples build upon the previous examples within a chapter, and each example contains

☐ an explanation of the nature of the example

☐ the sample SAS program for you to submit

☐ a sample of the output you should see on your display

☐ a description or an interpretation of the results.

For some examples, SAS/GRAPH software is used to plot the results. You should be aware that SAS/GRAPH software does have system-specific characteristics. For further information and assistance, you may want to consult your SAS/GRAPH software documentation or the SAS Software Consultant at your site.

Additional Documentation

SAS Institute provides many publications about products of the SAS System and how to use them on specific hosts. For a complete list of SAS publications, you should refer to the current *Publications Catalog*. The catalog is produced twice a year. You can order a free copy of the catalog by writing to the address or calling the telephone number below:

> SAS Institute Inc.
> Book Sales Department
> SAS Campus Drive
> Cary, NC 27513
> 919-677-8000

SAS/ETS Software Documentation

In addition to *SAS/ETS Software: Applications Guide 2*, you will find these other documents helpful when using SAS/ETS software:

□ *SAS/ETS Software: Applications Guide 1, Version 6, First Edition* (order #A56008) provides applications and examples showing how to use the SAS/ETS software for time series modeling and forecasting, financial reporting, and loan analysis.

□ *SAS/ETS User's Guide, Version 6, First Edition* (order #A5849) provides detailed reference information on SAS/ETS procedures.

□ *SAS System for Forecasting Time Series, 1986 Edition* (order #A5612) provides examples of univariate and multivariate time series modeling and forecasting. An accompanying diskette (order #A5629) contains the SAS DATA steps and raw data for the examples in the book.

Documentation for Other SAS Software

The SAS System includes many software products in addition to SAS/ETS software. Several books about other software products that may be of particular interest to you are listed here:

□ *SAS/GRAPH Software: Introduction, Version 6, First Edition* (order #A56019) gets you started with SAS/GRAPH software if you are unfamiliar with it.

□ *SAS/GRAPH Software: Reference, Version 6, First Edition, Volume 1* and *Volume 2* (order #A56020) provides detailed reference information on SAS/GRAPH software.

□ *SAS Language and Procedures: Introduction, Version 6, First Edition* (order #A56074) gets you started if you are unfamiliar with the SAS System.

□ *SAS Language and Procedures: Usage, Version 6, First Edition* (order #A56075) provides new users task-oriented examples of the major features of base SAS software.

□ *SAS Language and Procedures: Usage 2, Version 6, First Edition* (order #A56078) provides intermediate level, task-oriented examples of the major features of base SAS software.

□ *SAS Language: Reference, Version 6, First Edition* (order #A56076) provides detailed reference information about all elements of base SAS software except for procedures.

□ *SAS Procedures Guide, Version 6, Third Edition* (order #A56080) provides detailed reference information about the procedures in base SAS software.

□ *SAS/STAT User's Guide, Version 6, Fourth Edition, Volume 1* and *Volume 2* (order #A56045) documents all procedures in Release 6.06 SAS/STAT software.

□ *SAS System for Linear Models, Third Edition* (order #A56140) describes uses of SAS procedures for regression, analysis-of-variance models, analysis of covariance, multivariate linear models, and univariate and multivariate repeated-measures analysis of variance.

□ *SAS System for Regression, Second Edition* (order #A56141) describes SAS procedures for performing regression analyses.

Part 1
Econometric Modeling

Chapter 1 Background Topics

Introduction

This book is organized in three parts: econometric modeling, simulation, and forecasting. Often, these tasks are performed sequentially. The model is fitted to the data, then simulated with historical data, and finally used for forecasting. In this book, these tasks are performed with economic models and data; however, they are also appropriate for sociology, psychology, and other specialized fields of study.

Whether you are an economist, sociologist, or psychologist, you typically follow the same general steps of applied research:

1. Define the question or goal.

2. Collect, refine, and transform the relevant data as required.

3. Perform preliminary analyses of the data.

4. Determine a suitable model, fit the model, and interpret the fitted model.

5. When simulation is required, assess how well the fitted model simulates the historical data.

6. When forecasting is required, use the fitted model.

7. Prepare the findings for presentation.

In some cases, you must repeat some or all of the general steps to arrive at the final model or to answer your research questions.

Figure 1.1 shows an overview of research tasks and illustrates how SAS software can be used to help answer research questions.

Figure 1.1
An Overview of
Applied Research

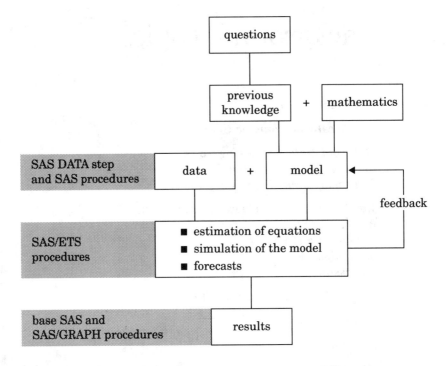

Empirical Questions or Goals

Empirical analysis always begins with a question or a goal. For example, you might have a goal of developing a simulation model to evaluate proposed changes in policy. The implied question is What if? Another goal might be to develop a forecasting model for tax revenues and then to forecast five years into the future.

Your goals for analysis differ depending on how you plan to use your model. For example, if your model is designed to estimate one or more parameters, you may not be interested in its ability to forecast future values of the dependent variable. However, if your model is designed to simulate relationships between variables for what-if analysis, you may not be interested in the magnitude and hypothesis tests of individual parameters.

Furthermore, the goal of your analysis usually indicates which type of analysis is appropriate. If your model is designed to answer questions about the magnitude of parameters or the importance of variables in the relationship, then estimation is most important. If your model is designed for simulation (policy analysis, what-if analysis, and goal-seeking simulation), then simulation is most important. If your model is designed to produce forecasts (future values of dependent variables), then forecasting is most important.

Data and Data Processing

To answer empirical economic questions, you need relevant data. Economic data are of the following three forms:

time series data
> are collected on one economic unit in successive, equally spaced time periods.

cross-sectional data
> are collected in one time period on several economic units.

time series cross-sectional data
> are collected on several economic units across several time periods. These data are also known as panel data.

You can obtain data from a wealth of resources, including government agencies and private companies, or you may need to collect new data through a survey. Many data sets are available on tapes or floppy disks. You can use the CITIBASE procedure in SAS/ETS software to extract time series data from the CITIBASE database and store them in a SAS data set. For reference information on PROC CITIBASE, see the *SAS/ETS User's Guide, Version 6, First Edition*.

In Release 6.08 of the SAS System, the DATASOURCE procedure extracts time series data from many data vendors and stores them in a SAS data set. The following vendor databases are supported:

□ Citicorp Database Services (CITIBASE)

□ Haver Analytics

□ International Monetary Fund

□ U.S. Bureau of Labor Statistics

□ U.S. Bureau of Economic Analysis

□ Standard & Poor's Compustat Services

□ Center for Research in Securities Prices (CRSP).

Refining and Transforming Data

Before estimating your model, you may want to use a DATA step to tailor your data set. You can use the DATA step to

□ transform data

□ create new variables

□ delete variables or observations

□ create new data sets

□ label variables

□ title the data and the output.

If your economic data require additional refining and transforming, you may want to use the following SAS/ETS procedures:

ARIMA   extends time series data, in addition to identifying, estimating, and forecasting ARIMA models.

EXPAND   converts time series data from one sampling interval or frequency to another, and interpolates between data points to fill in missing values.

X11   seasonally adjusts a quarterly or monthly time series using methods developed by the U.S. Bureau of the Census.

Examples of these tasks are found in *SAS/ETS Software: Applications Guide 1, Version 6, First Edition*. Reference information and mathematical details for these procedures are found in the *SAS/ETS User's Guide*.

Performing Preliminary Analyses

Preliminary analyses can reveal much about each individual variable and its relationship to other variables. As part of your initial analysis, you may want to use other SAS procedures, including the following:

CORR   computes correlation coefficients between variables.

GPLOT   creates high-resolution, two-dimensional plots. Several variables can be plotted on the same graph using the OVERLAY option.

G3D   creates high-resolution, three-dimensional plots.

MEANS   calculates summary statistics including means, variances, standard deviations, and sums.

PLOT   creates line-printer, two-dimensional plots. Several variables can be plotted on the same plot using the OVERLAY option.

SORT   sorts SAS data sets in ascending or descending order by one or more variables.

UNIVARIATE   produces descriptive statistics on data series.

Additionally, you may want to perform specialized preliminary analyses. For example, many time series methods require the analyzed series to be stationary; that is, the distribution of the time series is not time dependent. Many SAS procedures are available for specialized analyses. For examples of tests for time series stationarity, see *SAS/ETS Software: Applications Guide 1* and *SAS System for Forecasting Time Series, 1986 Edition* by Brocklebank and Dickey.

Empirical Analysis Questions and Tasks

Models for estimation can be diverse: they can consist of a single equation or a system of equations; they can be linear or nonlinear; and they can require restrictions on parameters. SAS/ETS software enables you to estimate and test hypotheses for all these types of models.

The development of your model is influenced not only by the characteristics of your data, but also by other questions:

- □ How many equations are required to model the relationship?

- □ If more than one equation is required, what relationships exist among the equations? For example, are the equations simultaneously determined?

- □ If your model consists of more than one equation, how many of the equations should be estimated? Only one? The whole system?

- □ What is the optimal number of independent variables to include in each equation?

- □ Are transformations of variables and equations appropriate?

- □ Is the model inherently nonlinear? That is, is there no appropriate transformation that would yield a linear model (in terms of the parameters)?

- □ Are any restrictions on parameters implied by theory? By physical realities?

- □ What are likely problems with the residuals? For example, do you anticipate problems with autocorrelation (lack of independence) or heteroskedasticity (nonconstant variance)?

Relevant SAS/ETS Procedures

The questions of interest, the goals of the analysis, and the type of data required affect your choice of statistical methods and SAS/ETS procedures. The following is a list of SAS/ETS estimation procedures and their major features. The BY statement in all of these procedures enables you to fit separate models for cross-sectional variables and other variables.

ARIMA	fits time series models that allow for an error term generated by an autoregressive integrated moving average (ARIMA) process (Box-Jenkins models). This includes transfer function models, and some distributed lag models.
AUTOREG	performs simple or multiple regression, allowing for a serially correlated error term that is generated by an autoregressive process.
FORECAST	forecasts time series using trend-adjusted autoregressive or exponential smoothing models.
MODEL	estimates, simulates, and forecasts single- or multiple-equation, linear or nonlinear models.
PDLREG	performs multiple regression with polynomial distributed lags and can include an error term generated by an autoregressive process.
SPECTRA	computes periodograms, smoothed spectral density estimates, and related statistics, including two white noise tests for a stationary time series.
STATESPACE	models the autocorrelation of a stationary vector time series in state space models.

SYSLIN	estimates parameters in interdependent systems of linear equations using least-squares and maximum-likelihood estimation methods.
TSCSREG	estimates parameters of time series cross-sectional models allowing for three common error structures:

□ variance components

□ first-order autoregressive with contemporaneous correlation process

□ mixed variance-component moving-average process.

Clearly, the accuracy and quality of your data affect the quality of your results; they also may affect your choice of estimation technique. For example, knowledge that some explanatory variables are measured with error implies that ordinary least squares is inappropriate.

Econometric Modeling

After preparing your data and performing preliminary analysis, you are ready to estimate your model. Typically, economic models are fitted using least-squares regression or maximum-likelihood estimation methods. Regression estimation methods relate one or more right-hand side (independent) variables to each left-hand side (dependent) variable. For example, a regression model can model consumption expenditures as a linear function of disposable income.

Regression models can be useful if you want to

□ develop a cause-and-effect model and estimate, test, and restrict the model parameters.

□ explain, simulate, and forecast the movements of one or more variables.

□ conduct policy experiments or what-if analyses.

□ solve for values of right-hand side variables (that is, goal-seeking analysis).

□ test economic theories.

Regression models require right-hand side, explanatory variables. If right-hand side variables are unavailable or unknown, then a time series method may be more appropriate. See Harvey (1981). Simple time series methods fit the time series to its own past values. For example, electricity consumption can be modeled on past values. More complex time series methods can relate several time series to each other and also include right-hand side variables. For example, construction contracts for new houses can be modeled on past values, mortgage interest rates, and housing starts.

Time series models can be useful if you want to

□ develop a model and estimate the parameters of the process underlying the time series

□ forecast the future behavior of the underlying process

□ develop a model of the relationships between various time series

□ forecast what effect changes in one time series may have on the future behavior of other time series.

Some questions are still more complex, requiring combinations of regression and time series methods. These combinations include time series cross-sectional methods and transfer functions. Time series cross-sectional models are often designed to compare the behavior of several cross-sectional groups across time. See Hsiao (1986). For example, electricity consumption over time and across several states can be modeled as a time series cross-sectional model. Time series cross-sectional data sets typically provide more data and degrees of freedom and more often generate efficient parameter estimates than either time series or cross-sectional data alone. Transfer functions enable you to incorporate the variability of the right-hand side variables into the forecasts of the dependent variable for more realistic forecasts. To fit a transfer function, you fit a time series model to the right-hand side variables, in addition to fitting a regression model to the dependent variable.

In general, when estimating models, you perform some or all of the following tasks. For some models, you may perform iterations of these tasks:

□ Select the appropriate estimation technique.

□ Examine the magnitude of the estimated parameters.

□ Perform individual and joint hypothesis tests of significance, that is, t and F tests.

□ Examine summary measures of goodness of fit, including R^2 and adjusted R^2.

□ Perform tests on the residuals to assess their conformance with standard error assumptions for ordinary least-squares (OLS) regression.

□ Plot predicted and actual values for comparison.

After estimating your model, you may want to test and validate it with individual and joint parameter hypothesis tests. Tests of the residuals may also assist in assessing the acceptability of your model. Additionally, some statistical tests are designed for use with certain types of data and do not provide useful information with other types. For example, the Durbin-Watson d statistic, used to test for correlation between time series residuals, does not provide useful information with cross-sectional data.

You can also use goodness-of-fit statistics to evaluate competing models. As you explore models, you may learn more about the relationship among the variables, and that knowledge may assist you in fine-tuning the model. The amount of information you desire from the model and the desired accuracy imply much about the effort required.

Simulation

You can validate your model through simulations with historical and conjectural data sets. You then assess the model's ability to re-create historical patterns or respond in appropriate directions. In general, when simulating models you perform the following tasks:

□ Simulate the model with historical data as a benchmark for simulations with conjectural data.

□ Examine goodness-of-fit statistics, and Theil statistics and their decompositions.

□ Perform what-if analysis; that is, solve for dependent variables with specific values of independent variables.

□ Perform policy analysis; that is, compare extrapolated status quo solution values with values resulting from a policy change.

□ Perform goal-seeking simulation; that is, solve for independent variables with specific values of dependent variables and other independent variables.

The MODEL and SIMLIN procedures are particularly useful for simulation. The SOLVE statement in PROC MODEL simulates or forecasts a model with input values you provide. The SIMLIN procedure reads a model file created in a SAS/ETS procedure and computes the reduced form. If you provide input data, then PROC SIMLIN uses the model to generate predicted values.

Forecasting

After you have fine-tuned your model, you are ready to apply it to the real world, either as tests of theory or as input for the decision-making process. Often, input for decisions consists of forecasted values. When forecasting models, you perform some or all of the following tasks:

□ Forecast using historical data, which provides a benchmark to assess the model's ability to forecast.

□ Examine goodness-of-fit statistics, and Theil statistics and their decompositions.

□ Acquire or create future values of the independent variables.

□ Forecast future values of the dependent variable or variables.

□ Calculate confidence intervals around forecasted values.

For some questions, you proceed from estimating to simulating and then to forecasting. You may want to continue iterating through the research process by applying your findings to new, even more realistic models.

Presenting Your Findings

After you have fitted, tested, and utilized your model, you may want to prepare your findings for presentation in plots, tables, and lists. In this book, you create plots with the following procedures:

PLOT   produces scatter plots.

GPLOT   produces high-resolution, two-dimensional plots.

G3D   produces high-resolution, three-dimensional plots.

For reference information on PROC PLOT, see the *SAS Procedures Guide, Version 6, Third Edition*. For reference information on the GPLOT and G3D procedures, see *SAS/GRAPH Software: Reference, Version 6, First Edition, Volume 1* and *Volume 2*.

In this book, you list data set observations with the PRINT procedure. For reference information on PROC PRINT, see the *SAS Procedures Guide*.

You may also want to use the REPORT and COMPUTAB procedures to create tables. For more information on PROC REPORT, see the *SAS Guide to the REPORT Procedure: Usage and Reference, Version 6, First Edition*. For reference information on PROC COMPUTAB, see the *SAS/ETS User's Guide*. For applications of the COMPUTAB procedure, see *SAS/ETS Software: Applications Guide 1*.

Chapter Summary

This chapter introduced SAS/ETS software procedures and discussed background topics to the research process. Preparing your data is crucial prior to its use in model estimation. Preliminary analysis of your data may reveal additional modeling considerations and refinement. Depending on the use of your model, the estimation, simulation, and forecasting goals may be very different. Lastly, the SAS procedures for presenting your findings were discussed.

Learning More

□   For full reference information on SAS/ETS procedures, see the *SAS/ETS User's Guide, Version 6, First Edition*.

□   For applications of SAS/ETS software for time series analysis, see *SAS/ETS Software: Applications Guide 1*. Also see *SAS System for Forecasting Time Series, 1986 Edition*, by Brocklebank and Dickey.

□   For reference information on the GPLOT and G3D procedures in SAS/GRAPH software, see *SAS/GRAPH: Reference, Version 6, First Edition, Volume 1* and *Volume 2*. Also see *SAS/GRAPH Software: Introduction, Version 6, First Edition*.

□   For more information on the CORR, MEANS, PLOT, SORT, and UNIVARIATE procedures, see the *SAS Procedures Guide, Version 6, Third Edition*.

□   For usage and reference information on the REPORT procedure, see *SAS Guide to the REPORT Procedure: Usage and Reference, Version 6, First Edition*.

References

Bails, D.G. and Peppers, L.C. (1982), *Business Fluctuations: Forecasting Techniques and Applications*, Englewood Cliffs, NJ: Prentice-Hall, Inc.

Harvey, A. (1981), *The Econometric Analysis of Time Series*, New York: John Wiley & Sons, Inc.

Hsiao, Cheng (1986), *Analysis of Panel Data*, New York: Cambridge University Press.

Johnston, J. (1984), *Econometric Methods, Third Edition*, New York: McGraw-Hill, Inc.

Koutsoyiannis, A. (1977), *Theory of Econometrics, Second Edition*, Totowa, N.J.: Barnes and Noble Books.

Pindyck, R. and Rubinfeld, D. (1991), *Econometric Models and Economic Forecasts, Third Edition*, New York: McGraw-Hill, Inc.

Chapter **2** Fitting OLS Regression Models

Introduction

This chapter reviews the ordinary least-squares (OLS) regression model and the role it plays in econometric analysis. Two examples, the Capital Asset Pricing Model (CAPM) and the Cobb-Douglas (CD) production function, illustrate how you can use OLS for econometric applications. In the first example, you use the AUTOREG procedure in SAS/ETS software to fit a CAPM, involving one left-hand side variable and one right-hand side variable. In the second example, you use the SYSLIN procedure in SAS/ETS software to fit a CD production function involving one left-hand side variable and two right-hand side variables.

In both examples, you assess the fit of your models using scatter plots and goodness-of-fit statistics. You also perform hypothesis tests on the parameters and fit the CD production function with a restriction on the parameter values.

Overview of OLS Regression

Ordinary least-squares (OLS) regression is a statistical technique for fitting a line to a set of data points. You can use OLS techniques to fit production functions (for example, the Cobb-Douglas production function), financial models (for example, the Capital Asset Pricing Model), supply and demand schedules, and models of learning and growth. After fitting your model, you may want to assess how well it fits the data. You may also want to perform statistical tests on the model parameters.

Regression analysis is concerned with cause and effect, that is, how the dependent variable responds to changes in the independent variable or variables. For example, when fitting a production function, you might want to know how output responds to changes in input levels. The inputs are the independent variables, and the output is the dependent variable. Similarly, you might want to fit a CAPM to find how a company's stock returns are affected by a change in the return of the market. The return of the market is the independent variable, and the return of the stock is the dependent variable.

The Regression Model

The multiple regression model with k independent variables and $k+1$ parameters to be estimated can be written as

$$Y_i = b_0 + b_1 X_{1,i} + b_2 X_{2,i} + \ldots + b_k X_{k,i} + \varepsilon_i$$

where

Y_i	is the value of the dependent or response variable for the ith observation.
b_0	is the intercept parameter to be estimated. If all k independent variables are zero, then $Y = b_0$.
$b_1, b_2, \ldots, b_k$	are the slope parameters to be estimated.
$X_{1,i}, X_{2,i}, \ldots, X_{k,i}$	are values of the independent or input variables for the ith observation.
ε_i	is the error associated with the ith observation.
n	is the number of observations.

The regression variables, the X's and Y, have various names, including the following:

Y	left-hand side variable, regressand, dependent variable, response variable, and endogenous variable
X's	right-hand side variables, regressors, independent variables, input variables, predetermined variables, explanatory variables, and exogenous variables.

Each estimated slope parameter, b_j, is interpreted as the change in the dependent variable, Y, resulting from a one-unit change in the regressor variable X_j *holding all of the other regressors constant.* For example, b_2 measures the change in Y associated with a one-unit change in X_2 while all the remaining regressors are held fixed. Thus, b_2 can be interpreted as the partial derivative of Y with respect to X_2, $\partial Y / \partial X_2$.

The error term, ε, represents the net effect of all forces not explicitly modeled. The true error values are estimated by the residuals, $\hat{\varepsilon}$, which are the differences between the actual Y values and those generated by the estimated equation, $\hat{Y}$. They have the form

$$\hat{\varepsilon}_i = Y_i - \hat{Y}_i = Y_i - \hat{b}_0 - \sum_{j=1}^{k} \hat{b}_j X_{j,i} \quad .$$

The least-squares objective is to find estimates of the parameters that minimize the sum of the squared residuals (SSE), where

$$SSE = \sum_{i=1}^{n} \hat{\varepsilon}_i^2 \quad .$$

The OLS regression model requires the following assumptions:

□ The model is correctly specified in terms of the right-hand side variable or variables and is linear in form (in terms of the parameters).

□ The errors are independent, identically distributed random variables with zero mean ($E(\varepsilon_i)=0$) and have a constant and finite variance ($Var(\varepsilon_i)=\sigma^2$).

□ The X values are fixed (as if you had chosen them), are not all the same value, have a finite variance, and are uncorrelated with the errors.

□ No exact linear relationship exists between two or more of the independent variables.

□ The additional assumption of a normal distribution of the errors allows the use of t and F distributions for hypothesis testing.

Violations of these assumptions can cause serious problems for estimating the model, testing the parameters, and interpreting the results.

For details of OLS regression formulas, required assumptions, and properties of OLS estimators, see Pindyck and Rubinfeld (1991) or Johnston (1984).

Fitting a Capital Asset Pricing Model

This section presents the steps to fit and test the standard Capital Asset Pricing Model (CAPM) using the AUTOREG procedure through the OLS method. The CAPM provides you with a formula for the expected return on an asset under the assumption that you know the return of the market. Securities analysts and investors use the CAPM to adjust their portfolio of assets. In this example, the CAPM is fitted using real data for the Tandy Corporation.

The Standard CAPM

The CAPM is an equation for predicting the return on assets. Investors are assumed to be interested only in the return on their assets and are actively searching for the highest return for a given level of risk. The relevant measure of risk and the relationship between expected return and risk for any asset (or portfolio of assets) can be determined by the CAPM. The basic time series CAPM equation, as developed by Black, Jensen, and Scholes (1972), is

$$R_i - R_f = \alpha + \beta(R_M - R_f) + \varepsilon_i$$

where

α   is the intercept parameter, often called Alpha in the finance literature. On average Alpha is expected to be zero.

β   is the slope parameter, often called Beta in the finance literature. It is the portion of an asset *i*'s return that is dependent on the market's rate of return and is interpreted as systematic, nondiversifiable risk.

ε   is the error term, interpreted as diversifiable risk (holding additional assets can eliminate this risk).

R_i is the return on asset *i* in time period *t*,

$$R_{i,t} = \frac{P_t + d_t - P_{t-1}}{P_{t-1}}$$

where P_t is the price of the asset at time period *t*, d_t is the dividends (if any) paid in time period *t*, and P_{t-1} is the price of the asset at time period $t-1$.

R_f is the return on a risk-free asset. The return on 30-day U.S. Treasury bills is often used in empirical data analysis.

$R_i - R_f$ is the risk premium of asset *i*, (that is, the excess return over the risk-free rate that investors require to compensate them for the additional risk of investing in asset *i*).

R_M is the return on the market portfolio (all assets). The Center for Research on Securities Prices (CRSP) at the University of Chicago provides an R_M based on the value-weighted transactions of all stocks listed on the New York and American Stock exchanges.

$R_M - R_f$ is the overall market's risk premium.

The relationship between the asset's expected return and market return is assumed to be linear. The higher an asset's Beta value, the riskier it is, and the higher its expected return should be. Furthermore, the relationship between the expected returns on any two assets is the difference in their Beta values.

   For more information about the CAPM, see Markowitz (1959), Sharpe (1985), and Black, Jensen, and Scholes (1972).

Introducing the TANDY Data Set

Before you can fit a CAPM regression, you need to create a SAS data set containing data on the market's rate of return, the risk-free rate of return, and an asset's rate of return. The asset chosen for this example is the common stock of the Tandy Corporation. Tandy markets personal computers and electronic hardware through Radio Shack stores. Data on the Tandy Corporation, and many other assets, are available from the Center for Research on Securities Prices.

The following DATA step reads monthly data from January 1978 through December 1987. You complete the DATA step by creating new variables containing the risk premiums for the Tandy Corporation's stock and the market. This DATA step creates a SAS data set named TANDY, reads data values into the variables R_M, R_F, and TANDY, and creates the dependent variable, R_TANDY, and the independent variable, R_MKT. The LABEL statement attaches meaningful labels to the variables.

```
    /* Creating the TANDY Data Set */
data tandy;
   input r_m r_f tandy aa;

      /* Creating New Variables */
   r_tandy = tandy - r_f;
   r_mkt = r_m - r_f;

   /* Labeling New Variables */
   label r_m='Market Rate of Return'
     r_f='Risk-Free Rate of Return'
     tandy='Rate of Return for Tandy Corporation'
     r_tandy='Risk Premium for Tandy Corporation'
     r_mkt='Risk Premium for Market';
   cards;
-.045 .00487 -.075   .010 .00494 -.004   .050 .00526  .124
 .063 .00491  .055   .067 .00513  .176   .007 .00527 -.014
 .071 .00528  .194   .079 .00607  .222   .002 .00645 -.100
-.189 .00685 -.206   .084 .00719  .086   .015 .00690  .085
 .058 .00761 -.046   .011 .00761 -.135   .123 .00769  .122
 .026 .00764 -.094   .014 .00772 -.148   .075 .00715  .096
-.013 .00728  .006   .095 .00789  .250   .039 .00802 -.005
-.097 .00913 -.037   .116 .00819  .170   .086 .00747  .037
 .124 .00883  .032   .112 .01073  .143  -.243 .01181 -.105
 .080 .00753 -.038   .062 .00630  .256   .086 .00503  .041
 .065 .00602  .446   .025 .00731  .167   .015 .00860  .157
 .006 .00895 -.015   .092 .01137  .212  -.056 .00977  .022
-.014 .01092 -.139  -.009 .01096  .082   .067 .01025  .299
-.008 .01084  .092   .064 .01255  .136  -.003 .01128 -.167
-.033 .01154  .032  -.031 .01169 -.063  -.164 .01054 -.008
 .062 .01003  .241   .069 .00816 -.037  -.039 .00740 -.046
-.079 .00949  .059  -.101 .00946 -.101  -.028 .01067 -.051
 .041 .00972  .053   .003 .00908 -.163  -.078 .00914  .023
-.006 .00714  .050   .122 .00503  .017   .008 .00563 -.026
 .136 .00620  .454   .049 .00614  .273   .014 .00648 -.042
 .065 .00646  .091   .028 .00599  .032   .043 .00686 -.004
 .097 .00652  .084   .080 .00649 -.010   .048 .00673 -.168
-.017 .00714 -.123  -.034 .00668 -.048   .000 .00702 -.083
-.082 .00678 -.058   .066 .00683  .082  -.012 .00693  .095
-.029 .00712 -.190  -.030 .00672 -.100   .003 .00763 -.008
-.003 .00741  .120  -.058 .00627 -.231   .005 .00748 -.037
-.058 .00771  .029   .146 .00852  .079   .000 .00830 -.100
-.035 .00688 -.096  -.019 .00602  .027  -.001 .00612  .005
 .097 .00606  .170   .012 .00586  .119   .008 .00650  .094
-.010 .00601 -.133   .019 .00512  .091  -.003 .00536  .087
```

```
 .012 .00562 -.119    .005 .00545  .063   -.055 .00571 -.011
 .026 .00577  .098    .059 .00540  .021    .013 .00479  .098
-.009 .00548 -.040    .049 .00523  .096    .048 .00508 -.047
-.009 .00444 -.058    .049 .00469  .094    .004 .00478 -.092
-.076 .00458 -.078    .049 .00343  .018   -.047 .00416 -.108
 .018 .00418  .242    .000 .00420  .094   -.005 .00382 -.023
 .148 .00454  .130    .065 .00437  .174    .037 .00423 -.118
-.025 .00207 -.119    .004 .00438 -.026    .038 .00402  .045
 .055 .00455  .087    .015 .00460  .027   -.015 .00520  .088
-.260 .00358 -.246   -.070 .00288 -.190    .073 .00277  .040
;
```

Once the data set is created, the PRINT procedure can be used to print the first several observations. The following is an interpretation of the PROC PRINT statements:

PROC PRINT
   invokes the PRINT procedure. The following options of the PROC PRINT statement are specified:

   DATA=*SAS-data-set*   specifies the data set. For this example, the TANDY data set is specified.

   (OBS=*number*)   specifies the number of observations to print. For this example, the first five observations are printed.

   LABEL   specifies the variable labels be printed.

VAR
   specifies the variables to print.

TITLE
   titles printed output.

The following SAS example code produces Output 2.1.

```
    /* Printing the First Five Observations */
proc print data=tandy (obs=5) label;
    var r_tandy r_mkt r_m r_f tandy;

       /* Titling the Data Set */
    title 'TANDY Corporation CAPM Example';
    title2 'First Five Observations TANDY Data';
run;
```

Output 2.1
The First Five Observations of the TANDY Data Set

```
                      TANDY Corporation CAPM Example
                      First Five Observations TANDY Data

                                                           Rate of
             Risk Premium      Risk       Market   Risk-Free   Return for
             for Tandy       Premium    Rate of    Rate of     Tandy
     OBS     Corporation    for Market   Return     Return    Corporation

      1       -0.07987       -0.04987    -0.045     .00487     -0.075
      2       -0.00894        0.00506     0.010     .00494     -0.004
```

(continued)

Output 2.1
(continued)

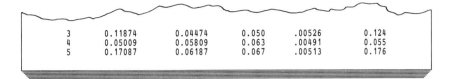

```
3      0.11874      0.04474      0.050      .00526      0.124
4      0.05009      0.05809      0.063      .00491      0.055
5      0.17087      0.06187      0.067      .00513      0.176
```

Interpretation of output

Output 2.1 confirms the creation of the TANDY data set and enables you to check your data for errors. It is good practice to confirm that newly created data sets contain the proper number of observations and variables, and that the correct values have been entered.

Plotting the TANDY Data Set

By plotting the dependent variable versus the independent variable, you can visually assess the appropriateness of your proposed model. The CAPM implies a linear model is appropriate. You should expect to observe some evidence of a linear trend in the TANDY data.

If the theory underlying your model and the findings of previous empirical studies do not suggest a model, then scatter plots of the data may suggest a model. When you plot some data sets, you may find visual evidence that a quadratic model or some other model is more appropriate.

The following SAS statements plot R_TANDY versus R_MKT. Note that you can specify up to ten TITLE statements to title your output. The following is an interpretation of the remaining SAS statements:

PROC PLOT
  invokes the PLOT procedure. The following options of the PLOT statement are specified:

  DATA=   specifies the TANDY data set be used.

  VPCT=   specifies the percentage of the page for the vertical height of the plot.

PLOT
  plots the dependent variable, R_TANDY, versus the independent variable, R_MKT, with the symbol "a".

The following SAS example code generates Output 2.2:

```
proc plot data=tandy vpct=65;
   plot r_tandy * r_mkt = 'a';
   title2 'Plot of Risk Premiums';
   title3 'Tandy Corporation versus the Market';
run;
```

Output 2.2
Plotting the Tandy
Corporation Risk
Premium Versus
the Market Risk
Premium

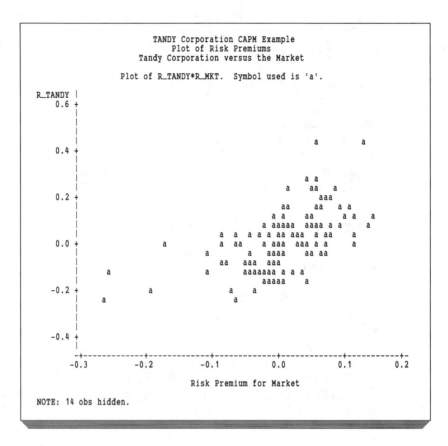

```
                    TANDY Corporation CAPM Example
                        Plot of Risk Premiums
                   Tandy Corporation versus the Market

                Plot of R_TANDY*R_MKT.  Symbol used is 'a'.

 R_TANDY |
    0.6  +
         |
         |
         |
         |                                             a        a
    0.4  +
         |
         |
         |                                      a a
         |                                   a   aa  a
    0.2  +                                       aaa
         |                                 aa      aa   a a
         |                               a a    aa       a a   a
         |                               a aaaaa aaaa a a       a
         |                           a a  a a aa aaa  a aa    a
    0.0  +                  a        a  aa   a aaa  aaa a a      a
         |                           a    a  aaaa    aa aa
         |                        aa   aaa  aaa
         |              a        a     aaaaaaa a a a
         |                                 aaaaa     a
   -0.2  +           a             a a
         |        a                      a
         |
         |
   -0.4  +
         |
         -+------------+------------+------------+------------+-----------+-
         -0.3        -0.2         -0.1          0.0          0.1         0.2

                           Risk Premium for Market

NOTE: 14 obs hidden.
```

Interpretation of output

The plot of the TANDY data set in Output 2.2 indicates that there is a positive relationship between the risk premium of the market and the risk premium of the Tandy Corporation's stock. This positive relationship seems reasonable: as the market returns increase, so should the return of most stocks, including the Tandy Corporation's.

Based on this visual evidence, a linear model between R_TANDY and R_MKT is reasonable. The next section shows you how to fit a linear CAPM to the TANDY data.

Fitting the CAPM to TANDY Data

The following statements use PROC AUTOREG to fit the CAPM to the TANDY data:

PROC AUTOREG
> invokes the AUTOREG procedure. The DATA= option specifies the TANDY data set be used.

MODEL
> specifies the model to be fitted. For this example, the dependent variable is R_TANDY, and the independent variable is R_MKT. By default, the AUTOREG procedure fits an OLS model. The DWPROB option requests the *p*-value (significance level) of the Durbin-Watson *d* statistic used in testing for autocorrelation of residuals.

The following SAS example code generates Output 2.3:

```
proc autoreg data=tandy;
   model r_tandy = r_mkt / dwprob;
run;
```

Output 2.3
Output from
Fitting the CAPM
for the Tandy
Corporation

```
                      TANDY Corporation CAPM Example

                           Autoreg Procedure

Dependent Variable = R_TANDY    Risk Premium for Tandy Corporation


                      Ordinary Least Squares Estimates

              SSE          1.317402   DFE               118
              MSE          0.011164   Root MSE     0.105662
              SBC          -191.299   AIC          -196.874
              Reg Rsq        0.3191   Total Rsq      0.3191
              Durbin-Watson  1.8914   PROB<DW        0.2739


        Variable    DF      B Value   Std Error   t Ratio Approx Prob

        Intercept    1   0.01065900     0.00970     1.099      0.2740
        R_MKT        1   1.05000106     0.14118     7.437      0.0001
```

Interpretation of output

The printed regression output in Output 2.3 contains two sections:

□ summary statistics for the model such as SSE, MSE, the Durbin-Watson *d* statistic, and its *p* value

□ parameter estimates and associated hypothesis test statistics.

From Output 2.3, you see that the estimated model is

R_TANDY = .010659 + 1.05 R_MKT

The intercept, $\hat{\alpha}$=.010659, is the value of R_TANDY if R_MKT=0. If $\hat{\alpha}$ is consistently greater than zero, then the Tandy stock would be returning an amount greater than expected. You would expect investors to purchase the Tandy Corporation stock, causing its price to rise and its return to fall.

The slope, $\hat{\beta}$=1.05, is the rate of change of R_TANDY as R_MKT changes. For example, if the return of the market above the risk-free rate increases by 1.0%, then you would expect the return of TANDY above the risk-free rate to increase by 1.05%.

Assessing the Fit of the Model

It is important to know how closely your model fits the data. SAS regression procedures automatically print statistics of fit. The key items are

□ the error sum of squares (SSE), the mean square error (MSE), and the root mean square error (Root MSE). The smaller the SSE, MSE, and Root MSE, the better the fit. The MSE in Output 2.3 is .011164; the Root MSE is .105662.

□ Schwarz's Bayesian criterion (SBC) and Akaike's information criterion (AIC). Akaike's information criterion (1974), Harvey's additional theory (1981), and Schwarz's Bayesian criterion (SBC) (1978) measure goodness of fit for a given estimation method, taking into account the number of parameters used to obtain that fit. The better the fit, the smaller both the SBC and AIC are.

You use MSE, Root MSE, AIC, and SBC to compare the fit of competing models to the same data.

□ The regression R^2 (Reg Rsq) and Total R^2 (Total Rsq) are measures of fit. R^2 in the two-variable model represents the proportion of the total variation of Y explained by the regression of Y on the independent variable, X. The R^2 of the OLS regression fitting the CAPM in Output 2.3 is .3191. This means that about 32% of the variation in the risk premium of the Tandy Corporation stock can be explained by the risk premium of the market. This is a reasonable value for CAPM regressions.

Note that Reg Rsq and Total Rsq are the same for OLS models. They differ when you specify a SAS/ETS regression procedure to weight the data, for example, to correct for autocorrelation or heteroskedasticity. For details on autocorrelation and heteroskedasticity, see Chapter 4, "Violations of the OLS Error Assumptions."

□ the Durbin-Watson d statistic and the p value (PROB<DW) for the d statistic.

The Durbin-Watson d statistic tests for autocorrelation and lack of independence of residuals, which is a common problem in time series data. The d statistic ranges from 0 to 4. A value close to 2.0 indicates you cannot reject the null hypothesis of no autocorrelation. In general, values close to 0 indicate positive autocorrelation, and values close to 4.0 indicate negative autocorrelation. The most common form of autocorrelation in economic data is first-order positive autoregression.

The calculated value of the d statistic in the CAPM for the Tandy Corporation is 1.8914 and has a p value of .2739. This value indicates that for this model, you cannot reject the null hypothesis of independent (nonautocorrelated) residuals at typically chosen levels of significance, that is, .10, .05, and .01. Moreover, the p value, .2739, indicates that you cannot reject the null hypothesis at levels of significance below .2739.

For a discussion of autocorrelation, see Chapter 3, "Autoregressive Models," in *SAS/ETS Software: Applications Guide 1, Version 6, First Edition*. For discussions of the Durbin-Watson test and violations of error term assumptions, see Chapter 4, "Violations of the OLS Error Assumptions," in this book.

Testing the Model

After fitting a model, you may want to test hypotheses about the model parameters. This section discusses the types of hypotheses you can test.

Individual parameter *t*-tests
The AUTOREG procedure automatically performs *t*-tests to test whether each parameter differs from zero. The parameter estimates, their standard errors, the *t*-statistics, and *p* values are displayed in Output 2.4.

Output 2.4
Parameter
Estimates,
Standard Errors,
t Ratios, and
p Values of
Output 2.3
Reprinted

```
                        TANDY Corporation CAPM Example

                              Autoreg Procedure

Dependent Variable = R_TANDY    Risk Premium for Tandy Corporation

      Variable      DF      B Value    Std Error    t Ratio Approx Prob

      Intercept      1     0.01065900   0.00970      1.099    0.2740
      R_MKT          1     1.05000106   0.14118      7.437    0.0001
```

The *p* values of these tests are .2740 and .0001, respectively. These *t*-statistics indicate that α is not different from zero at the .05 level while β is. You can conclude that changes in R_MKT affect the level of R_TANDY.

TEST statement with the SYSLIN procedure

In Output 2.4, the estimate of β is 1.05. When β is greater than 1, the Tandy Corporation returns are more volatile than market returns over the estimated period. To attract investors, an asset with returns more volatile than market returns must offer a higher average return than the market as compensation for the risk. To test the hypothesis that the Tandy stock had returns equal to the market ($\hat{\beta} = 1.0$) against the hypothesis that it did not, you can use the TEST statement in PROC SYSLIN.

The following SAS example code performs this *F* test. Specifying the NOPRINT option of the PROC SYSLIN statement suppresses the standard regression output. Output 2.5 shows the result.

```
proc syslin data=tandy noprint;
   model r_tandy = r_mkt;
   test r_mkt = 1;
run;
```

Output 2.5
Testing Whether $\hat{\beta}$
Equals 1.0

```
                        TANDY Corporation CAPM Example

                             SYSLIN Procedure
                      Ordinary Least Squares Estimation

Test:
     Numerator:     0.0014   DF:     1   F Value:   0.1254
     Denominator: 0.011164   DF:   118   Prob>F:    0.7239
```

Interpretation of output

In Output 2.5, the *F* statistic that β=1.0 is 0.1254 with an associated *p* value of .7239. There is little evidence that β is different from 1.0. Thus, there is little evidence that the returns of the Tandy stock were any more or any less volatile than the returns of the market.

Plotting Residuals and Predicted Values

You can use plots and graphs to make quick visual checks on the fit of your model and its assumptions. In the following sections, you create a scatter plot of residuals versus R_MKT with the PLOT procedure in base SAS software. You then create a high-resolution graph of the predicted and actual values with the GPLOT procedure in SAS/GRAPH software. The following sections discuss how to

□ Create an output data set containing the dependent variables, the residuals, and the predicted values.

□ Plot residuals versus the independent variable, R_MKT.

□ Plot actual and predicted values with upper and lower confidence limits versus R_MKT.

Creating the Output Data Set

By specifying options of the OUTPUT statement of PROC AUTOREG, you can create an output data set, TANDYOUT, containing predicted values, residual values, and upper and lower confidence limits. The OUTPUT statement follows the MODEL statement in PROC AUTOREG. The NOPRINT option of the MODEL statement suppresses the standard printed output. Use the following options of the OUTPUT statement:

OUT=*SAS-data-set*
> creates and names the output data set. For this example, the output data set is named TANDYOUT.

PREDICTED=*name*
P=*name*
> specifies that the predicted values be included in the output data set, in the variable specified. In this example, the predicted values are stored in the output data set as the variable P.

RESIDUAL=*name*
R=*name*
> specifies that the residual values be included in the output data set in the variable specified. In this example, the output data set stores the residual values in the variable R.

UCL=*name* and LCL=*name*
> request that the upper and lower confidence limits be included in the output data set. These confidence limits around the individual predicted values reflect the variation in the parameter estimates and the error term. For this example, these upper and lower confidence limits are named U and L, respectively.
>
> For confidence limits reflecting only the variation of the parameters, that is, the structural portion of the model, specify the LCLM=*name* and UCLM=*name* options.

ALPHACLI=*number*
> adjusts the confidence level of the confidence limits generated from both the structural and error parts of the model. For this example, the confidence limits at the $\alpha = .10$ level (often called 90% confidence limits) are specified for individual predicted values.

To adjust the confidence level of the confidence limits generated from only the structural part of the model, specify the ALPHACLM= option.

The following SAS example code creates the output data set TANDYOUT and prints the first five observations of the listed variables in Output 2.6.

```
proc autoreg data=tandy;
   model r_tandy = r_mkt / noprint;
   output out=tandyout p=p r=r ucl=u lcl=l alphacli=.10;
run;

proc print data=tandyout (obs=5) label;
   var r_tandy p r u l;
   title 'TANDY Corporation CAPM Example';
   title2 'First Five Observations of the';
   title3 'TANDYOUT Data Set';
run;
```

Output 2.6
Confirming the Contents of the Output Data Set TANDYOUT

```
                         TANDY Corporation CAPM Example
                          First Five Observations of the
                               TANDYOUT Data Set

           Risk Premium
             for Tandy
     OBS    Corporation        P           R          U          L

      1      -0.07987      -0.041705   -0.038165    0.13470   -0.21811
      2      -0.00894       0.015972   -0.024912    0.19187   -0.15993
      3       0.11874       0.057636    0.061104    0.23376   -0.11849
      4       0.05009       0.071654   -0.021564    0.24796   -0.10465
      5       0.17087       0.075623    0.095247    0.25199   -0.10074
```

Plotting the Residuals with PROC PLOT

Scatter plots of residuals can reveal obvious patterns which may suggest further analysis. The following SAS example code using PROC PLOT plots the residuals versus the independent variable. The VREF= option in the PLOT statement adds a reference line on the vertical axis. The plot appears in Output 2.7.

```
proc plot data=tandyout vpct=70;
   plot r * r_mkt = '*' / vref=0.0;   /* vertical reference line */
   title2 'OLS Residuals versus Market Risk Premium';
   title3;
run;
```

Output 2.7
Plot of Residuals from the TANDY CAPM Regression

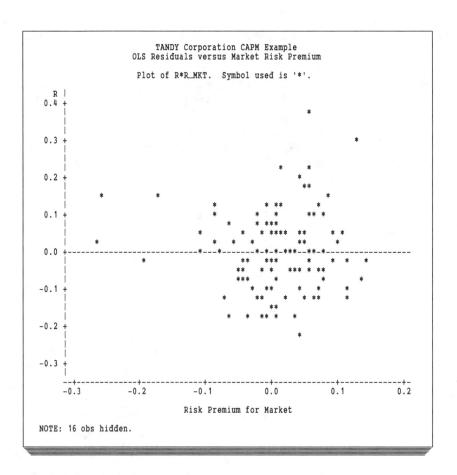

```
                    TANDY Corporation CAPM Example
               OLS Residuals versus Market Risk Premium

                  Plot of R*R_MKT.   Symbol used is '*'.

    R |
   0.4 +                                              *
       |
       |
   0.3 +                                                        *
       |
       |                                         *     *
   0.2 +                                             *
       |                                             **
       |            *              *               *         *
   0.1 +                             *        *   *        ** *
       |                             *      * ***
       |                       *     * ****  **    * *
       |              *        *  *  *        **     *
   0.0 +-------------------------*---*--------*-*-*-***-**-*-----------------
       |                          **  ***             *
       |                         **  * *  *** * **
       |                         ***    *           *
  -0.1 +                      *      * **  * * **    *
       |                           * **    * *  **   *
       |                              **
  -0.2 +                      *   *  ** *    *
       |                                   *
       |
  -0.3 +
       |
       --+-------------+-------------+-------------+-------------+-------------+-
        -0.3          -0.2          -0.1          0.0           0.1           0.2

                        Risk Premium for Market

NOTE: 16 obs hidden.
```

Interpretation of output

The residual scatter plot displayed in Output 2.7 does not reveal any obvious patterns; the residuals appear randomly distributed about the reference line.

Some residual scatter plots show no obvious pattern even though a statistical relationship exists. To protect against this, you may want to formally test whether the residuals violate the standard OLS error assumptions. Often, you want to test for autocorrelation (lack of independence) and heteroskedasticity (greater dispersion over some range of the data).

The PROC AUTOREG output displayed in Output 2.3 shows that the Durbin-Watson d statistic is not significant, indicating there is little evidence of autocorrelated residuals. You can test heteroskedasticity with the White Test, as discussed in Chapter 4.

Plotting Actual and Predicted Values

Plots of predicted and actual values can assist you in visually assessing the goodness of fit of your model. In general, for any given level of significance, the smaller the confidence interval width (the upper minus the lower confidence limit), the more precise the parameter estimates.

Using PROC PLOT

The following SAS example code using PROC PLOT plots the actual and predicted values with confidence intervals versus the independent variable, R_MKT. The output from this SAS program is not shown.

```
proc plot data=tandyout;
   plot

      /* Plotting R_TANDY vs R_MKT, Points Labeled 'a' */
   r_tandy * r_mkt = 'a'

      /* Plotting Predicted R_TANDY, p, vs R_MKT */
   p * r_mkt = 'p'

      /* Plotting Upper Confidence Limit, u, vs R_MKT */
   u * r_mkt = 'u'

      /* Plotting Lower Confidence Limit, l, vs R_MKT */
   l * r_mkt = 'l' / overlay;

   title2 'Actual and Predicted Risk Premium';
   title3 'versus Market Risk Premium';
run;
```

Using PROC GPLOT

You can use PROC GPLOT to create high-resolution, two-dimensional graphs, interpolate between data points, include vertical and horizontal reference lines, and overlay plots.

You should be aware that PROC GPLOT does have system-specific characteristics and requires that you specify a device driver and possibly additional options for some systems. You can specify a device driver to run SAS/GRAPH software (including PROC GPLOT) with the following GOPTIONS statement:

```
goptions device=device-driver-name;
```

For more information on specifying device drivers, see *SAS/GRAPH Software: Reference, Version 6, First Edition, Volume 1 and Volume 2.*

All of the PROC GPLOT examples in this book are run with the following graphics options. To make sure that your graphs look as much as possible like the examples in this book, submit the following program statement:

```
goptions reset=global
         gunit=pct
         cback=white border
         htitle=6
         htext=3
         ftext=swissb
         colors=(black);
```

In chapters containing more than one PROC GPLOT example, the PROC GPLOT code is preceded by

```
goptions reset=symbol;
```

This GOPTIONS statement resets the symbols for each plot. After ending your SAS/GRAPH session, the graphics options are reset to the default values.

For full reference information about the GOPTIONS statement and PROC GPLOT, see Chapter 12, "The GOPTIONS Statement," and Chapter 31, "The GPLOT Procedure," in *SAS/GRAPH Software: Reference.*

Prior to using PROC GPLOT in this example, use the SORT procedure to sort the data by the variable R_MKT. The DATA step uses array processing to create one data record per data point and a legend for the plot. The DO statement designates a group of statements to be executed as a unit until a matching END statement is encountered.

After sorting the data and using array processing, you use PROC GPLOT to plot the actual and predicted values with confidence intervals versus the independent variable, R_MKT. The following is an interpretation of the statements:

PROC GPLOT
  invokes the interactive GPLOT procedure. The DATA= option specifies REGDATA as the input data set.

PLOT
  specifies the variables to be plotted. The following options of the PLOT statement are specified:

  HAXIS=   specifies major tick marks for the horizontal axis.

  HMINOR=   specifies the number of minor tick marks between each major tick mark on the horizontal axis.

  VAXIS=   specifies major tick marks for the vertical axis.

  VMINOR=   specifies the number of minor tick marks between each major tick mark on the vertical axis.

SYMBOL
  creates symbols for the graph. The following options of the SYMBOL statement are specified:

  I=JOIN   interpolates between each point.

  V=   creates a symbol for the plotted variable.

  FONT=   specifies a font.

  L=   specifies the type of interpolation line between points.

AXIS
  specifies the axes of the graph. The following options of the AXIS statement are specified:

  LABEL=   labels the axes.

  ANGLE=   specifies the angle of the axes labels, where 0=horizontal and 90=vertical.

  ORDER=   specifies the range and order of major tick marks on the axes.

TITLE
> specifies the graph title.

QUIT
> ends the interactive GPLOT session.

You may need to change some options to match the requirements of your specific device driver or to produce desired results. The following SAS program produces the plot shown in Output 2.8.

```
      /* Sorting the Data */
proc sort data=tandyout;
   by r_mkt;
run;

      /* Creating Arrays for Plotting the Data */
data regdata(keep=y_value pt_type r_mkt);
   set tandyout;
   label pt_type='Observation Type';
   array regvar{4} r_tandy p l u;
   array varlabel{4} $12 _temporary_
     ('Actual' 'Predicted' 'Lower Limits' 'Upper Limits');
   do i=1 to 4;
      y_value=regvar{i};      /* create 1 record per data point */
      pt_type=varlabel{i};    /* label type of data point       */
      output;
   end;
run;

      /* Plotting the Data */
proc gplot data=regdata;
   plot y_value*r_mkt=pt_type / haxis=axis1 hminor=4 vaxis=axis2 vminor=4;
   symbol1 v=* h=3.5 pct font=swissb color=black;
   symbol2 i=join font=swissb l=2 color=blue;
   symbol3 i=join font=swissb l=1 color=green;
   symbol4 i=join font=swissb l=2 color=red;
   axis1 order=(-.3 to .15 by .05);
   axis2 label=(angle=90 'Tandy Corp. Risk Premium')
         order=(-.5 to .5 by .25);
   title1 "Actual and Predicted Values";
   title2 "with Upper and Lower Confidence Limits";
run;
quit;
```

Output 2.8
Plot of Actual and
Predicted Values
with Confidence
Intervals

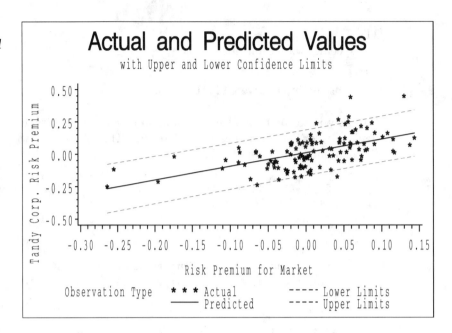

Interpretation of output

Output 2.8 shows that the actual returns are distributed around the predicted values and that they appear to have a constant variance. The scatter plot displays

□ the actual data values as asterisks

□ the estimated line (predicted values) as a solid line

□ the $\alpha=.10$ (90%) upper and lower confidence limits as dashed lines.

The 90% confidence limits provide a range of the Tandy Corporation's risk premium values that you expect to contain the actual value, on average, 90% of the time.

Fitting a Production Function

This section shows you how to fit a multiple regression model, test hypotheses about the parameters, and refit the model with restrictions placed on the estimated parameters using PROC SYSLIN. These tasks are illustrated using a Cobb-Douglas production function. A Cobb-Douglas production function allows the inputs to display diminishing marginal productivity, allows for input substitution, and includes a scale parameter to account for technology.

The Cobb-Douglas Production Function

The Cobb-Douglas (CD) production function was used by Cobb and Douglas to study the value shares of capital and labor in the value of national output (1928). Suppressing the observational subscript *i* the CD production function is

$$Y = a\ L^{b_1}K^{b_2}v$$

where the variables are

Y   an index of the U.S. GNP in constant dollars

L   a labor-input index

K   a capital-input index

v   a multiplicative random error.

The parameters are

a   a technology parameter

b_1 intensity of labor use parameter

b_2 intensity of capital use parameter.

In this form, the model is nonlinear and, therefore, computationally difficult to estimate. You can linearize the model by taking natural logarithms of both sides of the equation:

$$\ln(Y) = b_0 + b_1\ln(L) + b_2\ln(K) + \varepsilon$$

where $b_0=\ln(a)$ and $\varepsilon=\ln(v)$. The transformed model requires all the usual assumptions of multiple linear regression. If the theory underlying your model indicates that *v* and not ε is distributed normally, then your model should be estimated in its original form through nonlinear techniques, which are described in Chapter 7, "Fitting Nonlinear Models."

Recall that the estimated parameters are interpreted as partial derivatives of the dependent variable with respect to the independent variables. In the model transformed by taking natural logarithms, the estimated parameters are further interpreted as elasticities, that is, ratios of percentage rates of changes.

For more information about the CD production function and its use, see Cobb and Douglas (1928) or microeconomics texts.

Introducing the PROD Data Set

You first need to create a SAS data set containing values for GNP (Y), labor input (L), and capital input (K). The PROD data set contains variables Y, L, and K, which are annual observations from 1946 through 1967, as described in Christensen and Jorgenson (1970).

The following SAS example code creates the PROD data set containing new variables created with the natural logarithmic function, LOG, in assignment statements. A PROC PRINT step prints the first five observations, shown in Output 2.9.

```
data prod;
   input y l k aa;
      ln_y = log(y);
      ln_l = log(l);
      ln_k = log(k);
   label ln_y = 'Natural Log of US GNP Index'
      ln_l = 'Natural Log of Labor-Input Index'
      ln_k = 'Natural Log of Capital-Input Index';
   cards;
274.0 213.4  97.2    279.9 223.6 105.9    297.6 228.2 113.0
297.7 221.9 114.9    328.9 228.8 124.1    351.4 239.0 134.5
360.4 241.7 139.7    378.9 245.2 147.4    375.8 237.4 148.9
406.7 245.9 158.6    416.3 251.6 167.1    422.8 251.5 171.9
418.4 245.1 173.1    445.7 254.9 182.5    457.3 259.6 189.0
466.3 258.1 194.1    495.3 264.6 202.3    515.5 268.5 205.4
544.1 275.4 215.9    579.2 285.3 225.0    615.6 297.4 236.2
631.1 305.0 247.9
;

proc print data=prod (obs=5) label;
   var y ln_y l ln_l k ln_k;
   title 'Cobb-Douglas Production Function Example';
   title2 'First Five Observations of PROD Data Set';
run;
```

Output 2.9
The First Five Observations of the PROD Data Set

```
               Cobb-Douglas Production Function Example
                First Five Observations of PROD Data Set

                          Natural              Natural              Natural
                          Log of US            Log of               Log of
                          GNP                  Labor-Input          Capital-Input
     OBS   Y    Index     L      Index     K        Index
      1   274.0  5.61313  213.4  5.36317   97.2    4.57677
      2   279.9  5.63443  223.6  5.40986  105.9    4.66250
      3   297.6  5.69575  228.2  5.43022  113.0    4.72739
      4   297.7  5.69609  221.9  5.40223  114.9    4.74406
      5   328.9  5.79575  228.8  5.43285  124.1    4.82109
```

Fitting the CD Production Function

You can use the PROD data set to estimate a national CD production function. The following SAS example code using PROC SYSLIN fits the transformed model. The following is an interpretation of the SAS statements:

PROC SYSLIN
  invokes the SYSLIN procedure. The DATA= option requests the PROD data set.

MODEL

specifies the equation to be fit. For this example, the dependent variable is LN_Y, and the two independent variables are LN_L and LN_K.

The following SAS example code fits the linearized Cobb-Douglas production function. Output 2.10 shows the result.

```
proc syslin data=prod;
   model ln_y = ln_l ln_k;
run;
```

Output 2.10
Multiple
Regression
Example, a
National
Cobb-Douglas
Production
Function

```
               Cobb-Douglas Production Function Example

                          SYSLIN Procedure
                    Ordinary Least Squares Estimation
  Model: LN_Y
  Dependent variable: LN_Y Natural Log of US GNP Index

                         Analysis of Variance

                            Sum of        Mean
        Source      DF     Squares       Square      F Value     Prob>F

        Model        2     1.28373      0.64187     1757.188     0.0001
        Error       19     0.00694      0.00037
        C Total     21     1.29067

                 Root MSE      0.01911     R-Square      0.9946
                 Dep Mean      6.02384     Adj R-SQ      0.9941
                 C.V.          0.31728

                        Parameter Estimates

                      Parameter      Standard     T for H0:
        Variable  DF   Estimate         Error    Parameter=0    Prob > |T|

        INTERCEP   1   -2.232172      0.650909      -3.429        0.0028
        LN_L       1    0.943981      0.168588       5.599        0.0001
        LN_K       1    0.597394      0.058141      10.275        0.0001

                        Variable
        Variable  DF     Label

        INTERCEP   1   Intercept
        LN_L       1   Natural Log of Labor-Input Index
        LN_K       1   Natural Log of Capital-Input Index
```

Interpretation of output

Output 2.10 from PROC SYSLIN contains two main sections:

□   Analysis of Variance containing the usual statistics

□   Parameter Estimates containing the estimates, the degrees of freedom, standard errors, *t*-tests, and *p* values.

From the output, you can see that the estimated model is

LN_Y = − 2.232172 + .943981 LN_L + .597394 LN_K

The intercept, $\hat{b}_0 = -2.232172$, is a scale parameter measuring technology use. Over time, Y changes through growth in K, L, and technology. Growth in Y not attributable to L and K is due to growth in technology.

The first slope parameter, $\hat{b}_1 = .943981$, is the labor input elasticity. If the labor input is increased by 1% (while the capital input is held constant), then you expect the GNP index to rise by .944%.

The second slope parameter, $\hat{b}_2 = .597394$, is the capital input elasticity. If the capital input is increased by 1% (while the labor index is held constant), then you expect the GNP index to rise by .597%.

Assessing the Fit of the Model

You can measure the goodness of fit of multiple regression models with the R^2 and adjusted R^2. You can interpret R^2 as the proportion of the variation in LN_Y explained by the model. In Output 2.10, the R^2 is .9946, implying that the model explains 99.46% of the variation in the dependent variable.

In terms of R^2, adjusted R^2 is defined as

$$\text{adjusted } R^2 = 1 - (1 - R^2)\frac{n-1}{n-k}$$

where n is the number of observations and k is the number of independent variables.

R^2 is always greater than or equal to adjusted R^2 (Adj R-SQ). In Output 2.10, the adjusted R^2 is .9941. R^2 does not take into account the number of independent variables you use in the model, whereas the adjusted R^2 does. Adjusted R^2, in effect, reduces R^2 proportionally to the number of independent variables in the model.

Testing the Model

In multiple regression models, there are many hypothesis tests you may want to perform involving one or more estimated parameters. Examples of such tests include the following:

□ Are all slope parameters equal to zero?

□ Are any individual parameters different from zero?

□ Is a linear combination of two (or more) parameters different from zero?

The first and second tests are automatically performed for you by PROC SYSLIN and are listed as "F Value" and "T for HO: Parameter=0," respectively, in the regression output. The third test can be performed with a TEST statement in PROC SYSLIN.

The model F test

The first test you want to perform on the estimated model is: Are all of the slope parameters equal to zero? In other words, is there a statistically significant linear relationship between the dependent variable and any of the independent variables? The F statistic (labeled "F value") and its p value (labeled "Prob>F") are automatically calculated for you as part of the regression analysis in the Analysis of Variance section. In Output 2.10, the F statistic is 1757.188 with a p value $p<.0001$. After performing this joint test, you know that at least one and possibly both of the parameters differ from zero. You can perform individual t-tests to test each estimated parameter.

For more information about the derivation and form of the *F* tests, see Pindyck and Rubinfeld (1991, pp. 110—117) or Johnston (1984, pp. 212—225).

Individual parameter *t* tests

The SYSLIN procedure automatically tests whether each parameter differs from zero with individual *t*-tests. The *t*-statistics (labeled "T for HO: Parameter=0") for the parameters in Output 2.10 are reprinted in Output 2.11.

Output 2.11
Parameter Estimates, Standard Errors, t Statistics, and p Values Reprinted from Output 2.10

```
                    Cobb-Douglas Production Function Example

                              SYSLIN Procedure
                       Ordinary Least Squares Estimation

        Model: LN_Y
        Dependent variable: LN_Y Natural Log of US GNP Index

                              Parameter Estimates

                          Parameter      Standard     T for HO:
            Variable  DF    Estimate         Error   Parameter=0    Prob > |T|

            INTERCEP   1   -2.232172      0.650909        -3.429        0.0028
            LN_L       1    0.943981      0.168588         5.599        0.0001
            LN_K       1    0.597394      0.058141        10.275        0.0001

                          Variable
            Variable  DF   Label

            INTERCEP   1   Intercept
            LN_L       1   Natural Log of Labor-Input Index
            LN_K       1   Natural Log of Capital-Input Index
```

The *t*-tests in Output 2.10 have low *p* values (labeled "Prob > | T | ") of .0028, .0001, and .0001, respectively. These *t*-statistics indicate that each parameter is different from zero at the .01 level.

Testing a linear combination of parameters

You may want to test a linear combination of the estimated parameters with the TEST statement. For example, you could test the returns to scale of an estimated production function. If the input variables L and K of the production function $Y=f(L,K)$ are multiplied by a nonzero factor, p, the production function exhibits constant returns to scale if $pY=f(pL,pK)$. For example, a doubling of all inputs doubles the output.

For the CD production function, constant returns to scale occur only if $b_1+b_2=1$. Moreover, if a CD production function exhibits constant returns (and the input markets are assumed to be competitive), then the parameters b_1 and b_2 are the input shares of cost for the output.

You can test whether a CD production function exhibits constant returns to scale with a TEST statement in PROC SYSLIN. Note that you can suppress the standard regression output by specifying the NOPRINT option in the MODEL statement.

```
proc syslin data=prod;
   model ln_y = ln_l ln_k / noprint;
   test ln_l + ln_k = 1;
run;
```

Note that TEST statements follow MODEL statements in PROC SYSLIN. The previous code generates Output 2.12.

Output 2.12
Testing a Linear Combination of the Estimated Parameters

```
                   Cobb-Douglas Production Function Example

                             SYSLIN Procedure
                     Ordinary Least Squares Estimation

   Test:
       Numerator:   0.008298   DF:    1   F Value:  22.7155
       Denominator: 0.000365   DF:   19   Prob>F:    0.0001
```

Interpretation of output

The F statistic of Output 2.12 has a value of 22.7155 and p value of .0001. This indicates the null hypothesis, $b_1 + b_2 = 1$, should be rejected. The production function does not reflect constant returns to scale.

For additional information on testing linear combinations of the estimated parameters, see Johnston (1984, pp. 181—189).

Fitting a Restricted Model

In estimating production functions, you may want to impose the restriction of constant returns to scale. In the log-log, two-input CD production function, constant returns to scale can be imposed by restricting $b_1 + b_2 = 1$.

You can impose a linear restriction on the parameters of the model with a RESTRICT statement of the form

```
restrict ln_l + ln_k = 1;
```

The following SAS example code using a RESTRICT statement in PROC SYSLIN restricts the sum of b_1 and b_2 to one.

```
proc syslin data=prod;
   model ln_y = ln_l ln_k;
   restrict ln_l + ln_k = 1;
run;
```

Note that RESTRICT statements in PROC SYSLIN follow MODEL statements. The previous code generates Output 2.13.

Output 2.13
Restricting a
Linear
Combination of
the Estimated
Parameters

```
                    Cobb-Douglas Production Function Example

                              SYSLIN Procedure
                      Ordinary Least Squares Estimation

Model: LN_Y
Dependent variable: LN_Y Natural Log of US GNP Index

                          Analysis of Variance

                              Sum of        Mean
        Source       DF      Squares      Square    F Value      Prob>F

        Model         1      1.27543     1.27543   1674.037      0.0001
        Error        20      0.01524     0.00076
        C Total      21      1.29067

              Root MSE      0.02760    R-Square      0.9882
              Dep Mean      6.02384    Adj R-SQ      0.9876
              C.V.          0.45822

                          Parameter Estimates

                     Parameter     Standard    T for H0:
        Variable DF   Estimate        Error   Parameter=0    Prob > |T|

        INTERCEP  1   0.869683     0.015557       55.904       0.0001
        LN_L      1   0.147937     0.033097        4.470       0.0002
        LN_K      1   0.852063     0.033097       25.745       0.0001
        RESTRICT -1   0.015327     0.004644        3.300       0.0036

                     Variable
        Variable DF  Label

        INTERCEP  1  Intercept
        LN_L      1  Natural Log of Labor-Input Index
        LN_K      1  Natural Log of Capital-Input Index
        RESTRICT -1
```

Interpretation of output

The estimated slope parameters in the unrestricted model displayed in
Output 2.10 are $\hat{b}_1 = .943981$ and $\hat{b}_2 = .597394$. Their sum is greater than one.
The estimated slope parameters in the restricted model displayed in Output 2.13
are $\hat{b}_1 = .147937$ and $\hat{b}_2 = .852063$. Their sum is exactly 1.0. The estimated
production function now has constant returns to scale.

The t-test of this linear restriction has a t-statistic (labeled "T for H0:
Parameter=0") of 3.300 with a p value of .0036 and is different from zero at the
.05 level. You conclude that the restriction is active and binding, that is, it is
constraining the magnitudes of the estimated parameters.

The restriction has a negative degree of freedom because there is one fewer
independent parameter to estimate. For example, if b_1 is estimated, then
$b_2 = 1 - b_1$. If a restriction cannot be applied, PROC SYSLIN sets the restriction
parameter, RESTRICT, to zero, and degrees of freedom are listed as zero.

The restriction parameter, RESTRICT, reflects the rate of change of SSE as
the restriction is changed. Specifically, if the restriction is changed by a small
amount, γ, then SSE is changed by RESTRICT $\times 2\gamma$. If the restriction parameter
is zero, the restricted estimates are the same as the unrestricted estimates, and a
change in either direction increases the SSE.

For more information about linear restrictions of estimated parameters, see
Johnston (1984, pp. 204–207), and Pringle and Raynor (1971).

Chapter Summary

This chapter has given an overview of the AUTOREG and SYSLIN procedures in SAS/ETS software. Simple and multiple regression analyses using real economic data were presented. These examples demonstrated how to

□   create new variables

□   list (print) data sets

□   fit models using the AUTOREG and SYSLIN procedures

□   assess the fit of models

□   plot data using PROC PLOT

□   test the estimated parameters individually and jointly

□   plot residuals using PROC PLOT

□   plot predicted and actual values and confidence limits using the GPLOT procedure in SAS/GRAPH software

□   restrict parameters.

Learning More

□   For more information on analysis of variance (ANOVA), see Chapter 2, "Introduction to Analysis-of-Variance Procedures," and Chapter 13, "The ANOVA Procedure," in *SAS/STAT User's Guide, Version 6, Fourth Edition, Volume 1.*

□   The GOPTIONS statement and PROC GPLOT are discussed in Chapter 12, "The GOPTIONS Statement," and Chapter 31, "The GPLOT Procedure," in *SAS/GRAPH Software: Reference.*

□   Logarithmic transformations and other data step transformations are discussed in Chapter 11, "SAS Functions," in *SAS Language: Reference, Version 6, First Edition.*

□   The PLOT procedure is discussed in Chapter 25, "The PLOT Procedure," in the *SAS Procedures Guide, Version 6, Third Edition.*

□   The REG procedure is discussed in Chapter 36, "The REG Procedure," in the *SAS/STAT User's Guide, Version 6, Fourth Edition, Volume 2.*

□   For more information on autoregressive models, see *SAS/ETS Software: Applications Guide 1, Version 6, First Edition.*

□   For more information on the AUTOREG and SYSLIN procedures see the *SAS/ETS User's Guide, Version 6, First Edition.*

□   SET and TITLE statements are discussed in Chapter 9, "SAS Language Statements," in *SAS Language: Reference.*

□   For a detailed discussion of regression models, see *SAS System for Regression, Second Edition* by Rudolf J. Freund and Ramon C. Littell (1991).

References

Akaike, H. (1974), "A New Look at the Statistical Model Identification," IEEE Transaction on Automatic Control, AC-19, 716—723.

Berndt, E.R. (1991), *The Practice of Econometrics: Classic and Contemporary*, Reading, MA: Addison-Wesley.

Black, F., Jensen, M., and Scholes, M. (1972), "The Capital Assest Pricing Model: Some Empirical Tests," *Studies in the Theory of Capital Markets*, ed. M. Jensen, New York: Praeger, 79—121.

Christensen, L.R. and Jorgenson, D.W. (1970), "U.S. Real Product and Real Factor Input 1929—1967," *Review of Income and Wealth* (March).

Cobb, C. and Douglas, P. (1928), "A Theory of Production," *American Economic Review*, 18(1), Supplement, 139—165.

Harvey, A.C. (1981), *Time Series Models*, New York: John Wiley & Sons, Inc.

Johnston, J. (1984), *Econometric Methods, Third Edition*, New York: McGraw-Hill, Inc.

Markowitz, H. (1959), *Portfolio Selection: Efficient Diversification of Investments*, New York: John Wiley & Sons.

Pindyck, R.S. and Rubinfeld, D.L. (1991), *Econometric Models and Economic Forecasts, Third Edition*, New York: McGraw-Hill, Inc.

Pringle, R.M. and Raynor, A.A. (1971), *Generalized Inverse Matrices with Applications to Statistics*, New York: Hafner Publishing Company.

Schwarz, G. (1978), "Estimating the Dimension of a Model," *Annals of Statistics*, 6, 461—464.

Sharpe, W.F. (1985), *Investments, Third Edition*, Englewood Cliffs, NJ: Prentice-Hall, Inc.

Chapter **3** Using Dummy Variables

Introduction

While developing econometric models, you may discover some data points away from the main cluster of points. These outlying points influence the magnitude of the estimated parameters and may produce an overall poor fit of the model to the data. Often, these outlying points reflect a structural change or a qualitative difference over that range of data. Examples of structural changes are wars, time periods, seasons, political administrations, and major changes in government policy. Examples of qualitative differences are gender, occupation, and level of education. Structural changes and qualitative differences affect the estimated intercept, the slope (or slopes) or both.

Qualitative differences and structural changes occur for many reasons, and they may be identified through

☐ major events affecting the modeled relationship

☐ previous empirical findings

☐ theoretical implications.

If you suspect qualitative differences or structural changes have occurred, then you can add intercept-shifting and slope-shifting dummy variables to your model and test individually and jointly for their effects.

Note: Simply adding a dummy variable to account for outlying observations, without a reason or an event, may improve the apparent fit of the model but does not add to your understanding of the modeled relationship.

In this chapter, the SYSLIN procedure in SAS/ETS software

□   fits a Keynesian consumption function and a Capital Asset Pricing Model (CAPM) with real economic data through the technique of ordinary least squares (OLS)

□   creates residuals to check for structural change in modeled relationships

□   uses dummy variables to account for qualitative differences and structural changes in modeled relationships

□   performs Chow F tests on the dummy variables with the TEST statement.

In the following example, you fit a Keynesian consumption function without an intercept-shifting dummy variable, investigate the lack of fit of the initial model, and fit a new model with an intercept-shifting dummy variable.

Fitting a Consumption Function

Consumer spending typically accounts for about 60% of the annual U.S. gross national product (GNP). To adjust the economy, macroeconomic planners want a reliable model of consumers' behavior. Consumers' gross income minus taxes yields the consumers' disposable income, which may be spent (that is, consumed) or saved. Consumption functions relate the level of consumption to the level of disposable income.

John Maynard Keynes theorized a relationship between consumption and disposable income (1936). A linear model of the following form was proposed:

$$C = a + b(DI)$$

where

a   is the subsistence level of consumption; if DI=0, then C=a.

b   is the slope of the consumption function, also called the marginal propensity to consume (MPC). As DI changes by \$1, C changes by \$b, where $0 \leq b \leq 1$.

The Keynesian consumption function is estimated with time series data. A common problem of time series models is autocorrelated residuals, which you want to test for and correct if necessary. Autocorrelation is discussed in Chapter 3, "Autoregressive Models," in *SAS/ETS Software: Applications Guide 1, Version 6, First Edition*, and Chapter 4, "Violations of the OLS Error Assumptions," of this book.

Introducing the ACON Data Set

You can explore the relationship between consumption and disposable income with the ACON data set. The ACON data set consists of annual observations of real data from 1929 through 1960: per capita U.S. disposable income (DI) and consumption (C) expenditures in 1982 dollars. The data are from the U.S.

Department of Commerce's *Statistical Abstracts of the U.S.* (1990). The following SAS example code creates the ACON data and uses PROC PRINT to print the first five observations. Output 3.1 shows the results.

```
     /* Creating the ACON Data Set */
data acon;
    input yr di c @@;
    label di='Real per Capita Disposable Inc. in 1982$'
          c='Real per Capita Consumption in 1982$';
    cards;
29 4091 3868    30 3727 3569    31 3534 3400    32 3043 3081
33 2950 3013    34 3100 3088    35 3359 3236    36 3738 3523
37 3836 3628    38 3557 3517    39 3812 3667    40 4017 3804
41 4528 3981    42 5138 3912    43 5276 3949    44 5414 4026
45 5285 4236    46 5115 4632    47 4820 4625    48 5000 4650
49 4915 4661    50 5220 4834    51 5308 4853    52 5379 4915
53 5515 5029    54 5505 5066    55 5714 5287    56 5881 5349
57 5909 5370    58 5908 5357    59 6027 5531    60 6036 5561
;

     /* Printing the First Five Observations */
proc print data=acon (obs=5) label;
    var yr di c;
    title 'Annual Consumption Function Example';
    title2 'First Five Observations of ACON Data';
run;
```

Output 3.1
The First Five Observations of the ACON Data Set

```
                Annual Consumption Function Example
                First Five Observations of ACON Data

                            Real per
                             Capita        Real per
                           Disposable       Capita
                            Inc. in      Consumption
             OBS    YR       1982$          in 1982$

              1     29        4091           3868
              2     30        3727           3569
              3     31        3534           3400
              4     32        3043           3081
              5     33        2950           3013
```

Plotting the Data

Prior to fitting the model, you may want to plot the data. Scatter plots enable you to visually examine the data for trends and patterns. The PLOT procedure's PLOT statement plots the vertical axis variable versus the horizontal axis variable. The OVERLAY option of the PLOT statement requests the plotting of multiple variables in one scatter plot.

The following SAS example code plots the variables C and DI versus YR and C versus DI, as displayed in Output 3.2.

```
    /* Plotting C and DI vs Year */
proc plot data=acon vpct=60;
   plot c  * yr = 'c'
        di * yr = 'd' / overlay;
   title2 'Consumption and Disposable Income';
   title3 'versus Year';
run;

    /* Plotting C vs DI */
proc plot data=acon vpct=60;
   plot c * di;
   title2 'Consumption versus Disposable Income';
   title3;
run;
```

Output 3.2
Scatter Plots of DI
and C Versus YR
and C Versus DI

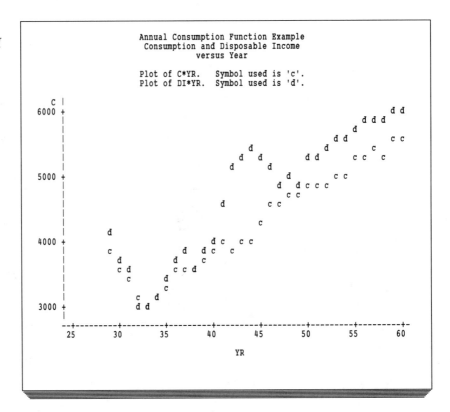

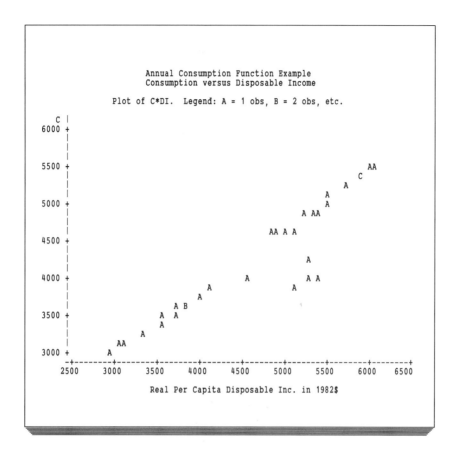

Interpretation of output

In the first scatter plot of Output 3.2, disposable income (DI) and consumption (C) appear to be highly correlated. The difference between DI and C, savings, is small during the 1930s (the great depression years), large in the first half of the 1940s (the years of U.S. involvement in World War II), and almost constant throughout the 1950s.

In the second scatter plot of Output 3.2, C versus DI, there appears to be a strong linear trend except for four outlying points which correspond to the years of U.S. involvement in World War II. A linear model seems appropriate, and you can expect a good fit except during those years.

Fitting the Keynesian Consumption Function

The following SAS example code using PROC SYSLIN fits the Keynesian consumption function and tests for autocorrelation with the Durbin-Watson *d* statistic. The following is an interpretation of the statements:

PROC SYSLIN
    invokes the SYSLIN procedure. The DATA= option specifies ACON as the input data set.

MODEL

> fits the Keynesian consumption function with OLS. In this example, the dependent variable, C, is specified on the left-hand side of the equation and the independent variable, DI, is specified on the right-hand side of the equation. The DW option requests the Durbin-Watson *d* statistic.

The following code generates Output 3.3.

```
proc syslin data=acon;
   model c=di / dw;
run;
```

Output 3.3
*Output from
Keynesian
Consumption
Function
Estimation*

```
                    Annual Consumption Function Example

                              SYSLIN Procedure
                      Ordinary Least Squares Estimation

   Model: C
   Dependent variable: C Real Per Capita Consumption in 1982$
                            Analysis of Variance

                            Sum of          Mean
         Source      DF    Squares         Square     F Value    Prob>F

         Model        1 17523278.845  17523278.845    209.062    0.0001
         Error       30 2514559.0296   83818.63432
         C Total     31 20037837.875

              Root MSE      289.51448     R-Square     0.8745
              Dep Mean     4288.06250     Adj R-SQ     0.8703
              C.V.            6.75164

                           Parameter Estimates

                      Parameter     Standard    T for H0:
    Variable   DF     Estimate         Error    Parameter=0   Prob > |T|

    INTERCEP    1    696.200077    253.634813      2.745         0.0101
    DI          1      0.762922      0.052765     14.459         0.0001

                        Variable
    Variable   DF      Label

    INTERCEP    1    Intercept
    DI          1    Real Per Capita Disposable Inc. in 1982$

                   Durbin-Watson              0.326
                   (For Number of Obs.)          32
                   1st Order Autocorrelation  0.823
```

Interpretation of output

From Output 3.3, you see the following:

□ The estimated model is

C = 696.200 + .7629 DI .

□ The fit of the model appears to be quite good. The R^2 (R-Square) is .8745. This means that disposable income, DI, explains over 87% of the variation in consumption, C.

□ The magnitude of the estimated DI slope parameter, the marginal propensity to consume (MPC), is .7629.

□ The *t* statistic of the DI slope parameter is 14.459 and is significant with a *p* value<.0001. Be aware that hypothesis tests can be misleading in models with autocorrelated residuals. Often, positive autocorrelation causes the accuracy of statistical tests to be less than the indicated level.

□ The Durbin-Watson *d* statistic (0.326) indicates positive autocorrelation of the residuals for a properly specified model. Although it is not shown on the output, this *d* statistic is significant at the .01 level.

  The *d* statistic has a range from zero to four. Uncorrelated residuals generate a *d* statistic of two. Positively autocorrelated residuals generate a *d* statistic between zero and two. The closer the correlation is to one, the closer the *d* statistic is to zero. Negatively autocorrelated residuals generate a *d* statistic between two and four. The closer the correlation is to minus one, the closer the *d* statistic is to four.

  The Durbin-Watson test assumes the model has been correctly specified. Thus, this result implies positive autocorrelation in a properly specified model. This result may also signify a more fundamental problem—misspecification of the model. Before concluding that a correction for autocorrelation is the best strategy for improving the fit of your model, you may find it is worthwhile to examine the OLS residuals and the historical setting of your model.

Examining Residuals

To create an output data set containing the residuals, you add these options and statements to the previous example code. The OUT= option of the PROC SYSLIN statement creates an output data set. Note that you must also use an OUTPUT statement. For this example, the output data set is named ACN_OUT. The NOPRINT option suppresses the printed regression output. The OUTPUT statement performs as follows. Output 3.4 shows the results.

OUTPUT

  creates the output data set ACN_OUT. The following options of the OUTPUT statement are specified:

RESIDUAL=	names the OLS residuals, RESID, and includes them in the output data set ACN_OUT.
PREDICTED=	names the predicted values, P, and includes them in the output data set ACN_OUT.

The following SAS example code creates the residuals and predicted values and then prints them in Output 3.4.

```
proc syslin data=acon out=acn_out noprint;
   model c=di / dw;
   output residual=resid predicted=p;
run;

proc print data=acn_out;
   var yr c p resid;
   title2 'Printout of ACN_OUT Data Set';
run;
```

Output 3.4
Listing the Residuals

```
                Annual Consumption Function Example
                    Printout of ACN_OUT Data Set

        OBS    YR      C        P        RESID

         1     29    3868    3817.32     50.684
         2     30    3569    3539.61     29.388
         3     31    3400    3392.37      7.632
         4     32    3081    3017.77     63.227
         5     33    3013    2946.82     66.179
         6     34    3088    3061.26     26.741
         7     35    3236    3258.86    -22.856
         8     36    3523    3548.00    -25.004
         9     37    3628    3622.77      5.230
        10     38    3517    3409.91    107.085
        11     39    3667    3604.46     62.540
        12     40    3804    3760.86     43.141
        13     41    3981    4150.71   -169.713
        14     42    3912    4616.10   -704.095
        15     43    3949    4721.38   -772.379
        16     44    4026    4826.66   -800.662
        17     45    4236    4728.24   -492.245
        18     46    4632    4598.55     33.452
        19     47    4625    4373.49    251.514
        20     48    4650    4510.81    139.188
        21     49    4661    4445.96    215.036
        22     50    4834    4678.65    155.345
        23     51    4853    4745.79    107.208
        24     52    4915    4799.96    115.040
        25     53    5029    4903.72    125.283
        26     54    5066    4896.09    169.912
        27     55    5287    5055.54    231.461
        28     56    5349    5182.95    166.053
        29     57    5370    5204.31    165.692
        30     58    5357    5203.55    153.454
        31     59    5531    5294.33    236.667
        32     60    5561    5301.20    259.800
```

Interpretation of output

The residuals are the actual values minus the predicted values. Notice that the residuals are almost all positive, except for observations 13 through 17, which correspond to the years 1941 through 1945. The residuals for the period 1942 through 1945 are large in magnitude and correspond to the period of U.S. involvement in World War II.

Plotting Predicted and Actual Values

The following SAS example code uses the GPLOT procedure in SAS/GRAPH software to produce a high-resolution plot of the predicted and actual values versus the independent variable, DI. Output 3.5 shows the results. For details on global settings and discussion of required steps, see Chapter 2, "Fitting OLS Regression Models," of this book and Chapter 9, "The Axis Statement," and Chapter 31, "The GPLOT Procedure," in *SAS/GRAPH, Software: Reference, Version 6, First Edition, Volume 1* and Volume 2.

```
goptions reset=symbol;

proc gplot data=acn_out;
    plot c*di=1
        p*di=2 / overlay haxis=axis1 vaxis=axis2;
    symbol1 h=1.5 pct v=* font=swissb color=black;
    symbol2 i=join h=1.5 pct font=swissb l=1 color=blue;
    axis1 label=(h=3.5 pct 'Per Capita Disposable Income')
        order=(2500 to 6500 by 500) minor=(number=4);
    axis2 label=(h=3.5 pct angle=90 'Per Capita Consumption')
        order=(2500 to 6000 by 500) minor=(number=4);
    title 'Actual and Predicted C versus DI';
    title2 '(in real 1982 dollars)';
run;
```

Output 3.5
Plot of Actual and Predicted Values of the Keynesian Consumption Function

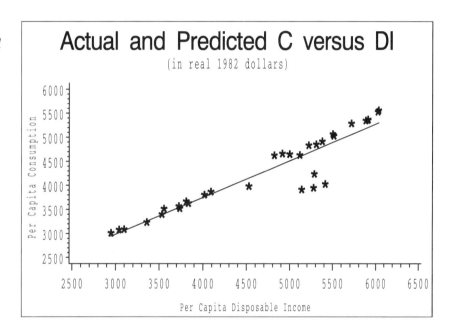

The following SAS example code uses the PLOT procedure to plot the residuals versus time in years (YR). The VREF= option of the PLOT statement is used to create a vertical reference line at zero.

```
proc plot data=acn_out vpct=60;
    plot resid*yr='*' / vref=0;
    title2 'Residuals versus Year';
    title3 'Model without Intercept Dummy';
run;
```

Output 3.6
Plot of Residuals
Versus Year

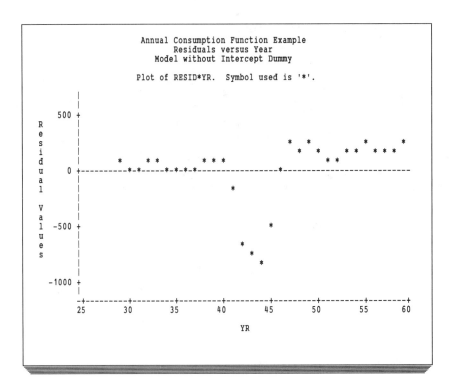

Interpretation of output

In the PROC GPLOT plot of Output 3.5, most of the actual consumption values are above the fitted line. There are four points, away from the main cluster, lying well below and to the right of the fitted line. These four points pull the fitted line down causing a poor fit to the data.

The PROC PLOT plot of the residuals in Output 3.6 reveals that these four outlying points correspond to the period 1942 through 1945, the years of United States involvement in World War II. The poor fit suggests that this period is structurally different from other years. The next step is to add a dummy variable to the consumption function to account for the effect of war years on consumption expenditures.

Using a Dummy Variable as an Intercept Shifter

You can use a dummy variable to shift the intercept during the war years and account for the lower level of consumption. The slope coefficient on disposable income, the MPC, is assumed to remain constant. If you include an intercept-shifting dummy variable, WWII_DUM, your model becomes

$$C = a + b(DI) \qquad \text{for all years except 1942 through 1945}$$

$$C = a + \gamma \text{ WWII\_DUM} + b(DI) \text{ for the years 1942 through 1945.}$$

You can define WWII_DUM in a DATA step with a value of one in the years 1942 through 1945, and a value of zero elsewhere.

```
if 41<yr<46 then wwii_dum=1;
else wwii_dum=0;
```

To refit the model with the intercept-shifting dummy variable, WWII_DUM, the MODEL statement in PROC SYSLIN becomes

```
model c=di wwii_dum /dw;
```

The following SAS example code creates an intercept-shifting dummy variable for the period 1942 through 1945 and fits the Keynesian consumption function. By using a SET statement, you can add the new variable WWII_DUM to the data set. Output 3.7 shows the results.

```
    /* Adding Intercept Dummy Variable to Consume Data */
data acon1;
    set acon;

    /* Creating Intercept Dummy Variable */
    if 41<yr<46 then wwii_dum = 1;
    else wwii_dum = 0;
    label wwii_dum='Intercept Dummy for WWII, 1942-1945';
run;

    /* Fitting Model and Storing Predicted Values */
proc syslin data=acon1 out=acn_out1;
    model c=di wwii_dum /dw;
    output p=p;
run;
```

Output 3.7
Keynesian Consumption Function Estimation with an Intercept-Shifting Dummy Variable for World War II

```
                      Annual Consumption Function Example

                              SYSLIN Procedure
                      Ordinary Least Squares Estimation

Model: C
Dependent variable: C Real Per Capita Consumption in 1982$
                          Analysis of Variance

                              Sum of        Mean
         Source      DF      Squares       Square     F Value    Prob>F

         Model        2  19828362.115  9914181.0576   1372.528   0.0001
         Error       29  209475.75982   7223.30206
         C Total     31  20037837.875

              Root MSE      84.99001     R-Square     0.9895
              Dep Mean    4288.06250     Adj R-SQ     0.9888
              C.V.           1.98201

                           Parameter Estimates

                        Parameter    Standard    T for H0:
         Variable  DF     Estimate      Error    Parameter=0   Prob > |T|

         INTERCEP   1   503.357059    75.235654      6.690       0.0001
         DI         1     0.825982     0.015887     51.992       0.0001
         WWII_DUM   1  -832.346149    46.593845    -17.864       0.0001

                         Variable
         Variable  DF     Label

         INTERCEP   1   Intercept
         DI         1   Real Per Capita Disposable Inc. in 1982$
         WWII_DUM   1   Intercept Dummy for WWII, 1942-1945

                         Durbin-Watson            2.199
                         (For Number of Obs.)        32
                         1st Order Autocorrelation -0.113
```

Interpretation of output

The estimated model in Output 3.6 is

$$C = \$503.36 + .826 \; DI \qquad \text{for all years except 1942 through 1945}$$

$$C = \$503.36 - \$832.35 + .826 \; DI \qquad \text{for the years 1942 through 1945.}$$

Comparing Outputs 3.3 and 3.7, you can see the following:

□ The fit of the model is improved: R^2(R-Square) and adjusted R^2(Adj R-SQ) rise while the root mean square error (Root MSE) falls. Output 3.7 displays the estimated model and statistical tests. The following table shows this comparison.

Table 3.1
Comparing the Keynesian Consumption Function Models

Goodness-of-Fit Statistics	With Dummy (Output 3.7)	Without Dummy (Output 3.3)
R-Square	.9895	.8745
Adj R-Square	.9888	.8703
Root MSE	84.9900	289.5145

□ The t statistic of the slope parameter, disposable income (DI), increases from 14.459 in Output 3.3 to 51.992 in Output 3.7.

□ The t statistic for the test that the intercept dummy variable, WWII_DUM, is different from zero is -17.864, which is significant at the .01 level. This test result indicates that WWII_DUM is important to the model. WWII_DUM shows you that annual real per capita consumption (in 1982 dollars) was lower by about $832.35 during the years 1942 through 1945.

□ The Durbin-Watson d statistic in Output 3.7 is 2.199 and is not significant at the .05 level. The apparent autocorrelation problem vanishes with the addition of the dummy variable to account for the structural change in consumption during World War II.

To calculate the predicted level of C given DI, you would

□ use the first equation in all years except 1942 through 1945. For example, if per capita DI is $4,000, then C is expected to be

$$C = \$503.36 + (.826 \times \$4,000)$$
$$C = \$503.36 + \$3,304 = \$3,807.36 \quad .$$

□ use the second equation for the years 1942 through 1945. For example, if per capita DI is $4,000, then C is expected to be

$$C = \$503.36 - \$832.35 + (.826 \times \$4,000)$$
$$C = -\$328.99 + \$3,304 = \$2,975.01$$

Plotting the Improved Fit of the Model

The GPLOT procedure in SAS/GRAPH software creates a graph showing the
improved fit of the model. The actual C values and the predicted values generated
in your model with the intercept dummy, WWII_DUM, are graphed versus the
independent variable, DI. By creating a new variable for the predicted values
during the WWII years, you can create a separate line for them. Output 3.8
shows the results.

```
data acn_out2;
   set acn_out1;
   if 41<yr<46 then
   do;
      p_wwii=p;   /* separate predicted values for WWII years */
      p=.;        /* exclude predicted values for WWII years  */
   end;
run;

goptions reset=symbol;

proc gplot data=acn_out2;
   plot c*di=1
        p*di=2       /* all years except WWII */
        p_wwii*di=3  /* WWII years            */
                 /overlay haxis=axis1 vaxis=axis2;
   symbol1 h=3.5 pct v=* font=swissb color=black;
   symbol2 font=swissb l=1 i=join color=blue;
   symbol3 font=swissb l=1 i=join color=green;
   axis1 label=(h=3 pct 'Per Capita Disposable Income')
         order=(2500 to 6500 by 500) minor=(number=4);
   axis2 label=(h=2.6 pct angle=90 'Per Capita Consumption')
         order=(2500 to 6000 by 500) minor=(number=4);
   title1 'Actual and Predicted C versus DI';
   title2 'WWII_DUM Added to the Model';
   title3 '(in real 1982 dollars)';
run;
quit;
```

Output 3.8
Actual and New
Predicted Values
from the Model
with WWII_DUM
Added

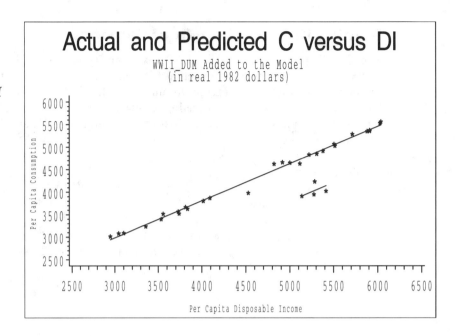

You can use PROC PLOT to plot the residuals of the refitted model versus time in years. Output 3.9 shows the results.

```
proc plot data=acn_out1 vpct=60;
   plot resid1*yr='*' / vref=0;
   title2 'Residuals versus Year';
   title3 'Model with Intercept Dummy, WWII_DUM';
run;
```

Output 3.9
Plot of Residuals
Versus Year

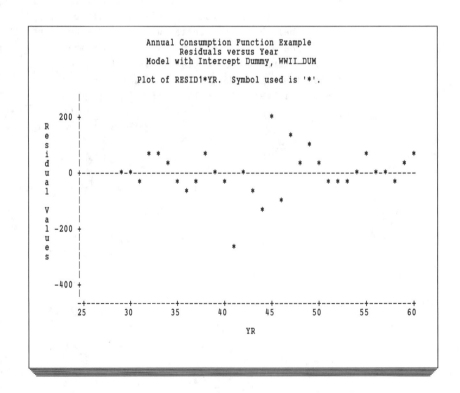

Interpretation of output

To visually compare and contrast the fit of the Keynesian consumption function with and without an intercept-shifting dummy variable, you compare Output 3.8 with Output 3.5.

In the model with the intercept-shifting dummy variable, the actual values during the period 1942 through 1945 now have corresponding predicted values, as displayed in the PROC GPLOT plot of Output 3.8. Overall, the residual values of the model with the intercept-shifting dummy variable are smaller in magnitude and have few outlying values, as displayed in the PROC PLOT plot. In particular, note the difference in the vertical axis scale of the residual plots in Output 3.6 and Output 3.9.

Using Intercept and Slope Dummies

You can use dummy variables to shift both the intercept and the slope of your model to account for major events that change the underlying structure of the model. This section shows you how to fit the Capital Asset Pricing Model (CAPM), developed in Chapter 2, to General Public Utilities (GPU), the parent holding company of the Three Mile Island Nuclear Power Plant.

On March 28, 1979, an accident occurred at Three Mile Island. Was the fit of the CAPM to GPU prior to the accident appropriate for the postaccident period? To answer this question you must fit the model with intercept and slope dummies, and then perform hypothesis tests on the estimated parameters.

This section performs the following tasks:

□ applies the CAPM to GPU

□ plots the GPU data

□ creates intercept and slope dummy variables

□ fits the CAPM to the GPU data

□ plots the actual and predicted values

□ jointly tests the intercept and slope dummy variables.

The Standard CAPM

The CAPM is an equation for predicting the return on assets. The basic time series CAPM equation is

$$R_i - R_f = \alpha + \beta(R_M - R_f) + \varepsilon_i$$

where α and β are parameters to be estimated, R_i is the asset's return, R_f is the risk-free asset's return, R_M is the market's return, and ε_i is the random error term. The CAPM is discussed in more detail in Chapter 2.

Before fitting the CAPM to GPU, you need to create a SAS data set, GPU, and examine a scatter plot of the data. The following sections show you how to perform these tasks.

Introducing the GPU Data Set

The GPU data set contains for the period January 1976 through June 1980 the market return, R_M, the return on the risk-free asset (30-day U.S. Treasury Bills), R_F, and the return on GPU. The data are available from the Center for Research on Securities Prices.

In the following SAS example code, the DATA step creates the GPU data set, creates a DATE variable new variables (R_GPU and R_MKT), and labels the variables. The FORMAT statement creates a DATE variable. The example code generates Output 3.10. For a discussion of FORMAT statements, see *SAS Language: Reference, Version 6, First Edition.*

```
data gpu;
   format date monyy.;
   input date:monyy5. r_m r_f gpu @@;
      r_gpu = gpu - r_f;
      r_mkt = r_m - r_f;
   label r_m='Market Rate of Return'
         r_f='Risk-Free Rate of Return'
         gpu='Rate of Return for Gen. Public Utilities'
         r_gpu='Risk Premium for Gen. Public Utilities'
         r_mkt='Risk Premium for Market';
   cards;
JAN76  .156 .00369  .05412   FEB76  .069 .00369 -.01429
MAR76  .010 .00390  .01449   APR76 -.012 .00383 -.01886
MAY76  .005 .00415 -.01493   JUN76  .016 .00431  .01515
JUL76 -.017 .00416  .05493   AUG76 -.016 .00389  .05797
SEP76  .007 .00412  .04110   OCT76 -.029 .00386 -.01737
NOV76  .000 .00355  .00685   DEC76  .111 .00345  .06122
JAN77  .015 .00372  .02154   FEB77 -.012 .00362 -.05769
MAR77  .008 .00367  .02041   APR77  .004 .00359  .02240
MAY77 -.005 .00394  .04000   JUN77  .070 .00400  .02564
JUL77 -.002 .00435  .02824   AUG77 -.023 .00445  .02659
SEP77  .008 .00476  .02424   OCT77 -.051 .00473 -.03243
NOV77  .083 .00450  .04375   DEC77  .039 .00467  .00000
JAN78 -.045 .00487 -.06874   FEB78  .010 .00494  .01974
MAR78  .050 .00526  .02581   APR78  .063 .00491 -.00931
MAY78  .067 .00513 -.03247   JUN78  .007 .00527 -.00671
JUL78  .071 .00528  .04405   AUG78  .079 .00607 -.04636
SEP78  .002 .00645  .03472   OCT78 -.189 .00685 -.07651
NOV78  .084 .00719  .04478   DEC78  .015 .00690  .00000
JAN79  .058 .00761  .05429   FEB79  .011 .00761 -.05556
MAR79  .123 .00769 -.04412   APR79  .026 .00764 -.33077
MAY79  .014 .00772 -.17241   JUN79  .075 .00715  .15714
JUL79 -.013 .00728 -.01235   AUG79  .095 .00789  .00000
SEP79  .039 .00802 -.07692   OCT79 -.097 .00913 -.08333
NOV79  .116 .00819  .00000   DEC79  .086 .00747  .07813
JAN80  .124 .00883 -.05797   FEB80  .112 .01073 -.24615
MAR80 -.243 .01181 -.30612   APR80  .080 .00753  .38235
MAY80  .062 .00630  .06383   JUN80  .086 .00503 -.06000
;

proc print data=gpu (obs=5);
   var date gpu r_m r_f r_gpu r_mkt;
```

```
    title 'General Public Utilities CAPM Example';
    title2 'First Five Observations GPU Data Set';
run;
```

Output 3.10
The First Five
Observations of
the GPU Data Set

```
                    General Public Utilities CAPM Example
                      First Five Observations GPU Data Set

    OBS    DATE      GPU       R_M      R_F       R_GPU      R_MKT

     1     JAN76    0.05412   0.156    .00369    0.05043    0.15231
     2     FEB76   -0.01429   0.069    .00369   -0.01798    0.06531
     3     MAR76    0.01449   0.010    .00390    0.01059    0.00610
     4     APR76   -0.01886  -0.012    .00383   -0.02269   -0.01583
     5     MAY76   -0.01493   0.005    .00415   -0.01908    0.00085
```

Plotting the GPU Data Set

If the Three Mile Island accident affected the risk premium of GPU, R_GPU, you should expect to observe a visible difference in a plot of R_GPU versus time. The HREF= option of the PLOT statement creates a horizontal reference line at March 1979. The following statements produce Output 3.11.

```
proc plot data=gpu vpct=65;
    plot r_gpu * date = "*" / href='01MAR79'd;
    title2 'GPU Risk Premium versus Time';
run;
```

Output 3.11
The Risk Premium
of GPU, R_GPU
Plotted Versus
Time (DATE)

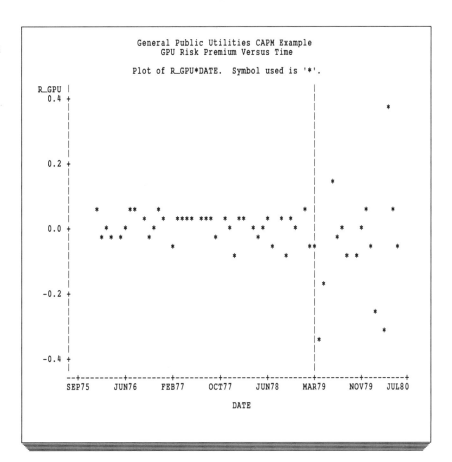

Interpretation of output

In the scatter plot of Output 3.11, the horizontal axis of the scatter plot is time, and the vertical axis is the risk premium of GPU, R_GPU. The horizontal reference line is drawn at the last observation prior to the accident. All points to the left of the line are preaccident; all points to the right of the line are post-accident. The scatter plot shows that R_GPU is closely grouped prior to the accident and more widely dispersed after the accident.

Greater dispersion of the data in some regions can cause the error variances to differ, which violates a standard OLS error assumption. (See Chapter 2 for a list of OLS error assumptions.) The problem of nonconstant error variances is called *heteroskedasticity* and is discussed in Chapter 4. For this example, we assume that correcting for heteroskedasticity is not the best approach, and that allowing the intercepts and slopes to differ for the two periods is a better approach.

Fitting the CAPM to GPU

Applying the CAPM to GPU yields the following equation:

$$R\_GPU = \alpha + \beta(R\_MKT) + \varepsilon$$

where

R_GPU   is the GPU risk premium, $R\_GPU = GPU - R\_F$.

α is the intercept.

β is the slope parameter.

R_MKT   is the market risk premium, $R\_MKT = R\_M - R\_F$.

ε is the error term.

You can add intercept and slope dummies to the CAPM model for GPU. The model becomes

$$R\_GPU = \alpha + \gamma INT\_DUM + \beta_0(R\_MKT) + \beta_1(SLP\_DUM) + \varepsilon$$

where the new variables and parameters are defined as follows:

γ is the parameter for the intercept dummy variable, INT_DUM.

INT_DUM   is an intercept dummy variable with the value zero for the period prior to the accident, JAN76 to MAR79, and the value one for the period after the accident, APR79 to JUN80.

β_0 is the slope parameter, also known as β in the finance literature.

β_1 is the slope parameter associated with the slope dummy variable, SLP_DUM.

SLP_DUM   is the slope dummy variable, $SLP\_DUM = INT\_DUM \times R\_MKT$.

The following SAS example code creates dummy variables (INT_DUM and SLP_DUM), fits the CAPM with intercept- and slope-shifting dummy variables using PROC SYSLIN, and creates the GPU_OUT output data set containing the predicted values, P. The fitted model is shown in Output 3.12. The predicted and actual values are plotted in Output 3.13.

```
        /* Creating Slope Dummy Variable */
data gpu1;
   set gpu;

     /* Three Mile Island Dummy Variable, INT_DUM is 0 */
     /* prior to MAR79, and 1 for APR79 and after.     */
   if date > '01MAR79'd then int_dum = 1;
   else int_dum = 0;

        /* Slope Dummy */
   slp_dum = int_dum * r_mkt;
   label int_dum='Intercept Dummy'
         slp_dum='Slope Dummy';
run;

     /* Fitting Model with Slope Dummy Variable */
proc syslin data=gpu1 out=gpu_out;
   model r_gpu = r_mkt int_dum slp_dum;
   output predicted=p;
run;
```

Output 3.12
Fitting the CAPM
to GPU Data with
Intercept and
Slope Dummies

```
                  General Public Utilities CAPM Example

                             SYSLIN Procedure
                      Ordinary Least Squares Estimation

Model: R_GPU
Dependent variable: R_GPU Risk Premium for Gen. Public Utilities

                          Analysis of Variance

                          Sum of        Mean
        Source      DF    Squares       Square      F Value    Prob>F

        Model        3    0.13132       0.04377       5.139     0.0036
        Error       50    0.42587       0.00852
        C Total     53    0.55719

               Root MSE       0.09229    R-Square       0.2357
               Dep Mean      -0.01273    Adj R-SQ       0.1898
               C.V.        -725.16814

                          Parameter Estimates

                        Parameter     Standard     T for H0:
        Variable  DF     Estimate       Error     Parameter=0    Prob > |T|

        INTERCEP   1    -0.001697     0.015393       -0.110       0.9126
        R_MKT      1     0.252145     0.257812        0.978       0.3328
        INT_DUM    1    -0.074897     0.029326       -2.554       0.0137
        SLP_DUM    1     0.571875     0.361013        1.584       0.1195

                           Variable
        Variable  DF       Label

        INTERCEP   1    Intercept
        R_MKT      1    Risk Premium for Market
        INT_DUM    1    Intercept Dummy
        SLP_DUM    1    Slope Dummy
```

Interpretation of output

In Output 3.12, the fitted CAPM for GPU is

$$R\_GPU = -.001697 + .252145(R\_MKT) \qquad \text{preaccident, JAN76}-\text{MAR79}$$

$$R\_GPU = -.076594 + .82402(R\_MKT) \qquad \text{postaccident, APR79}-\text{JUN80.}$$

where the intercept for the post-accident period is the sum of preaccident intercept, α, and the intercept dummy, γ; thus,

$$-.076594 = -.001697 - .074897 \quad .$$

The post-accident slope is the sum of the preaccident slope, β_0, and β_1, the estimated parameter of the slope dummy variable, SLP_DUM; thus,

$$.82402 = .252145 + .571875 \quad .$$

The goodness of fit statistics are as follows:

□ R-Square is .2357.

□ Adj R-SQ is .1898.

R-Square statistics are typically low for CAPM regressions.

The results of the individual *t*-tests (for the null hypotheses that each is different from zero) indicate that α and β_0 are no different from zero at the .20 level while both the intercept dummy, γ, and the slope dummy, β_1, are different from zero.

Since the post-accident β for GPU is higher, investors view GPU as a riskier investment. The economic interpretation of the negative intercept dummy, γ, is that the expected return on GPU is lower after the accident for *all* levels of market return. In fact, when the market return is zero, the expected return on GPU after the accident is $-.07659$.

Plotting the Model

You can use PROC GPLOT to graph the predicted values of the fitted model. Separate lines are created for the pre- and post-accident periods.

Prior to plotting, you use a DATA step and the SORT and FORMAT procedures. The DATA step creates the GPU_OUT1 data set and uses array processing to separate the predicted values by type (before the Three Mile Island accident and after). PROC SORT sorts the data, and PROC FORMAT formats the data for the legend in the PROC GPLOT plot.

The following SAS example code shows you how to plot the actual and predicted values and create separate lines for the pre- and post-accident periods, as displayed in Output 3.13.

```
   /* Separating Pre and Post Accident Values */
data gpu_out1(keep=y_value pt_type r_mkt);
   set gpu_out;
   label pt_type='Observation Type';
   array regvar(2) r_gpu p;
   do i=1 to 2;
      y_value=regvar(i);
```

```
         pt_type=i+2*(date > '01MAR79'd);
      output;
      end;
run;

   /* Sorting the Data */
proc sort data=gpu_out1
   by y_value pt_type;
run;

   /* Formatting the Data */
proc format;
   value ptfmt 1='Actual pre TMI'
               2='Predict pre TMI'
               3='Actual post TMI'
               4='Predict post TMI';
run;

goptions reset=symbol;

   /* Plotting the Data */
proc gplot data=gpu_out1
   plot y_value*r_mkt=pt_type / haxis=axis1 vaxis=axis2;
   symbol1 h=3 pct v=plus color=black;
   symbol2 font=swissb l=1 i=join color=blue;
   symbol3 h=3 pct v=circle color=green;
   symbol4 font=swissb l=3 i=join color=red;
   axis1 order=(-.3 to .2 by .1) minor=(number=1);
   axis2 label=(angle=90 'GPU Risk Premium')
         order=(-.4 to .4 by .1) minor=(number=1);
   title1 'Risk Premiums, GPU versus MKT';
   title2 'Actual and Predicted';
   format pt_type ptfmt.;
run;
quit;
```

Output 3.13
Actual and
Predicted Values
for the Two-Line
Model

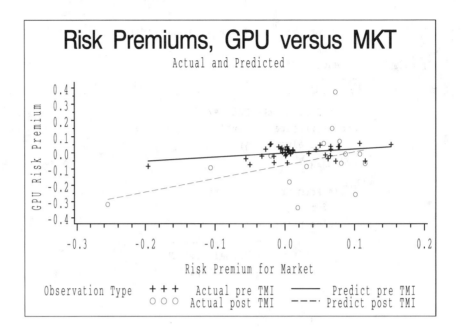

In Output 3.13, the values of R_GPU are given separate symbols for the two periods. The lines show the predicted values of the fitted model. The solid line and plus sign (labeled pre TMI), refer to the preaccident period. The dashed line and circle (labeled post TMI) refer to the postaccident period.

Output 3.13 provides further visual evidence that there was a structural change in the return of GPU after the accident. To formally test whether the two periods differ, you can use a Chow F test, as described in the next section.

Performing a Chow *F* Test

There are several joint tests you could perform on the dummy variables. They include

□ an analysis-of-variance F test, also known as a Chow F test

□ a likelihood ratio test

□ a Wald test

□ a Lagrangian Multiplier test.

The likelihood ratio test, the Wald test, and the Lagrangian Multiplier test are useful for nonlinear parameter tests and restrictions, and for non-normally distributed errors. The Chow test is applicable for linear restrictions of a linear model and is used in the following example to jointly test the intercept and slope dummy variables.

You can use a Chow F test to jointly test whether the parameter, γ, of the intercept dummy, INT_DUM, and the parameter, β_1, of the slope dummy, SLP_DUM, are zero. The null hypothesis that γ and β_1 are jointly zero is equivalent to the hypothesis that the estimated model has identical parameter values before and after the accident. If you cannot reject the null hypothesis that the parameters of the dummy variables are jointly zero, then you should estimate the model without the dummy variables. In that case, the expected returns of GPU are no different in the pre- and post-accident periods. If you can reject the null hypothesis and the parameters of the dummy variables are jointly different from zero, then you should use the fitted model with the dummy variables. In this case, you conclude that expected returns for GPU are different in the pre- and post-accident periods.

The following SAS example code using the TEST statement of PROC SYSLIN performs this Chow F test. When you specify the NOPRINT option of the MODEL statement, you suppress the printed regression output. The test, labeled CHOWTEST, performs the Chow F test with the null hypothesis that the parameters of INT_DUM and the slope dummy, SLP_DUM, are jointly zero; the alternative hypothesis is that they are not. Output 3.14 shows the results.

```
proc syslin data=gpu1;
   model r_gpu = r_mkt int_dum slp_dum / noprint;
   chowtest:test slp_dum = int_dum = 0;
run;
```

Output 3.14
Chow F Test for the GPU CAPM Regression with Intercept and Slope Dummies

```
                    General Public Utilities CAPM Example

                              SYSLIN Procedure
                      Ordinary Least Squares Estimation

     Test: CHOWTEST
        Numerator:   0.031224   DF:    2   F Value:   3.6660
        Denominator: 0.008517   DF:   50   Prob>F:    0.0327
```

Interpretation of output

In Output 3.14, the results of the Chow F test, labeled CHOWTEST, are shown. The F statistic is 3.6660 and has a p value of .0327 implying the two dummy variables are jointly different from zero at the .05 level. You can conclude that the Three Mile Island accident did affect the CAPM as applied to GPU for the 15-month period following the accident.

If the Chow F statistic had not been significant, then you would have been unable to reject the null hypothesis that the parameters were the same in both periods. In that case, your appropriate estimation strategy would have been to pool the data over the whole period and to fit a model without dummy variables.

An Alternative Approach for Performing Chow *F* Tests

Economists sometimes use an alternative strategy for performing Chow F tests. To employ this strategy, you perform the following steps:

1. Plot the data to visually search for structural changes and qualitative differences.

2. Add dummy variables as required and estimate the model with the entire data set.

3. Plot or list (or both) the residuals of the initial model and check for outliers.

4. Examine the theoretical implications of the model for groups of observations that may have a different relationship (that is, a different intercept or slope) with the dependent variable.

5. Examine the historical and institutional setting of the model for events that may have caused a structural change in the modeled relationship.

6. Re-estimate the model with the separate portions of the data or with newly collected data.

7. Perform Chow F tests for the appropriateness of pooling the data and using the model fit with the entire data set.

The following SAS example code generates these parameter estimates and the sums of squares needed to perform a Chow F test. The output from this code is not shown.

```
    /* Sorting the Data */
proc sort data=gpu;
    by int_dum;
run;

    /* Fitting a Regression Line Over Entire Period */
proc syslin data=gpu;
    model r_gpu = r_mkt;
run;

    /* Fitting Regression Lines Over Sub-periods */
proc syslin data=gpu;
    model r_gpu = r_mkt;
    by int_dum;
run;
```

For details on Chow tests see Pindyck and Rubinfeld (1991, pp. 115—117), Maddala (1977, pp. 194—201), and Chow (1960).

Using Separate Models

If the theory underlying your model indicates that the qualitative differences or structural change result in different error variances for the groups or periods, then you may want to estimate separate models. You can also test the error variances of the two models for equality (see Quandt 1960). Note that if the error variances are constant (or can be reasonably assumed so), then the separate models and the model with dummy variables for the structural changes are equivalent. For a discussion of estimation problems caused by nonconstant error variances, see Chapter 4.

Furthermore, if you believe that the error variance is different in the two periods, you may want to use a Wald test to jointly test the dummy variables. For details of an appropriate test, see Ohtani and Kobiyashi (1986).

Chapter Summary

This chapter discussed the use of dummy variables as intercept and slope shifters. Dummy variables can account for outliers and improve the fit of a model. Chow F tests were used to test the importance of the dummy variables. Finally, a discussion of criteria for using a separate model was presented.

Learning More

□ The GPLOT procedure is discussed in Chapter 31, "The GPLOT Procedure," in *SAS/GRAPH, Software, Reference, Version 6, First Edition, Volume 2.*

□ The PLOT procedure is discussed in Chapter 25, "The PLOT Procedure," of the *SAS Procedures Guide, Version 6, Third Edition.*

□ For more information on autoregressive models, see *SAS/ETS Software: Applications Guide 1, Version 6, First Edition.*

□ For more information on PROC SYSLIN, see the *SAS/ETS User's Guide, Version 6, First Edition.*

□ SET and TITLE statements are discussed in Chapter 9, "SAS Language Statements," in *SAS Language: Reference, Version 6, First Edition.*

□ The SORT procedure is discussed in Chapter 31, "The Sort Procedure," of the *SAS Procedures Guide.*

References

Chow, G.C. (1960), "Tests of Equality Between Sets of Coefficients in Two Linear Regressions," *Econometrica*, 28, 591—605.

Johnston, J. (1984), *Econometric Methods, Third Edition*, New York: McGraw-Hill, Inc.

Kennedy, P. (1992), *A Guide to Econometrics, Third Edition*, The MIT Press, Cambridge, Massachusetts.

Keynes, J.M. (1936), *General Theory of Employment, Investment and Money*, New York: Macmillan Publishing Co., Inc.

Kmenta, J. (1986), *Elements of Econometrics, Second Edition*, New York: Macmillan Publishing Co., Inc.

Maddala, G.S. (1977), *Econometrics*, New York: McGraw-Hill, Inc.

Ohtani, K. and Kobiyashi, M. (1986), "A Bounds Test for Equality between Sets of Coefficients in Two Linear Regression Models under Heteroskedasticity," *Econometric Theory*, 2, 220—231.

Pindyck, R.S. and Rubinfeld, D.L. (1991), *Econometric Models and Economic Forecasts, Third Edition*, New York: McGraw-Hill, Inc.

Quandt, R.E. (1960), "Test of the Hypothesis That a Linear Regression System Obeys Two Separate Regimes," *Journal of the American Statistical Association*, 55, 324—330.

U.S. Bureau of Economic Analysis, *Survey of Current Business*, July issues, various years, U.S. Government Printing Office, Washington, D.C.

U.S. Department of Commerce (1990), *Statistical Abstracts of the U.S.*, Washington, D.C.: U.S. Government Printing Office.

Chapter 4 Violations of the OLS Error Assumptions

Introduction

There are many circumstances in which data, particularly economic data, do not follow the error assumptions required for ordinary least-squares (OLS) estimation. Classical OLS regression assumes the individual error terms are identically distributed (identical means and variances) from a normal population, independent of each other, and uncorrelated with the right-hand side variables. This chapter discusses the effect of violations in the classical error assumptions of independence across time and constant variance (*homoskedasticity*). It discusses methods of testing for these violations. It also suggests some standard approaches to mitigate or eliminate their effects because violations of either of these assumptions can cause serious estimation and interpretation problems. The impact of errors that do not conform to the first two assumptions is that OLS estimation produces imprecise parameter estimates. For mathematical details, see Pindyck and Rubinfeld (1991), Johnston (1984), and Kmenta (1986). The estimation problems caused by errors correlated with right-hand side variables are discussed in Chapter 6, "Fitting Systems of Linear Equations."

In this chapter, you use the AUTOREG procedure in SAS/ETS software to fit a Monetarist model of inflation, test the residuals for autocorrelation, and then make corrections. Also in this chapter, you use the MODEL and SYSLIN procedures in SAS/ETS software to fit a model of state and local government expenditures, test for the constancy of the error variance, and make corrections.

Autocorrelation across Time

An autocorrelated error structure occurs whenever the errors corresponding to observations across time periods are not independent. Such errors are often referred to as *serially correlated errors* and occur often in time series data.

The discussion that follows assumes your data were collected at uniform time intervals: 0, 1, 2, . . . t, $t+1$, $t+2$, . . . T. If your data were not collected at uniform time intervals or have missing values, see the discussion of the EXPAND procedure in Chapter 2, "Manipulating Time Series Data," in *SAS/ETS Software: Applications Guide 1, Version 6, First Edition.*

The autocorrelated error structure does not lead to biased or inconsistent parameter estimates of a correctly specified model. However, OLS estimation with an autocorrelated error structure does lead to parameter estimates that are not efficient, and subsequent statistical tests of the estimated parameters are not valid. For example, OLS estimation and positive autocorrelation of the error structure results in underestimation of the standard errors of the parameters. Furthermore, t and F statistics as well as R^2 tend to be overestimated.

Checking for Autocorrelation

A Monetarist model of long-run inflation (as measured by the consumer price index, CPI) was developed by Selden (1975). In his model, which is fitted with time series data, Selden hypothesized that inflation depends on past changes in M1, the narrowly defined money supply.

Selden's inflation model has the form

$$P_t = B_0 + B_1 M_{t-k} + \varepsilon_t$$

P   refers to the long-run (three-year) percentage rate of change in the consumer price index, 1972=100.

M   refers to the long-run (three-year) percentage rate of change in the M1 money supply, consisting primarily of currency and coins in circulation and checking account deposits.

k represents the length of the lag from changes in M to changes in P.

ε_t is an error term, which follows the classic regression assumptions.

Selden selected a lag length of $k=14$ quarters, since this value maximized the R^2 of the OLS estimated equation, which is

$$P = .24 + 1.04\,M \quad .$$

As estimated, the model implies that increases in the long-run M1 money supply induce long-run inflation. Conversely, decreases in M1 induce reductions in long-run inflation. This implication is of great interest for advocates and detractors of monetary policy. However, because the model is estimated with time series data and OLS, there may be inaccuracies in the estimated parameters and in subsequent tests of significance due to autocorrelation.

The next section introduces the INFLATE data set, used to fit Selden's model, and then illustrates estimation and interpretation problems with autocorrelated error structures.

Introducing the INFLATE Data Set

The INFLATE data set contains quarterly observations from first quarter 1950 through the second quarter 1971 on the U.S. Consumer Price Index (1972=100) and the U.S. money supply as measured by M1.

The following SAS example code creates the INFLATE data set and prints the first five observations. Output 4.1 shows the results. For a description of the date creation function INTNX, see *SAS Language: Reference, Version 6, First Edition.*

```
data inflate;
   input cpi m1 @@;
   retain date '1oct49'd;
   date=intnx('qtr',date,1);
   format date yyq.;
   cards;
52.3 112.033  52.7 113.667  54.3 114.933  55.2 115.933
56.9 117.133  57.2 118.200  57.2 119.700  57.8 121.900
57.7 123.500  57.6 124.533  58.0 125.800  58.6 127.067
58.7 127.567  58.9 128.433  59.1 128.633  58.8 128.733
59.5 129.100  59.7 129.400  59.6 130.633  59.9 131.967
60.4 133.500  60.8 134.300  61.2 134.867  61.5 135.100
62.0 135.567  62.5 135.933  63.2 135.967  63.8 136.600
64.5 136.867  64.8 136.933  65.4 136.967  65.4 136.233
65.7 136.067  65.8 137.633  66.2 139.000  66.4 140.700
67.0 142.600  67.4 143.800  67.7 144.533  68.0 143.633
68.4 143.000  68.6 142.767  68.8 143.900  68.9 144.233
68.8 144.833  69.2 146.033  69.5 146.867  69.6 148.300
70.2 149.167  70.4 149.833  70.6 149.533  71.0 150.433
71.3 151.833  71.4 153.333  71.6 154.800  72.1 156.400
72.3 157.333  72.5 158.833  72.9 161.433  73.1 163.400
73.7 164.500  74.1 165.800  74.6 167.700  74.9 170.500
75.7 173.333  76.6 175.467  77.0 175.267  77.7 175.467
78.2 177.167  78.5 179.733  79.2 183.867  80.2 186.600
81.2 189.100  82.1 192.767  82.9 196.667  84.0 200.667
85.0 204.067  86.0 206.167  87.4 207.333  88.5 208.533
89.8 210.367  90.9 213.133  91.7 215.833  93.0 218.667
94.4 222.400  95.7 228.000
;
proc print data=inflate (obs=5);
   var date cpi m1;
   title 'INFLATION Model Example';
   title2 'First Five Observations INFLATE Data';
run;
```

Output 4.1
The First Five
Observations of
the INFLATE Data
Set

```
                      INFLATION Model Example
                  First Five Observations INFLATE Data

          OBS    DATE    CPI      M1

           1     50Q1    52.3    112.033
           2     50Q2    52.7    113.667
           3     50Q3    54.3    114.933
           4     50Q4    55.2    115.933
           5     51Q1    56.9    117.133
```

Plotting OLS Residuals

Plotting the data (either dependent variable versus the independent variables or versus time) is not reliable for identifying autocorrelated error structures. However, by plotting the OLS residuals, you can quickly check for obvious autocorrelation problems. You can create residuals and store them in a data set as you fit your model.

The following SAS example code creates and plots the OLS residuals of Selden's model. The code is presented in the following three parts: the DATA step, the AUTOREG procedure, and the PLOT procedure.

The DATA step uses the INFLATE data set to create the percentage changes in CPI and M1, then lags the percentage changes in M1, labels the newly created variables, and lastly, subsets the data—deleting the missing values created in the lagging process.

```
data inflate1;
set inflate;

    /* Calculating Percentage Changes in P and M */
p=100*(cpi-lag12(cpi))/lag12(cpi);
m=100*(m1-lag12(m1))/lag12(m1);

    /* Calculating Lag in Money Supply M1 */
m_lag14=lag14(m);

   /* Labeling Variables */
label p='Quarterly % Change in Prices'
      m='Quarterly % Change in Money Supply, M1'
      m_lag14='M1 Money Supply Lagged 14 Quarters';

   /* Subsetting Data */
if date < '1JAN58'D then delete;
run;
```

You use PROC AUTOREG and the INFLATE1 data set to fit the model from 58Q1 through 71Q2 with OLS and create the residuals to be used for plotting. The following is an interpretation of the statements:

PROC AUTOREG
   invokes the AUTOREG procedure. The DATA= option specifies INFLATE1 as the input data set.

MODEL
> specifies the model to be fitted. The dependent variable, P, is on the left-hand side of the model, and the independent variable, M_LAG14, is on the right-hand side of the model. The NOPRINT option suppresses the printed output.

OUTPUT
> creates an output data set. The OUT= option names the output data set, INFL_OUT. The other options of the OUTPUT statement are interpreted as follows:

> R=   requests that the residuals, based on both the structural and time series parts of the model, be stored in the output data set in a variable named RESID.

> P=   requests that the predicted values, based on both the structural and autoregressive parts of the model, be stored in the output data set in a variable named PRED.

The following SAS program produces the data set INFL_OUT.

```
    /* Fitting of the Model by OLS */
proc autoreg data=inflate1;
   model p = m_lag14 / noprint;
   output out=infl_out r=resid p=pred;
run;
```

You can use PROC PLOT and the INFL_OUT data set to plot the residuals versus time. The VREF= option of the PROC PLOT statement adds a vertical reference line at the value 0.0. The following statements generate Output 4.2.

```
    /* Plotting Residuals Versus Time */
proc plot data=infl_out vpct=55;
   plot resid * date = '*' / vref=0.0;
   title 'INFLATION Model Example';
   title2 'OLS Residuals versus Time';
run;
```

Output 4.2
Plots of Residuals
Showing
Autocorrelation

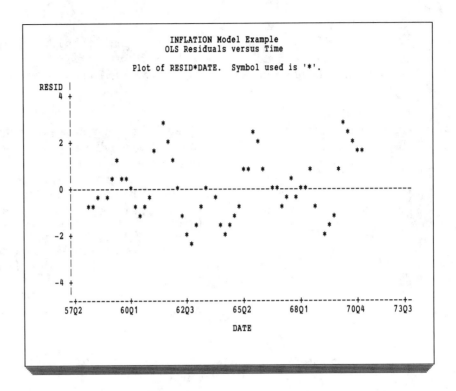

Interpretation of output

Randomly distributed errors present no patterns in scatter plots versus time or in chronological lists. The residuals in Output 4.2 tend to be grouped in fours and fives: one set all negative, the next set all positive. Patterns of this form indicate positive autocorrelation.

Testing for Autocorrelation

Often, you may want to test for autocorrelated residuals. The Durbin-Watson d statistic detects autocorrelation, and is defined as

$$d = \frac{\sum\limits_{t=2}^{T} \left(\hat{\varepsilon}_t - \hat{\varepsilon}_{t-1}\right)^2}{\sum\limits_{t=1}^{T} \hat{\varepsilon}_t^2}$$

where the $\hat{\varepsilon}$'s are the residuals from the fitted equation.

The d statistic is approximately equal to $2(1-\rho)$, where ρ is the correlation coefficient between errors in time period t and those in time period $t-1$. If there is no autocorrelation, then $\rho=0$ and the statistic is close to two. When ρ approaches one, the d statistic is close to zero, and when ρ approaches -1, the d statistic is close to four.

The Durbin-Watson test is not exact. The sequence of error terms used to calculate the d statistic depends on itself and on the sequence of values of the independent variable or variables. In tables of critical values for the d statistic, two values are given, d_l and d_u. The following table lists the conclusions you should make from the d statistic value.

	If the Magnitude of the *d* statistic is . . .	Then . . .
Table 4.1 *Interpretations of Durbin-Watson d Statistic Values*	$4 - d_l < d < 4$	reject the null hypothesis; negative autocorrelation
	$4 - d_u < d < 4 - d_l$	result is indeterminate
	$d_u < d < 4 - d_u$	accept null hypothesis
	$d < d < d_u$	result is indeterminate
	$0 < d < d_l$	reject null hypothesis; positive autocorrelation

▶ *Caution* . . . . **The Durbin-Watson test was designed to detect first-order autoregressive errors.** This is only one type of autocorrelation and seems to be the most common. Moreover, the Durbin-Watson bounds do not hold when lagged values of the dependent variable appear on the right-hand side of the regression. Also, for incorrectly specified regression models, the Durbin-Watson *d* statistic may lie in the critical region even though no real autocorrelation is present. Some economists use the *d* statistic as a lack-of-fit statistic; a use that is justified for models assumed to exhibit no autocorrelation. ▲

For additional information on the Durbin-Watson *d* statistic, see Chapter 3, "Autoregressive Models," of *SAS/ETS Software: Applications Guide 1* or Pindyck and Rubinfeld (1991), and Bartles and Goodhew (1981). For details on the derivation of the Durbin-Watson test, see Durbin and Watson (1950 and 1951).

In Release 6.07 or higher of SAS/ETS software, the AUTOREG and PDLREG procedures print the generalized Durbin-Watson *d* statistics and the level of significance by specifying the DW= and the DWPROB options of the model statement.

Testing the Inflation Model for Autocorrelation

The following SAS example code uses PROC AUTOREG and the INFLATE1 data to fit the model and test for autocorrelation. The following is an interpretation of the options of the MODEL statement:

DW=*n*   prints the generalized Durbin-Watson *d* statistics. For this example, DW=4, specifying that the first- through fourth-order generalized *d* statistics be printed.

DWPROB   prints the *p* values of the generalized *d* statistics.

The following SAS example code fits the inflation model and then tests for autocorrelation, as displayed in Output 4.3.

```
proc autoreg data=inflate1;
   model p = m_lag14 / dw=4 dwprob;
run;
```

Output 4.3
Testing the
Inflation Model for
Autocorrelation

```
                        INFLATION Model Example

                          Autoreg Procedure

Dependent Variable = P        Quarterly % Change in Prices


                   Ordinary Least Squares Estimates

        SSE            93.43755    DFE              52
        MSE            1.796876    Root MSE    1.340476
        SBC            190.832     AIC         186.8541
        Reg Rsq        0.8767      Total Rsq     0.8767

                   Durbin-Watson Statistics

                Order     DW      PROB<DW
                  1     0.4397    0.0001
                  2     1.1989    0.0010
                  3     1.9329    0.4665
                  4     2.4382    0.9751


    Variable    DF      B Value    Std Error   t Ratio Approx Prob

    Intercept    1    0.23667426    0.44652     0.530    0.5983
    M_LAG14      1    1.04137217    0.05416    19.229    0.0001
```

Interpretation of output

In Output 4.3, the first generalized d statistic in the OLS model is .4397 with a p value of .0001. The second generalized d statistic is 1.1989 with a p value of .001. These test results imply significant positive autocorrelation in a correctly specified model.

You may want to continue checking and analyzing the form of autocorrelation present. You can use the ARIMA procedure in SAS/ETS software to identify the autocorrelation process of a series. For examples, see Chapter 8, "Fitting Time Series Cross-Sectional Models," and Chapter 16, "Combining Forecasting Methods." For additional examples and discussion, see *SAS/ETS Software: Applications Guide 1* and the *SAS/ETS User's Guide, Version 6, First Edition*.

Assuming the model is correctly specified, a correction for autocorrelation is appropriate. The following sections show you how to correct the model for first-order autoregression, and then for second-order autoregression. Notice the change in magnitude of the estimated slope parameter as the corrections are made.

Correcting for Autoregression

Several approaches have been developed to adjust for autoregressive error structures. One strategy devised by Cochrane and Orcutt is to estimate the autoregressive parameters from the OLS residuals, transform the data (to correct for the autoregression), and then re-estimate by OLS (1949). This approach can be performed in iterations by alternating the estimation of the model parameters and the autoregression parameters until they converge. Prais and Winsten accounted for data transformation anomalies that occur in the first k observations of the data transformations for kth order autoregression (1954).

PROC AUTOREG enables you to estimate the model parameters and account for autoregression with the estimation strategies of maximum likelihood, the Yule-Walker method, and unconditional least squares. Examples are shown below using maximum-likelihood estimation.

A first-order autoregressive version of the Monetarist inflation model is

$$P_t = B_0 + B_1 \, \text{M\_LAG14}_t + v_t$$

where the error term v_t is defined as

$$v_t = \varepsilon_t - \varphi_1 v_{t-1}$$

The term ε_t is a sequence of independent normal error terms (conforming to the classical regression error assumptions), and φ_1 is the autoregressive parameter. A second order autoregressive error process has the form

$$v_t = \varepsilon_t - \varphi_1 v_{t-1} - \varphi_2 v_{t-2} \quad .$$

A *p*th order autoregressive error process has the form

$$v_t = \varepsilon_t - \varphi_1 v_{t-1} - \varphi_2 v_{t-2} - \ldots - \varphi_p v_{t-p} \quad .$$

The *p*th order autoregressive model contains *p* autoregressive parameters.

Note that this definition of the autoregressive process causes the signs of the autoregressive parameters to be reversed from what you would have expected otherwise. For details on the estimation methods of the ARIMA and AUTOREG procedures, see Chapter 3, "Autoregressive Models," in *SAS/ETS Software: Applications Guide 1*, or Chapter 7, "The ARIMA Procedure," and Chapter 8, "The AUTOREG Procedure," of the *SAS/ETS User's Guide, Version 6, First Edition*.

Also note that the %AR macro in SAS/ETS software enables you to correct for autoregression in PROC MODEL, which allows you great flexibility in model specification. An example of using the %AR macro in PROC MODEL is presented in the next section. For more information on use of the %AR macro, see the *SAS/ETS User's Guide*.

Correcting for First-Order Autoregression

Seaks (1984) noted the significant, positive autocorrelation present in Selden's inflation model. Knowing that OLS estimation with autocorrelated data would yield inaccurate statistical tests, Seaks re-estimated the model using maximum-likelihood estimation and corrected for first-, then second-order autoregression.

You can correct the inflation model for first-order autoregression by specifying the following options of the MODEL statement in PROC AUTOREG:

NLAG=

> specifies the order of autoregression or lists the subset of autoregressive parameters to be fitted. For example, NLAG=3 fits a third-order autoregressive process; all three autoregressive parameters are fitted. If you specify NLAG=(1 3), only the first and third parameters are fitted.
>
> Note that if you do not specify an NLAG= length, PROC AUTOREG does not fit an autoregressive model.

METHOD=

specifies an estimation method. You can specify the following methods:

ML   is maximum-likelihood estimation.

YW   is Yule-Walker estimation.

ULS   is unconditional least-squares estimation.

For this example, the ML method is specified.

MAXIT=

specifies the maximum number of iterations. With iterated estimation, the regression parameters and the autoregression parameter or parameters are alternatively estimated until convergence is reached. The default number of iterations is 15.

CONVERGE=

specifies the convergence criteria of the estimation. Convergence is obtained when the absolute value of the change in the autoregression parameter or parameters between iterations is less than the specified value. The default value is .001.

The following SAS example code uses PROC AUTOREG to fit the inflation model with a correction for first-order autoregression, as displayed in Output 4.4.

```
proc autoreg data=inflate1;
   model p = m_lag14 / nlag=1 method=ml maxit=40 converge=.0001
                       dw=1 dwprob;
   run;
```

Output 4.4
*The Inflation
Model Corrected
for AR(1)*

```
                        INFLATION Model Example

                          Autoreg Procedure

Dependent Variable = P          Quarterly % Change in Prices


                    Ordinary Least Squares Estimates

             SSE            93.43755    DFE              52
             MSE            1.796876    Root MSE    1.340476
             SBC             190.832    AIC         186.8541
             Reg Rsq          0.8767    Total Rsq     0.8767
             Durbin-Watson    0.4397    PROB<DW       0.0001


        Variable     DF      B Value    Std Error   t Ratio Approx Prob

        Intercept     1    0.23667426    0.44652      0.530     0.5983
        M_LAG14       1    1.04137217    0.05416     19.229     0.0001


                    Estimates of Autocorrelations

   Lag  Covariance  Correlation -1 9 8 7 6 5 4 3 2 1 0 1 2 3 4 5 6 7 8 9 1

     0   1.730325    1.000000  |                    |********************|
     1   1.319112    0.762349  |                    |***************     |
```

(continued)

Output 4.4
(continued)

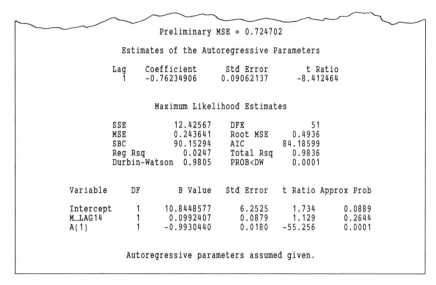

```
                    Preliminary MSE = 0.724702

            Estimates of the Autoregressive Parameters

        Lag    Coefficient     Std Error      t Ratio
         1     -0.76234906    0.09062137    -8.412464


                  Maximum Likelihood Estimates

        SSE         12.42567    DFE              51
        MSE          0.243641   Root MSE      0.4936
        SBC         90.15294    AIC         84.18599
        Reg Rsq      0.0247     Total Rsq     0.9836
        Durbin-Watson 0.9805    PROB<DW       0.0001


    Variable    DF     B Value    Std Error   t Ratio Approx Prob

    Intercept    1   10.8448577     6.2525     1.734     0.0889
    M_LAG14      1    0.0992407     0.0879     1.129     0.2644
    A(1)         1   -0.9930440     0.0180   -55.256     0.0001


          Autoregressive parameters assumed given.
```

```
                    INFLATION Model Example

                      Autoreg Procedure

    Variable    DF     B Value    Std Error   t Ratio Approx Prob

    Intercept    1   10.8448577     3.9691     2.732     0.0086
    M_LAG14      1    0.0992407     0.0873     1.137     0.2608
```

Interpretation of output

From the Ordinary Least Squares Estimates section of Output 4.4, the OLS estimated slope parameter on the lagged changes in the money supply was 1.04 and was significantly different from zero at the .01 level. However, the Durbin-Watson d statistic indicated significant positive autocorrelation.

In the Maximum Likelihood Estimates section, the magnitude of the estimated slope parameter on the lagged changes in the money supply has fallen to 0.099 and is no longer significantly different from zero, having a t statistic of only 1.137. The first-order autoregression parameter is estimated to be −0.762349 and is significant. Notice the Durbin-Watson d statistic is .9805 and is significant (at the .01 level), indicating the residuals are still autocorrelated and are not independent. A correction for second-order autoregression is specified next.

Correcting for Second-Order Autoregression

You can request a correction for second-order autoregression by specifying NLAG=2 as an option in the MODEL statement, as shown in the following example code:

```
proc autoreg data=inflate1;
   model p = m_lag14 / nlag=2 method=ml maxit=40 dw=1 dwprob;
run;
```

The output generated by the above code correcting for second-order autoregression is displayed in Output 4.5.

Output 4.5
Correcting for
Second-Order
Autoregression

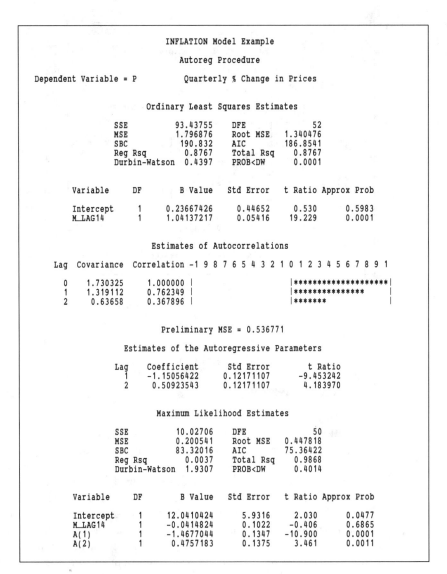

```
                          INFLATION Model Example

                            Autoreg Procedure

Dependent Variable = P          Quarterly % Change in Prices


                      Ordinary Least Squares Estimates

              SSE         93.43755    DFE              52
              MSE          1.796876   Root MSE   1.340476
              SBC         190.832     AIC        186.8541
              Reg Rsq       0.8767    Total Rsq    0.8767
              Durbin-Watson 0.4397    PROB<DW      0.0001


        Variable    DF      B Value    Std Error  t Ratio Approx Prob

        Intercept    1   0.23667426     0.44652     0.530    0.5983
        M_LAG14      1   1.04137217     0.05416    19.229    0.0001


                    Estimates of Autocorrelations

  Lag  Covariance  Correlation -1 9 8 7 6 5 4 3 2 1 0 1 2 3 4 5 6 7 8 9 1

    0   1.730325    1.000000 |                   |********************|
    1   1.319112    0.762349 |                   |***************     |
    2   0.63658     0.367896 |                   |*******            |


                  Preliminary MSE = 0.536771

          Estimates of the Autoregressive Parameters

          Lag    Coefficient    Std Error     t Ratio
           1     -1.15056422    0.12171107   -9.453242
           2      0.50923543    0.12171107    4.183970


                  Maximum Likelihood Estimates

              SSE         10.02706    DFE              50
              MSE          0.200541   Root MSE   0.447818
              SBC         83.32016    AIC        75.36422
              Reg Rsq       0.0037    Total Rsq    0.9868
              Durbin-Watson 1.9307    PROB<DW      0.4014


        Variable    DF      B Value    Std Error  t Ratio Approx Prob

        Intercept    1   12.0410424      5.9316     2.030    0.0477
        M_LAG14      1   -0.0414824      0.1022    -0.406    0.6865
        A(1)         1   -1.4677044      0.1347   -10.900    0.0001
        A(2)         1    0.4757183      0.1375     3.461    0.0011
```

```
                        INFLATION Model Example

                          Autoreg Procedure

             Autoregressive parameters assumed given.

        Variable    DF      B Value    Std Error  t Ratio Approx Prob

        Intercept    1   12.0410424      4.2608     2.826    0.0068
        M_LAG14      1   -0.0414824      0.0959    -0.433    0.6670
```

Interpretation of output

The d statistic in Output 4.5 of the model corrected for second-order
autoregression is 1.9307 and is not significant at the .05 level.

The estimated slope parameters, R^2s, t statistics, and Durbin-Watson
d statistics from the OLS model, the model corrected for first-order
autoregression, and the model corrected for second-order autoregression are
compared in the following table.

Table 4.2
Comparing Inflation Models, OLS, AR(1) Corrected, and AR(2) Corrected

Statistics and Parameter	OLS	Corrected for First-Order Autoregression	Corrected for Second-Order Autoregression
Reg R-Square	.8767	.0247	.0037
M_lag14 Parameter Estimate	1.04	.099	−.041
t statistic	19.229	1.129	−.406
Durbin-Watson *d* statistic	.44	.9805	1.93

After correcting for second-order autoregression, the apparent relationship between long-run changes in M1 (M_lag14) and inflation (P) vanishes. Using OLS estimation in the presence of an autoregressive error structure can result in misleading parameter estimates and levels of significance.

%AR Macro for PROC MODEL

You can use the %AR macro to correct models for autoregression within PROC MODEL. The model to be fitted follows the EXOGENOUS statement. The following is an interpretation of the statements:

PROC MODEL
> invokes the MODEL procedure. The DATA= option requests the INFLATE1 data set.

PARAMETERS
> specifies the parameters to be estimated.

ENDOGENOUS
> identifies the endogenous variables.

EXOGENOUS
> identifies the exogenous variables.

%AR (*name, nlag, endolist*)
> requests the %AR macro. The three arguments of the %AR macro are interpreted as follows:

> | | |
> |---|---|
> | *name* | specifies a prefix to the autoregressive parameters. For this example, the prefix AR is specified. |
> | *nlag* | specifies the order of the autoregression correction, or the list of autoregressive parameters to be fitted. For this example, a second-order process is specified. |
> | endolist | specifies the list of equations to which the autoregressive process is to be applied. |

FIT
> specifies the equations to be fitted. The equation P= defines the equation to be fitted. In PROC MODEL, you must write out equations to be fitted with all parameters, variables, and arithmetic operators.

The following SAS example code fits the inflation model to the INFLATE1 data set with a correction for second-order autoregression.

```
proc model data=inflate1;
   parameters b0 b1;
   endogenous p;
   exogenous m_lag14;
   p = b0 + b1*m_lag14;
   %ar(ar,2,p)
   fit p;
run;
```

For more information about PROC MODEL, see Chapter 7, "Fitting Nonlinear Models," in this book or Chapter 13, "The MODEL Procedure," in the *SAS/ETS User's Guide*.

Heteroskedasticity

Heteroskedasticity occurs when the error terms do not have a constant variance. Cross-sectional data (data collected in the same time period over geographic regions, firms, individuals, and so on) exhibit heteroskedasticity more than time series data do. For example, the variance of expenditures may not be constant across all levels of income (variance of expenditures often tends to increase with income), but is often constant over time within a particular income level. Over time, economic data often change in roughly the same order of magnitude and may be less likely to have unequal variances.

Heteroskedasticity causes the OLS estimates of the parameter variances to be biased. This, in turn, leads to unreliable t and F tests of the parameters.

Examining Data for Heteroskedasticity

It is important to establish that heteroskedasticity is a problem before correcting for it. A quick, intuitive approach to assessing the constancy of the variance of the errors is to plot the data and the OLS residuals. Data and OLS residuals that display greater dispersion (variance) in some areas may be heteroskedastic.

Introducing the EXPEND Data Set

The EXPEND data set contains cross-sectional data by states from U.S. Bureau of the Census data from 1970. It contains the following variables:

EXP   is state and local government expenditures.

POP   is state population.

AID   is per capita government aid for education.

INCOME   is per capita personal income.

The following SAS example code creates the EXPEND data set, labels the variables, titles the data set, and prints the first five observations, as displayed in Output 4.6.

```
data expend;
   input exp pop aid income @@;
   label exp='State & Local Govt Exp in Million of $'
         pop='State Population in Thousands'
         aid='Per Capita Govt Aid for Education in $'
         income='Per Capita Personal Income in $';
   cards;
  698    325 570 5222    368    346 369 4269    411    460 235 3703
  543    533 180 5209    571    571 170 5222    475    634 201 4128
  521    680 195 3766    587    716 252 4083    512    755 180 3711
  526    774 123 4279    940    816 202 5153    699    969 184 4513
  704   1026 186 3664    823   1076 277 3512    821   1127 196 3741
 1052   1528 134 4451   1250   1795 252 3624   1523   1963 150 4273
 1014   2008 199 3345   1766   2185 201 4339   1427   2256 255 3188
 1551   2268 132 4535   1920   2364 183 4600   1767   2633 190 3837
 1512   2688 153 3500   2108   2884 113 4316   2546   3080 145 5414
 2063   3306 181 3634   3070   3418 184 4601   2104   3521 193 3476
 2691   3738 196 3565   3528   3877 163 4343   3392   4048 135 5017
 2446   4072 175 3708   3757   4526 116 4279   3197   4733 178 3956
 3156   4747 151 4307   3037   4765 131 4396   2938   5221 141 3868
 3457   5286 103 4364   5166   5796 190 4825   4771   7347 114 4450
 5911   7349 141 5379   7799   9013 147 4982   6867  10722 112 4572
 8935  11244 156 5162   7246  11604 141 4085   8840  11905 136 4545
22750  18367 240 5275  20052  20411 200 5087
;

proc print data=expend (obs=5) label;
   var exp pop aid income;
   title 'Government Expenditure Model';
   title2 'First Five Observations EXPEND Data';
run;
```

Output 4.6
The First Five
Observations of
the EXPEND Data
Set

```
                     Government Expenditure Model
                     First Five Observations EXPEND Data

                                          Per Capita
                     State &                Govt Aid
                   Local Govt     State       for      Per Capita
                     Exp in    Population  Education    Personal
      OBS         Million of $  in Thousands  in $    Income in $

        1            698          325         570        5222
        2            368          346         369        4269
        3            411          460         235        3703
        4            543          533         180        5209
        5            571          571         170        5222
```

Plotting Heteroskedastic Data

By plotting the data, you can visually check for regions where the data display greater dispersion. The following SAS example code plots the variable EXP (the dependent variable in subsequent examples) versus POP, AID, and INCOME, in separate scatter plots. Output 4.7 shows the results.

```
proc plot data=expend vpct=55;
   plot exp * (pop aid income) = '*';
   title2 'Dependent versus Independent Variables';
run;
```

Output 4.7
Plots of the
EXPEND Data Set

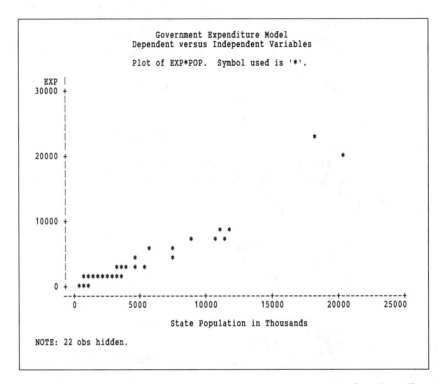

(continued)

Output 4.7
(continued)

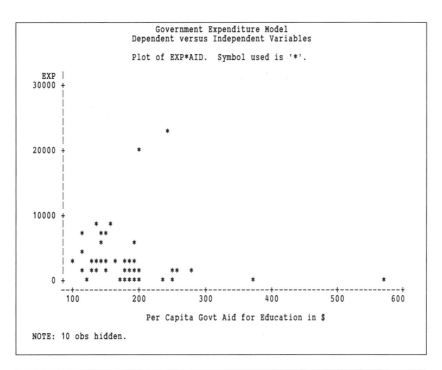

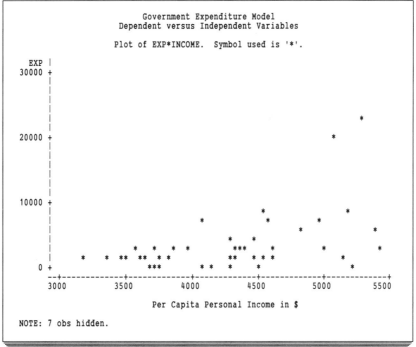

Interpretation of output

In Output 4.7, expenditures (EXP) plotted versus population (POP) and income (INCOME) show greater dispersion at higher levels of POP and INCOME; EXP plotted versus per capita government aid (AID) seems to display greater variability at lower levels of AID. From the visual evidence of these scatter plots, EXP may have a nonconstant variance with all of the variables.

Visual inspection of scatter plots can reveal an obvious change in the dispersion of the data. However, a better approach for visual inspection for heteroskedasticity is to examine a scatter plot of the OLS residuals plotted against the right-hand side variables of the regression model.

In the following section, a multiple regression model relating EXP to POP, AID, and INCOME is fitted, then the residuals are plotted.

Fitting the Government Expenditure Model

The following multiple regression model hypothesizes that EXP depends linearly on POP, AID, and INCOME:

$$EXP = \beta_0 + \beta_1\,POP + \beta_2\,AID + \beta_3\,INCOME + \varepsilon \ .$$

The following SAS example code uses PROC AUTOREG to fit the model, creates an output data set named EXP_OUT containing the residuals, RESID, and the predicted values, PRED. Output 4.8 shows the results.

```
proc autoreg data=expend;
   model exp = pop aid income;  /* Fitting the model        */
   output out = exp_out         /* Output data set creation */
           p = pred             /* Create predicted values  */
           r = resid;           /* Create residuals         */
run;

proc print data=exp_out (obs=5);
run;
```

Output 4.8
Fitting an OLS
Model to the
EXPEND Data Set

```
                     Government Expenditure Model
                          Autoreg Procedure
Dependent Variable = EXP       State & Local Govt Exp in Million of $

                   Ordinary Least Squares Estimates

              SSE        57392203   DFE                46
              MSE         1247657   Root MSE     1116.985
              SBC        855.2117   AIC          847.5637
              Reg Rsq      0.9384   Total Rsq      0.9384
              Durbin-Watson 1.4500


     Variable    DF     B Value    Std Error    t Ratio Approx Prob

     Intercept    1  -4112.75226      1240.1     -3.316      0.0018
     POP          1  0.949681823    0.040288     23.572      0.0001
     AID          1      6.50813         2.2      2.935      0.0052
     INCOME       1  0.530009197    0.284974      1.860      0.0693
```

(continued)

Output 4.8
(continued)

```
                      Government Expenditure Model

        OBS     PRED      RESID     EXP    POP    AID    INCOME

         1    2673.24   -1975.24    698    325    570     5222
         2     879.95    -511.95    368    346    369     4269
         3    -183.86     594.86    411    460    235     3703
         4     325.71     217.29    543    533    180     5209
         5     303.61     267.39    571    571    170     5222
```

Interpretation of output

In Output 4.8 the estimated model is

$$EXP = -4112.752 + .94968 \, POP + 6.50813 \, AID + .53001 \, INCOME \quad.$$

The R^2, .9384, indicates a reasonable fit of the data. Because the data are cross-sectional in a single time period, correlation of residuals across time is not a problem; thus, the Durbin-Watson *d* statistic does not provide useful information.

The *t* statistics indicate that the slope parameters are all significantly different from zero at the .10 level. However, heteroskedastic errors would invalidate the *t*-tests. The next section plots the residuals and provides visual evidence of heteroskedasticity.

Plotting Heteroskedastic Residuals

Plotting the residuals, their absolute values, and the squared residuals versus the independent variables provides a visual check on the constancy of the error variance and may offer insight as to which variable is associated with the heteroskedasticity. The greater the dispersion of the residuals, the greater the estimated error variance.

▶ *Caution* .... *While plotting is a useful tool for data analysis, a serious problem with visual inspections for significant changes in variables and functions of variables is that the eye can misinterpret.*
A scatter plot that appears to be a random distribution with one or two outliers here and there may actually contain patterns. Alternatively, a scatter plot that appears to be a distinct pattern may not be significantly different from a random distribution. ▲

The following SAS example code using the output data set EXP_OUT and PROC PLOT to generate a scatter plot of the residuals versus each of the independent variables. Output 4.9 shows the results.

```
proc plot data=exp_out vpct=55;
   plot resid * (pop aid income) / vref=0.0;
   title2 'Residuals versus Independent Variables';
run;
```

Output 4.9
*Plots of OLS
Residuals Versus
Regressors*

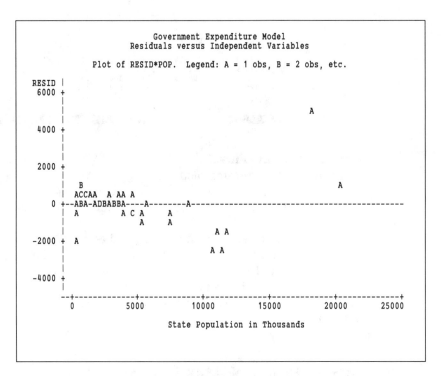

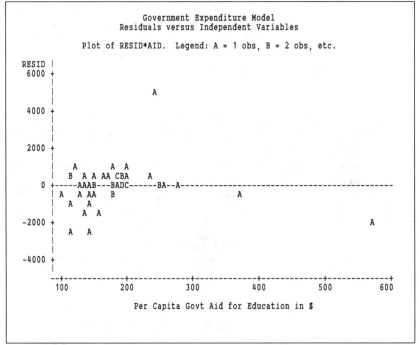

(continued)

Output 4.9
(continued)

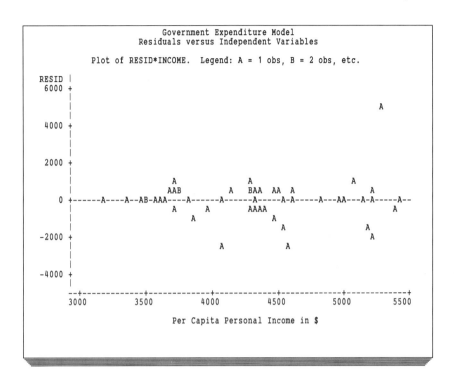

```
                           Government Expenditure Model
                         Residuals versus Independent Variables

                    Plot of RESID*INCOME.  Legend: A = 1 obs, B = 2 obs, etc.

        RESID |
         6000 +
              |
              |                                                                A
              |
         4000 +
              |
              |
         2000 +
              |
              |                A              A              A
              |                AAB          A BAA   AA  A            A
            0 +------A----A--AB-AAA----A------A------A-----A-A-----A---AA---A-A-----A--
              |                A    A         AAAA                              A
              |                  A            A
              |                            A                          A
        -2000 +                                                       A
              |
              |                   A          A
        -4000 +
              |
              --+-------------+-------------+-------------+-------------+-------------+
              3000          3500          4000          4500          5000          5500

                              Per Capita Personal Income in $
```

Interpretation of output

The plots of the residuals in Output 4.9 reveal

□   a greater dispersion (variance) as POP increases

□   roughly the same dispersion for AID and INCOME.

For illustrative purposes, focus on POP as the independent variable associated
with the heteroskedasticity.

Other useful OLS residual plots

Plotting the absolute value of the residuals versus the independent variables and
the squared residuals versus the independent variables may also reveal patterns of
increased dispersion of the residuals. You can obtain these plots using the MODEL
procedure in SAS/ETS software and PROC PLOT. The SAS example code shown
next generates these plots. The NOPRINT option of the PROC MODEL statement
suppresses the standard output.

Note that PROC MODEL uses the suffix *.name* to refer to equations, residuals,
errors, and predicted values. For example, the equation to be fitted is EXP (in
reference to the dependent variable), and residuals generated by this equation are
RESID.EXP. The variable RESID.EXP may be transformed and used in
programming statements within PROC MODEL.

The following SAS example code uses PROC MODEL to fit the model and
create the output data set EXP_OUT1 containing the variables RESID_AB and
RESID2, the absolute values and squared values of the residuals, respectively. The
model to be fitted is written with arithmetic operators after the EXOGENOUS
statement. Lastly, PROC PLOT plots RESID_AB and RESID2 versus population
(POP).

The following is an interpretation of the statements:

PROC MODEL
> invokes the MODEL procedure. The following options of the PROC MODEL statement are specified:

> DATA=   requests the EXPEND data set.

> NOPRINT   suppresses the normal printed output.

PARAMETERS
> identifies the parameters to be estimated. For this example, they are b_0, b_1, b_2, and b_3.

ENDOGENOUS
> identifies endogenous variables. For this example, the variable EXP is endogenous.

EXOGENOUS
> identifies the exogenous variables. For this example, POP, AID, and INCOME are exogenous.

RESID_AB
> creates the absolute values of the residuals within PROC MODEL.

RESID2
> creates the squares of the residuals within PROC MODEL.

FIT
> identifies the equation to be fitted. The OUT= option creates an output data set. For this example, the output data set is named EXP_OUT1.

OUTVARS
> requests that the variables created within PROC MODEL, RESID_AB and RESID2, be included in the output data set, EXP_OUT1.

For more information about the use of variables generated in PROC MODEL and programming within PROC MODEL, see Chapter 13, "The MODEL Procedure," in the *SAS/ETS User's Guide*.

```
    /* Creating Squares and Absolute Values of Residuals */
proc model data=expend noprint;
    parameters b0 b1 b2 b3;
    endogenous exp;
    exogenous pop aid income;
    exp = b0 + b1*pop + b2*aid + b3*income;
    resid_ab = abs(resid.exp);
    resid2 = resid.exp**2;
    fit exp / out=exp_out1;
    outvars resid_ab resid2;
run;
```

After creating the output data set EXP_OUT1 with PROC MODEL, PROC PLOT plots the absolute value and square of the residuals versus population (POP), as displayed in Output 4.10.

```
                    /* Plotting Squares and Absolute Values of Residuals */
              proc plot data=exp_out1 vpct=55;
                  plot (resid_ab resid2) * pop;
                  title2 'Absolute Value and Square of Residuals';
                  title3 'versus Population, POP';
              run;
```

Output 4.10
*Plots of Absolute
Value and Square
of Residuals versus
POP*

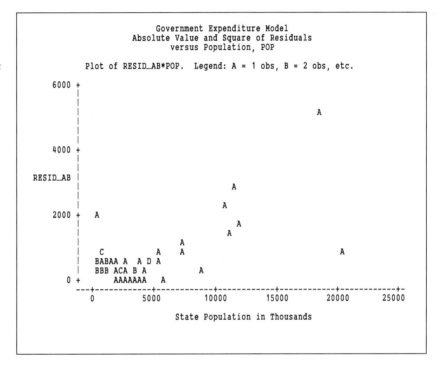

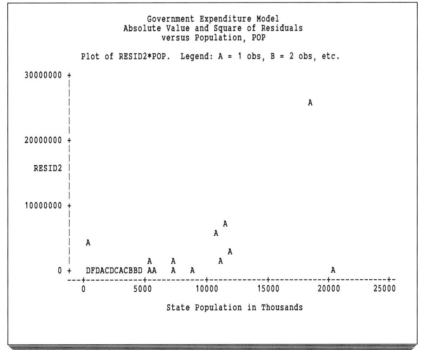

Interpretation of output

The plots in Output 4.10 reveal a greater residual dispersion as population increases. Using the squared residuals can cause a large vertical scale with most of the points lying on or near the horizontal axis and a few apparent outliers sprinkled on the rest of the plot. Using the absolute value of the residuals avoids the large vertical scale problem. Both may obscure asymmetry of the residuals about the horizontal axis. Which residual transformation you choose to use is a matter of personal preference.

In all cases after visual assessment indicates nonconstancy of the error variance, formal statistical tests are in order. The next section discusses the White test for heteroskedasticity.

Testing for Heteroskedasticity

Several tests for heteroskedasticity have been developed. This section presents the White test, which tests the null hypothesis of *homoskedasticity* (constant variance of the errors) with the alternative hypothesis of heteroskedasticity of the specified form.

The steps you must follow to perform a White test are as follows:

1. Fit the OLS model using the MODEL procedure in SAS/ETS software.

2. Calculate and square the OLS residuals in programming statements within PROC MODEL.

3. Store the residuals in an output data set using the OUT= option of the FIT statement.

4. Regress the squared residuals against the variable or variables thought to be associated with the heteroskedasticity using PROC AUTOREG or another regression procedure of your choice.

5. Under the null hypothesis of homoskedasticity, the number of observations, n, times the R^2 of the test regression is distributed as a chi square with one degree of freedom per slope parameter in the test regression.

For mathematical details of the White test, see White (1980).

Using the White Test for Linear Trend

The following regression equation can be used for testing if heteroskedasticity is linearly related to population:

$$\hat{\varepsilon}_i^2 = g_0 + g_1\text{POP}_i + v_i \quad .$$

The following SAS example code using the MODEL and AUTOREG procedures performs a White test. The NOPRINT option of the PROC MODEL statement suppresses the normal printed output. Output 4.11 shows the results.

```
   /* Creating the Squared OLS Residuals */
proc model data=expend noprint;
   parameters b0 b1 b2 b3;
   endogenous exp;
   exogenous pop aid income;
```

```
      exp = b0 + b1*pop + b2*aid + b3*income;
      resid2 = resid.exp**2;
      fit exp / out=exp_out2;
      outvars resid2;
   run;

      /* Performing the White Test */
   proc autoreg data=exp_out2;
      model resid2 = pop;
   run;
```

Output 4.11
White Test of
Heteroscedasticity
Linearly Related to
Population

```
                        Government Expenditure Model

                           Autoreg Procedure

Dependent Variable = RESID2

                     Ordinary Least Squares Estimates

             SSE            4.679E14   DFE               48
             MSE            9.748E12   Root MSE     3122190
             SBC            1643.081   AIC         1639.257
             Reg Rsq          0.3411   Total Rsq     0.3411
             Durbin-Watson    2.5102


      Variable     DF     B Value    Std Error   t Ratio Approx Prob

      Intercept    1   -949225.244    6.10E+05    -1.557     0.1262
      POP          1       505.376    1.01E+02     4.985     0.0001
```

Interpretation of output

From Output 4.11, you use the R^2 of the test regression for the White test. The statistic, $n(R^2)$ is distributed as a chi square with one degree of freedom. For OLS regressions, the regression R^2 (Reg Rsq) and total R^2 (Total Rsq) are identical. The White test statistic for this regression is 50(.3411) or 17.055. The critical value of the chi square distribution with one degree of freedom is 6.6349 at the .01 level. You reject the null hypothesis of homoskedasticity at the .01 level in favor of the alternative hypothesis of heteroskedasticity that is linearly related to population.

Using the White Test for Proportionality

Because the intercept term is not significantly different from zero at the .10 level, you may want to test whether heteroskedasticity is proportional to population.

$$\hat{\varepsilon}_i^2 = g\,\text{POP}_i + v_i \quad .$$

You use the EXP_OUT2 output data set, created in Output 4.11, and the NOINT option of the MODEL statement in PROC AUTOREG to perform the White test for heteroskedasticity proportional to an independent variable. Output 4.12 shows the results.

```
      /* Performing the White Test */
   proc autoreg data=exp_out2;
      model resid2 = pop / noint;
   run;
```

Output 4.12
White Test of Heteroscedasticity Proportional to Population

```
                        Government Expenditure Model

                           Autoreg Procedure

Dependent Variable = RESID2


                      Ordinary Least Squares Estimates

          SSE          4.915E14    DFE               49
          MSE          1.003E13    Root MSE     3167194
          SBC          1641.631    AIC         1639.719
          Reg Rsq        0.3666    Total Rsq     0.3666
          Durbin-Watson  2.4255

    NOTE: No intercept term is used. R-squares are redefined.



        Variable   DF      B Value    Std Error   t Ratio Approx Prob
        POP         1   396.540418      74.455      5.326      0.0001
```

Interpretation of output

From Output 4.12, you use the R^2 of the test regression for the White test. The statistic, $n(R^2)$ is distributed as a chi square with one degree of freedom. The White test statistic for this regression is 50(.3666) or 18.33. The critical value of the chi square distribution with one degree of freedom is 6.6349 at the .01 level. You reject the null hypothesis of homoskedasticity at the .01 level in favor of the alternative hypothesis of heteroskedasticity that is proportionally related to population.

In subsequent examples, the government expenditure model is corrected for heteroskedasticity under the assumption that the heteroskedasticity is proportionally related to population.

Using the White Test for Quadratic Form

You are not limited to testing for the forms of heteroskedasticity presented in the preceding examples. White suggests that if there is only one right-hand variable associated with heteroskedasticity, you may want to include its square to allow for nonlinearities. If there are two right-hand variables you believe are associated with heteroskedasticity, you may want to include both of their squares and a crossproduct term. In general, for each slope parameter estimated in the White test regression, there is one degree of freedom in the Chi-square test statistic, $n(R^2)$.

An example of a White test for a more complex form of heteroskedasticity in the EXPEND data set is where the error variance is believed to be a quadratic polynomial of population and income (POP, INCOME, their squares, and a crossproduct term). The null hypothesis of this test is that the error variances are homoskedastic (have a constant variance); the alternative hypothesis is that the error variances follow a quadratic of population and income. The test regression equation becomes

$$\hat{\varepsilon}_i^2 = g_0 + g_1 POP_i + g_2 POP_i^2 + g_3 INCOME_i + g_4 INCOME_i^2 + g_5 POP\_INC_i + v_i$$

where POP_INC is the crossproduct term, the product of POP and INCOME.

To perform this White test, use the following SAS example code:

```
    /* Creating Squares and Crossproduct for White Test */
data expend1;
set expend;
        pop2 = pop**2;
        income2 = income**2;
        pop_inc = pop*income;
run;

    /* Fitting Model and Creating Squared Residuals */
proc model data=expend1;
    parameters b0 b1 b2 b3;
    endogenous exp;
    exogenous pop aid income;
    exp = b0 + b1*pop + b2*aid + b3*income;
    resid2 = resid.exp**2;
    fit exp / out=exp_out3;

        /* Adding Variables to Output Data */
    id pop2 income2 pop_inc;
    outvars resid2;
run;

        /* Performing a White Test */
proc autoreg data=exp_out3;
    model resid2 = pop pop2 income income2 pop_inc;
run;
```

The output generated by the previous SAS example code is not shown. As in the previous example, you multiply the R^2 value by n to calculate the White test Chi-square value. In this case, the critical value has five degrees of freedom.

Correcting for Heteroskedasticity

Once you have determined that heteroskedasticity is present and you have determined its form, then you can select the appropriate correction strategy.

One approach to correcting for heteroskedasticity involves transforming or weighting the data to stabilize the variance. You can transform your data by using SAS data steps or by using the WEIGHT statements in the MODEL and SYSLIN procedures in SAS/ETS software.

The error variance may be related to an independent variable. One often-hypothesized form is that the error variances are proportional to the square of an independent variable:

$$\text{Var}(\varepsilon_i) = \sigma^2 X_i^2$$

where the error variance, σ^2, is equal to a nonzero (and finite) constant. This form of heteroskedasticity can be corrected by a simple data transformation, weighting by the factor $1/X_i$. In the two-variable model this becomes

$$Y_i^* = \frac{Y_i}{X_i} \quad X_i^* = \frac{1}{X_i} \quad \text{and} \quad \varepsilon_i^* = \frac{\varepsilon_i}{X_i} \quad .$$

This transformation yields the model

$$Y_i^* = b_0 \frac{1}{X_i} + b_1 + \varepsilon_i^* \quad .$$

Notice that in the transformed model, the parameters change roles: b_0 becomes a slope parameter, and b_1 becomes the intercept. Redefining the equation parameters and employing X^* yields the completely transformed equation

$$Y_i^* = b_0^* + b_1^* X_i^* + \varepsilon_i^* \quad .$$

The finite magnitude of the nonzero (but constant) error variance, σ^2, is not important to the estimation process.

Using a Transformation

Assuming the error variance is proportional to the square of population, $\mathrm{Var}(\varepsilon_i) = \sigma^2 X_i^2$, the following transformation and SAS example code eliminates the heteroskedasticity. Output 4.13 shows the results.

```
    /* Creating Transformed Variables */
data expend2;
set expend;
    expcorr = exp/pop;
    popcorr = 1/pop;
    aidcorr = aid/pop;
    inccorr = income/pop;
run;

    /* OLS Regression of Transformed Data */
proc autoreg data=expend2;
    model expcorr = popcorr aidcorr inccorr;
run;
```

Output 4.13
Government Expenditure Model Corrected for Heteroskedasticity with DATA Step Data Transformations and PROC AUTOREG

```
                    Government Expenditure Model

                         Autoreg Procedure

Dependent Variable = EXPCORR


                  Ordinary Least Squares Estimates

               SSE           0.703758   DFE              46
               MSE           0.015299   Root MSE   0.123689
               SBC          -55.6253    AIC         -63.2734
               Reg Rsq        0.7650    Total Rsq    0.7650
               Durbin-Watson  1.9329


       Variable    DF     B Value    Std Error   t Ratio Approx Prob

       Intercept    1    0.745480     0.025959    28.717     0.0001
       POPCORR      1  -794.872653    136.15      -5.838     0.0001
       AIDCORR      1    0.697125       0.14       4.936     0.0001
       INCCORR      1    0.162152     0.032115     5.049     0.0001
```

Interpretation of output

In Output 4.13, the R^2 of the transformed model is .7650 while the R^2 of the untransformed model in Output 4.8 is .9384. The lower R^2 of the transformed model does not indicate that the transformation was incorrect. The R^2 of the transformed equation is not a useful measure of the goodness of fit of the original relationship.

A better approach is to use the original relationship and the efficiently estimated parameters (of the transformed equation) to calculate the residuals:

$$\hat{\varepsilon}_i = Y_i - \hat{Y}_i$$

$$= Y_i + 794.8727 - .7455(POP) - .6971(AID) - .1622(INCOME)$$

where the transformed intercept is used as the slope parameter of population and vice versa. See the previous discussion of the model transformation. R^2 is the square of the simple correlation between Y_i and $\hat{Y}_i$, or in terms of the sums of squares

$$R^2 = 1 - \frac{SSE}{TSS}$$

where SSE, the error sum of squares, and TSS, the total sum of squares, are

$$SSE = \sum_{i=1}^{n} \hat{\varepsilon}_i^2$$

$$TSS = \sum_{i=1}^{n} (Y_i - \overline{Y})^2 \quad .$$

The R^2, as calculated in the next example, is .9488. See Output 4.14.

R^2 is difficult to interpret and compare among several fitted models. Some models are generated with transformed data; others are generated with untransformed data. For more information, see Johnston (1984).

Using a WEIGHT Statement

You can also correct for heteroskedasticity with a WEIGHT statement in PROC MODEL or PROC SYSLIN. WEIGHT statements in PROC MODEL follow FIT statements. Specify the equation you want to fit (in terms of untransformed variables), then specify a WEIGHT statement naming the variable you wish to use for the data transformation. After transforming the data, you can fit the model through the OLS technique.

The following example uses PROC SYSLIN and the EXPEND data set. It assumes that the error variance is proportional to the square of state population. Follow these steps to run a weighted regression:

1. Create a weight variable (for example, WT=1/POP**2;) in the DATA step.

2. Specify the model with a MODEL statement.

3. Use a WEIGHT statement after the MODEL statement.

The following SAS example code creates a weight variable, prints the first five weight values, and fits a weighted regression. A SET statement is used to add the weight variable to the original data. Output 4.14 shows the results.

```
                    /* Creating Weight Variable, WT */
data expend3;
set expend;
   wt = 1/pop**2;
run;


                    /* Printing Five Observations of POP and WT */
proc print data=expend3 (obs=5) label;
   var pop wt;
   title2 'First Five Observations EXPEND3 Data';
run;


                    /* Performing Weighted Regression */
proc syslin data=expend3;
   model exp = pop aid income;
   weight wt;
run;
```

Output 4.14
Government
Expenditure Model
Corrected for
Heteroskedasticity
with a WEIGHT
Statement in PROC
SYSLIN

```
                          Government Expenditure Model
                       First Five Observations EXPEND3 Data

                                State
                             Population
                  OBS       in Thousands          WT

                   1            325           .0000094675
                   2            346           .0000083531
                   3            460           .0000047259
                   4            533           .0000035200
                   5            571           .0000030671
```

```
                          Government Expenditure Model

                               SYSLIN Procedure
                        Ordinary Least Squares Estimation

Model: EXP
Dependent variable: EXP State & Local Govt Exp in Million of $

                             Analysis of Variance

                                 Sum of        Mean
          Source        DF       Squares       Square      F Value     Prob>F

          Model          3      13.03313      4.34438      283.963     0.0001
          Error         46       0.70376      0.01530
          C Total       49      13.73688

                    Root MSE     0.12369      R-Square     0.9488
                    Dep Mean   659.93756      Adj R-SQ     0.9454
                    C.V.         0.01874

                             Parameter Estimates

                       Parameter      Standard     T for H0:
          Variable  DF   Estimate        Error    Parameter=0   Prob > |T|

          INTERCEP   1  -794.872653   136.150611     -5.838       0.0001
          POP        1     0.745480     0.025959     28.717       0.0001
          AID        1     0.697125     0.141224      4.936       0.0001
          INCOME     1     0.162152     0.032115      5.049       0.0001
```

(continued)

Output 4.14
(continued)

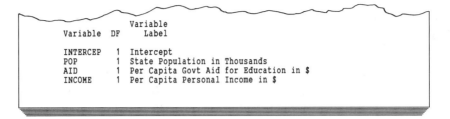

```
                      Variable
         Variable  DF    Label

         INTERCEP   1  Intercept
         POP        1  State Population in Thousands
         AID        1  Per Capita Govt Aid for Education in $
         INCOME     1  Per Capita Personal Income in $
```

Interpretation of output

The parameter values and tests of significance in Output 4.14 are the same as in Output 4.13. There are the following differences in the outputs of the two examples:

□ The intercept and the slope parameter for POP in the weighted regression are switched.

□ The R^2s are different. See the discussion following Output 4.13.

Be careful in comparing R^2s of models based on different data. Recall that OLS estimation is equivalent to maximizing a fitted equation's R^2. Transforming the data and re-estimating often reduces the resulting equation's R^2. Econometric models are designed to estimate values other than an R^2. Avoid placing too much emphasis on any single summary statistic.

For additional discussion of R^2 and weighted regressions, see the *SAS/ETS User's Guide* and Pindyck and Rubinfeld (1991, p. 132).

Chapter Summary

This chapter presented the impact of and strategies for identifying and dealing with the effects of error assumption violations. This chapter also provided examples of econometric analysis with heteroskedastic and autoregressive error structures.

Learning More

□ For more information on time series modeling, see *SAS/ETS Software: Applications Guide 1* and *SAS System for Forecasting Time Series, 1986 Edition* by Brocklebank, J.C. and Dickey, D.A.

□ For additional information on the AUTOREG, MODEL, and SYSLIN procedures, see the *SAS/ETS User's Guide*.

□ The PLOT procedure is discussed in Chapter 25, "The Plot Procedure," in the *SAS Procedures Guide, Version 6, Third Edition*.

References

Bartles, R. and Goodhew, J. (1981), "The Robustness of the Durbin-Watson Test," *Review of Economics and Statistics*, 63, 136—139.

Cochrane, D. and Orcutt, G.H. (1949), "Application of Least Squares Regressions to Relationships Containing Autocorrelated Error Terms," *Journal of the American Statistical Association*, 44, 32—61.

Durbin, J. (1960), "Estimation of Parameters in Time-Series Regression Models," *Journal of the Royal Statistical Society*, Series B, 22, 139—153.

Durbin, J. and Watson, G.S. (1950), "Testing for Serial Correlation in Least Squares Regression I," *Biometrika*, 37, 409—428.

Durbin, J. and Watson, G.S. (1951), "Testing for Serial Correlation in Least Squares Regression II," *Biometrika*, 38 159—178.

Johnston, J. (1984), *Econometric Methods, Third Edition*, New York: McGraw-Hill, Inc.

Judge, G. et al. (1985), *The Theory and Practice of Econometrics*, New York: John Wiley & Sons, Inc.

Kennedy, P. (1992), *A Guide to Econometrics, Third Edition*, Cambridge, MA: MIT Press.

Kmenta, J. (1986), *Elements of Econometrics, Second Edition*, New York: Macmillan Publishing Co., Inc.

Maddala, G.S. (1977), *Econometrics*, New York: McGraw-Hill, Inc.

Pindyck, R.S. and Rubinfeld, D.L. (1991), *Econometric Models and Economic Forecasts, Third Edition*, New York: McGraw-Hill, Inc.

Prais, S.J. and Winsten, C.B. (1954), "Trend Estimators and Serial Correlation," *Cowles Commission Discussion Paper,* No. 383, Chicago.

Savin, N.E. and White, K.J. (1978), "Estimation and Testing for Functional Form and Autocorrleation," *Journal of Econometrics*, 8, 1—12.

Seaks, T.G. (1984), "Selden's Model of Inflation: A Reexamination," *Journal of Macroeconomics*, 6(1), 103—107.

Selden, R.T. (1975), "Monetary Growth and the Long-Run Rate of Inflation," *American Economic Review Papers and Proceedings*, 65, 125—128.

Selden, R.T. (1981), "Inflation and Monetary Growth: Experience in Fourteen Countries of Europe and North America Since 1958," *Federal Reserve Bank of Richmond Economic Review*, 67(6), 19—35.

White, H. (1980), "A Heteroskedasticity-Consistent Covariance Matrix Estimator and a Direct Test for Heteroskedasticity," *Econometrica*, 48, pp. 817—838.

Chapter 5 Fitting Regression Models with Lagged Variables

Introduction

Models with lagged variables arise because the adjustment due to a change in a regressor variable may not be complete from one observation period to the next. In general, the shorter the interval between observations, the more likely the effects will be distributed across several observations.

Models that fit lagged effects are called *lag models*. For example, the Koyck lag model fits an infinite lag with one parameter. Another example is the Almon polynomial distributed lag model, which fits a polynomial function to lagged effects.

Fitting lag models enables you to

☐ include effects of independent variables from previous periods

☐ conserve degrees of freedom

☐ solve multicollinearity problems caused by including several lags of an independent variable as right-hand side variables in the proposed model.

In this chapter, you use real data to fit, test, and restrict lag models of consumption and investment expenditures. You use the AUTOREG procedure in SAS/ETS software to fit and test an infinite lag model to consumption expenditures. Infinite lag models are also known as Koyck or geometric lag models. You also use the PDLREG procedure in SAS/ETS software to fit, test, and restrict an Almon polynomial distributed lag model to investment expenditures.

Moreover, you can use the AUTOREG and PDLREG procedures to correct for autoregression, a common problem of time series data.

Infinite Lag Regression Models

This section uses PROC AUTOREG to fit and test an infinite lag, habit persistence model of consumption based on the Keynesian consumption function. The Keynesian consumption function is introduced in Chapter 3, "Using Dummy Variables."

Economic theory suggests that consumers do not immediately adjust their consumption expenditures as their disposable income changes. Past values of disposable income, DI, affect the current level of consumption, C. For example, you might want to spread a windfall gain across several months. In general, your disposable income of the past several months may affect the level of this month's consumption expenditures.

In infinite lag form, the habit persistence consumption model has the form

$$C_t = b_0 + b_1(\mathrm{DI}_t + w\mathrm{DI}_{t-1} + w^2\mathrm{DI}_{t-2} + \ldots + \varepsilon_t$$

where $0 < w < 1$.

You can interpret the model as follows: the current value of C depends on the current value of DI and, in decreasing amounts, on the past values of DI. Over time, the weights on the past values of DI never become zero, but at some point their effect becomes negligible.

A serious problem of this model is that it cannot be fitted since it requires the estimation of an infinite number of parameters. You can transform the model to an estimable form as follows. Lag the model one period to yield

$$C_{t-1} = b_0 + b_1(\mathrm{DI}_{t-1} + w\mathrm{DI}_{t-2} + w^2\mathrm{DI}_{t-3} + \ldots) + \varepsilon_{t-1} \ .$$

Then, use the Koyck transformation (1954) to multiply the lagged model by w and subtract it from the original expression to obtain

$$C_t - wC_{t-1} = b_0(1 - w) + b_1\mathrm{DI}_t + v_t$$

or

$$C_t = b_0(1 - w) + wC_{t-1} + b_1\mathrm{DI}_t + v_t$$

where $v_t = \varepsilon_t - w\varepsilon_{t-1}$. The estimable model is

$$C_t = b_0^* + wC_{t-1} + b_1\,\mathrm{DI}_t + v_t$$

where $b_0^* = b_0(1-w)$. Note that the transformed model has only three parameters to be estimated (w, b_0^*, and b_1). The structural parameter, b_0, can be easily recovered.

The habit persistence model of consumption is equivalent to an adaptive expectations model and stock adjustment models. For details, see Pindyck and Rubinfeld (1991, pp. 204—210).

The MCON data set will be used to fit and test an infinite lag model.

Introducing the MCON Data Set

Before fitting the habit persistence consumption model, you need to create a SAS data set containing consumption, C, and disposable income, DI. For this example, both C and DI are monthly series from September 1982 through June 1990, and were collected from the July issues of the *Survey of Current Business*. The monthly CPI (1982 through 1984=100) was provided by the Council of Economic Advisors. C and DI are deflated to real terms by the CPI. The MCON data set includes

C_N   national per capita consumer expenditures

DI_N   national per capita disposable income

CPI   consumer price index (1982 through 1984=100).

The following SAS example code creates the MCON data set with the new variables C (real consumption), DI (real disposable income), and C_1 (real consumption lagged one month). A FORMAT statement assigns a date format to the DATE variable. Output 5.1 shows the results.

```
data mcon;
   format date monyy.;
   input date:monyy5. di_n c_n cpi @@;
     c = c_n/cpi;
    di = di_n/cpi;
    c_1 = lag(c);
   label di='Real Disposable Income in Billions 1982$'
         c='Real Consumption in Billions of 1982$'
         c_1='1 Month Lagged Real C in Billions 1982$';
   cards;
SEP82 2283.2 2140.1  .979   OCT82 2299.8 2157.9  .982
NOV82 2321.7 2178.7  .980   DEC82 2332.7 2188.1  .976
JAN83 2344.3 2196.9  .978   FEB83 2339.2 2202.4  .979
MAR83 2353.7 2219.3  .979   APR83 2382.0 2249.9  .986
MAY83 2397.4 2276.9  .992   JUN83 2406.9 2296.3  .995
JUL83 2438.6 2318.1  .999   AUG83 2433.2 2329.8 1.002
SEP83 2457.7 2332.4 1.007   OCT83 2499.1 2366.2 1.010
NOV83 2528.7 2378.4 1.012   DEC83 2555.9 2402.9 1.013
JAN84 2585.2 2437.2 1.019   FEB84 2614.3 2414.2 1.024
MAR84 2635.9 2440.8 1.026   APR84 2637.8 2469.6 1.031
MAY84 2637.0 2489.7 1.034   JUN84 2653.5 2510.7 1.037
JUL84 2675.9 2508.1 1.041   AUG84 2688.0 2522.3 1.045
SEP84 2709.4 2547.3 1.050   OCT84 2710.9 2540.7 1.053
NOV84 2725.5 2585.2 1.053   DEC84 2749.5 2588.1 1.053
JAN85 2771.2 2620.3 1.055   FEB85 2764.6 2633.6 1.060
MAR85 2757.9 2653.6 1.064   APR85 2832.9 2654.0 1.069
MAY85 2890.2 2701.1 1.073   JUN85 2829.2 2693.7 1.076
JUL85 2835.1 2709.8 1.078   AUG85 2837.4 2742.1 1.080
SEP85 2847.5 2788.4 1.083   OCT85 2877.2 2764.0 1.087
NOV85 2887.5 2781.1 1.090   DEC85 2933.7 2818.2 1.093
JAN86 2944.9 2828.6 1.096   FEB86 2958.1 2819.2 1.093
MAR86 2974.6 2822.1 1.088   APR86 3010.6 2837.0 1.086
MAY86 3004.5 2859.1 1.089   JUN86 3004.2 2858.3 1.095
JUL86 3013.5 2882.5 1.095   AUG86 3022.2 2903.4 1.097
```

```
SEP86 3037.0 2967.1 1.102    OCT86 3047.4 2937.4 1.103
NOV86 3061.2 2944.5 1.104    DEC86 3081.4 3002.4 1.105
JAN87 3112.3 2965.1 1.112    FEB87 3149.5 3030.0 1.116
MAR87 3157.6 3039.5 1.121    APR87 3044.2 3065.0 1.127
MAY87 3163.6 3073.4 1.131    JUN87 3169.2 3101.3 1.135
JUL87 3192.5 3123.5 1.138    AUG87 3213.9 3158.9 1.144
SEP87 3227.0 3152.5 1.150    OCT87 3293.7 3158.5 1.153
NOV87 3281.6 3165.5 1.154    DEC87 3331.6 3193.7 1.154
JAN88 3341.9 3225.3 1.157    FEB88 3381.4 3235.1 1.160
MAR88 3412.6 3266.2 1.165    APR88 3399.3 3268.6 1.171
MAY88 3441.8 3295.5 1.175    JUN88 3477.0 3331.8 1.180
JUL88 3507.4 3345.2 1.185    AUG88 3516.8 3370.1 1.190
SEP88 3536.0 3374.3 1.198    OCT88 3585.0 3414.8 1.202
NOV88 3560.8 3427.8 1.203    DEC88 3590.8 3448.6 1.205
JAN89 3618.6 3460.8 1.211    FEB89 3669.1 3475.7 1.216
MAR89 3697.5 3479.4 1.223    APR89 3676.5 3518.9 1.231
MAY89 3696.2 3527.5 1.238    JUN89 3719.3 3539.0 1.241
JUL89 3740.1 3569.0 1.244    AUG89 3741.0 3597.8 1.246
SEP89 3749.0 3599.6 1.250    OCT89 3772.9 3605.0 1.256
NOV89 3802.1 3618.1 1.259    DEC89 3823.9 3653.4 1.261
JAN90 3861.2 3687.3 1.274    FEB90 3886.1 3695.0 1.280
MAR90 3915.9 3706.9 1.287    APR90 3915.5 3715.8 1.289
MAY90 3927.7 3717.4 1.292    JUN90 3945.7 3752.2 1.299
;

proc print data=mcon (obs=5);
   title 'Monthly Consumption Function Example';
   title2 'First Five Observations MCON Data';
run;
```

Output 5.1
First Five
Observations of
the MCON Data
Set

```
                    Monthly Consumption Function Example
                      First Five Observations MCON Data

 OBS     DATE     DI_N     C_N     CPI       C         DI        C_1

   1     SEP82   2283.2   2140.1  0.979   2186.01   2332.18       .
   2     OCT82   2299.8   2157.9  0.982   2197.45   2341.96    2186.01
   3     NOV82   2321.7   2178.7  0.980   2223.16   2369.08    2197.45
   4     DEC82   2332.7   2188.1  0.976   2241.91   2390.06    2223.16
   5     JAN83   2344.3   2196.9  0.978   2246.32   2397.03    2241.91
```

Interpretation of output

Output 5.1 confirms the creation of the MCON data set. In general, you want to print out a partial listing of newly created data sets to confirm that they contain the proper date format and the variables created in the DATA step.

Fitting an Infinite (Koyck) Lag Model

The estimable Koyck infinite lag model is

$$C_t = b_0^* + wC_{t-1} + b_1 DI_t + v_t$$

where $b_0^* = b_0(1-w)$, and $0 < w < 1$.

The estimated parameters can be used to determine the impact of an additional dollar of DI on C at various periods. If DI changes by one dollar, b_1 measures the initial impact on C. After the second period, the effect is $b_1 + w b_1$. After T periods the effect is

$$b_1 \sum_{s=0}^{T-1} w^s = \frac{b_1(1 - w^T)}{(1 - w)} \quad .$$

As T increases, w^T approaches zero, so the long-run effect of a one-dollar increase in DI on C is $b_1/(1-w)$. This long-run effect is analogous to the marginal propensity to consume (MPC) of the Keynesian consumption models discussed in Chapter 3 of this book.

Because the Koyck lag consumption function model is fit with time series data, you want to check for autocorrelation; that is, lack of independence of the residuals across time. However, because a lagged dependent variable, C_{t-1}, is included as a right-hand side variable, the Durbin-Watson d statistic is inappropriate. You should use the Durbin h statistic, which is defined as follows:

$$h = \hat{\varphi} \sqrt{\frac{T}{1 - (T \times \text{Var}(\hat{w}))}}$$

where $\hat{\varphi}$ is the estimate of the first-order autoregression parameter, T is the number of observations, and $\text{Var}(\hat{w})$ is the estimated variance of the slope parameter, w, which is associated with the lagged endogenous variable, C_{t-1}. The Durbin h statistic is normally distributed with mean of 0 and variance of 1. If $1 < T \times \text{Var}(\hat{w})$, then the Durbin h statistic cannot be calculated and the Durbin t statistic is appropriate. For details about the Durbin h and t statistics, see Durbin (1970).

The following SAS example code uses PROC AUTOREG to fit the Koyck lag consumption function model and perform the appropriate test for first-order autocorrelation. The LAGDEP= option of the MODEL statement specifies the lagged dependent variable and prints the Durbin h or t statistics, whichever is appropriate. Output 5.2 shows the results.

```
proc autoreg data=mcon;
   model c=c_1 di / lagdep=c_1;
run;
```

Output 5.2
Output from the
Koyck Lag Model

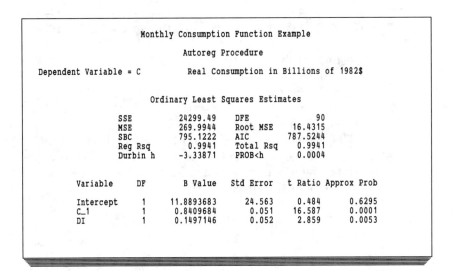

```
                      Monthly Consumption Function Example

                              Autoreg Procedure

Dependent Variable = C          Real Consumption in Billions of 1982$


                      Ordinary Least Squares Estimates

                SSE        24299.49   DFE               90
                MSE        269.9944   Root MSE      16.4315
                SBC        795.1222   AIC          787.5244
                Reg Rsq      0.9941   Total Rsq      0.9941
                Durbin h   -3.33871   PROB<h         0.0004


        Variable    DF      B Value   Std Error   t Ratio Approx Prob

        Intercept    1   11.8893683    24.563      0.484      0.6295
        C_1          1    0.8409684     0.051     16.587      0.0001
        DI           1    0.1497146     0.052      2.859      0.0053
```

Interpretation of output

The estimated model is

$$C = 11.88937 + .84097 \; C\_1 + .149715 \; DI \quad .$$

Note the following items from Output 5.2:

□ The slope parameter of C_1, .8409684, is w in the estimable specification. The intercept, $\overset{.}{b_0}$, is 11.889368 or $b_0(1-w)$; so that the structural parameter, b_0, is 74.7610.

□ If per capita disposable income, DI, changes by one dollar, then the impact after one month on per capita consumption, C, is a .149715 dollars increase (15 cents) in C. After two months, the impact is $.149715 \times (1 + .840968)$ or .27562 dollars. The long-run effect is $.149715/(1 - .840968)$ or .94141 (94 cents). From this model we would conclude that the marginal propensity to consume is about .94 (for this time period and model).

□ The p values, Approx Prob, of the estimated parameters are .6295, .0001, and .0053 for the intercept, the slope parameter of C_1, and the slope parameter of DI, respectively. The slope parameters of C_1 and DI are significantly different from zero at the .01 level.

□ The Durbin h statistic is -3.33871, and has a p value of .0004. The Durbin h statistic is significant and indicates the presence of positive autocorrelation in a properly specified model.

Be aware that the residuals of infinite lag models (Geometric, Koyck, Exponential, and so on) often exhibit autocorrelation. This tendency is a major shortcoming of infinite lag models. For additional information, see Maddala (1977, pp. 359–373).

Refitting the Model

The significant Durbin h statistic in Output 5.2 indicates the presence of autocorrelation. The most common form of autocorrelation is first-order autoregression, often denoted AR(1), which we assume is reasonable for the purposes of this example.

As an alternative estimation strategy, you may want to specify a high-order autoregressive process, test for significance of the autoregressive parameters, and sequentially reduce the order of the process until the highest-order autoregressive parameter is significant.

You can use PROC AUTOREG to correct the Koyck lag model for autoregression. The options of the MODEL statement that have not been interpreted previously are as follows:

METHOD=

specifies the estimation method. You can specify the following methods:

ML   is maximum-likelihood estimation.

YW   is Yule-Walker estimation.

ULS   is unconditional least-squares estimation.

For this example, Yule-Walker estimation is specified.

NLAG=

specifies the order of the autoregressive process to be fitted. Additionally, you can specify a list of subset lags to be fitted. For example, NLAG=(1 3) fits an autoregressive process with first and third lags. Note that the default is zero, in which case PROC AUTOREG does not fit an autoregressive process.

The following SAS example code generates Output 5.3. Only the final model is shown. The output produced from OLS estimation is not shown.

```
proc autoreg data=mcon;
   model c=c_1 di / method=yw nlag=1;
run;
```

Output 5.3

The Koyck Lag Model Corrected for First-Order Autoregression

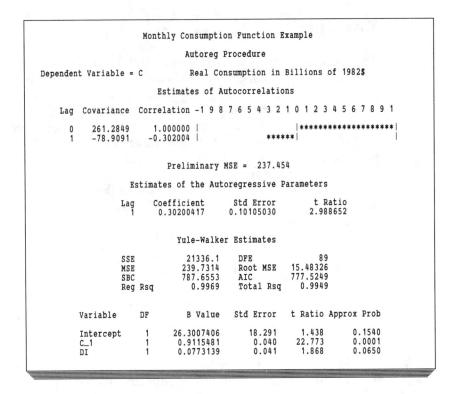

```
                        Monthly Consumption Function Example
                               Autoreg Procedure
Dependent Variable = C          Real Consumption in Billions of 1982$
                          Estimates of Autocorrelations

Lag  Covariance  Correlation -1 9 8 7 6 5 4 3 2 1 0 1 2 3 4 5 6 7 8 9 1

 0    261.2849    1.000000  |                   |********************|
 1    -78.9091   -0.302004  |             ******|                    |


                       Preliminary MSE = 237.454
               Estimates of the Autoregressive Parameters

       Lag   Coefficient      Std Error       t Ratio
        1     0.30200417      0.10105030      2.988652


                        Yule-Walker Estimates

         SSE        21336.1    DFE              89
         MSE       239.7314    Root MSE    15.48326
         SBC       787.6553    AIC        777.5249
         Reg Rsq     0.9969    Total Rsq    0.9949


    Variable      DF      B Value    Std Error   t Ratio Approx Prob

    Intercept      1    26.3007406    18.291      1.438     0.1540
    C_1            1     0.9115481     0.040     22.773     0.0001
    DI             1     0.0773139     0.041      1.868     0.0650
```

Interpretation of output

The structural portion of the estimated model is

$$C = 26.30074 + .91155 \; C\_1 + .077314 \; DI \quad .$$

The error term of the estimated model is

$$v_t = -.3020 \; v_{t-1} + \varepsilon_t$$

where ε_t is assumed to follow the OLS error term assumptions.
Note the following items from Output 5.3:

□ The intercept has more than doubled in magnitude from Output 5.2.

□ The slope parameter of C_1 is larger, while the slope parameter of DI is smaller. Both are still significantly different from zero at the .10 level.

□ The *p* values (Approx Prob) of the estimated parameters are .1540, .0001, and .0650 for the intercept, the slope parameter of C_1, and the slope parameter of DI, respectively. The slope parameter of C_1 remains significantly different from zero at the .01 level, while the slope parameter of DI is significantly different from zero at the .10 level.

You may want to continue the research process and further refine the Koyck lag consumption function model. For example, you may want to continuing checking for higher orders of autoregression, or different forms of autocorrelation, and making corrections as required.

Alternatively, because the MCON data set contains monthly data, you may want to fit a model with an error term, v_t, of the following form:

$$v_t = -\varphi_1 v_{t-1} - \varphi_{12} v_{t-12} - \varphi_{13} v_{t-13} + \varepsilon_t$$

where φ_{12} is the autoregressive parameter for the correlation between a month and its value in the preceding year, and ε_t conforms to the standard OLS error assumptions.

You can fit the previous model with the following MODEL statement in PROC AUTOREG.

```
model c=c_1 di / nlag=(1 12 13);
```

The output from this SAS example code is not shown.

Note that you can model autoregressive processes, moving average processes, and mixed autoregressive and moving average processes with the ARIMA procedure in SAS/ETS software. For applications and examples, see *SAS/ETS Software: Applications Guide 1, Version 6, First Edition*, and for full reference information on PROC ARIMA, see the *SAS/ETS User's Guide, Version 6, First Edition*.

Polynomial Distributed Lag Models

PDL models assume the lag coefficients (the weights for each period) can be specified by a continuous function (the polynomial), and the lag function itself can be approximated at discrete points in time.

In fitting a PDL model, the following questions must be resolved:

1. What is the length of the lag?

2. What is the degree of polynomial for the lag?

The length of the lag must be at least as great as the degree of polynomial being fitted. For example, a lag length of two requires three data points (the current value and two lagged values). You can fit a quadratic polynomial, but not a cubic in this case.

This section uses PROC PDLREG to fit, test, and restrict a PDL investment model developed by Shirley Almon (1965). Almon's model of capital expenditures formalized the generally accepted notion that investment takes time and planning: many current capital expenditures were planned months or even years in advance, funds were allocated, and only later does the investment in new capital assets occur. Thus, capital expenditures, CAP_EXP, depends on current and past levels of appropriations, APPRO. The PDL model has the form

$$CAP\_EXP_t = \alpha + w_0\ APPRO_t + w_1\ APPRO_{t-1} + \ldots + w_P\ APPRO_{t-P} + \varepsilon_t$$

where

α is the intercept.

w_i are the lag parameters, where i runs from 0 to P. w_0 is the slope parameter of the current value of APPRO, w_1 is the slope parameter of the one-period lagged value of APPRO, and so on.

P   is the length of the lag.

ε is the random error term.

and $w_i = c_0 + c_1 i + c_2 i^2 + \ldots + c_D i^D$ where

D   is the degree of the lag.

c are polynomial coefficients for the lag parameters.

After introducing the data set used in fitting PDL models, the remainder of this section discusses PDL models as follows:

1. fitting an initial model

2. correcting for autoregression

3. exploring the lag length of the model

4. using endpoint restrictions

5. exploring the degree of the model.

Introducing the ALMON Data Set

In this example, you fit PDL models with the same data set, labeled ALMON, used by Almon in her original study (1965). The ALMON data set includes quarterly observations from the National Industrial Conference Board for the years 1953—1967 on capital expenditures, CAP_EXP, and appropriations, APPRO.

The following SAS example code creates the ALMON data set and uses the INTNX function to create a DATE variable. The INTNX function is described in *SAS Language: Reference, Version 6, First Edition*. PROC PRINT lists the first five observations, as displayed in Output 5.4.

```
data almon;
   input cap_exp appro @@;
   retain date '1oct52'd;
   date=intnx('qtr',date,1);
   format date yyq.;
   label cap_exp='Capital Expenditures'
      appro='Appropriations';
   cards;
2071 1660   2077 1926   2078 2181   2043 1897   2062 1695
2067 1705   1964 1731   1981 2151   1914 2556   1991 3152
2129 3763   2309 3903   2614 3912   2896 3571   3058 3199
3309 3262   3446 3476   3466 2993   3435 2262   3183 2011
2697 1511   2338 1631   2140 1990   2012 1993   2071 2520
2192 2804   2240 2919   2421 3024   2639 2725   2733 2321
2721 2131   2640 2552   2513 2234   2448 2282   2429 2533
2516 2517   2534 2772   2494 2380   2596 2568   2572 2944
2601 2629   2648 3133   2840 3449   2937 3764   3136 3983
```

```
          3299 4381    3514 4786    3815 4094    4093 4870    4262 5344
          4531 5433    4825 5911    5160 6109    5319 6542    5574 5785
          5749 5707    5715 5412    5637 5465    5383 5550    5467 5465
          ;

          proc print data=almon (obs=5);
             var date cap_exp appro;
             title 'Almon Polynomial Distributed Lag Example';
             title2 'First Five Observations ALMON Data';
          run;
```

Output 5.4
First Five
Observations of
the ALMON Data
Set

```
                   Almon Polynomial Distributed Lag Example
                      First Five Observations ALMON Data

             OBS     DATE     CAP_EXP     APPRO

              1      53Q1      2071        1660
              2      53Q2      2077        1926
              3      53Q3      2078        2181
              4      53Q4      2043        1897
              5      54Q1      2062        1695
```

Fitting PDL Models

You can use PROC PDLREG or the %PDL macro of PROC MODEL to fit
polynomial distributed lag (PDL) models:

□ PROC PDLREG fits polynomial distributed lag models by computing the lag
coefficients with an orthogonal reparameterization of each independent effect
for which you specify a lag structure.

□ The %PDL macro in PROC MODEL fits PDL models within complex systems
of equations or in a system of nonlinear equations. The macro does not use
the orthogonal reparameterization of each independent effect. In general, the
estimated polynomial parameters differ in the two approaches. The fit of the
macro could be obtained from a complex set of linear restrictions of the
lagged regressor values and OLS estimation.

For comparison, Output 5.5 presents the fit using PROC PDLREG and
Output 5.10 presents the fit using the %PDL macro.

Fitting a PDL Model with PROC PDLREG

To fit a PDL model, you must specify a lag length, P, and the degree of the lag, D.
Since the ALMON data set is aggregated to the national level, the lag structure is
expected to have all positive values, increase steadily, reach a peak, and then
decrease steadily. A lag polynomial of degree two, a quadratic, should be
sufficient. Furthermore, it is assumed that an eight-period lag (two years) is the
maximum expected lag between capital appropriations and capital expenditures.

The basic PROC PDLREG code is

```
proc pdlreg data=SAS-data-set;
   model y = x z(p,d,q);
run;
```

where

Y   is the dependent variable.

X   is an independent variable with no lagged effects. Including independent variables with no lagged effects is optional.

Z   is an independent variable with lagged effects.

Note that this is the basic PROC PDLREG syntax. You may include additional independent variables with or without lagged effects, provided you have sufficient degrees of freedom.

You can specify a polynomial lag for an independent variable as follows:

P   is the number of lags (the lag length). The default is zero, for which PROC PDLREG performs an OLS estimation.

D   is the maximum degree of the lag polynomial. The default is p.

Q   is the minimum degree of the lag polynomial. The default is d.

You do not have to specify D and Q in the MODEL statement to fit a PDL model, but at a minimum you must specify P. The default of D is P, and the default of Q is D.

When D>Q, PROC PDLREG fits more than one distributed lag model. For example, if D=4 and Q=2, three models will be fitted: a quartic, a cubic, and a quadratic.

PROC PDLREG should be used only for ordered and equally spaced time series data. Note that variables lagged P times will have missing values for the first P observations. PROC PDLREG skips observations at the beginning of the data set that have missing values.

The following statements fit a quadratic eight-period lag model to the ALMON data. The following is an interpretation of the statements:

PROC PDLREG
    invokes the PDLREG procedure. The DATA= option specifies the ALMON data set.

MODEL
>
> specifies the model to be fit. For this example, the dependent variable is
> CAP_EXP. APPRO is the independent variable with lagged effects. An
> eight-quarter lag effect of APPRO with a maximum degree polynomial of two
> and a minimum-degree polynomial of two with the (8,2,2) specification is
> requested. The following options of the MODEL statement are specified:

DW= requests the printing of the generalized *d* statistics used for testing for autocorrelation. For this example, first- through fourth-order generalized *d* statistics are requested.

DWPROB requests the printing of the *p* values of the generalized *d* statistics.

The following SAS example code fits a PDL model as an eight-quarter quadratic lag, as displayed in Output 5.5.

```
proc pdlreg data=almon;
   model cap_exp = appro(8,2,2) / dw=4 dwprob;
run;
```

Output 5.5
Eight-Quarter
Quadratic
Polynomial Lag
Model Output

```
                   Almon Polynomial Distributed Lag Example

                            PDLREG Procedure

Dependent Variable = CAP_EXP    Capital Expenditures

                  ❶ Ordinary Least Squares Estimates

            SSE        779726.1    DFE              48
            MSE        16244.29    Root MSE    127.4531
            SBC        663.3782    AIC         655.5732
            Reg Rsq      0.9886    Total Rsq     0.9886

                  ❷ Durbin-Watson Statistics

                    Order    DW      PROB<DW
                      1     0.4730    0.0001
                      2     1.0256    0.0001
                      3     1.5153    0.0332
                      4     1.7798    0.2773

 ❸ Variable      DF      B Value    Std Error   t Ratio Approx Prob

    Intercept     1    73.0733450      58.283     1.254      0.2160
    APPRO**0      1     0.3211620    0.005861    54.795      0.0001
    APPRO**1      1    -0.0724313       0.014    -5.036      0.0001
    APPRO**2      1    -0.0907790       0.029    -3.138      0.0029

              Parameter    Std      t    Approx
 ❹ Variable       Value   Error   Ratio    Prob

    APPRO(0)     0.09618   0.017   5.71   0.0001
    APPRO(1)     0.12304   0.007  18.36   0.0001
    APPRO(2)     0.13955   0.006  25.30   0.0001
    APPRO(3)     0.14572   0.009  16.08   0.0001
    APPRO(4)     0.14154   0.010  13.69   0.0001
    APPRO(5)     0.12701   0.009  14.50   0.0001
    APPRO(6)     0.10215   0.005  18.89   0.0001
    APPRO(7)     0.06693   0.008   8.19   0.0001
    APPRO(8)     0.02137   0.019   1.13   0.2637
```

(continued)

Output 5.5
(continued)

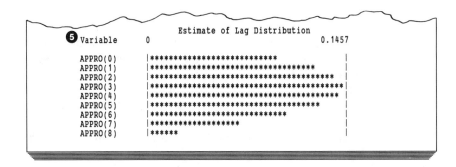

```
                              Estimate of Lag Distribution
❺ Variable      0                                        0.1457

   APPRO(0)    |****************************              |
   APPRO(1)    |*********************************         |
   APPRO(2)    |*************************************      |
   APPRO(3)    |**************************************    *|
   APPRO(4)    |*************************************      |
   APPRO(5)    |************************************       |
   APPRO(6)    |****************************              |
   APPRO(7)    |*******************                       |
   APPRO(8)    |******                                    |
```

Description of output

The circled numbers in Output 5.5 correspond to the numbered items in the following list:

❶ presents the goodness-of-fit statistics, which are described in Chapter 2, "Fitting OLS Regression Models."

❷ lists the first- through fourth-order generalized Durbin-Watson *d* statistics and their associated *p* values.

❸ presents the fitted model:

□ estimates of the intercept and the constant, linear, and quadratic terms of the PDL model, APPRO**0, APPRO**1, and APPRO**2

□ lists the parameter standard errors, STD ERROR

□ lists the individual *t* statistics, T RATIO, and their associated *p* values.

❹ lists the estimated lag coefficients, APPRO(_), their standard errors, *t* statistics of individual *t* tests, and the associated *p* values

❺ displays a plot of the lag coefficients labeled "Estimate of Lag Distribution." You can use the visual evidence of the plot to assess the appropriateness of the specified degree of the polynomial lag. For example, if you specify a quadratic polynomial lag, and the true lag polynomial is a quadratic polynominal, then you would expect to see a quadratic curve in the plot. However, if the true lag polynomial is linear, then you would see little evidence of a quadratic curve in the plot.

Interpretation of output

The fitted model is

$$CAP\_EXP_t = 73.0733 + .09618\ APPRO_t + .12304\ APPRO_{t-1} +$$
$$.13955\ APPRO_{t-2} + \ldots + .02137\ APPRO_{t-8}$$

The polynomial distributed weights are generated by the following equation:

$$w_i = 0.32116 - 0.07243\ i - 0.09078\ i^2\ .$$

PROC PDLREG computes the Almon polynomial coefficients using an orthogonal reparameterization of the lagged effects of APPRO on CAP_EXP. For details on the computational method see, Chapter 15, "The PDLREG Procedure," in the *SAS/ETS User's Guide*.

The standard regression statistics (R^2, MSE, SSE, and so on) indicate a good fit of the data. For example, the R^2 implies approximately 98.9% of the variation in capital expenditures are explained by the PDL model of appropriations.

You want to check the plot of the lag coefficients, which provides visual evidence of the estimated lag structure. The plot in Output 5.5 reveals the expected pattern: the coefficients are all positive, steadily increase, reach a peak, and then steadily decrease.

The first three generalized Durbin-Watson *d* statistics are significant at the .05 level while the fourth is not. These *d* statistics indicate positive autocorrelation (lack of independence of time series residuals) in a properly specified model. The effects of positive autocorrelation include underestimation of the parameter standard errors and of the *p* values for the *t*-tests. Before making a detailed assessment of the hypothesized lag structure, you should correct for autocorrelation or respecify the model.

For additional information on the effects of autocorrelation in lag models see Maddala (1977, 1992).

You have several strategies for improving the fit of the model and mitigating the effects of autocorrelation. Estimation strategies you can pursue include

□ correcting for autocorrelation as described in Chapter 4, "Violations of the OLS Error Assumptions"

□ checking for misspecification and specifying a new model, perhaps like the model displayed in Output 3.5 and Output 3.6 in Chapter 3. For example, if you believe seasonal variation in the quarterly data is responsible for the apparent autocorrelation. You could account for the seasonality by using three dummy variables (for second, third, and fourth quarters with the first quarter as a base).

As a contrast to the respecification approach shown in Chapter 3, we follow the first strategy in subsequent examples. In this case, we assume a form for the autocorrelation, then refit the model making the appropriate correction. For the purposes of this example, we assume the autocorrelation is second-order autoregression, often denoted AR(2).

Thus, a general error term for the PDL model, v_t is assumed to be

$$v_t = \varepsilon_t - \varphi_1 v_{t-1} - \varphi_2 v_{t-2}$$

where ε_t conforms to the OLS error term assumptions. The autoregressive parameters to be estimated are φ_1 and φ_2. The general error term, v_t depends on its own values of the past two periods, and a random term, ε_t.

Note that the ALMON data set has been analyzed in other ways. For additional analysis of the ALMON data set, see Chapter 15, "The PDLREG Procedure," in the *SAS/ETS User's Guide, Version 6, First Edition*; Maddala and Rao (1971); and Almon (1965). You may want to compare and contrast the estimation strategies and fitted models.

Correcting the PDL Model for Autoregression

You use the NLAG= option of the MODEL statement of PROC PDLREG to correct for second-order autoregression. The following new options of the MODEL statement of PROC PDLREG are specified:

METHOD=
specifies an estimation method. For this example, the Yule-Walker, YW, estimation method is specified.

NLAG=
specifies the order of the autoregressive process, or the subset of lags to be fitted. For this example, a correction for second-order autoregression is specified.

The following SAS example code fits the eight-quarter quadratic polynomial model to the ALMON data set and corrects for autoregression.

```
proc pdlreg data=almon;
   model cap_exp = appro(8,2,2) / method=yw nlag=2 dw=1 dwprob;
run;
```

Part of the output generated by the previous code is displayed in Output 5.6. The OLS estimation (displayed in Output 5.5) is not shown.

Output 5.6

The Quadratic, Eight-Quarter Almon PDL Model Corrected for Second-Order Autoregression

```
                  Almon Polynomial Distributed Lag Example

                            PDLREG Procedure

Dependent Variable = CAP_EXP     Capital Expenditures

                       Estimates of Autocorrelations

   Lag  Covariance  Correlation -1 9 8 7 6 5 4 3 2 1 0 1 2 3 4 5 6 7 8 9 1
     0   14994.73     1.000000  |                    |********************|
     1   11321.2      0.755012  |                    |***************     |
     2    6406.694    0.427263  |                    |*********           |
```

```
                  Almon Polynomial Distributed Lag Example

                            PDLREG Procedure

                       Preliminary MSE = 5736.135

              Estimates of the Autoregressive Parameters

        Lag    Coefficient      Std Error      t Ratio
         1     -1.00573487     0.13907488    -7.231607
         2      0.33207861     0.13907488     2.387769


                       Yule-Walker Estimates

        SSE            294144.2   DFE                46
        MSE            6394.439   Root MSE     79.96523
        SBC            621.6651   AIC          609.9576
        Reg Rsq          0.9646   Total Rsq      0.9957
        Durbin-Watson    1.9402   PROB<DW        0.3501
```

(continued)

Output 5.6
(continued)

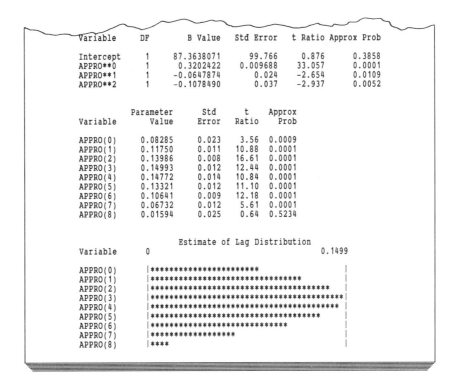

Variable	DF	B Value	Std Error	t Ratio	Approx Prob
Intercept	1	87.3638071	99.766	0.876	0.3858
APPRO**0	1	0.3202422	0.009688	33.057	0.0001
APPRO**1	1	-0.0647874	0.024	-2.654	0.0109
APPRO**2	1	-0.1078490	0.037	-2.937	0.0052

Variable	Parameter Value	Std Error	t Ratio	Approx Prob
APPRO(0)	0.08285	0.023	3.56	0.0009
APPRO(1)	0.11750	0.011	10.88	0.0001
APPRO(2)	0.13986	0.008	16.61	0.0001
APPRO(3)	0.14993	0.012	12.44	0.0001
APPRO(4)	0.14772	0.014	10.84	0.0001
APPRO(5)	0.13321	0.012	11.10	0.0001
APPRO(6)	0.10641	0.009	12.18	0.0001
APPRO(7)	0.06732	0.012	5.61	0.0001
APPRO(8)	0.01594	0.025	0.64	0.5234

```
                            Estimate of Lag Distribution
    Variable         0                                       0.1499

    APPRO(0)    |***********************                    |
    APPRO(1)    |*********************************          |
    APPRO(2)    |**************************************     |
    APPRO(3)    |*******************************************|
    APPRO(4)    |******************************************* |
    APPRO(5)    |************************************       |
    APPRO(6)    |****************************               |
    APPRO(7)    |******************                         |
    APPRO(8)    |****                                       |
```

Interpretation of output

In Output 5.6, note the following items:

□ The R^2 goodness-of-fit statistics of Output 5.6 indicate a good fit of the data. Reg Rsq (.9646) is the R^2 of the transformed (corrected) model, and Total Rsq (.9957) is constructed from the sum of squares of the untransformed dependent variable and the final residual estimates. For details on the formulas, see Chapter 8, "The AUTOREG Procedure," in the *SAS/ETS User's Guide*.

□ The Durbin-Watson *d* statistic is 1.9402 and has a *p* value of .3501. For our purposes, we conclude that the correction for second-order autoregression is sufficient.

□ The first set of *t*-tests is used to evaluate the hypothesized lag structure, the degree of the polynomial.

□ The second set of *t*-tests is used to evaluate the hypothesized lag length.

□ The model corrected for second-order autoregression exhibits a pronounced peak near the center of the lag. The first seven lag parameters are significantly different from zero at the .05 level; the eighth is not. This suggests a seven-quarter lag model.

Fitting a PDL Model with a Shorter Lag Length

The theory underlying your model may suggest the appropriate length of lag, or at least a range of lag lengths to explore. Your data may also influence the length of lag of your final model. For example, if you specify a lag of eight quarters in length and only the first four quarters have estimated parameters significantly different from zero, you should refit the model with a shorter lag length. If you fitted a lag of three quarters and all of the estimated lag parameters are significantly different from zero, you might want to explore models with longer lag lengths.

If theory offers no range of lag lengths, you may want to fit different lag lengths and select the optimal length based on some or all of the following: adjusted R-square (Adj R^2), or a minimum standard error (MSE) criterion, or *t* statistics of the estimated lag parameters.

For additional information, including a list of caveats of PDL model estimation, see Maddala (1992).

The following SAS example code fits the quadratic PDL model with a seven-period lag and corrects for second-order autoregression.

```
proc pdlreg data=almon;
   model cap_exp = appro(7,2,2) / method=yw nlag=2 dw=1 dwprob;
run;
```

Part of the output generated by the previous code is displayed in Output 5.7. The OLS estimation is not shown.

Output 5.7
The Quadratic, Seven-Quarter Almon PDL Model Corrected for Second-Order Autoregression

```
                  Almon Polynomial Distributed Lag Example

                           PDLREG Procedure

Dependent Variable = CAP_EXP     Capital Expenditures

                      Estimates of Autocorrelations

   Lag  Covariance  Correlation -1 9 8 7 6 5 4 3 2 1 0 1 2 3 4 5 6 7 8 9 1

    0    15178.12    1.000000 |                    |********************|
    1    11254.31    0.741482 |                    |***************     |
    2    6309.114    0.415671 |                    |********            |
```

```
                  Almon Polynomial Distributed Lag Example

                           PDLREG Procedure

                      Preliminary MSE = 6226.766

                 Estimates of the Autoregressive Parameters

          Lag   Coefficient      Std Error        t Ratio
           1    -0.96238365     0.13924144      -6.911618
           2     0.29791882     0.13924144       2.139584
```

(continued)

Output 5.7
(continued)

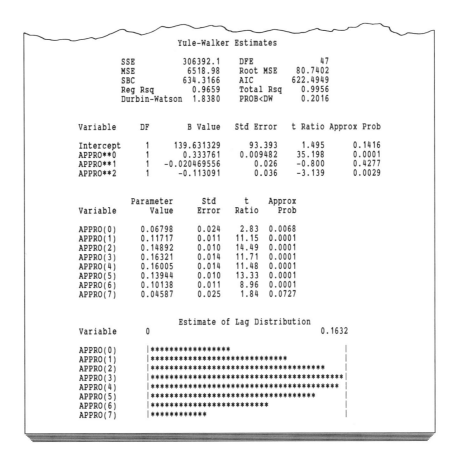

```
                              Yule-Walker Estimates

              SSE           306392.1   DFE                  47
              MSE            6518.98    Root MSE        80.7402
              SBC            634.3166   AIC             622.4949
              Reg Rsq        0.9659     Total Rsq        0.9956
              Durbin-Watson  1.8380     PROB<DW          0.2016


     Variable     DF      B Value   Std Error   t Ratio Approx Prob

     Intercept    1    139.631329     93.393      1.495      0.1416
     APPRO**0     1      0.333761   0.009482     35.198      0.0001
     APPRO**1     1     -0.020469556    0.026     -0.800     0.4277
     APPRO**2     1     -0.113091      0.036      -3.139     0.0029


                  Parameter    Std      t     Approx
     Variable        Value    Error    Ratio   Prob

     APPRO(0)      0.06798    0.024    2.83    0.0068
     APPRO(1)      0.11717    0.011   11.15    0.0001
     APPRO(2)      0.14892    0.010   14.49    0.0001
     APPRO(3)      0.16321    0.014   11.71    0.0001
     APPRO(4)      0.16005    0.014   11.48    0.0001
     APPRO(5)      0.13944    0.010   13.33    0.0001
     APPRO(6)      0.10138    0.011    8.96    0.0001
     APPRO(7)      0.04587    0.025    1.84    0.0727


                         Estimate of Lag Distribution
     Variable     0                                      0.1632

     APPRO(0)    |****************                       |
     APPRO(1)    |****************************           |
     APPRO(2)    |************************************** |
     APPRO(3)    |***************************************|
     APPRO(4)    |***************************************|
     APPRO(5)    |***********************************     |
     APPRO(6)    |*************************               |
     APPRO(7)    |***********                             |
```

Interpretation of output

In Output 5.7, the polynomial constant, APPRO**0, and the quadratic, APPRO**2, are significant at the .05 level, while the intercept and the linear term, APPRO**1, are not. Even though the linear term is not significant, it should not be dropped from the model. Exclude polynomial terms from the highest degree to the lower degrees if the highest degree is not significant. The magnitude of the polynomial coefficients changes slightly from the eight-period lag of Output 5.6 to the seven-period lag of Output 5.7.

The plot of the lag parameters, labeled Estimate of Lag Distribution, reveals the expected pattern, and the magnitudes of the lag coefficients, APPRO(_), change slightly. All lag coefficients are significantly different from zero at the .05 level except for the last lag coefficient, which is significant at the .10 level.

The goodness-of-fit statistics indicate a good fit of the data. The Reg Rsq is .9659 and Total Rsq is .9956. The *d* statistic is 1.8380, has a *p* value of .2016, and is not significant at the .05 level.

Endpoint Restrictions in PDL Models

You may wish to restrict the effects of the lagged values to a given period. For example, if the theory underlying your PDL model implies a lag should have no effect after a period of a given length, then an endpoint restriction can be used to set the lag parameter equal to zero for the period following the specified lag.

The options FIRST, LAST, and BOTH of the MODEL statement in PROC PDLREG restrict the lag effect to zero in the period prior to the start of the lag, in the period just after the lag, or both.

The following SAS example code refits the second-order autoregressive corrected PDL model of Output 5.7 using the LAST option. In this example, the LAST option restricts the estimated parameter of the period following the lag (the eighth period) to zero.

```
proc pdlreg data=almon;
   model cap_exp = appro(7,2,2,last) / method=yw nlag=2 dw=1 dwprob;
run;
```

Part of the output generated by the previous code is displayed in Output 5.8. The OLS estimation is not shown.

Output 5.8

The Quadratic, Seven-Quarter Almon PDL Model Corrected for Second-Order Autoregression, and the Eighth-Quarter Effect Restricted to Zero

```
                    Almon Polynomial Distributed Lag Example

                              PDLREG Procedure

Dependent Variable = CAP_EXP     Capital Expenditures

                       Estimates of Autocorrelations

   Lag  Covariance  Correlation -1 9 8 7 6 5 4 3 2 1 0 1 2 3 4 5 6 7 8 9 1

     0   15291.04    1.000000 |                    |********************|
     1   11468.45    0.750011 |                    |***************     |
     2   6563.232    0.429221 |                    |*********           |

                       Preliminary MSE = 6068.569

                 Estimates of the Autoregressive Parameters

        Lag    Coefficient      Std Error       t Ratio
         1     -0.97852848     0.13747472     -7.117879
         2      0.30468610     0.13747472      2.216306

                        Yule-Walker Estimates

             SSE          307984.8   DFE              48
             MSE           6416.35   Root MSE    80.10212
             SBC         630.6588    AIC         620.8073
             Reg Rsq      0.9640     Total Rsq   0.9956
             Durbin-Watson 1.9195    PROB<DW      0.3050

        Variable    DF      B Value    Std Error   t Ratio Approx Prob

        Intercept    1     130.4488     9.35E+01     1.395    0.1693
        APPRO**0     1  0.3350880608    9.35E-03    35.829    0.0001
        APPRO**1     1  -0.013861562    2.35E-02    -0.589    0.5584
        APPRO**2     1  -0.094054156    1.44E-02    -6.521    0.0001

        Restriction DF      L Value    Std Error   t Ratio Approx Prob

        APPRO(8)    -1   84974.1885    1.39E+05     0.613    0.5425
```

(continued)

Output 5.8
(continued)

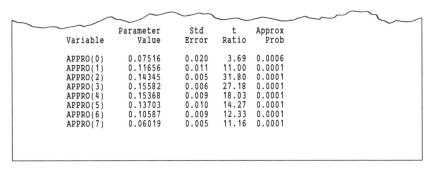

```
                   Parameter    Std     t    Approx
        Variable     Value     Error  Ratio   Prob

        APPRO(0)    0.07516    0.020   3.69   0.0006
        APPRO(1)    0.11656    0.011  11.00   0.0001
        APPRO(2)    0.14345    0.005  31.80   0.0001
        APPRO(3)    0.15582    0.006  27.18   0.0001
        APPRO(4)    0.15368    0.009  18.03   0.0001
        APPRO(5)    0.13703    0.010  14.27   0.0001
        APPRO(6)    0.10587    0.009  12.33   0.0001
        APPRO(7)    0.06019    0.005  11.16   0.0001
```

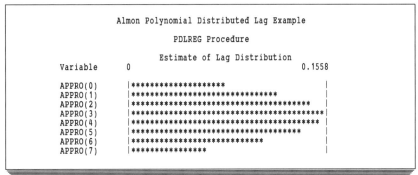

```
              Almon Polynomial Distributed Lag Example

                       PDLREG Procedure

                   Estimate of Lag Distribution
        Variable    0                                  0.1558

        APPRO(0)    |*******************                     |
        APPRO(1)    |******************************          |
        APPRO(2)    |**************************************** |
        APPRO(3)    |*****************************************|
        APPRO(4)    |****************************************|
        APPRO(5)    |************************************    |
        APPRO(6)    |***************************             |
        APPRO(7)    |***************                         |
```

Interpretation of output

The models of Output 5.7 and Output 5.8 yield similar results; yet, the following are differences worth noting:

□ The restriction that the eighth-period lag weight (parameter) is zero is not significant at the .05 level or even at the .20 level, yet it does affect the fit.

□ The polynomial coefficients (the APPRO**0, APPRO**1, and APPRO**2) differ slightly in value, but the significance of APPRO**2 increases, from a t statistic of -3.139 (with p value .0029) in Output 5.7 to a t statistic of -6.521 (with p value .0001) in Output 5.8.

□ The plot of the lag parameters reveals the expected quadratic pattern, and the parameter estimates change slightly in magnitude.

□ Finally, the model of Output 5.8 is more parsimonious. The restriction conserves a degree of freedom (note the negative degree of freedom). Knowing that the eighth-period effect is equal to zero implies one less independent parameter to fit. For examples, see Pindyck and Rubinfeld (1991) or Kmenta (1986).

The d statistic is 1.9195, and has a p value of .3050.

The goodness-of-fit statistics indicate that both of the models fit the data quite well, as shown in the following table.

Table 5.1
Comparing Almon PDL Models

Statistic	Unrestricted Output 5.7	Restricted Output 5.8
Reg R-Square	.9659	.9640
MSE	6518.98	6416.35

Depending upon your choice of goodness-of-fit criteria either model could be selected. However, the restricted model is the model of choice because

□ The individual *t* statistics are larger in absolute magnitude for the restricted model, except for APPRO**1.

□ The aggregated nature of the data implies a smoothness in the lag structure, and the eighth-period lag is not significantly different from zero as shown in Output 5.6.

Interpretation of the final model

The final PDL model of investment is a quadratic PDL model with a seven-period lag, the eighth-period lag restricted to zero, and is corrected for second-order autoregression. The fitted model is

$$\text{CAP\_EXP}_t = 130.4488 + .07516\ \text{APPRO}_t + .11656\ \text{APPRO}_{t-1} + .14345\ \text{APPRO}_{t-2} + \ldots + .06019\ \text{APPRO}_{t-7} + v_t$$

where the second-order autoregressive error term, v_t, is given by the following equation:

$$v_t = 0.97853\ v_{t-1} - 0.30469\ v_{t-2} + \varepsilon_t$$

and ε_t conforms to the OLS error assumptions.

The polynomial weights are determined by the following equation:

$$w_i = 0.33509 - 0.01386\ i - 0.09405\ i^2 \quad .$$

The model shows that an increase in this period's capital appropriations will have immediate and lagged impacts in capital expenditures.

The model can be used to answer questions such as

□ Given an increase in appropriations, what percent of the total impact on capital expenditures will occur after four quarters?

□ After appropriations increase, how long will it take for at least 75% of the total effect on capital expenditures to occur?

These questions can be answered by calculating the percentage of impact in each period of a change in appropriations on expenditures. First sum the lag coefficients, then divide each lag coefficient by that sum. This process will standardize the lag coefficients. For this model, the answers are

□ 68%, obtained from summing the first five standardized coefficients (lags 0 through 4).

□ five quarters, as the sum of the first six standardized coefficients is .82479.

Exploring the Degree of the PDL Model

Often you want to explore the degree of the polynomial lag. Theory may suggest that once the lag effect has peaked, it should taper off. Highly aggregated data is likely to behave in this fashion. For less aggregated data, individual events, or local conditions may imply different lag structures. Examples of other lag structures include continually declining weights (see the section on Infinite or Koyck lags) and multiple peaks, which suggest a cubic or even a quartic polynomial lag model.

In general, you may want to initially estimate a polynomial lag of a high degree and then examine the t statistic of the highest degree. If the highest degree is not significantly different from zero (at your selected level of significance), refit the model with a polynomial of one less degree. Continue fitting with lower degree polynomials until the highest degree is significantly different from zero.

For comparison purposes with Output 5.7, the following SAS example code fits a seven quarter cubic PDL model corrected for second order autoregression.

```
proc pdlreg data=almon;
   model cap_exp = appro(7,3,3) / nlag=2 dw=1 dwprob;
run;
```

Part of the output generated by the previous code is displayed in Output 5.9. The OLS estimation is not shown.

Output 5.9
Seven-Quarter, Cubic Almon Polynomial Distributed Lag Model

```
                    Almon Polynomial Distributed Lag Example

                              PDLREG Procedure

Dependent Variable = CAP_EXP     Capital Expenditures

                          Estimates of Autocorrelations

   Lag  Covariance  Correlation -1 9 8 7 6 5 4 3 2 1 0 1 2 3 4 5 6 7 8 9 1
     0   14177.57    1.000000  |                   |********************|
     1   10367.27    0.731245  |                   |***************     |
     2    6469.318   0.456307  |                   |********            |
```

(continued)

Output 5.9
(continued)

```
                    Almon Polynomial Distributed Lag Example

                              PDLREG Procedure

                         Preliminary MSE = 6409.207

                  Estimates of the Autoregressive Parameters

               Lag    Coefficient      Std Error        t Ratio
                1      -0.85447873     0.14533311      -5.879450
                2       0.16852644     0.14533311       1.159587


                          Yule-Walker Estimates

              SSE         302188.9    DFE               46
              MSE         6569.323    Root MSE       81.05136
              SBC         637.3936    AIC            623.6015
              Reg Rsq       0.9651    Total Rsq        0.9957
              Durbin-Watson 1.7794    PROB<DW          0.1503


     Variable      DF       B Value      Std Error    t Ratio  Approx Prob

     Intercept      1     148.637022        96.530      1.540      0.1305
     APPRO**0       1       0.333200      0.009694     34.373      0.0001
     APPRO**1       1      -0.013250783      0.025     -0.534      0.5957
     APPRO**2       1      -0.103450         0.034     -3.058      0.0037
     APPRO**3       1       0.074991022      0.048      1.554      0.1271


                      Parameter     Std        t      Approx
     Variable          Value       Error     Ratio     Prob

     APPRO(0)         0.03678      0.033      1.12     0.2689
     APPRO(1)         0.13801      0.016      8.55     0.0001
     APPRO(2)         0.17712      0.022      8.20     0.0001
     APPRO(3)         0.17258      0.015     11.16     0.0001
     APPRO(4)         0.14284      0.016      9.12     0.0001
     APPRO(5)         0.10637      0.022      4.88     0.0001
     APPRO(6)         0.08163      0.016      5.00     0.0001
     APPRO(7)         0.08709      0.034      2.57     0.0136


                         Estimate of Lag Distribution
     Variable      0                                       0.1771

     APPRO(0)    |********                               |
     APPRO(1)    |*********************************      |
     APPRO(2)    |*****************************************|
     APPRO(3)    |****************************************|
     APPRO(4)    |**********************************     |
     APPRO(5)    |************************               |
     APPRO(6)    |******************                     |
     APPRO(7)    |*******************                    |
```

Interpretation of output

The quadratic term of the polynomial lag model is significant at the .01 level. The cubic term is not significantly different from zero at the .10 level. Except for APPRO(0), all of the estimated lag parameters are significant at the .05 level. Also, in the cubic model the seventh-quarter lag parameter is larger than the sixth-quarter lag parameter. This result is unexpected for data aggregated to the national level. Economic theory suggests a smoother lag structure: the seventh-quarter parameter should be smaller than the sixth. The plot of the lag distribution clearly shows this unacceptable pattern. You should refit this model as before, as a quadratic model.

Using the %PDL Macro

The model of Output 5.5 could have been fitted with the %PDL macro in PROC MODEL. PROC PDLREG uses an orthogonal reparameterization of the lag effects; the %PDL macro does not. For details on the computational methods of the MODEL and PDLREG procedures, see the *SAS/ETS User's Guide*.

The following SAS example code generates a PDL model within PROC MODEL. The statements are interpreted as follows.

PROC MODEL
invokes the MODEL procedure. The DATA= option requests the ALMON data set.

PARAMETERS
specifies the parameters to be estimated. In this example, the intercept, INT, is estimated separately from the lagged effects.

ENDOGENOUS
specifies the endogenous (or in this case, the left-hand side variable), CAP_EXP.

%PDL(_, ,)
invokes the %PDL macro. The arguments of the %PDL macro are as follows:

pdlname	names the effect. In this example, the PDL effect is named APPROPDL.
nlags	specifies the lag length. In this example, the lag length is eight quarters.
degree	specifies the degree of the polynomial lag. In this example, the polynomial degree is two (a quadratic polynomial).
R=*code*	specifies an optional code for endpoint restrictions. Codes are FIRST, LAST, and BOTH, to restrict the lag effect in the period preceding the lag, the period following the lag, or both.

FIT
requests the fitting (estimation) of the CAP_EXP equation. CAP_EXP= specifies the model to be estimated. The %PDL requests the specified %PDL macro be applied to the variable APPRO.

The following SAS example code generates Output 5.10.

```
proc model data=almon;
   parameters int;  /* int = intercept */
   endogenous cap_exp;
   %pdl(appropdl,8,2)
   cap_exp = int + %pdl(appropdl,appro);
   fit cap_exp;
run;
```

Output 5.10
*The PDL Model
Fitted with the
%PDL Macro in
PROC MODEL*

```
                  Almon Polynomial Distributed Lag Example

                            MODEL Procedure

                            Model Summary

                  Model Variables        1
                     Endogenous          1
                  Parameters             4
                  Equations              1

                  Number of Statements  10

                  Program Lag Length     8

            Model Variables: CAP_EXP

            Parameters: INT APPROPDL_0 APPROPDL_1 APPROPDL_2

            Equations: CAP_EXP
```

```
                  Almon Polynomial Distributed Lag Example

                            MODEL Procedure

                       The Equation to Estimate is:

        CAP_EXP = F( INT(1), APPROPDL_0, APPROPDL_1, APPROPDL_2 )


                     The estimation lag length is 8.
```

```
                  Almon Polynomial Distributed Lag Example

                            MODEL Procedure
                            OLS Estimation

                        OLS Estimation Summary

                  Dataset Option      Dataset
                  DATA=               ALMON

                  Parameters Estimated      4

                        Minimization Summary
                  Method                GAUSS
                  Iterations                1

                  Final  Convergence  Criteria
                  R                         0
                  PPC                 5.5E-13
                  RPC(INT)           723497.5
                  Object            0.9986784
                  Trace(S)         16244.2943
                  Objective Value  14994.7332

                        Observations Processed
                  Read                     60
                  Solved                   52
                   First                    9
                   Last                    60
                  Lagged                    8
```

```
                  Almon Polynomial Distributed Lag Example

                            MODEL Procedure
                            OLS Estimation

                 Nonlinear OLS Summary of Residual Errors

                  DF   DF
       Equation Model Error     SSE      MSE    Root MSE R-Square Adj R-Sq

       CAP_EXP    4    48    779726   16244.3  127.45311   0.9886   0.9878
```

(continued)

Output 5.10
(continued)

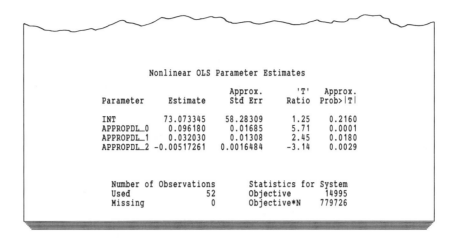

```
                   Nonlinear OLS Parameter Estimates

                              Approx.    'T'   Approx.
         Parameter   Estimate  Std Err  Ratio  Prob>|T|

         INT          73.073345  58.28309   1.25   0.2160
         APPROPDL_0    0.096180   0.01685   5.71   0.0001
         APPROPDL_1    0.032030   0.01308   2.45   0.0180
         APPROPDL_2   -0.00517261 0.0016484 -3.14   0.0029


         Number of Observations      Statistics for System
         Used                52      Objective         14995
         Missing              0      Objective*N      779726
```

Interpretation of output

The model shown in Output 5.10 is similar to the model shown in Output 5.5: the degrees of freedom are equivalent, also equivalent are SSE, MSE, Root MSE, R-Square, and the estimated intercept. However, the polynomial coefficients are very different. PROC PDLREG uses an orthogonal reparameterization of the lag effects, and the %PDL macro does not.

For a full explanation of PROC MODEL output, see Chapter 13, "The MODEL Procedure," in the *SAS/ETS User's Guide,* and for applications of PROC MODEL, see Chapter 7, "Fitting Nonlinear Models," in this book. For more information about the %PDL Macro, see Chapter 6, "Topics in Nonlinear and Linear Modeling" and Chapter 13 in *SAS/ETS User's Guide.*

Chapter Summary

The following topics were presented in this chapter:

□ fitting infinite (geometric or Koyck) lag models

□ fitting polynomial distributed lag (PDL) models

□ correcting for autoregression in PDL models

□ restricting the lag endpoints of PDL models

□ selecting lag length and degree of the lag in PDL models.

You have seen how to use PROC PDLREG and the %PDL macro with PROC MODEL to estimate and test polynomial distributed lag model parameters.

Other Relevant SAS Publications

For additional information on the AUTOREG, MODEL, and PDLREG procedures and the %PDL macro in PROC MODEL see the *SAS/ETS User's Guide, Version 6, First Edition.*

For additional information on date formatting, see *SAS Language: Reference, Version 6, First Edition.*

For applications and examples of modeling autoregressive processes, moving average processes, and mixed autoregressive and moving average processes, see *SAS/ETS Software: Applications Guide 1, Version 6, First Edition.*

For full reference information on PROC ARIMA, see the *SAS/ETS User's Guide, Version 6, First Edition.*

References

Almon, S. (1965), "The Distributed Lag between Capital Appropriations and Expenditures," *Econometrica*, 33, 178—196.

Council of Economic Advisers (1991), *Economic Report of the President*, Washington, D.C.: U.S. Government Printing Office.

Durbin, J. (1970), "Testing for Serial Correlation in Least-Squares Regression When Some of the Regressors Are Lagged Dependent Variables," *Econometrica*, 38, 410—421.

Griliches, Z. (1967), "Distributed Lags: A Survey," *Econometrica*, 35, 16—49.

Johnston, J. (1984), *Econometric Methods, Third Edition*, New York: McGraw-Hill Book Company.

Kmenta, J. (1986), *Elements of Econometrics, Second Edition*, New York: Macmillan Publishing Co., Inc.

Koyck, L.M. (1954), *Distributed Lags and Investment Analysis*, Amsterdam, Netherlands: North-Holland.

Maddala, G.S. (1977), *Econometrics*, New York: McGraw-Hill Book Company.

Maddala, G.S. (1992), *Introduction to Econometrics, Second Edition*, New York: Macmillan Publishing Company, Inc.

Maddala, G.S. and Rao, A.S. (1971), "Maximum Likelihood Estimation of Solow's and Jorgenson's Distributed Lag Models," *The Review of Economics and Statistics*, 80—88.

Pindyck, R.S. and Rubinfeld, D.L. (1991), *Econometric Models and Economic Forecasts, Third Edition*, New York: McGraw-Hill Book Company.

U.S. Bureau of Economic Analysis, *Survey of Current Business*, Washington, D.C.: U.S. Government Printing Office.

Chapter **6** Fitting Systems of Linear Equations

Introduction

A system of equations can model the interrelated behavior of jointly determined variables. Suppose you want to estimate price (P) and quantity (Q) from a typical supply and demand system. P and Q are simultaneously determined; that is, any change that affects one affects the other. In most supply and demand systems, the quantity demanded is a function of price and demand shifters, and quantity supplied is a function of price and supply shifters. In the following system, the demand equation has been solved for Q, and the supply equation has been solved for P:

Demand: Q = f(P, demand shifters) + ε_D

Supply: P = g(Q, supply shifters) + ε_S

where f and g are linear functional operators, and ε_D and ε_S are the random errors associated with the equations. The variables P and Q are called *endogenous*, or dependent, because they are determined within the system. The equation shifters are called *exogenous*, or independent, because they are determined outside the system.

In this supply and demand system, a change in a shifter affects both P and Q simultaneously. This implies that P and Q are correlated with both error terms, violating a basic assumption of ordinary least-squares (OLS) estimation. If you estimate one or more equations of this system through OLS, then the resulting parameter estimates are biased, a problem known as *simultaneous equation bias*.

To determine whether simultaneous equation bias is a problem, consider the causation sequence. If causation runs only from right-hand side variables to left-hand side variables, then a single equation can model the relationship, and there is no bias. However, if the causation runs in both directions, then the variables are simultaneously determined, and OLS estimation is no longer appropriate.

When estimating one or more equations from a system of equations, there are several commonly-used strategies for avoiding simultaneous estimation bias. You can

□ simultaneously estimate all the equations by a systems method, including the following statistical methods: SUR (Seemingly Unrelated Regressions), ITSUR (Iterated SUR), 3SLS (Three Stage Least Squares), IT3SLS (Iterated 3SLS), and FIML (Full Information Maximum Likelihood).

□ use general form estimation to estimate the system.

□ estimate one of the equations by a statistical technique that accounts for the simultaneous equation bias, including the following statistical methods: 2SLS (Two Stage Least Squares), K-Class (K-Class Estimators), MELO (Minimum Expected Loss Estimation), and LIML (Limited Information Maximum Likelihood).

□ solve for the reduced form equations (that is, solve each equation for an endogenous variable in terms of exogenous variables), and then estimate each equation by OLS. This approach has the disadvantage of requiring you to re-solve the system (by hand or through the SYSLIN procedure in SAS/ETS software) to obtain the structural parameter estimates from the reduced form parameter estimates. Depending on whether a system is under-identified, just-identified, or over-identified, you cannot obtain estimates for some parameters, you can obtain one estimate per parameter, and you can obtain multiple estimates for some parameters, respectively. For additional information on conditions for identification of equations, see Pindyck and Rubinfeld (1991).

The following table summarizes the estimation techniques available in the MODEL and SYSLIN procedures in SAS/ETS software. A check indicates that the estimation technique is available.

	Single Equation					System of Equations				
	OLS	2SLS	K-Class	MELO	LIML	SUR	ITSUR	3SLS	IT3SLS	FIML
PROC MODEL	√	√				√	√	√	√	
PROC SYSLIN	√	√	√	√	√	√	√	√	√	√

In this chapter, you estimate two systems of linear equations. You simultaneously estimate the equations of the Klein Model 1, a small model of the United States economy, with PROC MODEL. You first estimate the Klein Model by SUR, then by an instrumental method, 3SLS, and finally by 3SLS with the %AR macro to correct for autoregression. You also use the MODEL and SYSLIN procedures to estimate a supply and demand model of the United States pork market. First, you estimate the supply and demand model in general form equations with 2SLS. Next, you estimate only the demand equation by LIML.

A Small Model of the U.S. Economy

For purposes of this example, suppose you are an economist or a fiscal analyst for the Roosevelt administration in 1941. Your job entails estimating a small model of the economy that can be used for policy analysis. You ask Professor Lawrence Klein for assistance. Professor Klein has developed a small model of the economy, suitable for estimation and policy analysis.

In the following examples, the Klein Model 1 is specified with three equations and four identities. The equations are a consumption equation, an investment equation, and a private sector demand for labor equation. They are

$$C = a_1 + a_2 P + a_3 P\_1 + a_4 WT$$
$$I = b_1 + b_2 P + b_3 P\_1 + b_4 K\_1$$
$$WP = c_1 + c_2 X + c_3 X\_1 + c_4 TIME$$

where the variables are defined as follows:

C   is consumer expenditures.

P   is profits.

P_1   is profits lagged one period.

WT   is the total wage bill (the sum of private and government wages).

I   is investment expenditures.

K_1   is the capital stock lagged one period.

WP   is the private wage bill.

X   is total output of private industry.

X_1   is total output of private industry lagged one period.

TIME   is a linear, annual time trend.

The equations are simultaneously determined because endogenous variables appear on the right-hand side of the equations. The four identities are production, profit, capital, and total wages. They are

PRODUCT: $X = C + I + G$
PROFIT: $P = X - WP - T$
CAPITAL: $K = K\_1 + I$
WAGE: $WT = WP + WG$

where the remaining variables are defined as follows:

G   is Government Expenditures.

T   is Taxes.

WG   is the Government Wage Bill.

K   is the Capital Stock.

There are seven endogenous variables (C, I, WP, X, P, WT, and K), and seven exogenous variables (TIME, T, G, WG, P_1, K_1, and X_1). For details on the Klein Model 1, see Klein (1950).

In estimating the Klein Model 1, check for the following:

□ nonzero cross-equation error covariance, which suggests SUR estimation

□ autocorrelation (for which you should correct)

□ correlation of an independent variable and the error terms (for which you should correct).

Each of the previous items is discussed as you proceed through the Klein Model 1 examples. After the Klein data set is introduced, the model is fit first by SUR, next by 3SLS, and finally by 3SLS with a correction for first-order autoregression.

Introducing the KLEIN Data Set

Before fitting the Klein Model 1, you must create a data set that contains annual values from 1919 through 1941 on the following variables: YEAR, C, P, WP, I, K, X, WG, G, and T. All the variables are defined previously except for YEAR, which is an annual time trend, and X, which is total output of private industry.

The following statements create and print the first five observations of the KLEIN data set, as displayed in Output 6.1.

```
    /* Creating the KLEIN Data Set */
data klein;
    input year c p wp i k x wg g t;
        time = year-1919;
        p_1 = lag(p);
        x_1 = lag(x);
        k_1 = lag(k);
        wt = wp+wg;
    label c = 'Consumer Expenditures'
        p = 'Profits'
        wp= 'Private Wage Bill'
        i = 'Investment Expenditures'
        k = 'Capital Stock'
        k_1='Capital Stock Lagged One Period'
        x = 'Total Output of Private Industry'
        wg= 'Government Wage Bill'
        g = 'Government Expenditures'
        t = 'Taxes';
    cards;
1919  .    .    .    .   180.1  .    .     .    .
1920 39.8 12.7 28.8  2.7 182.8 44.9 2.2   2.4  3.4
1921 41.9 12.4 25.5 -.2  182.6 45.6 2.7   3.9  7.7
1922 45.0 16.9 29.3  1.9 184.5 50.1 2.9   3.2  3.9
1923 49.2 18.4 34.1  5.2 189.7 57.2 2.9   2.8  4.7
1924 50.6 19.4 33.9  3.0 192.7 57.1 3.1   3.5  3.8
1925 52.6 20.1 35.4  5.1 197.8 61.0 3.2   3.3  5.5
1926 55.1 19.6 37.4  5.6 203.4 64.0 3.3   3.3  7.0
1927 56.2 19.8 37.9  4.2 207.6 64.4 3.6   4.0  6.7
```

```
1928 57.3 21.1 39.2  3.0 210.6 64.5 3.7  4.2  4.2
1929 57.8 21.7 41.3  5.1 215.7 67.0 4.0  4.1  4.0
1930 55.0 15.6 37.9  1.0 216.7 61.2 4.2  5.2  7.7
1931 50.9 11.4 34.5 -3.4 213.3 53.4 4.8  5.9  7.5
1932 45.6  7.0 29.0 -6.2 207.1 44.3 5.3  4.9  8.3
1933 46.5 11.2 28.5 -5.1 202.0 45.1 5.6  3.7  5.4
1934 48.7 12.3 30.6 -3.0 199.0 49.7 6.0  4.0  6.8
1935 51.3 14.0 33.2 -1.3 197.0 54.4 6.1  4.4  7.2
1936 57.7 17.6 36.8  2.1 199.8 62.7 7.4  2.9  8.3
1937 58.7 17.3 41.0  2.0 201.8 65.0 6.7  4.3  6.7
1938 57.5 15.3 38.2 -1.9 199.9 60.9 7.7  5.3  7.4
1939 61.6 19.0 41.6  1.3 201.2 69.5 7.8  6.6  8.9
1940 65.0 21.1 45.0  3.3 204.5 75.7 8.0  7.4  9.6
1941 69.7 23.5 53.3  4.9 209.4 88.4 8.5 13.8 11.6
;

    /* Printing the KLEIN Data Set */
proc print data=klein (obs=5) label;
    var year c i wp k x g t wg p;
    title 'KLEIN Model 1 Example';
    title2 'First Five Observations KLEIN Data';
run;
```

Output 6.1
*The First Five
Observations of
the KLEIN Data
Set*

```
                            KLEIN Model 1 Example
                        First Five Observations KLEIN Data

                                           Private              Total Output
                    Consumer    Investment   Wage     Capital    of Private
    OBS   YEAR     Expenditures Expenditures  Bill      Stock      Industry

     1    1919          .            .         .       180.1         .
     2    1920        39.8          2.7      28.8      182.8        44.9
     3    1921        41.9         -0.2      25.5      182.6        45.6
     4    1922        45.0          1.9      29.3      184.5        50.1
     5    1923        49.2          5.2      34.1      189.7        57.2


            Government              Government
    OBS    Expenditures   Taxes     Wage Bill    Profits

     1          .            .          .           .
     2         2.4          3.4        2.2        12.7
     3         3.9          7.7        2.7        12.4
     4         3.2          3.9        2.9        16.9
     5         2.8          4.7        2.9        18.4
```

Estimating the System by the SUR Method

You can use PROC MODEL to estimate the Klein Model 1 by the method of seemingly unrelated regressions (SUR) estimation. In the Klein Model 1, unmodeled events simultaneously affect endogenous variables through the error terms. For example, New Deal fiscal policies such as the Social Security Act affected, at least, both consumption expenditures and private wages. These unmodeled events imply that the error terms across equations are contemporaneously correlated. SUR estimation incorporates the additional information from the cross-equation, correlated error terms.

SUR estimation requires two stages. In the first stage, OLS residuals are used to estimate the cross-equation error covariances. In the second stage, regression parameters are estimated through generalized least squares using the estimated covariances. If the cross-equation error covariances are zero, then OLS and SUR estimates are equivalent. If the cross-equation error covariances are nonzero, then SUR parameter estimates have smaller standard errors than do the OLS parameter estimates. For additional information about SUR estimation, see Zellner (1962).

The following statements print the dependency structure of the model and fit the Klein Model 1 by the techniques of OLS and SUR. In this example, the model equations and identities are entered following the PARMS statement. In PROC MODEL, you must write out equations to be fit with all parameters, variables, and arithmetic operators. Note that PROC MODEL can generate lagged values with a lag function. In this example, the equations to be estimated follow the PARMS statement. The statements are interpreted as follows:

PROC MODEL
invokes the MODEL procedure. The following options of the PROC MODEL statement are specified:

DATA=	specifies the KLEIN data set as input for PROC MODEL.
OUTMODEL=	creates an output file, named KL_MOD, containing the fitted model for use in subsequent chapters.
GRAPH	prints a graph of the dependency structure of the model.

PARAMETERS
PARMS
specifies the parameters to be estimated.

ENDOGENOUS
ENDO
specifies the endogenous variables.

EXOGENOUS
EXO
specifies the exogenous variables.

ID
specifies the variables to be included in the output data set.

FIT
specifies the model to be fit. The following options of the FIT statement are specified:

DW	requests the Durbin-Watson d statistic.
SUR	requests the estimation technique of seemingly unrelated regressions.
CORRS	prints the correlation matrix of residuals.

Output 6.2 displays the output generated by the following SAS example code:

```
/* Invoking PROC MODEL */
proc model data=klein outmodel=kl_mod graph;
   parms a1-a4 b1-b4 c1-c4;

      /* Model Equations */
   c=a1+a2*p+a3*lag(p)+a4*wt;
   i=b1+b2*p+b3*lag(p)+b4*lag(k);
   wp=c1+c2*x+c3*lag(x)+c4*time;

      /* Identities */
   x=c+i+g;
   p=x-wp-t;
   k=lag(k)+i;
   wt=wp+wg;

      /* Endogenous and Exogenous Variables */
   endo c i wp x p wt k;
   exo p_1 k_1 x_1 time t g wg;

      /* Variable Included in Output Data Set */
   id year;

      /* Estimating the Model */
   fit c i wp / dw sur covs;
run;
```

Output 6.2
Fitting the Klein
Model 1 through
the SUR Method

```
               KLEIN Model 1 Example

                  MODEL Procedure
               ❶ Model Summary

               Model Variables     14
                  Endogenous        7
                  Exogenous         7
               Parameters          12
               ID Variables         1
               Equations            7

               Number of Statements 7

               Program Lag Length    1

        Model Variables: C P WT I K WP X TIME G T WG P_1 K_1 X_1

        Parameters: A1 A2 A3 A4 B1 B2 B3 B4 C1 C2 C3 C4

        Equations: C I WP X P WT K
```

```
               KLEIN Model 1 Example

                  MODEL Procedure
               ❷ Model Structure Analysis
        (Based on Assignments to Endogenous Model Variables)

        Exogenous Variables: TIME G T WG P_1 K_1 X_1

        Endogenous Variables: C P WT I K WP X
```

(continued)

Output 6.2
(continued)

```
                    Adjacency Matrix for Graph of System

                                            1 1 1 1
         Variable      1 2 3 4 5 6 7 8 9 0 1 2 3 4
                                            * * * * * *
  C        1:  X X X . . . . . . . . . . .
  P        2:  . X . . X X . . X . . . . .
  WT       3:  . . X . X . . . . X . . . .
  I        4:  . X . X . . . . . . . . . .
  K        5:  . . . X X . . . . . . . . .
  WP       6:  . . . . X X X . . . . . . .
  X        7:  X . . X . . X . X . . . . .
  TIME     8:  * . . . . . . X . . . . . .
  G        9:  * . . . . . . . X . . . . .
  T       10:  * . . . . . . . . X . . . .
  WG      11:  * . . . . . . . . . X . . .
  P_1     12:  * . . . . . . . . . . X . .
  K_1     13:  * . . . . . . . . . . . X .
  X_1     14:  * . . . . . . . . . . . . X

              (Note: * = Exogenous Variable.)

NOTE: The System Consists of 1 Recursive Equations and 1 Simultaneous Blocks.

                    Block Structure of the System

                    Block 1: C P WT I WP X


                 Dependency Structure of the System

        Block 1 Depends On: TIME G T WG
        K        Depends On: Block 1 TIME G T WG
```

```
                       KLEIN Model 1 Example

                         MODEL Procedure

        Adjacency Matrix for Graph of System Including Lagged Impacts

                                                1 1 1 1
      Block  Variable      1 2 3 4 5 6 7 8 9 0 1 2 3 4
                                                * * * * * *
        1    C        1:  X L X . . . . . . . . . . .
        1    P        2:  . X . . . X X . . X . . . .
        1    WT       3:  . . X . . X . . . . X . . .
        1    I        4:  . L . X L . . . . . . . . .
        1    K        5:  . . . X L . . . . . . . . .
        1    WP       6:  . . . . . X L X . . . . . .
             X        7:  X . . X . . X . X . . . . .
             TIME     8:  * . . . . . . X . . . . . .
             G        9:  * . . . . . . . X . . . . .
             T       10:  * . . . . . . . . X . . . .
             WG      11:  * . . . . . . . . . X . . .
             P_1     12:  * . . . . . . . . . . X . .
             K_1     13:  * . . . . . . . . . . . X .
             X_1     14:  * . . . . . . . . . . . . X

                (Note: * = Exogenous Variable.)
```

```
                       KLEIN Model 1 Example

                         MODEL Procedure

                  The 3 Equations to Estimate are:

        C  = F( A1(1), A2, A3, A4(WT) )
        I  = F( B1(1), B2, B3, B4 )
        WP = F( C1(1), C2, C3, C4(TIME) )


                 The estimation lag length is 1.
```

```
                      KLEIN Model 1 Example

                       MODEL Procedure
                       SUR Estimation

               ❸ SUR Estimation Summary

          Dataset Option        Dataset
          DATA=                 KLEIN

          Parameters Estimated     12

                    Minimization Summary
          Method                    GAUSS
          Iterations                    1

          Final  Convergence  Criteria
          R                             0
          PPC                    1.94E-13
          RPC(C1)                 2.60057
          Object               0.04598528
          Trace(S)             2.72546179
          Objective Value      2.31689283

                  Observations Processed
          Read                         23
          Solved                       22
           First                        2
           Last                        23
          Used                         21
          Missing                       1
          Lagged                        1
```

```
                      KLEIN Model 1 Example

                       MODEL Procedure
                       SUR Estimation

           ❹ Nonlinear SUR Summary of Residual Errors
```

Equation	DF Model	DF Error	SSE	MSE	Root MSE	R-Square	Adj R-Sq	Durbin Watson
C	4	17	18.0993	1.06467	1.03183	0.9808	0.9774	1.346
I	4	17	17.4590	1.02700	1.01341	0.9308	0.9186	1.843
WP	4	17	10.7745	0.63379	0.79611	0.9864	0.9841	2.082

```
               Nonlinear SUR Parameter Estimates
```

Parameter	Estimate	Approx. Std Err	'T' Ratio	Approx. Prob>|T|
A1	15.984436	1.29903	12.30	0.0001
A2	0.230467	0.08523	2.70	0.0151
A3	0.067371	0.08550	0.79	0.4416
A4	0.795903	0.03919	20.31	0.0001
B1	13.040944	5.31461	2.45	0.0252
B2	0.439763	0.09537	4.61	0.0002
B3	0.368745	0.09911	3.72	0.0017
B4	-0.125913	0.02598	-4.85	0.0002
C1	-0.237276	1.12562	-0.21	0.8356
C2	0.409722	0.03028	13.53	0.0001
C3	0.174504	0.03464	5.04	0.0001
C4	0.156146	0.03062	5.10	0.0001

```
          Number of Observations     Statistics for System
          Used               21      Objective      2.3169
          Missing             1      Objective*N   48.6547


      ❺ Covariance of Residuals Matrix Used for Estimation

                    S        C        I       WP

                    C     1.0517   0.0553  -0.4704
                    I     0.0553   1.0103   0.1547
                    WP   -0.4704   0.1547   0.5885
```

(continued)

Output 6.2
(continued)

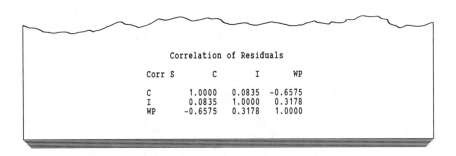

```
                         Correlation of Residuals

                 Corr S        C         I        WP

                 C         1.0000    0.0835   -0.6575
                 I         0.0835    1.0000    0.3178
                 WP       -0.6575    0.3178    1.0000
```

Interpretation of output

Output 6.2 displays the output from the MODEL procedure. There are five main sections of the printed output. The circled numbers correspond to the numbers in the following list.

❶ Model Summary

This section summarizes the model, presenting variables (endogenous and exogenous), parameters to be estimated, and model equations. Note that the lag length of variables, equations, and the model is one.

❷ Model Structure Analysis

This section, the exogenous and endogenous variables, prints matrices for the graph of the system, defines the block structure and the lag structure of the system, and lists the dependency structure of the system.

The first graph of the system is a matrix of the model variables and their dependencies. There is one block structure, consisting of the variables C, P, WT, I, WP, and X, that should be estimated simultaneously.

After the first graph, the Model Structure Analysis section lists the dependency structure of the model, which is the one block and one variable, K.

The second graph of the system includes the lagged impacts of the model variables and their dependencies. PROC MODEL tracks the use of lags in the model program and automatically determines the lag length of each equation and of the model as a whole. The program lag length is the maximum number of lags required in estimating the equations or computing any instrumental variable.

❸ SUR Estimation Summary

This section lists the data set used, the number of parameters estimated, the minimization method used, the number of iterations required to achieve convergence, the final convergence criteria, and the observations processed.

Note that the nonlinear estimation methods used in PROC MODEL reduce to the corresponding linear systems regression methods if the model is linear. Moreover, for linear models, the iterative methods converge on the first iteration, and PROC MODEL produces the same parameter estimates as PROC SYSLIN.

❹ Nonlinear SUR Summary of Residual Errors

This section presents the fitted model estimated by SUR. The estimated model is as follows:

$$C = 15.9844 + .2305\, P + .0674\, P\_1 + .7959\, WT$$
$$I = 13.0409 + .4398\, P + .3687\, P\_1 - .1259\, K\_1$$
$$WP = -.2373 + .4097\, X + .1745\, X\_1 + .1561\, TIME\ .$$

The individual *t*-tests are all significantly different from zero at the .05 level except for A3 and C1. The R^2s (R-Squares) and Adjusted R^2s (Adj R-Sqs) are all above .90, indicating the model is a good fit to the data. However, the Durbin-Watson *d* statistic for the C equation is 1.346. Although they are not shown in this output, the d_l and d_u values for 21 observations, at the .05 level of significance, are 1.026 and 1.669. To be conservative, you may want to correct the C equation for autocorrelation.

❺ Covariance and Correlation of Residuals Matrices
This section contains the covariance and correlation matrices of residuals. The first matrix is the covariances of residuals used for parameter estimation. The second matrix contains the estimates of the correlation between residuals of the estimated equations. The matrices are symmetric, and the off-diagonal terms are nonzero. The nonzero off-diagonal terms reveal the contemporaneous correlation of the error terms across equations and the appropriateness of SUR estimation.

Estimating the System by Instrumental Methods

The OLS and SUR estimations of the Klein Model 1 assume that the right-hand side variables are uncorrelated with the error terms. Because endogenous variables appear on the right-hand side of the model equations, you know that some of the right-hand side variables are correlated with the error terms. For example, in the consumption equation, WT appears as a right-hand side variable. But, WT depends on WP, an endogenous variable. Hence, WT is simultaneously determined with consumption expenditures and is correlated with the error term of that equation. Estimating the consumption equation by OLS produces biased parameter estimates.

Because some of the right-hand side variables are correlated with the error terms, OLS estimation is inappropriate. A method of estimating a system of linear equations is appropriate. You can use the maximum-likelihood estimation method of FIML or the instrumental variables method of 3SLS. For this example, the Klein Model 1 is fitted with 3SLS.

Instrumental variables methods require finding one or more replacement variables for each independent variable correlated with the error term. You want the replacement variable to be uncorrelated with the error term and highly correlated with the original variable. The number of instrumental variables you can use is limited by the number of remaining degrees of freedom, that is, the number of observations minus the number of estimated parameters.

When you use instrumental methods to fit a single-equation model, you use OLS twice. This method is known as two-stage least squares (2SLS). The first use of OLS is to regress the error-correlated variable against the replacement variables (the instrumental variables). The predictions from this first-stage regression replace the error-correlated variable(s) of the original model. The second use of OLS is to estimate the model parameters.

When you use instrumental methods to fit a system of equations, you use least squares three times. This method is called three-stage least squares (3SLS). The three uses of least squares are as follows:

1. Use the instrumental variables to create replacement variables for right-hand side variables correlated with the error term.

2. Estimate the error-covariance matrix.

3. Fit the model using the replacement variables from the first stage and the
    error-covariance matrix from the second stage.

For mathematical details of 3SLS estimation, see Kmenta (1986) and Zellner and
Theil (1962).

3SLS Estimation

Estimation by 3SLS accounts for the correlation between error terms caused by
unmodeled events and the correlation between right-hand side variables and the
error terms. The following SAS example code fits the Klein Model 1 with the
3SLS statistical technique. Statements and options that have not been previously
presented follow:

INSTRUMENTS
specifies the instrumental variables. In this example, all the
exogenous variables are specified as instrumental variables.

3SLS
requests that the model be fitted by the 3SLS statistical
technique.

FSRSQ
requests the R^2 statistics from the first-stage regressions.

```
proc model data=klein;
    parms a1-a4 b1-b4 c1-c4;
    c=a1+a2*p+a3*lag(p)+a4*wt;
    i=b1+b2*p+b3*lag(p)+b4*lag(k);
    wp=c1+c2*x+c3*lag(x)+c4*time;
    x=c+i+g;
    k=lag(k)+i;
    wt=wp+wg;
    endo c i wp x p wt k;
    exo p_1 k_1 x_1 time t g wg;
    id year;
    fit c i wp / dw 3sls fsrsq;
    instruments p_1 k_1 x_1 time t g wg;
run;
```

Output 6.3 displays part of the output generated by the previous code. The
model and estimation summaries are not displayed.

Output 6.3
*Fitting the Klein
Model 1 through
the 3SLS Method*

```
                        KLEIN Model 1 Example

                           MODEL Procedure
                           3SLS Estimation

                  Nonlinear 3SLS Summary of Residual Errors

                  DF    DF                                              Durbin
Equation  Model  Error      SSE      MSE    Root MSE  R-Square  Adj R-Sq  Watson
   C        4     17     18.6894  1.09938   1.04851    0.9801    0.9766   1.426
   I        4     17     42.6875  2.51103   1.58462    0.8308    0.8010   1.998
   WP       4     17     10.9245  0.64262   0.80164    0.9863    0.9838   2.154
```

(continued)

Output 6.3
(continued)

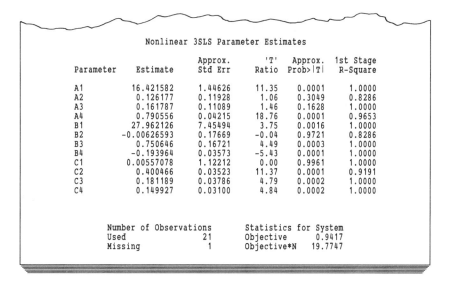

```
                     Nonlinear 3SLS Parameter Estimates

                              Approx.      'T'   Approx.  1st Stage
         Parameter  Estimate  Std Err    Ratio  Prob>|T|  R-Square

            A1      16.421582  1.44626    11.35   0.0001    1.0000
            A2       0.126177  0.11928     1.06   0.3049    0.8286
            A3       0.161787  0.11089     1.46   0.1628    1.0000
            A4       0.790556  0.04215    18.76   0.0001    0.9653
            B1      27.962126  7.45494     3.75   0.0016    1.0000
            B2      -0.00626593 0.17669   -0.04   0.9721    0.8286
            B3       0.750646  0.16721     4.49   0.0003    1.0000
            B4      -0.193964  0.03573    -5.43   0.0001    1.0000
            C1       0.00557078 1.12212    0.00   0.9961    1.0000
            C2       0.400466  0.03523    11.37   0.0001    0.9191
            C3       0.181189  0.03786     4.79   0.0002    1.0000
            C4       0.149927  0.03100     4.84   0.0002    1.0000


              Number of Observations      Statistics for System
              Used               21       Objective       0.9417
              Missing             1       Objective*N    19.7747
```

Interpretation of output

In Output 6.3, the estimated model is as follows:

$$C = 16.4216 + .1262\ P + .1618\ P\_1 + .7906\ WT$$
$$I = 27.9621 - .0063\ P + .7506\ P\_1 - .1940\ K\_1$$
$$WP = .0056 + .4005\ X + .1812\ X\_1 + .1499\ TIME\ .$$

Note the following items:

□ Eight of the individual *t*-tests are significantly different from zero at the .10 level. The parameters A2, A3, B2, and C1 are not.

□ The first stage R-Squares are less than 1.0 in four of twelve cases, indicating that some information was lost in the first-stage regressions.

□ The R-Squares and Adj R-Sqs of the consumption equation, C, and the private wages equation, WP, are above .90; they are above .80 for the investment equation, I. These values indicate the model is a reasonable fit to the data.

□ However, the Durbin-Watson *d* statistic for the C equation is 1.426, which is in the indeterminant range. To be conservative, you may conclude that the C equation should be corrected for autocorrelation.

The following example assumes that the autocorrelation of the consumption equation follows a first-order autoregressive process. The model is refitted with 3SLS, correcting the consumption equation for first-order autoregression.

3SLS Estimation with a Correction for First-Order Autoregression

You use the %AR macro to correct for autoregression in the MODEL procedure. The following statements produce Output 6.4. The %AR macro and the FIT statement are interpreted as follows:

%AR (*name, nlag, endolist*)
    contains three arguments:

name	specifies a prefix to the autoregressive parameters. For this example, the prefix AR_C is specified. PROC MODEL automatically adds a suffix for the order of the autoregressive parameter. Thus, the first-order autoregressive parameter becomes AR_C_L1.
nlag	specifies the order of the autoregressive process. This example uses a first-order process, AR(1).
endolist	specifies the list of equations to which the AR process is to be applied. This example applies the AR process to the equation with C as the dependent (left-hand side) variable. For details on the %AR macro, see the *SAS/ETS User's Guide, Version 6, First Edition*.

The following SAS example code fits the Klein Model 1 by 3SLS and corrects the consumption equation for first-order autoregression.

```
proc model data=klein;
   parms a1-a4 b1-b4 c1-c4;
   c=a1+a2*p+a3*lag(p)+a4*wt;
   i=b1+b2*p+b3*lag(p)+b4*lag(k);
   wp=c1+c2*x+c3*lag(x)+c4*time;
   x=c+i+g;
   p=x-wp-t;
   k=lag(k)+i;
   wt=wp+wg;
   %ar(ar_c,1, c)
   endo c i wp x p wt k;
   exo p_1 k_1 x_1 time t g wg;
   id year;
   fit c i wp / dw 3sls;
   instruments p_1 k_1 x_1 time t g wg;
run;
```

Output 6.4 displays part of the output generated by the previous code. Only the final model is presented.

Output 6.4
Fitting the System through 3SLS with an AR(1) Correction for the Consumption Equation

```
                           KLEIN Model 1 Example

                             MODEL Procedure
                             3SLS Estimation

                   Nonlinear 3SLS Summary of Residual Errors

                   DF   DF                                              Durbin
          Equation Model Error    SSE       MSE   Root MSE R-Square Adj R-Sq Watson

             C       5    16    46.9254   2.93284   1.71255   0.9502   0.9377  1.993
             I       4    17    33.6568   1.97981   1.40706   0.8666   0.8431  2.050
             WP      4    17    10.0169   0.58923   0.76761   0.9874   0.9852  1.990


                        Nonlinear 3SLS Parameter Estimates

                               Approx.    'T'     Approx.
          Parameter  Estimate  Std Err   Ratio   Prob>|T|  Label

          A1        31.331835   9.08718   3.45     0.0033
          A2         0.518435   0.28401   1.83     0.0867
          A3         0.495425   0.33104   1.50     0.1540
          A4         0.043891   0.46765   0.09     0.9264
          B1        22.433634   7.75806   2.89     0.0101
          B2         0.086736   0.18185   0.48     0.6395
          B3         0.659115   0.17210   3.83     0.0013
          B4        -0.166953   0.03723  -4.48     0.0003
          C1        -0.125563   1.14378  -0.11     0.9139
          C2         0.435511   0.03916  11.12     0.0001
          C3         0.151359   0.04268   3.55     0.0025
          C4         0.129567   0.03209   4.04     0.0009
          AR_C_L1    1.149017   0.09662  11.89     0.0001  AR(AR_C) C LAG1 PARAMETER


                     Number of Observations      Statistics for System
                     Used              21        Objective       0.5913
                     Missing            1        Objective*N    12.4167
```

Interpretation of output

In Output 6.4, the structural portion of the estimated model, fitted by the method of 3SLS, is as follows:

$$C = 31.3318 + .5184\ P + .4954\ P\_1 + .0439\ WT$$
$$I = 22.4336 + .0867\ P + .6591\ P\_1 - .1670\ K\_1$$
$$WP = -.1256 + .4355\ X + .1514\ X\_1 + .1296\ TIME\ .$$

Note the following items:

□ The correction for autoregression affects the residuals of the C equation, which affects the estimate of the error-covariance matrix, which in turn affects the magnitude of the estimated parameters. The C equation is most affected. You may want to compare the parameter estimates of Output 6.4 with those of Output 6.3.

□ Eight of the individual *t*-tests are significantly different from zero at the .10 level. The parameters A3, A4, B2, and C1 are not.

□ The R-Squares and Adj R-Sqs of the C and WP equations are above .90 and above .80 for the I equation. These values indicate the model is a reasonable fit to the data.

□ The Durbin-Watson *d* statistic for the C equation is 1.993, and although it is not shown on this output, it is not significant at the .05 level.

A Supply and Demand Model

A supply and demand model of the U.S. wholesale pork market is used to illustrate the method of 2SLS and general form equation estimation. Suppose you are an analyst for a company buying pork wholesale or trading in the pork futures market. The timing of your pork transactions is affected by the price of pork and the quantity available. The interaction of supply and demand simultaneously determines price and quantity.

Both the supply and demand schedules for pork include the price of pork and one or more exogenous variables. The demand schedule includes the demand shifter, B, the price of beef, because as beef prices change, you expect the quantity of pork demanded to change. The supply schedule includes the supply shifter, H, the number of hogs kept for breeding, because hogs are either bred or sold for pork. These exogenous variables shift the schedules. A structural model of the wholesale pork market follows.

Note that, in terms of economics, the third equation of the model insures that the market clears; that is, the quantity demanded equals the quantity supplied at the market price. In terms of statistics and mathematics, the third equation completes the system; that is, there are three endogenous variables (Qd_t, Qs_t, and P_t), and three equations are required to solve the system.

Demand: $Qd_t = d_0 + d_1 P_t + d_2 B_t + \varepsilon_{d,t}$

Supply: $Qs_t = s_0 + s_1 P_t + s_2 H_t + \varepsilon_{s,t}$

$Qs_t = Q_t = Qd_t$

where

d_0 and s_0	are the intercept parameters to be estimated.
d_1, d_2, s_1, s_2	are the slope parameters to be estimated.
Qd_t	is the annual quantity of pork demanded, in millions of pounds.
Qs_t	is the annual quantity of pork supplied, in millions of pounds.
P_t	is the annual (real) average price of pork in dollars.
B_t	is the annual (real) price of beef in dollars for the category, all weights, in 100-pound carlots.
H_t	is the annual number of hogs kept for breeding in thousands.
$\varepsilon_{s,t}, \varepsilon_{d,t}$	are the random error terms.

Before fitting the pork market model, you must first create the PORK data set.

Introducing the PORK Data Set

The following SAS example code creates the PORK data set containing new variables (P and B) to fit the model and prints the first five observations. The input variables, Q, TRN (nominal total revenue from pork sales), BN (nominal price of beef), EXPN (nominal total farm expenses), and H are from the U.S. Department of Agriculture's *Agricultural Statistics* (1990) while the CPI is provided by the Council of Economic Advisors. The CPI is used to deflate nominal values to account for the effects of inflation. YN is nominal personal income, from the Economic Report of the President. YN and EXPN are used later in subsequent examples.

```
data pork;
    input yr q trn yn h cpi expn bn;
        tr = trn/cpi;
        p = tr/q;
        y = yn/cpi;
        exp = expn/cpi;
        b = bn/cpi;
    label yr = 'Year'
        q = 'Quantity Produced in Millions of lbs'
        p = 'Average Pork Price Real $ per lb'
        y = 'Real Personal Income in Billions'
        h = 'Hogs Kept for Breeding in Thousands'
        cpi = 'US CPI 1982-1984 = 100'
        exp = 'US Farms Total Expenses in Millions'
        b = 'Real Price Beef, 100 lbs Carlots';
    cards;
65 18252.141    3732.747    552.0    7915    .315    33650    28.62
66 19148.989    4314.511    600.8    8752    .324    36508    35.44
67 20636.444    3921.254    644.5    8988    .334    38181    35.94
68 21034.221    3881.759    707.2    9252    .348    39525    37.30
69 20600.325    4700.280    772.9    9205    .367    42115    41.58
70 21822.826    4750.844    831.8   10630    .388    44424    44.72
71 22832.335    4144.396    894.0    9748    .405    47367    45.63
72 20918.802    5387.954    981.6    9147    .418    52315    51.41
73 20154.425    7736.731   1101.7    8988    .444    65562    65.78
74 19976.384    7166.161   1210.1    8823    .493    72210    53.48
75 16835.178    8183.583   1313.4    7358    .538    75043    43.09
76 18160.337    7756.478   1451.4    8388    .569    82741    52.00
77 19020.900    7543.411   1607.5    8688    .606    88885    51.55
78 19466.200    9038.467   1812.4    8857    .652   103249    74.61
79 22617.129    9294.814   2034.0   10368    .726   123305   100.48
80 23401.728    9157.469   2258.5    9481    .824   133139    92.45
81 21812.966   10000.500   2520.9    8358    .909   139444    84.06
82 19657.921   10836.950   2670.8    7414    .965   139954    78.96
83 21206.207    9914.131   2838.6    8113    .996   137897    78.48
84 20199.620    9816.436   3108.7    7401   1.039   143819    74.70
85 20166.989    9132.223   3325.3    6997   1.076   131926    74.13
86 19461.055    9823.886   3526.2    6435   1.096   125503    71.31
87 20445.529   10424.037   3766.4    7040   1.136   127693    83.70
88 21669.557    9283.451   4070.8    7530   1.183   132063    88.61
89 21849.658    9497.491   4384.3    7330   1.240   142566    94.43
;

proc print data=pork (obs=5) label;
    var yr q p b h;
    title 'Pork Market Supply and Demand Example';
    title2 'First Five Observations PORK Data';
run;
```

Output 6.5 displays the output generated by the previous code.

Output 6.5
The First Five
Observations of
YR, Q, P, B, and H
from the PORK
Data Set

```
                          Pork Market Supply and Demand Example
                             First Five Observations PORK Data

                          Quantity
                          Produced       Average Pork      Real Price       Hogs Kept
                          in Millions    Price Real        Beef, 100        for Breeding
          OBS    Year     of lbs         $ per lb          lbs Carlots      in Thousands

           1      65      18252.14       0.64924            90.857             7915
           2      66      19148.99       0.69541           109.383             8752
           3      67      20636.44       0.56891           107.605             8988
           4      68      21034.22       0.53030           107.184             9252
           5      69      20600.33       0.62170           113.297             9205
```

Estimating the System in General Form

General form equations are the model equations solved for the error terms. The general form equations of the pork model are as follows:

$$\varepsilon_{d,t} = -d_0 - d_1 P_t - d_2 B_t + Q d_t$$
$$\varepsilon_{s,t} = -s_0 - s_1 t \ \ - s_2 H_t + Q s_t \quad .$$

Estimating the model in general form has advantages. You do not have to rewrite (or normalize) some or all of the equations by deriving the reduced form. Rewriting the model may cause the error term to be transformed inappropriately. If the original model is nonlinear, then it may be impossible to derive the reduced form. Additionally, you do not have to solve for the structural parameters as in the case of fitting reduced-form models. Finally, restricting the parameters and performing hypothesis tests of the parameters is easier when the model can be estimated in the general form.

You can use PROC MODEL to fit a model in general equation form. The following are interpretations of statements that have not been described previously.

EQ.____
   are the general form equations. Q has been subtracted from the right-hand side. In this example, the equations are labeled DEMAND and SUPPLY.

FIT
   requests the fitting of the DEMAND and SUPPLY equations. Because P and Q are simultaneously determined and therefore correlated with the error term, the estimation method selected should account for this estimation problem. For this example, 2SLS is specified with the 2SLS option. Note that because of the equilibrium criteria, $Q s_t = Q_t = Q d_t$, the dependent variables are the same in both equations.

INSTRUMENTS
   identifies variables to be used in the first-stage regressions. In this example, the following variables are used as instruments: YR, Y, H, CPI, EXP, and B. In this example, H, EXP, and B are assumed to be uncorrelated with the residuals. Note that you may want to create a larger model in which the pork

market also influences the beef or poultry markets. In those cases, H, EXP, and B may not be acceptable instruments.

The following SAS example code fits the pork market model in the general equation form.

```
proc model data=pork;
   var p q h b;
   parms d0-d2 s0-s2;
   eq.demand = d0 + d1*p + d2*b - q;
   eq.supply = s0 + s1*p + s2*h - q;
   fit demand supply / 2sls;
   instruments yr y h cpi exp b;
run;
```

Output 6.6 displays part of the output generated by the previous code. The model summary has been omitted.

Output 6.6
General Form,
2SLS Estimation of
the Pork Market
Model

```
                   Pork Market Supply and Demand Example

                              MODEL Procedure
                              2SLS Estimation

                   Nonlinear 2SLS Summary of Residual Errors

                  DF    DF
       Equation  Model Error      SSE         MSE      Root MSE  R-Square  Adj R-Sq

       DEMAND      3    22     6300332     286378.7   535.14363
       SUPPLY      3    22     9779935     444542.5   666.74022


                       Nonlinear 2SLS Parameter Estimates

                                         Approx.      'T'     Approx.
            Parameter     Estimate       Std Err     Ratio    Prob>|T|

            D0           21574.15      558.88721     38.60     0.0001
            D1          -11086.79      922.84399    -12.01     0.0001
            D2           53.930094       5.61619      9.60     0.0001
            S0           17574.82        1122.6      15.66     0.0001
            S1           -8615.95        1037.8      -8.30     0.0001
            S2            0.928251       0.13012      7.13     0.0001


            Number of Observations       Statistics for System
            Used               25        Objective        391324
            Missing             0        Objective*N      9783090
```

Interpretation of output
In Output 6.6, the 2SLS fitted general form model is

$$Q_d = 21574.15 - 11086.79 \ P + 53.930094 \ B$$
$$Q_s = 17574.82 - 8615.95 \ P + .928251 \ H \ \ .$$

All the estimated parameters are significantly different from zero at the .01 level. Note that the supply equation has a negative slope with respect to price. This is not the expected sign, but the magnitude is less than the slope of the demand equation with respect to price, implying the system still achieves equilibrium through quantity adjustments. You may want to continue the research process and include additional supply and demand equation shifters and re-estimate the pork model, or you may want to respecify the model and use a different estimation method.

Estimating One Equation from a System by 2SLS

You may be interested in the factors affecting one equation in a system of equations. For example, you may be interested in the price sensitivity of the demand schedule; the supply relationship is unimportant. Because price and quantity are simultaneously determined, fitting the demand equation by OLS would yield biased parameter estimates. You should use either 2SLS or limited information maximum-likelihood (LIML) estimation to estimate one equation from a system of equations.

The following SAS example code using PROC SYSLIN estimates the demand equation of the pork market model with the LIML method.

```
proc syslin data=pork liml;
    instruments yr y h cpi exp b;
    model q = p b;
run;
```

Output 6.7 displays the output generated by the previous code.

Output 6.7
LIML Estimation
of the Pork Market
Demand Schedule

```
              Pork Market Supply and Demand Example

                         SYSLIN Procedure
             Limited-Information Maximum Likelihood Estimation

Model: Q
Dependent variable: Q Quantity Produced in Millions of lbs

                        Analysis of Variance

                             Sum of        Mean
         Source       DF     Squares      Square      F Value      Prob>F

         Model         2  42831513.837 21415756.919    72.597      0.0001
         Error        22  6489885.3931 294994.79060
         C Total      24  57366051.270

              Root MSE      543.13423    R-Square      0.8684
              Dep Mean   20453.91464    Adj R-SQ      0.8565
              C.V.          2.65540

                        Parameter Estimates

                      Parameter     Standard     T for H0:
         Variable DF   Estimate        Error   Parameter=0    Prob > |T|

         INTERCEP  1      21698      579.302725     37.455      0.0001
         P         1     -11516     1021.717264    -11.271      0.0001
         B         1   55.195176       5.825687      9.474      0.0001

                      Variable
         Variable DF    Label

         INTERCEP  1   Intercept
         P         1   Average Pork Price Real $ per lb
         B         1   Real Price Beef, 100 lbs Carlots
```

Interpretation of output

In Output 6.7, the LIML estimated demand equation is

$$Q = 21698 - 11516\,P + 55.195176\,B \quad .$$

The R^2 (R-Square) is .8684, and the adjusted R^2 (Adj R-SQ) is .8565. All the estimated parameters are significantly different from zero at the .01 level.

This fitted equation is similar to the fitted demand equation in Output 6.6. The estimated parameters are approximately the same magnitude and have similar t-statistics. The Root Mean Square Error (Root MSE) of the general form model is 535.14 and is 543.13 for the LIML model. On the criteria of smallest Root MSE, the general form demand model (estimated by 2SLS) provides a slightly better fit to the PORK data. In general, Nagar shows that 2SLS is often preferable to LIML for small sample estimation (1960).

Note that if you had used 2SLS to fit the demand equation, then you would have produced the same parameter estimates shown in Output 6.6.

Plotting an Estimated Equation

You can graph one or more estimated equations by creating an output data set containing the estimated model, then creating data points along one or more estimated equations, and finally, plotting the data points. This section takes you through the steps of plotting the demand schedule estimated in Output 6.7 for two levels of real beef prices per 100 pounds, B.

Creating an output data set
The following SAS example code shows you how to create an output data set containing the estimated model. The OUTEST= option creates an output data set, PORK_EST, containing the fitted model. The NOPRINT option suppresses the printed regression output.

```
proc syslin data=pork liml outest=pork_est;
   instruments yr y h cpi exp b;
   model q = p b / noprint;
run;

proc print data=pork_est;
   title2 'Fitted Pork Market Demand Data';
run;
```

Output 6.8 displays the output generated by the previous code.

Output 6.8
Creation of the Output Data Set Containing the Fitted Model

```
                    Pork Market Supply and Demand Example
                        Fitted Pork Market Demand Data

  OBS   _TYPE_    _MODEL_    _DEPVAR_   _SIGMA_     INTERCEP      YR        Y

   1     INST      FIRST        Q        653.105    -1884.15    206.454   -3.75563
   2     INST      FIRST        P          0.058        0.11      0.019    0.00005
   3     LIML        Q          Q        543.134    21697.83       .          .


  OBS       H          CPI        EXP         B         Q            P

   1      1.50267    7213.34   -0.037627   35.6108     -1           .
   2     -0.00012      -1.02    0.000004    0.0015      .         -1.00
   3         .           .         .       55.1952     -1      -11515.94
```

Creating data points
You can create points along the demand schedule with an iterative DO loop in a DATA step. The following SAS example code shows you how to create price and quantity points and then print the first five observations. The KEEP statement

specifies the variables to be kept in the new data set, PORK1. The IF-THEN statement eliminates the observations containing the instrumental variables estimation. Price coordinates are generated for pork prices from \$.25 to \$1.10 in \$.05 increments. The price coordinates are then used in the fitted model to create corresponding quantity coordinates. Q_EST1 values are the resulting quantity coordinates (or quantities demanded) as P changes, given that B is \$100 per 100 pounds. Q_EST2 values are the resulting quantities demanded as P changes, given that B is \$200 per 100 pounds.

```
data pork1;
   set pork_est;
   keep intercep q b p p_est q_est1 q_est2;
   if _n_ < 3 then delete;
   do p_est = .25 to 1.1 by .05;
   q_est1 = intercep + b*100 + p*p_est;  /* Beef prices low */
   q_est2 = intercep + b*200 + p*p_est;  /* Beef prices high */
   label p_est = 'Estimated Price'
         q_est1 = 'Estimated Quantity, Low Beef Price'
         q_est2 = 'Estimated Quantity, High Beef Price';
   output;
   end;
run;

proc print data=pork1 (obs=5);
   title2 'Pork Data for Demand Schedules';
run;
```

Output 6.9 displays the output generated by the previous code.

Output 6.9
Partial Listing of Data Points for Plotting the Demand Schedules

```
                        Pork Market Supply and Demand Example
                            Pork Data for Demand Schedules

                              Quantity                     Estimated Estimated
                   Real Price Produced  Average Pork       Quantity, Quantity,
                   Beef, 100  in Millions Price Real Estimated Low Beef High Beef
    OBS Intercept lbs Carlots  of lbs    $ per lb   Price    Price     Price

     1  21697.83   55.1952      -1      -11515.94   0.25   24338.36  29857.88
     2  21697.83   55.1952      -1      -11515.94   0.30   23762.56  29282.08
     3  21697.83   55.1952      -1      -11515.94   0.35   23186.76  28706.28
     4  21697.83   55.1952      -1      -11515.94   0.40   22610.97  28130.48
     5  21697.83   55.1952      -1      -11515.94   0.45   22035.17  27554.69
```

Plotting the demand schedules
You can use the PLOT procedure to plot the demand schedules contained in the PORK1 data set. The following SAS example code plots demand schedules for the cases of a low beef price (B=\$100) and a high beef price (B=\$200).

```
proc plot data=pork1 vpct=60;
   plot p_est * q_est1 = 'L'
        p_est * q_est2 = 'H' / overlay;
   title2 'Pork Demand Shift as Beef Price Changes';
run;
```

Output 6.10 displays the output generated by the previous code.

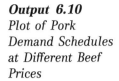

Output 6.10
Plot of Pork Demand Schedules at Different Beef Prices

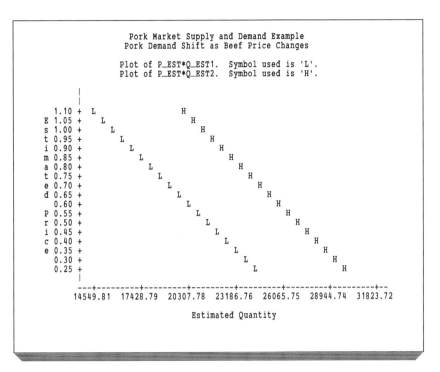

Interpretation of output

In Output 6.10, the vertical axis is price, and the horizontal axis is quantity. Prices range from \$.25 to \$1.10 per pound of pork, and the quantity demanded falls as price rises. The symbol L denotes the quantities of pork demanded for the beef price of \$100 per 100 pounds of beef. The symbol H denotes the quantities of pork demanded for the beef price of \$200 per 100 pounds of beef. Note that the higher beef price implies greater quantities of pork demanded.

Estimating Elasticities from Model Parameters

Economists are often interested in the own-price and cross-price elasticities (price sensitivity) of consumers. The own-price elasticity is $(\partial Q / \partial P) \times (P / Q)$, and the cross-price elasticity of pork for changes in beef prices is $(\partial Q / \partial B) \times (B / Q)$. The partial derivatives are actually the estimated slope parameters of the P and B variables from the demand equation of Output 6.9. You can calculate the elasticities for any point on the demand schedule. For a linear demand model (as in Output 6.7), the elasticities for the mean values of the data are often reported.

PROC MEANS calculates the mean values of Q, P, and B and creates the output data set PORK_OUT. DATA steps merge the PORK1 and PORK_OUT data sets, delete unnecessary data, and calculate the elasticities. PROC PRINT prints the elasticities.

```
proc means data=pork noprint;
   var q p b;
   output out=pork_out mean= q_mean p_mean b_mean;
run;
```

```
data pork2;
   merge pork1 pork_out;
   keep p b q_mean p_mean b_mean;
   if _n_ > 1 then delete;
run;

proc print data=pork2;
   title2 'Pork Data for Elasticities';
run;

data pork3;
   set pork2;
   p_elas = p*(p_mean/q_mean);
   b_elas = b*(b_mean/q_mean);
   label p_elas = 'Own Price Elasticity'
         b_elas = 'Cross-Price Elasticity (with Beef)';
run;

proc print data=pork3 label;
   var p_elas b_elas;
   title2 'Pork Demand Elasticities';
run;
```

Output 6.11 displays the output generated by the previous code.

Output 6.11
Data for Demand Elasticities and Calculated Elasticities

```
                    Pork Market Supply and Demand Example
                          Pork Data for Elasticities

     OBS       B          P         Q_MEAN      P_MEAN     B_MEAN

      1     55.1952   -11515.94    20453.91    0.57602    97.6454
```

```
                    Pork Market Supply and Demand Example
                          Pork Demand Elasticities

                                            Cross-Price
                              Own Price     Elasticity
                    OBS      Elasticity     (with Beef)

                     1        -0.32431        0.26350
```

Interpretation of output

In Output 6.11, the own-price elasticity of pork demand is negative: as price increases, the quantity demanded decreases. For the mean values of P and Q, the own-price elasticity is between 0 and −1, indicating that pork is an inelastic good. For a 1% increase in price, quantity demanded falls by about .32%. The cross-price elasticity is positive: as beef prices rise, so does pork consumption, as expected. Pork and beef are substitutes. For a 1% increase in the price of beef, the quantity of pork demanded increases by about .26%.

Chapter Summary

This chapter presented several examples of estimating multiple-equation models. Estimation methods for one equation within the system are 2SLS, IT2SLS, LIML, MELO, and K-Class; and systems estimation methods are SUR, ITSUR, FIML, 3SLS, and IT3SLS. The MODEL and SYSLIN procedures in SAS/ETS software estimate and test the parameters of one or more equations from a system of linear equations. The SUR and instrumental variables methods estimate system equations. This chapter also presented a method for plotting a fitted equation and a method of estimating elasticities from the data and the model parameters.

Learning More

For full reference information on PROC MODEL, PROC SYSLIN and the %AR MACRO, see the *SAS/ETS User's Guide, Version 6, First Edition.*

References

The Council of Economic Advisors (1991), *Economic Report of the President 1991*, Washington, D.C.: U.S. Government Printing Office.

Klein, L.R. (1950), *Economic Fluctuations in the United States 1921—41*, New York: John Wiley & Sons, Inc.

Kmenta, J. (1986), *Elements of Econometrics, Second Edition*, New York: MacMillan Publishing Company, Inc.

Maddala, G.S. (1977), *Econometrics*, New York: McGraw-Hill, Inc.

Nagar, A.L. (1960), "A Monte Carlo Study of Alternative Simultaneous Equation Estimators," *Econometrica*, 28, 573—590.

Pindyck, R.S. and Rubinfeld, D. L. (1991), *Econometric Models and Economic Forecasts, Third Edition*, New York: McGraw-Hill, Inc.

U.S. Department of Agriculture (1990), *Agricultural Statistics of the U.S.*, Washington, D.C.: U.S. Government Printing Office.

U.S. Department of Commerce (1990), *Statistical Abstracts of the U.S.*, Washington, D.C.: U.S. Government Printing Office.

Zellner, A. (1962), "An Efficient Method of Estimating Seemingly Unrelated Regressions and Tests for Aggregation Bias," *Journal of the American Statistical Association*, 57, 348—368.

Zellner A. and Theil, H. (1962), "Three Stage Least Squares: Simultaneous Estimation of Simultaneous Relations," *Econometrica*, 30, 54—78.

Chapter 7 Fitting Nonlinear Models

Introduction

You may need to fit nonlinear economic models to describe the behavior of economic data. For example, you may need to model the growth or acceptance of a new technology. Such growth curves are often modeled either by approximating the curve with a polynomial or by fitting a logistic curve. Modeling a constant elasticity of substitution (CES) production function is another example where you can rely on a nonlinear model.

Nonlinear models can generally be described as either inherently linear or inherently nonlinear. *Inherently linear models* are those that can be reduced to linear models by an appropriate transformation. For example, consider the Cobb-Douglas production function. In its nonlinear form, you can write the model as:

$$Y = b_0 \, X_1^{b_1} \, X_2^{b_2} \, \varepsilon \quad .$$

You can linearize this model by taking the natural logarithm on each side of the equal sign to obtain

$$\ln(Y) = \ln(b_0) + b_1 \ln(X_1) + b_2 \ln(X_2) + \ln \varepsilon \quad .$$

Expressed in this form, you assume that $\ln \varepsilon$, rather than ε, is distributed normally. If the theory underlying your model indicates this assumption is inappropriate, your model is inherently nonlinear and should be estimated through nonlinear techniques. For an example of how to fit a Cobb-Douglas model, see Chapter 2, "Fitting OLS Regression Models."

Models that you cannot reduce to linear models by any transformation are called *inherently nonlinear models*. The logistics growth curve is an example of an inherently nonlinear model:

$$Y = \frac{a}{1 + e^{b+cX}}$$

In this chapter, you learn how to use the MODEL procedure in SAS/ETS software to fit a growth curve to data by finding an appropriate polynomial model and by fitting a logistic curve. You also learn how to fit a nonlinear CES production function, how to assess the stability of the parameter estimates, and how to put restrictions on the parameters in the fitted model.

Fitting a Growth Curve

Polynomial and logistic models are often used to describe growth rates, such as the dispersion of technology and acceptance of new products. Knowledge of growth rates helps producers plan the timing of input purchases and storage or shipment of finished products. The introduction of the personal computer (PC) in the 1980s illustrates these business concerns.

This section introduces the PC data set, shows you how to plot the data and identify possible growth models, fits a polynomial model to the data, and fits a logistic model to the data.

Introducing the PC Data Set

The dispersion of personal computers in elementary schools in the United States during the 1980s occurred in three stages: initial use by a few front runners; gradual, then rapid acceptance; and finally, almost universal use. To model dispersion, you want a function that increases slowly at first, then rapidly, and finally stabilizes. Polynomial and logistic models are suitable candidates to model dispersion.

The PC data set contains the percentage of elementary schools in the United States with PCs between 1981 and 1988. The data are from the U.S. Department of Commerce's *Statistical Abstracts of the United States*.

The following SAS example code creates the PC data set, labels the variables, prints the PC data set, and titles the output, which appears in Output 7.1.

```
    /* Creating the PC Data Set */
data pc;
   input year percent @@;
      yr = year - 80;
   cards;
81 11.1 82 20.2 83 62.4 84 82.2 85 91.0 86 94.9 87 96.0 88 96.8
;
```

```
                 /* Printing the PC Data Set */
        proc print data=pc;
           var yr percent;
           title 'Logistic Curve Example';
           title2 'PC Data';
        run;
```

Output 7.1
Printing the PC Data Set

```
                        Logistic Curve Example
                               PC Data

                    OBS    YR    PERCENT

                     1      1      11.1
                     2      2      20.2
                     3      3      62.4
                     4      4      82.2
                     5      5      91.0
                     6      6      94.9
                     7      7      96.0
                     8      8      96.8
```

Plotting the PC Data Set

A good first step is to plot the data and determine whether the data suggest an appropriate model. You can use the GPLOT procedure in SAS/GRAPH software to plot the PC data. The following GPLOT statements produce Output 7.2.

PROC GPLOT
> invokes the interactive GPLOT procedure. The DATA= option specifies the PC data.

PLOT
> requests the plotting of the Y-axis variable versus the X-axis variable. The following options are specified:

> HAXIS   defines the horizontal axis.

> VAXIS   defines the vertical axis.

SYMBOL
> defines the plotting symbols used in the graph. The following options of the SYMBOL statement are specified:

> V=   specifies a symbol.

> H=   specifies the height of a symbol.

> FONT=   specifies a font.

> I=   specifies interpolation between points.

> L=   specifies the line type of the plot line.

AXIS
>   defines the horizontal and vertical axes. The following options of the AXIS statement are specified:

ORDER=	specifies the major tick marks and their spacing.
MINOR=	specifies the number of minor tick marks between major tick marks.
OFFSET=	specifies the amount of space between the first major tick mark from the axis and the amount of space between the last tick mark and the end of the axis.
LABEL=	labels the horizontal axis.

TITLE
>   titles the graph.

QUIT
>   ends the interactive GPLOT procedure.

The following SAS program plots PERCENT versus YEAR, as displayed in Output 7.2.

```
goptions reset=symbol;

proc gplot data=pc;
   plot percent*year / haxis=axis1 vaxis=axis2;
   symbol1 v=A h=1 font=swissb i=join l=1;
   axis1 order=(81 to 88 by 1) minor=none offset=(3);
   axis2 order=(0 to 100 by 10) minor=(number=3)
         label=(angle=90 'Percent of Schools');
   title 'Personal Computer Use';
run;
quit;
```

Output 7.2
Plotting the PC Data Set

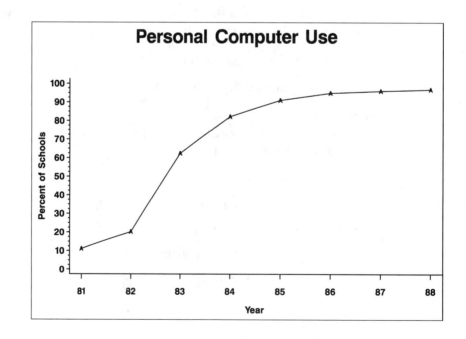

Interpretation of output

Examination of the scatter plot in Output 7.2, PERCENT versus YEAR, reveals a nonlinear relationship because there appear to be two bends in the curve. The pattern of the data suggests a quadratic or cubic polynomial model, or a logistic curve model.

Visual inspections are important and can reveal apparent nonlinearities, but you may want to use formal statistical tests for linearity. For more information, see Kmenta (1986) and Box and Cox (1964).

Fitting Polynomial Models

You can use polynomial models to approximate growth curves; they have the advantages of being easy to specify, fit, and interpret. An often-used strategy for fitting a polynomial model is to fit a higher-order model and then drop the highest-order term if it is not significantly different from zero. Continue reducing the order of the polynomial by one until the highest-order term is significantly different from zero.

A Cubic Model

The PC data have two bends in the curve, as shown in Output 7.2. The bends suggest you should first fit a cubic polynomial to the PC data as follows:

$$\text{PERCENT} = a + b\text{YR} + c\text{YR2} + d\text{YR3} + \varepsilon$$

where

a,b,c, and d	are parameters to be estimated.
YR	is a linear trend.
YR2	is a quadratic trend (YRxYR).
YR3	is a cubic trend (YRxYRxYR).
ε	is a random error term.

The following SAS example code shows you how to use PROC MODEL to fit this model. The SET statement is used to add quadratic and cubic terms to the PC data set. Note that the model is written out with the intercept and all arithmetic operators included following the PARAMETERS statement. The following is an interpretation of the remaining statements.

PROC MODEL
  invokes the MODEL procedure, and the DATA= option requests that the PC1 data set be used.

PARAMETERS
  identifies the parameters to be estimated.

FIT
  requests the equation with PERCENT as the left-hand side variable be fit.

The following SAS example code fits the cubic polynomial model to the PC1 data set. Output 7.3 shows the result. The model and estimation summaries are not shown.

```
    /* Adding Quadratic and Cubic Terms */
data pc1;
   set pc;
   yr2 = yr*yr;
   yr3 = yr2*yr;
title 'Logistic Curve Example';
title2;
run;

    /* Fitting the Cubic Polynomial Model */
proc model data=pc1;
   parameters a b c d;
      percent = a + b*yr + c*yr2 + d*yr3;
   fit percent;
run;
```

Output 7.3
A Cubic
Polynomial Model
of PC Dispersion

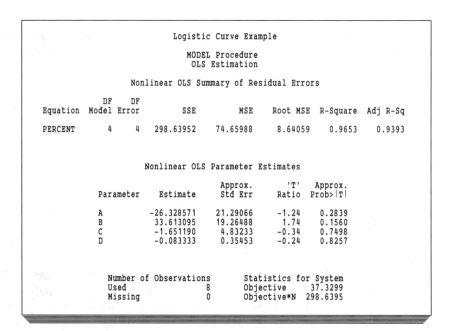

```
                         Logistic Curve Example

                           MODEL Procedure
                           OLS Estimation

                 Nonlinear OLS Summary of Residual Errors

                   DF   DF
Equation        Model Error       SSE        MSE    Root MSE  R-Square  Adj R-Sq

PERCENT            4    4     298.63952   74.65988   8.64059    0.9653    0.9393


                   Nonlinear OLS Parameter Estimates

                                       Approx.      'T'    Approx.
          Parameter     Estimate       Std Err     Ratio   Prob>|T|

          A           -26.328571      21.29066     -1.24    0.2839
          B            33.613095      19.26488      1.74    0.1560
          C            -1.651190       4.83233     -0.34    0.7498
          D            -0.083333       0.35453     -0.24    0.8257


              Number of Observations        Statistics for System
              Used               8          Objective      37.3299
              Missing            0          Objective*N   298.6395
```

Interpretation of output

In Output 7.3, the goodness of fit statistics indicate the cubic equation provides a reasonable fit; for example, the R-square is .9653, implying the model explains over 96% of the variance in the dependent variable. Yet, the *t*-statistics of the individual parameters are close to zero with large *p* values. None of the parameters are significantly different from zero at the .10 level. This result indicates a problem with *multicollinearity*, a lack of independent variation in the right-hand side (exogenous) variables. You should try dropping the cubic term and fitting a quadratic model to the PC data.

A Quadratic Model

You can fit a quadratic polynomial model with a slight modification of the SAS program used to produce Output 7.3. Note that the PARAMETERS statement of PROC MODEL can be abbreviated as PARMS. The following statements fit the quadratic polynomial model. Output 7.4 shows the result.

```
proc model data=pc1;
   parms a b c;
      percent = a + b*yr + c*yr2;
   fit percent;
run;
```

Output 7.4
A Quadratic Polynomial Model of PC Dispersion

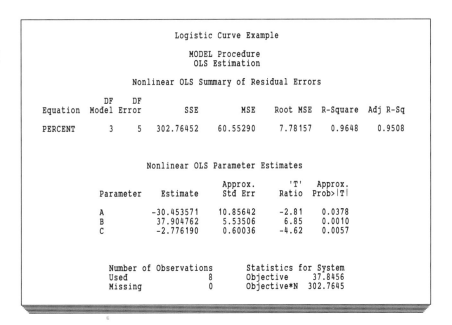

```
                        Logistic Curve Example

                          MODEL Procedure
                           OLS Estimation

                  Nonlinear OLS Summary of Residual Errors

                DF   DF
    Equation  Model Error      SSE        MSE     Root MSE  R-Square  Adj R-Sq

    PERCENT     3     5    302.76452   60.55290   7.78157    0.9648    0.9508


                      Nonlinear OLS Parameter Estimates

                                   Approx.     'T'    Approx.
               Parameter  Estimate  Std Err   Ratio   Prob>|T|

               A         -30.453571  10.85642  -2.81   0.0378
               B          37.904762   5.53506   6.85   0.0010
               C          -2.776190   0.60036  -4.62   0.0057


               Number of Observations      Statistics for System
               Used            8           Objective      37.8456
               Missing         0           Objective*N   302.7645
```

Interpretation of output

In Output 7.4, the fitted quadratic polynomial model is

PERCENT = −30.4536 + 37.9048 YR − 2.7762 YR2

The R^2 (R-Square) of this model is .9648, the adjusted R^2 (Adj R-Sq) is .9508 (higher than the Adj R-Sq of the cubic model), and the parameters are all significantly different from zero at the .05 level. Thus, the quadratic model is the polynomial model of choice.

Plotting the Predicted Values

You can plot the predicted and actual values of the quadratic model to visually assess the fit. You first use PROC MODEL to fit the model, create an output data set, and include the predicted values. Then, use PROC GPLOT to plot the predicted and actual values. The following is an interpretation of the previously undefined PROC MODEL statements used to create the output data set.

FIT

> specifies the equation to be fitted. The OUT= option creates the output data set PC_OUT.

PREDP=

> specifies a name for the predicted values.

OUTVARS

> specifies variables created by PROC MODEL to be included in the output data set. For this example, PREDP is included in the output data set.

ID

> specifies variables in the data set used by PROC MODEL to be included in the output data set. For this example, PERCENT and YEAR are included in the output data set.

The following SAS example code generates Output 7.5.

```
    /* Generating the PC_OUT Output Data Set */
proc model data=pc1 noprint;
   parms a b c;
      percent = a + b*yr + c*yr2;
   fit percent / out=pc_out;
   predp=pred.percent;
   outvars predp;
   id percent year;
run;

goptions reset=symbol;

   /* Creating Graph */
proc gplot data=pc_out;
   plot percent*year
        predp*year / overlay haxis=axis1 vaxis=axis2;
   symbol1 v=A h=1 font=swissb i=join l=1 color=black;
   symbol2 font=swissb i=join l=3 color=blue;
   axis1 label=(Year') order=(81 to 88 by 1) offset=(3) minor=none;
   axis2 label=(angle=90 'Percent of Schools')
                order=(0 to 100 by 10) minor=(number=3);
   title 'Actual and Predicted Percent vs. Year';
   title2 'Quadratic Polynomial Model';
run;
quit;
```

Output 7.5
The Actual and
Fitted Values of
the Quadratic
Polynomial Model

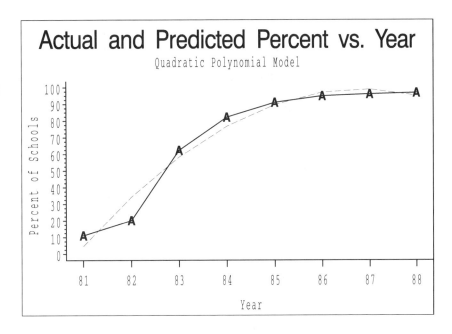

Interpretation of output

In Output 7.5, the solid line connects the actual data points, labeled A. The dashed line represents the predicted values from the quadratic model. This visual evidence indicates the quadratic model fits the data quite well. Moreover, the quadratic model is useful for interpolation. Predicted values between the actual observations seem reasonable. However, the fitted quadratic model would be inappropriate for predicting beyond the known range of data. The quadratic model predicts decreasing use of PCs and even negative percentages of usage by 1994. Thus, the quadratic polynomial model is of limited use for predicting beyond 1988.

Fitting a Logistic Curve Model

A logistic curve is often used to characterize growth rates. A logistic curve applied to the model of PC dispersion has the form

$$\text{PERCENT} = \frac{a}{1 + e^{b\,+\,c\text{YR}}} + \varepsilon$$

where e is the base of natural logarithms, approximately 2.71828. The following is an interpretation of the parameters.

a is the maximum value, expected to be a value near 100%.

b is a location parameter.

c is an initial growth rate (a negative value).

In this equation, the logistic curve limits mean values of the dependent variable to values between zero and a maximum defined by the parameter A.

The following SAS example code uses PROC MODEL to fit a logistic curve to the PC data. The following is an interpretation of the options of the FIT statement.

START=

provides starting values for parameters specified in the PARMS statement. PROC MODEL initially sets all parameter values equal to .0001, then calculates the direction of change and the optimal step size. Because you know that the parameter A can be no greater than 100 (but is much larger than .0001) and the parameter C is a small negative number, you provide starting values.

CONVERGE=

sets the convergence criteria for fitting the model. In this example, the convergence criteria is set at .05, which is well above the default value of .001. For initial attempts to fit nonlinear models, you want to use less stringent convergence criteria.

The following SAS example code generates Output 7.6.

```
proc model data=pc;
   parms a b c;
      percent = a/(1 + exp(b + c*yr));
   fit percent start=(a=100 c=-.005) / converge=.05;
run;
```

Output 7.6
Initial Attempt to Fit a Logistic Curve to the PC Data Set

```
                   Logistic Curve Example

                       MODEL Procedure
                  ❶ Model Summary

                  Model Variables        1
                  Parameters             3
                  Equations              1

                  Number of Statements   1

             Model Variables: PERCENT

             Parameters: A: 100  B C: -0.005

             Equations: PERCENT
```

```
                   Logistic Curve Example

                       MODEL Procedure

              The Equation to Estimate is:

                  PERCENT = F( A, B, C )
```

```
                   Logistic Curve Example

                       MODEL Procedure
                       OLS Estimation
    ❷
    ERROR: After 20 halvings of the GAUSS method parameter change vector the
           objective function was not improved.
           With the change vector below reduced by the factor 9.5367432E-7, the
           OBJECTIVE=1411.3183094, which is not less than the previous OBJECTIVE=
           1411.1864679.
```

(continued)

Output 7.6
(continued)

```
Failed GAUSS Method Change Vector At OLS Iteration 1
A:    868713 B:    17370 C:    44.9332


ERROR: The parameter estimates failed to converge for OLS after 1 iterations
       using CONVERGE=0.05 as the convergence criteria.

OLS Iteration 1: N=8 Objective=1411.1864679 MSE=2257.8983486 Nsubit=20 R=
               0.9865200453 PPC=171981958.24(B)
               A: 100 B: 0.0001 C: -0.005

    GAUSS Method Parameter Change Vector At OLS Iteration 1
    A:    868713 B:    17370 C:    44.9332


                    Collinearity Diagnostics

                         Condition  Var Prop  Var Prop  Var Prop
        Number  Eigenvalue  Number      A         B         C

          1     2.85750     1.0000   0.0000    0.0000    0.0000
          2     0.14250     4.4780   0.0000    0.0000    0.0000
          3   4.2414E-10    82080    1.0000    1.0000    1.0000

NOTE: The parameter estimation is abandoned. Check your model and data. If the
      model is correct and the input data are appropriate, try rerunning the
      parameter estimation using different starting values for the parameter
      estimates.
      PROC MODEL continues as if the parameter estimates had converged.
```

```
                    Logistic Curve Example

                      MODEL Procedure
                      OLS Estimation

    ❸ OLS Estimation Summary (Not Converged)

            Dataset Option      Dataset
            DATA=                   PC

            Parameters Estimated (    3)

                Minimization Summary
            Method               GAUSS
            Iterations               1
            Subiterations           40

            Final  Convergence  Criteria
            R               0.98652005
            PPC(B)            1.7198E8
            RPC                    .
            Object                 .
            Trace(S)         2257.89835
            Objective Value  1411.18647

                Observations Processed
            Read                     8
            Solved                   8
```

```
                    Logistic Curve Example
                  ❹ MODEL Procedure
                      OLS Estimation

   Nonlinear OLS Summary of Residual Errors (Estimates Not Converged)

              DF    DF
   Equation Model Error     SSE      MSE    Root MSE  R-Square  Adj R-Sq

   PERCENT    1    7      11289    1612.8   40.15949   -0.3116   -0.3116


      Nonlinear OLS Parameter Estimates (Not Converged)

                                  Approx.   'T'   Approx.
              Parameter  Estimate Std Err  Ratio  Prob>|T|
```

(continued)

Output 7.6
(continued)

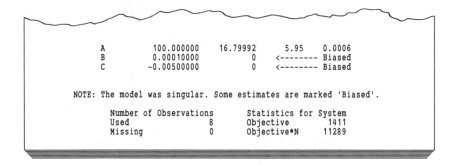

```
              A        100.000000    16.79992     5.95    0.0006
              B          0.00010000          0    <-------- Biased
              C         -0.00500000          0    <-------- Biased


    NOTE: The model was singular. Some estimates are marked 'Biased'.

         Number of Observations       Statistics for System
         Used                8        Objective             1411
         Missing             0        Objective*N          11289
```

Description of output

The circled numbers in the Output 7.6 correspond to the numbers in the following list:

1. The Model Summary describes the model variables, parameters, and equations. Here, the model consists of one endogenous variable, three parameters, and one equation. The Model Summary also lists the starting values assigned to the parameters A and C in the FIT statement.

2. This portion of the output gives the method used, an iteration history, and shows that **convergence was not achieved**. When convergence is not achieved, PROC MODEL lists the collinearity diagnostics.

3. The Estimation Summary describes the estimation, including the estimation method used (OLS), the data set used, the number of parameters estimated, the method used to minimize the objective function (GAUSS), the number of iterations and subiterations, the convergence criteria, and the number of observations used.

4. The Nonlinear OLS Summary describes the estimated model including the goodness of fit statistics (MSE, Root MSE, R-Square, and Adj R-Sq), the estimated parameters, their standard errors, t statistics, and p values. Lastly, the Nonlinear OLS Summary lists the number of observations used, the value of objective function, and the objective function times n.

Interpretation of output

Output 7.6 shows that the model did not converge. Given the current starting values, there is a problem with collinearity. The small eigenvalues listed under the heading "Collinearity Diagnostics" indicate little individual variation (high collinearity) in the rates of change of the parameters B and C. The very small eigenvalue $4.2414E-10$ indicates a severe collinearity problem for this model. Different parameter starting values may eliminate collinearity problems.

Refitting the Model

By selecting different starting values for B and C, you can mitigate the effect of collinearity. You can specify more than one starting value for parameters with the START= option by listing them with a space between each number. For example, the following FIT statement specifies one starting value for parameter A, two starting values for parameter B, and three starting values for parameter C.

```
fit percent start=(a=100 b=100 10 c=-.5 -1 -1.5);
```

This FIT statement creates a grid of six sets of starting values (1x2x3=6). PROC MODEL calculates the value of the objective function for each combination of parameter values and then uses the combination that produces the minimum value.

Even when you specify starting values, nonlinear algorithms may not converge. If you set the parameter starting values near the expected parameter estimates, you improve the chances of attaining convergence.

If you continue to have collinearity problems after specifying new starting values, you may want to use a different method of minimizing the objective function with the METHOD= option of the FIT statement. You can specify the GUASS (the default) and MARQUARDT (Marquardt-Levenberg) methods of minimizing the objective function. For details see the *SAS/ETS User's Guide, Version 6, First Edition*.

The following statements refit the logistic curve model creating a grid of starting values for the parameter estimates and specify the Marquardt-Levenberg method. The OUTMODEL= option of the PROC MODEL statement creates the output file PC_MOD containing the fitted model for later use. The following options of the FIT statement are specified.

START=
> creates a grid of starting values.

CONVERGE=
> specifies the convergence criteria. In this example, the convergence criteria is set at .0001.

METHOD=
> specifies the estimation method. In this example, the Marquardt-Levenberg method is used.

The following SAS example code generates Output 7.7.

```
proc model data=pc outmodel=pc_mod;
   parms a b c;
      percent = a/(1 + exp(b + c*yr));
   fit percent start=(a=100 b=100 10 c=-.5 -1 -1.5)
            / converge=.0001 method=marquardt;
run;
```

Output 7.7
A Logistic Curve Fit to the PC Data Set

```
                      Logistic Curve Example

                         MODEL Procedure

                         Model Summary

                Model Variables          1
                Parameters               3
                Equations                1

                Number of Statements     1

        Model Variables: PERCENT

        Parameters: A: 100   B: 100   C: -0.5

        Equations: PERCENT
```

```
                    Logistic Curve Example

                      MODEL Procedure

                 The Equation to Estimate is:

                   PERCENT = F( A, B, C )
```

```
                    Logistic Curve Example

                      MODEL Procedure
Initial Grid Search

NOTE: Grid search points tried: 6.
```

```
                    Logistic Curve Example

                      MODEL Procedure
                       OLS Estimation

                  OLS Estimation Summary

         Dataset Option        Dataset
         DATA=                  PC

         Parameters Estimated     3

                  Minimization Summary
         Method              MARQUARDT
         Iterations                  8
         Subiterations               5
         Average Subiterations    0.63

         Final  Convergence  Criteria
         R                    0.00008726
         PPC(C)               0.000021
         RPC(C)               0.000098
         Object               1.94708E-7
         Trace(S)             12.1879395
         Objective Value      7.61746217
         Lambda               1E-9

                Observations Processed
         Read                        8
         Solved                      8
```

```
                    Logistic Curve Example

                      MODEL Procedure
                       OLS Estimation

           Nonlinear OLS Summary of Residual Errors

              DF    DF
Equation    Model  Error      SSE       MSE     Root MSE  R-Square  Adj R-Sq

PERCENT       3      5     60.93970  12.18794   3.49112    0.9929    0.9901


              Nonlinear OLS Parameter Estimates

                                Approx.    'T'     Approx.
           Parameter  Estimate  Std Err   Ratio   Prob>|T|

               A      95.451766  1.88994   50.51   0.0001
               B       4.109726  0.44384    9.26   0.0002
               C      -1.528940  0.16746   -9.13   0.0003
```

(continued)

Output 7.7
(continued)

```
        Number of Observations          Statistics for System
        Used                    8       Objective       7.6175
        Missing                 0       Objective*N    60.9397
```

Interpretation of output

In Output 7.7, convergence is achieved. The final model is

$$\text{PERCENT} = \frac{95.4518}{1 + e^{(4.1097 - 1.5289\ \text{YR})}}$$

The *t*-statistics for the parameters of the logistic model in Output 7.7 are large in magnitude and are all significant at the .01 level.

The upper bound parameter, A, tells you that as YR gets large, PCs are dispersed to about 95.45% of U.S. elementary schools. This logistic model would not predict that PCs will be dispersed to 100% of the schools. Reasons for this result could be that some schools lack funding and that some school administrators prefer to not use PCs. The location parameter, B, tells you that if YR is zero (1980), then PCs are dispersed to about 1.5% of U.S. elementary schools. In practice, this parameter is of little interest. The parameter C is the proportionate rate of growth of dispersion, about 1.53%. The growth rate for any year is proportional to the current dispersion and the difference between the upper bound and the current dispersion.

The logistic model generates higher R-Square and Adj R-Sq and lower MSE and Root MSE than the quadratic polynominal model, as shown in the following table.

Table 7.1
Comparison of Logistic and Polynomial Models

Goodness-of-Fit Statistics	Logistic Model (Output 7.7)	Quadratic Polynomial Model (Output 7.4)
R-Square	.9929	.9648
Adj R-Square	.9901	.9508
MSE	12.1879	60.5529
Root MSE	3.4911	7.7816

Based on these criteria, the logistic model provides the superior fit.

Plotting the Fitted Curve

You can see how well your model fits the data by plotting the dependent variable and the predicted values versus YEAR. The following SAS example code:

□ fits the model (the NOPRINT option suppresses the printed output), and creates the output data set PC_OUT1 (the OUTVARS statement includes the predicted values in the output data set while the ID statement includes the actual dependent-variable values in the output data set)

□ uses the GPLOT procedure to create a high-resolution graph.

The following SAS example code generates Output 7.8.

```
    /* Fitting Model and Creating PC_OUT1 Output Data Set */
proc model data=pc noprint;
   parms a b c;
      percent = a/(1 + exp(b + c*yr));
   fit percent start=(a=100 b=100 10 c=-.5 -1 -1.5)
               / converge=.0001 method=marquardt out=pc_out1;
   predp=pred.percent;
   outvars predp;
   id percent year;
run;
quit;


goptions reset=symbol;

    /* Plotting Actual and Predicted Values */
proc gplot data=pc_out1;
   plot percent * year
        predp * year / overlay haxis=axis1 vaxis=axis2;
   axis1 order=(81 to 88 by 1) offset=(3) minor=none;
   axis2 label=(angle=90 'Percent of Schools') minor=(number=3)
        order=(0 to 100 by 10);
   symbol1 h=1 pct v=A font=swissb color=black;
   symbol2 font=swissb i=join l=3 color=blue;
   title 'Fit of Logistic Model';
run;
quit;
```

Output 7.8
A Plot of Actual and Predicted Percent of Elementary Schools with PCs

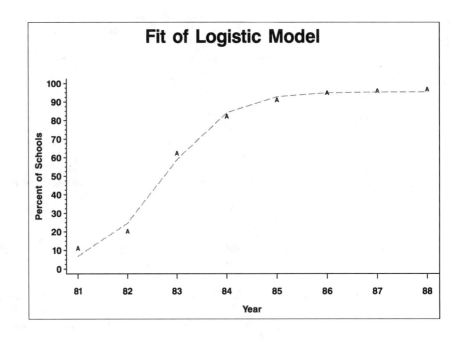

Description of output

In Output 7.8, the A's represent actual values, and the dashed line represents the predicted values. The plot indicates the logistic curve model is a good fit to the PC data set. This visual evidence enables you to confirm the appropriateness of the logistic model.

Fitting a Production Function

The Constant Elasticity of Substitution (CES) production function developed by Arrow, Chenery, Minhas, and Solow (1961) is a generalization of the Cobb-Douglas (CD) production function. (For a discussion of the CD production function, see Chapter 2). In general, production functions describe how inputs are combined to produce outputs. Given a set of input prices, there is an optimal input mix. As the relative price of inputs changes, the firm may want to change its input mix. The elasticity of substitution measures how easily firms may substitute one input for another while keeping production at the same level. If you use the CD production function, you assume that the elasticity of input substitution is 1. The CES production function allows the elasticity of input substitution to be a constant but not necessarily 1.

The CES production function has the form

$$Q_i = \gamma[\delta K_i^{-\rho} + (1-\delta)L_i^{-\rho}]^{-v/\rho} e^{\varepsilon_i}$$

where

Q_i is the output for the ith firm.

K_i is the capital input for the ith firm.

L_i is the labor input for the ith firm.

e the base of the natural logarithms ($e=2.71828\ldots$).

ε_i is the random error for the ith firm.

and

γ is an efficiency parameter (an indicator of the state of technology).

δ is a distribution parameter (defining the relative input shares).

v is the returns-to-scale parameter.

ρ is the parameter associated with the elasticity of substitution, which for CES production functions is $1/(1+\rho)$. As $\rho \to 0$, the CES production function reduces to the CD production function. As $\rho \to \infty$, the CES reduces to a Leontief (fixed proportions) production function.

Introducing the CES Data Set

Fitting the CES model to the widget-producing industry requires information on capital input (expenditures on plant and equipment), labor input (expenditures for wages), and output (number of widgets produced). The CES data set contains data on the capital and labor inputs and the outputs of the 25 firms producing widgets. The data are found in Kmenta (1986).

The following SAS program creates the CES data set, labels the variables, and uses PROC PRINT to print the first five observations, which are shown in Output 7.9.

```
data ces;
   input k l q @@;
   label k ='Capital Input'
      l ='Labor Input'
      q ='Output';
   cards;
8 23 106.00  9 14  81.08  4 38 72.80  2 97  57.34  6 11  66.79
6 43  98.23  3 93  82.68  6 49 99.77  8 36 110.00  8 43 118.93
4 61  95.05  8 31 112.83  3 57 64.54  6 97 137.22  4 93  86.17
2 72  56.25  3 61  81.10  3 97 65.23  9 89 149.56  3 25  65.43
1 81  36.06  4 11  56.92  2 64 49.59  3 10  43.21  6 71 121.24
;

proc print data=ces (obs=5) label;
   title 'CES Production Function Example';
   title2 'First Five Observations CES Data';
run;
```

Output 7.9
The First Five
Observations of
the CES Data Set

```
                   CES Production Function Example
                   First Five Observations CES Data

                      Capital   Labor
            OBS        Input     Input    Output

             1           8        23      106.00
             2           9        14       81.08
             3           4        38       72.80
             4           2        97       57.34
             5           6        11       66.79
```

Plotting the CES Data Set

You first use the G3GRID procedure in SAS/GRAPH software to create a data set that contains a rectangular grid of interpolated and smoothed values. You use the G3D procedure to produce a three-dimensional surface plot. The following is an interpretation of the statements.

PROC G3GRID
   invokes the G3GRID procedure. The OUT= option creates the output data set CES_GRID to be used for the surface plot.

GRID
   specifies K as the Y axis, L as the X axis, and Q as the Z axis. The following options of the FIT statement are specified:

   SPLINE   requests spline interpolation.

SMOOTH=   specifies a smoothing constant of .01.

AXIS   specifies the range of values and the increment between
               values.

PROC G3D
   invokes the G3D procedure. The DATA= option requests that the CES_GRID
   data set be used.

PLOT
   specifies K*L as the Y*X plane (the floor of the graph) and Q as the Z axis (the
   height of the plot). The following options of the PLOT statement are specified:

ROTATE=   specifies a 75-degree rotation of the graph about the Z
               axis.

TILT=   specifies an 80-degree tilt of the graph about the Y axis.

ZMIN=   specify the minimum and maximum values of the Z axis.
ZMAX=

YTICKNUM=   specify the number of major tick marks on the Y and X
XTICKNUM=   axes.

For details, see Chapter 39, "The G3D Procedure," and Chapter 40, "The
G3GRID Procedure," in *SAS/GRAPH Software: Reference*.

```
proc g3grid data=ces out=ces_grid;
   grid k*l=q / spline smooth=.01
                axis1=1 to 9 by .5
                axis2=10 to 100 by 10;
run;

proc g3d data=ces_grid;
   plot k*l=q / rotate=75 tilt=80
                zmin=10 zmax=160 yticknum=3 xticknum=5;
   title 'Two-Input Production Surface Plot';
run;
quit;
```

This code generates the plot displayed in Output 7.10.

Output 7.10
A 3-D Surface Plot of Output Produced by Combinations of Capital and Labor Inputs

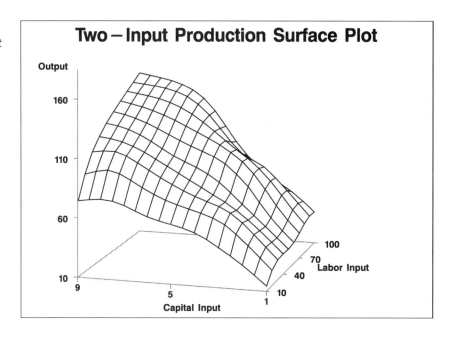

Interpretation of output

Output 7.10 reveals the nonlinear surface of output produced by inputs, capital, and labor. Cross-sections from front to back (holding capital constant) show the marginal physical product of labor. In general, for a given level of capital, more labor increases output but at a decreasing rate. Cross-sections from right to left (holding labor constant) show the marginal physical product of capital. Capital also exhibits diminishing marginal returns. Cross-sections at different output levels (cross-sections parallel to the capital and labor plane) are *isoquants*, different combinations of inputs that produce the same level of output.

Fitting the CES Production Function

Kmenta uses the CES data set to estimate a linearized CES production function (1986). Kmenta linearizes by first taking natural logarithms, next using a Taylor's series expansion around the parameter ρ, and, finally, dropping all terms involving a higher order than one of ρ. Using PROC MODEL, you can fit this nonlinear model without the complicated linearizing process used by Kmenta.

The following SAS example code uses PROC MODEL to fit the nonlinear CES production function. The model is written with all mathematical operators following the PARMS statement. Initial starting values for the parameters and a convergence criteria of .0001 are specified in the FIT statement.

```
proc model data=ces;
   parms g r v d;
      q = g*((d*k**r) + (1-d)*l**r)**(v/r);
   fit q start = (g=15 d=.6 r=-.3 v=.5) / converge =.0001;
run;
```

This code generates Output 7.11.

Output 7.11
Estimating the CES
Production
Function

```
                        CES Production Function Example

                              MODEL Procedure

                              Model Summary

                    Model Variables        1
                    Parameters             4
                    Equations              1

                    Number of Statements   1

          Model Variables: Q

          Parameters: G: 15  R: -0.3  V: 0.5  D: 0.6

          Equations: Q
```

```
                        CES Production Function Example

                              MODEL Procedure

                        The Equation to Estimate is:

                            Q = F( G, R, V, D )
```

```
                        CES Production Function Example

                              MODEL Procedure
                              OLS Estimation

                           OLS Estimation Summary

                    Dataset Option        Dataset
                    DATA=                     CES

                    Parameters Estimated      4

                          Minimization Summary
                    Method                  GAUSS
                    Iterations                  5
                    Subiterations               1
                    Average Subiterations    0.20

                    Final  Convergence  Criteria
                    R                  0.00002655
                    PPC(R)               0.000061
                    RPC(R)               0.000641
                    Object             7.12298E-8
                    Trace(S)           46.6646711
                    Objective Value    39.1983237

                          Observations Processed
                    Read                       25
                    Solved                     25
```

```
                        CES Production Function Example

                              MODEL Procedure
                              OLS Estimation

                    Nonlinear OLS Summary of Residual Errors

                    DF   DF
          Equation Model Error     SSE      MSE  Root MSE R-Square Adj R-Sq Label

          Q          4   21   979.9581 46.66467  6.83115   0.9537   0.9471 Output
```

(continued)

Output 7.11
(continued)

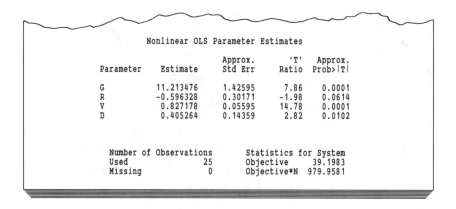

```
              Nonlinear OLS Parameter Estimates

                                Approx.     'T'    Approx.
          Parameter   Estimate  Std Err    Ratio  Prob>|T|
             G       11.213476  1.42595     7.86   0.0001
             R       -0.596328  0.30171    -1.98   0.0614
             V        0.827178  0.05595    14.78   0.0001
             D        0.405264  0.14359     2.82   0.0102


          Number of Observations       Statistics for System
          Used              25         Objective      39.1983
          Missing            0         Objective*N   979.9581
```

Interpretation of output

The estimated model in Output 7.11 is

$$Q = 11.213[.4053\ K^{-.5963} + .5947\ L^{-.5963}]^{-1.38712}$$

where $-1.38712 = -.827178 / .596328 = v / \rho$.

For comparison, Kmenta's linearized model estimates are

$$Q = 3.4456[.4723\ K^{-.4334} + .5277\ L^{-.4334}]^{-1.9024}$$

where $-1.9024 = .8245 / .4334 = v / o$, and Kmenta's estimated log γ is 1.2371, which is approximately 3.4456.

Output 7.11 indicates a good fit of the data: R-Square is .9537 and Adj R-Sq is .9471. All of the estimated parameters are significantly different from zero at the .10 level.

The returns to scale of the two models are about .82, indicating a doubling of the two inputs would increase output by about 82%. The two models differ in the following ways.

□ The input mix, associated with the parameter δ in Kmenta's linearized model implies a 47% capital and 53% labor mix while the nonlinear model indicates a 41% capital and 59% labor mix.

□ The elasticity of substitution, $1 / (1 + \rho)$, in Kmenta's linearized model is 1.765 while in the nonlinear model is 2.477. This means that the nonlinear model implies inputs can be more easily substituted for each other than in the linearized model.

□ The efficiency parameter γ indicates the state of technology (changes in output not attributable to more capital and labor) is approximately 3.45 in Kmenta's linearized model and 11.213 in the nonlinear model. The nonlinear fitted model indicates the methods of production are more different as the level of output changes than they are in Kmenta's linearized model.

With all nonlinear models, you want to check for sensitivity of the parameter estimates to starting values and your specified convergence criteria. The next section discusses approaches for checking the robustness of your estimated model.

Checking Parameter Stability

You may want to conduct sensitivity analysis on the estimated model. By changing your starting values and convergence criteria, you check the robustness of your parameter estimates. If the newly estimated parameters are close in value to those of the less stringent convergence criteria, your fitted nonlinear model is robust.

The following SAS example code refits the model of Output 7.11 with a wider grid of starting values and a smaller convergence criteria:

```
proc model data=ces;
   parms g r v d;
      q = g*(((d*k)**r) + ((1-d)*1)**r)**(v/r);
   fit q start = (g=50 5 d=.65 .55 r=-.2 -.4 v=.7 -.8)
                   / converge =.00005;
run;
```

Part of the output generated by the previous code is displayed in Output 7.12. The model and estimation summary portions of the output have been omitted.

Output 7.12
Refitting the CES
Production
Function as a
Check on
Robustness

```
                     CES Production Function Example

                            MODEL Procedure
                            OLS Estimation

                   Nonlinear OLS Summary of Residual Errors

                DF    DF
   Equation  Model  Error      SSE       MSE   Root MSE R-Square Adj R-Sq Label

      Q          4    21   979.9581  46.66467  6.83115    0.9537   0.9471 Output


                     Nonlinear OLS Parameter Estimates

                                     Approx.     'T'    Approx.
            Parameter    Estimate    Std Err    Ratio   Prob>|T|

               G        11.213491    1.42595     7.86    0.0001
               R        -0.596287    0.30170    -1.98    0.0614
               V         0.827183    0.05595    14.78    0.0001
               D         0.405283    0.14359     2.82    0.0102


            Number of Observations        Statistics for System
            Used              25          Objective     39.1983
            Missing            0          Objective*N  979.9581
```

Interpretation of output

Output 7.12 indicates the model converged and has the same MSE, R-Square, and Adj R-Square. The parameter estimates of this model are very close to those of Output 7.11.

Restricting Parameters of the Nonlinear Model

You may want to restrict a production function to having constant returns to scale. For production functions with constant returns to scale, k times all inputs results in k times the output. To restrict a CES production function to having constant returns to scale, the parameter v must equal 1.

To restrict a parameter value, you can follow either approach listed below.

□ Use direct substitution. For example, to obtain a constant returns to scale CES production function, replace *v* with 1 and drop *v* from the list of parameters.

□ Use a CONTROL statement in PROC MODEL to control the value of a parameter or a variable.

CONTROL statements also enable you to perform case studies and what-if analyses which are forms of simulation. For details on simulation, see Part 2, "Simulation."

The following SAS example code restricts the CES production function to constant returns to scale using a CONTROL statement.

```
proc model data=ces;
   parms g r v d;
   control v 1;
      q = g*((d*k**r) + (1-d)*l**r)**(v/r);
   fit q start = (g=5 50 d=.6 r=-.25) / converge =.001;
run;
```

The fitted model generated by the previous code is displayed in Output 7.13. Most of the model summary portion of the output has been omitted.

Output 7.13
Restricting the CES Production Function to Constant Returns to Scale

```
                    CES Production Function Example

                          MODEL Procedure
                          OLS Estimation

                 Nonlinear OLS Summary of Residual Errors

                 DF    DF
Equation Model Error      SSE      MSE   Root MSE R-Square Adj R-Sq Label

Q                3    22     1405 63.87732   7.99233   0.9336   0.9276 Output


                 Nonlinear OLS Parameter Estimates

                                   Approx.    'T'    Approx.
            Parameter    Estimate  Std Err   Ratio   Prob>|T|

               G         8.418848  0.83590   10.07    0.0001
               R        -0.133932  0.19351   -0.69    0.4961
               D         0.623893  0.09878    6.32    0.0001


            Number of Observations       Statistics for System
            Used             25          Objective      56.2120
            Missing           0          Objective*N       1405
```

Interpretation of output

In Output 7.13, the model parameters are estimated where the returns to scale parameter is set equal to one. The parameters *g* and *d* are significantly different from zero at the .10 level while the parameter *r* is not. (You may want to compare the estimated parameters in Outputs 7.11 and 7.12.) From these results, you conclude that restricting the CES production function to constant returns to scale is inappropriate for this data set.

Chapter Summary

This chapter discussed inherently linear and inherently nonlinear models, and has presented estimation strategies for nonlinear models. Providing starting values and less-stringent convergence for initial estimation attempts can assist you in attaining convergence. A logistic curve and CES production function were estimated. The CES production function was restricted to constant returns to scale and re-estimated. Finally, parameter sensitivity analysis was performed by varying the starting values and the convergence criteria.

Learning More

For more information about PROC MODEL and nonlinear modeling, see the *SAS/ETS User's Guide*.

For more information about the GPLOT, G3D, and G3GRID procedures, see *SAS/GRAPH Software: Reference, Version 6, First Edition, Volume 1* and *Volume 2* and *SAS/GRAPH Software: Usage, Version 6, First Edition*.

References

Arrow, K.J.; Chenery, H.B.; Minhas, B.S.; and Solow, R.M. (1961), "Capital-Labor Substitution and Economic Efficiency," *Review of Economics and Statistics*, (43)5, 225–254.

Box, G.E.P. and Cox, D.R. (1964), "An Analysis of Transformations," *Journal of the Royal Statistical Society, Series B*, 26, 211–243.

Kmenta, J. (1986), *Elements of Econometrics, Second Edition*, New York: Macmillan Publishing Company, Inc.

Maddala, G.S., (1992) *Introduction to Econometrics, Second Edition*, New York: Macmillan Publishing Company, Inc.

Pindyck, R.S. and Rubinfeld, D.L. (1991), *Econometric Models and Economic Forecasts, Third Edition*, New York: McGraw-Hill, Inc.

U.S. Department of Commerce, (1990) *Statistical Abstracts of the U.S.*, Washington, D.C.: U.S. Government Printing Office.

Chapter **8** Fitting Time Series Cross-Sectional Models

Introduction

You may need to analyze data collected over multiple time periods and multiple cross-sectional units. These data are known as time series cross-sectional (TSCS) data, or sometimes as panel data. For example, residential electricity sales for North Carolina, South Carolina, and Virginia over the period 1970 through 1988 is a time series cross-sectional data set. There are three cross-sectional units and 19 years of time series data. For comparison, a time series data set has observations across time on only one economic unit. A cross-sectional data set has observations across several economic units, but for only one time period.

You can use several approaches for regression analysis of TSCS data. For example, you could assume that all time periods are alike, pool the data across time, and perform a cross-sectional analysis. Alternatively, you could assume that all cross sections are alike, pool the data across the cross-sectional units, and perform a time series analysis. Pooling the data across either dimension may oversimplify your analysis.

Because TSCS data have properties of both cross-sectional data and time series data, a better approach is to use TSCS methods and analyze the data across both dimensions. Advantages of TSCS analysis include accounting for

☐ autocorrelation across time units (within cross sections)

☐ heteroskedasticity within cross sections (across time units)

□ contemporaneous spatial correlation among cross sections (across time units)

□ moving average components across time units (within cross-sections).

In this chapter, you learn how to use the TSCSREG procedure to fit a TSCS model to residential demand for electricity. In the process of fitting a model, you must identify the time series process, and check for cross-sectional correlation. You also learn how to select the most appropriate TSCS statistical method and how to add intercept-shifting dummy variables to improve the fit.

Methods of TSCS Analysis

You can estimate TSCS models with the TSCSREG procedure. PROC TSCSREG performs TSCS regression analysis by any of the following:

□ Fuller and Battese method

□ Parks method

□ Da Silva method

In each method, the residuals are used to provide an estimate of the covariance matrix. The regression parameters are then estimated by generalized least squares. The three methods are described in the following paragraphs.

The Fuller and Battese method is a variance component model in which the error term, $u_{i,t}$, has the following decomposition:

$$u_{i,t} = v_i + e_t + \varepsilon_{i,t}$$

where the v_i, e_t, and $\varepsilon_{i,t}$ are independently distributed with zero means and positive, finite variances. The v_i component is a cross-sectional error component, the e_t component is a time series error component, and $\varepsilon_{i,t}$ is a random error component. The Fuller and Battese method is appropriate when the error structure conforms to these assumptions. However, the Fuller and Battese method displays a general robustness to the underlying error structure.

The Parks method assumes a first-order autogressive error structure with contemporaneous correlations between the cross sections. The errors may be heteroskedastic within the same cross section, contemporaneously correlated across cross sections within the same time observation, and follow a first autoregressive process within the same cross section across time units. If your data and preliminary analysis indicate a higher-order autoregressive process or a moving average component, then the Parks method may be inappropriate.

The Da Silva method can be viewed as a mixed variance-component moving average model. The TSCS model is written in the following form:

$$Y_{i,t} = a_i + b_t + \beta X_{i,t} + \varepsilon_{i,t}$$

where

$Y_{i,t}$ is the value of the dependent variable for the *i*th cross-section in the *t*th time period.

a_i is a time invariant cross-sectional unit effect.

b_t is a cross-sectional unit invariant time effect.

β is the slope parameter associated with the independent variable, $X_{i,t}$.

$X_{i,t}$ is the value of the independent variable for the *i*th cross section in the *t*th time period.

$\varepsilon_{i,t}$ is a residual effect unaccounted for by the independent variable, the time effect, and the cross-sectional unit effect. $\varepsilon_{i,t}$ is assumed to be a finite moving average process.

The Da Silva method is appropriate when preliminary analysis indicates the presence of a moving average component. If your data and preliminary analysis indicate autocorrelation, heteroskedasticity, or spatial correlation are problems, then the Da Silva method may be inappropriate.

Modeling Electricity Demand

In modeling the residential demand for electricity, there are many interesting empirical questions you could examine:

□ Do price and income influence the residential demand for electricity?

□ Is the residential demand for electricity sensitive to changes in price and income?

□ Does demand differ across states?

A simple and general TSCS model of residential electricity demand can be described as

$$Q_{i,t} = a + bP_{i,t} + cY_{i,t} + u_{i,t}$$

where

$Q_{i,t}$ is the quantity of electricity demanded by residential consumers in the *i*th state for the *t*th year.

a, *b*, and *c*   are the parameters to be estimated.

$P_{i,t}$ is the average price of electricity to residential consumers in the *i*th state for the *t*th year.

i   is the cross-sectional index, i=1, 2, . . . , N.

t   is the time series index, t=1, 2, . . . , T.

$Y_{i,t}$ is the real annual income of residents in the *i*th state for the *t*th year.

$u_{i,t}$ is a general error term.

In econometric studies, it has traditionally been assumed that each residential consumer behaves as if the supply of electricity is infinitely elastic over a fairly large range. Thus, aggregating over consumers implies that changes in residential demand affect only quantity, not price. Therefore, in this model, price and quantity are not simultaneously determined; thus, the demand schedule can be estimated by OLS. For additional information on modeling energy demand schedules, see Bohi (1981).

Introducing the DEMAND Data Set

Electricity demand has been an important area of economic research. As electricity demand increases, more generating capacity is required. Because generating plants are costly to build and require long lead times, utility companies want to model electricity demand so they can forecast when additional capacity will be required. At some point, the growth of electricity demand makes it optimal to build a new plant.

Understanding electricity demand helps forecasters predict electricity usage more accurately. Price of electricity and income of consumers are variables likely to affect the level of demand. Price increases reduce the quantity demanded, while income increases raise the quantity demanded. These two variables can be used to create a fairly simple model of residential electricity demand. The DEMAND data set includes annual observations in North Carolina (NC), South Carolina (SC), and Virginia (VA) during the period from 1970 through 1988. The following variables are collected:

□ Q, residential electricity consumption, in trillions of BTUs (from *State Energy Data Report*, Consumption Estimates, DOE/EIA)

□ CPI, the consumer price index, 1982 through 1984=100 (from the Bureau of Labor Statistics, U.S. Department of Commerce). This is used to deflate nominal income and price to account for inflation.

□ PN, nominal average price (per million BTUs in dollars) of residential electricity (from State Energy Price and Expenditure Report, DOE/EIA)

□ YN, nominal per capita personal income in dollars (from July issues of *Survey of Current Business*).

Creating the DEMAND Data Set

The following SAS example code creates the DEMAND data set, labels the variables, and prints the first five observations. Note that nominal income and nominal price are deflated by the CPI to account for inflation. Output 8.1 shows the results.

```
data demand;
   input st year q cpi pn yn @@;

      /*     Creating Real P and Y by     */
      /* Deflating Nominal P and Y by CPI */
   p = pn/cpi;
   y = yn/cpi;

      /* Labeling Variables */
   label q = 'Sales in Trillions of BTUs'
      cpi = 'Consumer Price Index'
      p = 'Real Electricity Price'
      y = 'Real Personal Income';
```

```
      /* Labeling Cross-Sections */
  if st=1 then state = 'NC';
  if st=2 then state = 'SC';
  if st=3 then state = 'VA';
  cards;
1 1970  50.0  .388  5.47  3256  1 1971  53.9  .405  5.89  3424
1 1972  56.6  .418  6.30  3721  1 1973  63.1  .444  6.53  4258
1 1974  63.4  .493  8.03  4612  1 1975  64.8  .538  9.32  4943
1 1976  68.2  .569 10.44  5409  1 1977  74.6  .606 11.21  5935
1 1978  77.3  .652 12.02  6607  1 1979  77.2  .726 12.60  7359
1 1980  83.2  .824 13.91  7999  1 1981  85.1  .909 15.96  8646
1 1982  81.9  .965 18.50  9148  1 1983  86.1  .996 19.42  9982
1 1984  91.9 1.039 19.57 11001  1 1985  91.6 1.076 20.48 11664
1 1986 100.7 1.096 21.17 12453  1 1987 107.5 1.136 21.59 13353
1 1988 109.9 1.183 21.90 14304  2 1970  25.1  .388  5.66  2992
2 1971  26.8  .405  6.10  3142  2 1972  28.1  .418  6.52  3448
2 1973  31.7  .444  6.69  3885  2 1974  31.9  .493  8.30  4258
2 1975  33.6  .538  9.62  4665  2 1976  35.3  .569 10.48  5126
2 1977  38.6  .606 11.45  5628  2 1978  40.0  .652 11.35  6242
2 1979  39.0  .726 12.70  7027  2 1980  42.9  .824 13.69  7589
2 1981  44.6  .909 15.73  8109  2 1982  46.0  .965 17.61  8605
2 1983  47.1  .996 18.97  9288  2 1984  49.7 1.039 19.20 10171
2 1985  50.0 1.076 20.54 10734  2 1986  55.0 1.096 20.89 11336
2 1987  57.7 1.136 21.03 12078  2 1988  58.6 1.183 20.90 12926
3 1970  39.4  .388  6.13  3720  3 1971  41.1  .405  6.28  3899
3 1972  44.5  .418  6.51  4258  3 1973  50.1  .444  6.90  4868
3 1974  50.3  .493  9.06  5265  3 1975  54.2  .538 11.07  5770
3 1976  58.5  .569 11.12  6276  3 1977  62.1  .606 12.73  6865
3 1978  63.7  .652 13.30  7624  3 1979  63.9  .726 14.95  8605
3 1980  67.3  .824 17.80  9827  3 1981  70.2  .909 18.15 10385
3 1982  69.4  .965 19.81 11386  3 1983  73.7  .996 20.56 12505
3 1984  74.1 1.039 19.53 13498  3 1985  77.0 1.076 19.49 14467
3 1986  86.1 1.096 19.48 15456  3 1987  91.7 1.136 19.62 16539
3 1988  96.2 1.183 19.29 17675
;

  /* Printing the First Five Observations */
proc print data=demand (obs=5) label;
  var state year q p y;
  title 'TSCS Electricity Demand Example';
  title2 'First Five Observations DEMAND Data';
run;
```

Output 8.1
First Five Observations of the DEMAND Data Set

```
                         TSCS Electricity Demand Example
                         First Five Observations DEMAND Data

                              Sales in      Real        Real
                             Trillions  Electricity   Personal
         OBS   STATE   YEAR   of BTUs      Price       Income
          1     NC     1970    50.0      14.0979      8391.75
          2     NC     1971    53.9      14.5432      8454.32
          3     NC     1972    56.6      15.0718      8901.91
          4     NC     1973    63.1      14.7072      9590.09
          5     NC     1974    63.4      16.2880      9354.97
```

Plotting the Electricity Demand

You can plot electricity demand over time with the GPLOT procedure in
SAS/GRAPH software. The FORMAT procedure is used to format the cross
sections for the plot legend. The VALUE statement of the FORMAT procedure
defines a value format. For this example, the variable STATE has three values:
NC, SC, and VA. The following GPLOT statements produce Output 8.2 and are
interpreted as follows:

PROC GPLOT
>   invokes the GPLOT procedure. The DATA= option specifies DEMAND as the
>   input data set.

PLOT
>   requests the plotting of the Y-axis variable versus the X-axis variable. The
>   following options are specified:

>   HAXIS=   specifies the horizontal axis.

>   VAXIS=   specifies the vertical axis.

SYMBOL
>   defines the plotting symbols used in the graph. The following options of the
>   SYMBOL statement are specified:

>   V=   specifies a symbol.

>   FONT=   specifies a font.

>   I=   specifies interpolation between points.

>   L=   specifies the type of plotting line.

AXIS
>   defines the horizontal and vertical axes. The following options of the AXIS
>   statement are specified:

>   ORDER=   specifies the major tick marks and their spacing.

>   MINOR=   specifies the number of minor tick marks between major tick
>   marks.

>   OFFSET=   specifies the amount of space between the first major tick
>   mark from the axis, and the amount of space between the last
>   tick mark and the end of the axis.

>   LABEL=   labels the horizontal axis.

TITLE
>   titles the graph.

The following SAS example code graphs Q versus YEAR.

```
        /* Formatting the Cross-Sections */
    proc format;
       value stfmt 1='NC'
                   2='SC'
                   3='VA';
    run;
```

```
goptions reset=symbol;

  /* Plotting the Electricity Demand */
proc gplot data=demand;
  plot q*year=st / haxis=axis1 vaxis=axis2;
  symbol1 v=N font=swissb i=join l=1 color=black;
  symbol2 v=S font=swissb i=join l=1 color=blue;
  symbol3 v=V font=swissb i=join l=1 color=green;
  axis1 order=(1970 to 1988 by 2) minor=(number=1) offset=(3);
  axis2 order=(20 to 110 by 10) minor=(number=3)
  label=(angle=90 'Electricity Sales');
  title1 'Residential Demand for Electricity';
  title2 '(in trillions of BTU)';
  format st stfmt.;
run;
quit;
```

Output 8.2
Graphing
Residential
Electricity Demand
by States

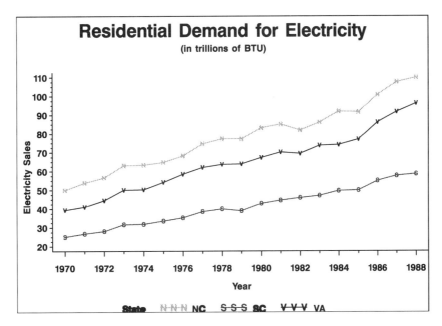

Interpretation of output

The graph of residential electricity demand displayed in Output 8.2 shows a difference in the base level of consumption across states. NC residential consumption is consistently the highest, SC consumption is the lowest, and VA consumption is between them.

This graph indicates that you need to include some form of cross-sectional analysis in the fitted model. Moreover, you need to check for time series effects within each cross section.

Determining the Appropriate Model

You can test for violations of the OLS error assumptions prior to fitting the TSCS model. Violations that you discover influence your choice of statistical technique to fit your model. The following sections test the residuals for autocorrelation and contemporaneous spatial correlation, and identify the time series process of the dependent variable Q. You can also test for heteroskedasticity; see Chapter 4, "Violations of the OLS Error Assumptions," for techniques of testing for heteroskedasticity.

Testing for Autocorrelation

When you have time series data, you should check for autocorrelation. You can use the SORT procedure and the SAS/ETS procedure AUTOREG to test for autocorrelation. The following is an interpretation of the SAS statements:

PROC AUTOREG
> invokes the AUTOREG procedure. The DATA= option specifies DEMAND as the input data set.

MODEL
> specifies the OLS model (as described previously) with the following options:

DW=	specifies the generalized Durbin-Watson tests for first- through fourth-order autocorrelation.
DWPROB	specifies the *p* values of the generalized Durbin-Watson statistics.

BY
> produces separate analyses for each of the states.

It is important to sort your data by cross section and then by time series within each cross section. Data sets sorted in other ways may produce misleading results.

The following SAS example code performs the Durbin-Watson tests on the OLS residuals for each state. Output 8.3 shows the results.

```
    /* Sorting the Data */
proc sort data=demand;
   by state year;
run;

    /* Checking for Autocorrelation */
proc autoreg data=demand;
   model q = p y / dw=4 dwprob;
   by state;
run;
```

Output 8.3 displays partial output for each state containing the generalized Durbin-Watson statistics and their associated *p* values. The OLS fitted models are not shown.

Output 8.3
The Generalized Durbin-Watson Statistics and p-Values for Each State

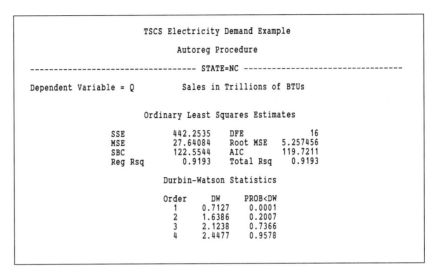

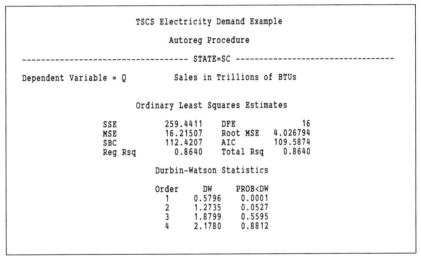

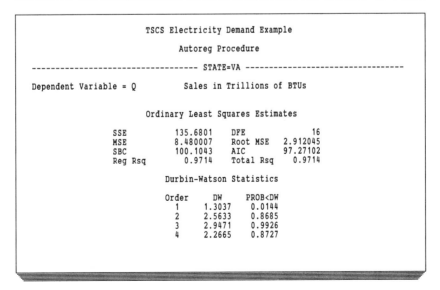

Interpretation of output

The generalized Durbin-Watson statistics and their associated p values in Output 8.3 show evidence of autocorrelation. The next step is to identify the type of process or the nature of the autocorrelation.

Identifying the Time Series Process

You can identify a time series process using the ARIMA procedure in SAS/ETS software. PROC ARIMA uses the Box-Jenkins method of identification, estimation, and forecasting. Time series processes may contain autoregressive components, moving average components, or a combination of the two. Be aware that the series must be stationarity before identification. You may need to difference the series to achieve stationarity.

You can identify the time series process with the autocorrelation function, the inverse autocorrelation function, and the partial autocorrelation function. For example, if the time series is an autoregressive process of the first order, AR(1), then the autocorrelation function will decay exponentially (see Output 8.4), while the inverse and partial autocorrelation functions will have a spike at the first lag and be essentially zero elsewhere. Another example is a moving average process of first order, MA(1). An MA(1) process has an autocorrelation function with a spike at the zero and first lags and is essentially zero elsewhere (see Output 8.5). The inverse and partial autocorrelation functions of the MA(1) process decay exponentially.

Output 8.4
Example of an Autocorrelation Function Decaying Exponentially

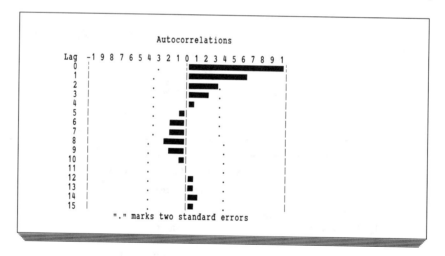

Output 8.5
Example of a
Partial
Autocorrelation
Function with a
Spike at Lag 1 and
a Drop to 0

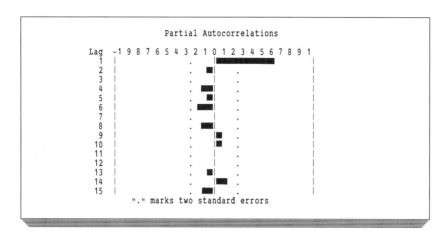

Note: Output 8.4 and Output 8.5 show results that have been altered slightly for emphasis. You cannot use SAS code to produce identical output.

The following statements show you how to produce autocorrelation plots with the ARIMA procedure:

PROC ARIMA

invokes the ARIMA procedure. The DATA= option specifies DEMAND as the input data set.

BY

produces separate analyses for each of the states.

IDENTIFY

computes statistics to help identify models to fit. The VAR= option names the variable containing the time series.

The following SAS example code identifies the time series process for each state.

```
proc arima data=demand;
   by state;
   identify var=q;
run;
quit;
```

Output 8.6 displays partial output from PROC ARIMA, the autocorrelation functions of Q in North Carolina.

Output 8.6
The PROC ARIMA
Identification of
the Regression
Time Series Model

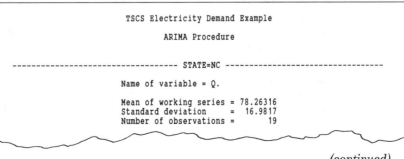

(continued)

Output 8.6
(continued)

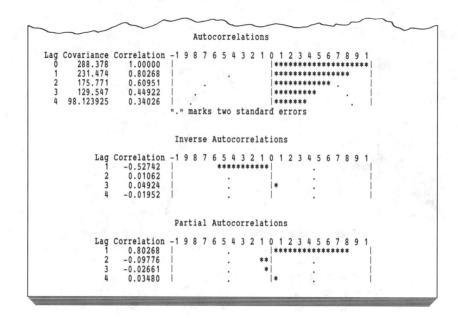

```
                              Autocorrelations

Lag Covariance Correlation -1 9 8 7 6 5 4 3 2 1 0 1 2 3 4 5 6 7 8 9 1
  0   288.378   1.00000   |                  |******************|
  1   231.474   0.80268   |                  |****************  |
  2   175.771   0.60951   |          .       |************ .    |
  3   129.547   0.44922   |           .      |*********      .  |
  4 98.123925   0.34026   |           .      |*******      .    |
                     "." marks two standard errors


                          Inverse Autocorrelations

Lag Correlation -1 9 8 7 6 5 4 3 2 1 0 1 2 3 4 5 6 7 8 9 1
  1   -0.52742   |           ***********|          .          |
  2    0.01062   |                  .   |          .          |
  3    0.04924   |                  .   |*         .          |
  4   -0.01952   |                  .   |          .          |


                          Partial Autocorrelations

Lag Correlation -1 9 8 7 6 5 4 3 2 1 0 1 2 3 4 5 6 7 8 9 1
  1    0.80268   |                  .   |****************     |
  2   -0.09776   |                  .  **|         .          |
  3   -0.02661   |                  .   *|         .          |
  4    0.03480   |                  .   |*        .          |
```

Interpretation of output

The PROC ARIMA identification for North Carolina is shown in Output 8.6. The remaining states have almost identical output. From Output 8.6, you can see that

□   the autocorrelation function declines exponentially

□   the inverse autocorrelation function has a spike at lag 1, and is essentially zero elsewhere

□   the partial autocorrelation function has a spike at lag 1, and is essentially zero elsewhere.

Based on these results, you conclude that the process is AR(1), and there is little evidence of a moving average component.

For more information on identification of time series processes, see Chapter 3, "Autoregressive Models," in *SAS/ETS Software: Applications Guide 1, Version 6, First Edition*; Chapter 7, "The ARIMA Procedure," of the *SAS/ETS User's Guide; Version 6, First Edition*; and Box and Jenkins (1976).

Checking for Cross-Sectional Correlation

Cross-sectional correlations occur if the data are correlated among the cross sections. You can expect the quantity of electricity demanded to be cross-sectionally correlated because residents move among the states and because electricity suppliers provide service in more than one state. Moreover, other factors (like similarly cold or hot weather) can cause correlations among the states. If cross-sectional correlations exist in the data, then TSCS statistical methods are required to account for them.

Before testing for cross-sectional correlations, you need to create a new data set that is organized differently from the DEMAND data set. The new data set should be arranged so that each observation has the quantities demanded for each state as a separate variable.

The following statements produce Output 8.7. You use the SORT and TRANSPOSE procedures and then a DATA step to reorganize the data. You can then use the CORR procedure to test for cross-sectional correlation. The statements perform as follows:

PROC SORT
    invokes the SORT procedure. The following options of the PROC SORT statement are specified:

DATA=	specifies DEMAND as the input data set.
OUT=	names the output data set, DEM_OUT.
KEEP=	specifies the variables to be kept, YEAR and Q.

BY
    specifies the variable to sort by, YEAR.

PROC TRANSPOSE
    invokes the TRANSPOSE procedure. The following options of the PROC TRANSPOSE statement are specified:

DATA=	specifies the DEM_OUT data set.
OUT=	names the output data set, DEM_OUT1.
DROP=	specifies the variables to be dropped.

BY
    specifies the variable for which separate observations are generated, YEAR.

RENAME
    renames the columns (variables) in the DEM_OUT1 data set.

PROC CORR
    invokes the CORR procedure and specifies DEM_OUT1 as the input data set.

VAR
    specifies the variables to be used.

The following SAS example code prints the first five observations of the reorganized data set to confirm its creation and performs the cross-sectional correlation analysis:

```
    /* Sorting the Data by Time Series ID */
proc sort data=demand out=dem_out (keep=year q);
    by year;
run;

    /* Transposing the Data */
    /* Rows Become Columns  */
proc transpose data=dem_out out=dem_out1 (drop=_name_ _label_);
    by year;
run;

    /* Renaming the Data Columns */
data dem_out2;
set dem_out1;
    rename col1=q_nc col2=q_sc col3=q_va;
run;
```

```
/* Printing the Data */
proc print data=dem_out2 (obs=5);
  title2 'First Five Observations DEM_OUT2 Data';
run;


/* Checking for Cross-Sectional Correlation */
proc corr data=dem_out2;
  var q_nc q_sc q_va;
run;
```

Output 8.7
Cross-sectional Correlation Analysis of the Demand for Residential Electricity

```
                    TSCS Electricity Demand Example
                  First Five Observations DEM_OUT2 Data

            OBS    YEAR    Q_NC    Q_SC    Q_VA

             1     1970    50.0    25.1    39.4
             2     1971    53.9    26.8    41.1
             3     1972    56.6    28.1    44.5
             4     1973    63.1    31.7    50.1
             5     1974    63.4    31.9    50.3
```

```
                    TSCS Electricity Demand Example

                        Correlation Analysis

         3 'VAR' Variables:   Q_NC      Q_SC      Q_VA


                          Simple Statistics

   Variable    N      Mean     Std Dev        Sum     Minimum     Maximum

   Q_NC       19   78.26316   17.44704       1487    50.00000   109.90000
   Q_SC       19   41.14211   10.29538   781.70000    25.10000    58.60000
   Q_VA       19   64.92105   16.22880       1234    39.40000    96.20000


   Pearson Correlation Coefficients / Prob > |R| under Ho: Rho=0 / N = 19

                       Q_NC            Q_SC            Q_VA

        Q_NC         1.00000         0.99522         0.99567
                     0.0             0.0001          0.0001

        Q_SC         0.99522         1.00000         0.99306
                     0.0001          0.0             0.0001

        Q_VA         0.99567         0.99306         1.00000
                     0.0001          0.0001          0.0
```

Interpretation of output

In Output 8.7, all of the Pearson correlation coefficients are greater than .99, and all are different from zero at the .01 level. You conclude that the quantity of electricity demanded is contemporaneously correlated across states. TSCS statistical methods are appropriate for analysis.

For additional information about the CORR procedure, see Chapter 15, "The CORR Procedure," in the *SAS Procedures Guide, Version 6, Third Edition.*

Fitting a Parks Model

The results so far show the quantity of electricity demanded follows autoregressive processes within cross sections, displays little evidence of a moving average component, and has contemporaneous cross-sectional correlation. Thus, the appropriate TSCS estimation method is the Parks method.

The following SAS statements sort the data by the cross-sectional variable (STATE) and then by the time series variable (YEAR), and then fit a Parks model to the DEMAND data. The following is an interpretation of the statements.

▶ *Caution* . . . . *Sort your data by cross-sections and by time within cross-sections prior to using PROC TSCSREG. Failure to use properly sorted data can yield misleading results.*

PROC SORT
> invokes the SORT procedure. The DATA= option specifies DEMAND as the input data set.

BY
> requests that the data be sorted first by STATE and then by YEAR (within STATE).

PROC TSCSREG
> invokes the TSCSREG procedure. The DATA= option specifies DEMAND as the input data set.

MODEL
> specifies the model to be fitted. Using options of the MODEL statement, you can specify the TSCS estimation method. The options are FULLER, PARKS, and DASILVA for the Fuller and Battese, Parks, and Da Silva methods, respectively. The following options of the MODEL statement are specified:

> PARKS   requests the Parks method.

> RHO   prints the autocorrelation coefficients.

ID
> specifies the cross-sectional index variable and the time series index variable.

The following SAS example code produces Output 8.8.

```
   /*   Sorting the Data                               */
   /* First by Cross-Section ID, Second by Time-Series ID   */
proc sort data=demand;
   by state year;
run;

   /* Fitting the TSCS Model */
proc tscsreg data=demand;
   model q = p y / parks rho;
   id state year;
run;
```

Output 8.8
The Fitted Parks
TSCS Model

```
                      TSCS Electricity Demand Example

                            TSCSREG Procedure
                          Parks Method Estimation

Dependent Variable: Q   Sales in Trillions of BTUs

                           Model Description

               Estimation Method         PARKS
               Number of Cross Sections  3
               Time Series Length        19

                     Variance Component Estimates

        SSE          52.94883    DFE               54
        MSE          0.980534    Root MSE     0.990219


                        Parameter Estimates

                      Parameter     Standard      T for H0:
         Variable  DF  Estimate      Error       Parameter=0  Prob > |T|

         INTERCEP  1   -9.581092    14.416696    -0.664583     0.5091
         P         1   -0.308510     0.378420    -0.815258     0.4185
         Y         1    0.006566     0.001025     6.407148     0.0001

                        Parameter Estimates

                                  Variable
                   Variable  DF   Label

                   INTERCEP  1    Intercept
                   P         1    Real Electricity Price
                   Y         1    Real Personal Income

                   First Order Autoregressive
                       Parameter Estimates

                    STATE              RHO

                     NC             0.960056
                     SC             0.960056
                     VA             0.922048
```

Interpretation of output

The fitted Parks model of Output 8.8 is

$$Q = -9.581092 - .308510\ P + .006566\ Y$$

The estimated slope parameter for income (Y) is different from zero at the .01 level of significance. The slope parameter for price (P) is a negative number, as you should expect in a demand equation, but is not significantly different from zero. Note the relatively large standard error of the intercept. This could be a result of omitted cross-sectional effects.

Accounting for Cross-Sectional Differences

Recall that Output 8.2 indicated there were different base levels of residential electricity consumption for states. The Parks model you fitted does not account for these differences. You should include cross-sectional intercept-shifting dummy variables in the Parks model.

After sorting your data by cross section (ST) and by time series (YEAR), you use a DATA step to add intercept-shifting dummy variables, SC_DUM and VA_DUM, to the DEMAND data set. The following SAS example code fits the

Parks model with cross-sectional intercept-shifting dummy variables. Output 8.9 shows the results.

```
    /* Creating Cross-Sectional Dummy Variables */
data demand1;
    set demand;
    if st=2 then sc_dum = 1;
    else sc_dum = 0;
    if st=3 then va_dum = 1;
    else va_dum = 0;
run;

    /* Fitting the TSCS Model */
proc tscsreg data=demand1;
    model q = sc_dum va_dum p y / parks rho;
    id state year;
run;
```

Output 8.9
The Fitted
Intercept-Shifting,
Parks TSCS Model

```
                        TSCS Electricity Demand Example

                               TSCSREG Procedure
                            Parks Method Estimation

Dependent Variable: Q    Sales in Trillions of BTUs

                              Model Description

                    Estimation Method          PARKS
                    Number of Cross Sections    3
                    Time Series Length         19


                         Variance Component Estimates

            SSE           54.335      DFE              52
            MSE         1.044904      Root MSE   1.022205


                            Parameter Estimates

                       Parameter     Standard     T for H0:
            Variable  DF  Estimate       Error   Parameter=0  Prob > |T|

            INTERCEP   1  -24.065310   8.463822    -2.843315      0.0064
            SC_DUM     1  -30.022337   2.961519   -10.137480      0.0001
            VA_DUM     1  -31.588255   3.403028    -9.282396      0.0001
            P          1    0.405863   0.315192     1.287669      0.2036
            Y          1    0.009506   0.000518    18.343957      0.0001

                            Parameter Estimates

                                        Variable
                    Variable  DF          Label

                    INTERCEP   1   Intercept
                    SC_DUM     1
                    VA_DUM     1
                    P          1   Real Electricity Price
                    Y          1   Real Personal Income


                        First Order Autoregressive
                            Parameter Estimates

                         STATE               RHO

                          NC             0.816014
                          SC             0.645939
                          VA             0.389814
```

Interpretation of output

The fit of the TSCS Parks model with intercept-shifting dummy variables in Output 8.9 is similar to the results of Output 8.8. The slope parameter of income is different from zero at the .05 level of significance, and the slope parameter of price is not. However, the intercept and both of the intercept-shifting dummy variables are different from zero at the .01 level. You can conclude that the intercept-shifting dummy variables are important to the model.

From this fitted model, you conclude that income does influence the residential demand for electricity and price does not. Thus, within the range of observed values of income and price, residential demand is sensitive to changes in income but not in price. Because the intercept-shifting dummy variables are different from zero at the .05 level, you can conclude that the base level of demand does differ across states.

Calculating and Plotting Predicted Values

To calculate the predicted values from the structural portion of your TSCS model, you must first create an output data set containing the parameter estimates. Next, the parameter estimates are renamed and merged with all input data observations in DATA steps. Then, the predicted values are calculated using array processing. Lastly, the predicted values are plotted using PROC GPLOT. The following SAS example code calculates the predicted values, then plots them.

```
    /* Creating OUTEST Data Set */
proc tscsreg data=demand1 noprint outest=dem_est
            (keep=_type_ intercep p y sc_dum va_dum);
    model q = sc_dum va_dum p y / parks;
    id st year;
run;

    /* Creating Parameter Estimate Data Set */
data dem_est1(drop=_type_);
    set dem_est(where=(_type_='PARMS')
    rename=(y=p_y p=p_p sc_dum=p_sc_dum va_dum=p_va_dum));
run;

    /* Creating Predicted Values */
data demand2;

        /*     Merging First Observation with All     */
        /* Observations to Calculate Predicted Values */
    if _n_=1 then set dem_est1;
    set demand1(keep=q st year p y);
    drop p_nc_dum;

        /* Setting NC_DUM Equal to Zero */
    retain p_nc_dum 0;
    array p_dum{3} p_nc_dum p_sc_dum p_va_dum;
    array pred_val{3} pred_nc pred_sc pred_va;
    array act_val{3} q_nc q_sc q_va;
    pred_val{st}=intercep + p*p_p + y*p_y + p_dum{st};
    act_val{st}=q;
run;
```

```
goptions reset=symbol;

   /* Plotting Actual and Predicted Values */
proc gplot data=demand2;
   plot q_nc*year=1
        q_sc*year=2
        q_va*year=3
        pred_nc*year=4
        pred_sc*year=5
        pred_va*year=6 / overlay haxis=axis1 vaxis=axis2;
   symbol1 h=2 pct v=N font=swissb i=join l=1 color=black;
   symbol2 h=2 pct v=S font=swissb i=join l=1 color=blue;
   symbol3 h=2 pct v=V font=swissb i=join l=1 color=green;
   symbol4 h=2 pct v=star color=red;
   symbol5 h=2 pct v=circle color=gray;
   symbol6 h=2 pct v=diamond color=lib; /* light blue */
   axis1 order=(1970 to 1988 by 2) minor=(number=1) offset=(3);
   axis2 order=(20 to 110 by 10) minor=(number=3)
         label=(angle=90 'Electricity Sales');
   title1 'Residential Demand for Electricity';
   title2 '(in trillions of BTU)';
run;
quit;
```

Output 8.10
Graphing Actual
and Predicted
Values by States
for the Parks
Model with
Intercept-Shifting
Dummy Variables

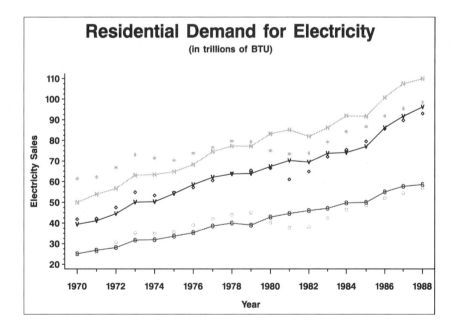

Interpretation of output

The graph in Output 8.10 indicates a reasonable fit of the cross-sectional effects. The three separate lines connect the actual data values by state. The asterisk, diamond, and circle symbols represent the predicted values for NC, VA, and SC, respectively. The three separate sets of predicted values generally follow the actual state consumption data. The predicted values for VA and SC appear to be quite close to the actual values.

Further Analysis

The predicted values in Output 8.10 tend to be above the actual values through 1979, and after 1979 they tend to be below the actual values. You may want to recalculate the predicted values using both the structural and autoregressive portions of the model. Alternatively, you may want to refit the model using the generally more robust Fuller and Battese estimation method, and compare estimates and predicted values.

As another alternative, you may want to account for specific effects with time-series intercept-shifting dummy variables. For example, you might want to add a dummy variable to account for higher energy prices starting in 1979. This dichotomous dummy variable can be created in a DATA step that includes the statements

```
if year >= 1980 then ts_dum = 1;
else ts_dum = 0;
```

Alternatively, you may want to create a dichotomous dummy variable to account for recessionary periods. This dichotomous dummy variable can be created in a DATA step that includes the statements

```
select (year);
when (1974, 1975, 1980, 1981, 1982, 1983) ts_dum=1;
otherwise ts_dum=0;
end;
```

For additional information on the use of dummy variables, see Chapter 3, "Using Dummy Variables."

You may want to calculate the price and income elasticities of demand. Recall that elasticities are ratios of percentage changes. For example, the income elasticity is the ratio of the percentage change in quantity demanded to the percentage change in income. For a calculation method, see Chapter 6, "Fitting Systems of Linear Equations."

Alternative TSCS Analyses

There are many ways to analyze time series cross-sectional data, and other SAS procedures may also be useful in fitting TSCS models. The following examples may not be appropriate for the electricity demand model of this chapter, but may be appropriate for other models and TSCS data sets.

For example, you can use PROC AUTOREG to fit a model with fixed effects across time and states to the hypothetical TEST data:

```
proc autoreg data=test;
   model q = p y / noint;
run;
```

Note that this model does not account for the cross-sectional differences of baseline response, nor does it account for autoregressive or moving average error processes within cross sections. Also, be aware that OLS models fitted without intercepts do not generate errors sums of squares, mean square errors, or R^2 statistics that are comparable with OLS models fitted with intercepts. For discussion of the caveats of comparing R^2s generated from models with and without intercepts, see Maddala (1992, p. 83).

Alternatively, after sorting your data by cross section and then by time series within cross sections, you can use the GLM procedure in SAS/STAT software and an ABSORB statement to absorb main effects (for example, cross-sectional differences), provided the main effects do not participate in interactions. This means that the effect can be adjusted out before the construction and solution of the rest of the model. This is particularly useful when the effect has many levels. The following SAS statements fit a model to the hypothetical TEST data set with the cross-sectional effects absorbed:

```
proc glm data=test;
   absorb st;
   model q = p y;
run;
```

Note that this model does not account for the autoregressive or moving average processes across time within cross sections.

As another alternative, you can perform analysis of covariance using PROC GLM and a CLASS statement. The NOINT option of the MODEL statement fits the model without an intercept. The SOLUTION option of the MODEL statement prints the solution to the normal equations, that is, the parameter estimates. Thus, a model with constant intercepts and varying slopes for the cross sections can be fitted using the following SAS statements:

```
proc glm data=test;
   class st;
   model q = st p y / noint solution;
run;
```

Note that this model does not account for the autocorrelation or moving average processes across time within cross sections. Furthermore, be aware that OLS models fitted without intercepts should not be compared with OLS models fitted with intercepts on the basis of error sums of squares, mean square errors, or R^2s.

Summary

This chapter showed you how to perform TSCS analysis with PROC TSCSREG. Preliminary analysis indicated that you should account for autoregression and spatial correlation, and PROC ARIMA was used to identify the time series process. The Parks method was shown to be appropriate for the DEMAND data set. The Parks model was fitted, and then intercept-shifting dummy variables were added to the model to account for cross-sectional effects. The actual and predicted values were plotted versus time to visually assess the fit. Finally, this chapter presented the SAS statements to fit additional time-series cross-sectional models.

Learning More

☐ For additional information on using the ARIMA and AUTOREG procedures, see Chapter 7, "The ARIMA Procedure," and Chapter 8, "The AUTOREG Procedure," in the *SAS/ETS User's Guide, Version 6, First Edition*.

☐ For additional information on identification of time series models, see Chapter 3, "Autoregressive Models," in *SAS/ETS Software: Applications Guide 1, Version 6, First Edition*.

☐ For additional information on the GLM Procedure in SAS/STAT software, see Chapter 24, "The GLM Procedure," in the *SAS/STAT User's Guide, Version 6, Fourth Edition*.

☐ For full reference information on PROC GPLOT, see *SAS/GRAPH Software: Reference, Version 6, First Edition, Volume 1* and *Volume 2* and *SAS/GRAPH Software Usage, Version 6, First Edition*.

☐ For additional information about the CORR procedure, see Chapter 15, "The CORR Procedure," in the *SAS Procedures Guide, Version 6, Third Edition*.

References

Bohi, D. (1981), *Analyzing Demand Behavior: A Study of Energy Elasticities*, John Hopkins University Press, Baltimore.

Box, G.E.P. and Jenkins, G.M. (1976), *Time Series Analysis: Forecasting and Control*, Holden-Day, San Francisco.

Da Silva, J.G.C. (1975), "*The Analysis of Cross-Sectional Time Series Data*," Ph.D. dissertation, Department of Statistics, North Carolina State University, Ann Arbor, MI: University Microfilms.

Fuller, W.A. and Battese, G.E. (1974), "Estimation of Linear Models with Crossed-Error Structure," *Journal of Econometrics*, 2(1), 67—78.

Hsiao, Cheng; (1986) *Analysis of Panel Data*, New York: Cambridge University Press.

Maddala, G.S. (1992), *Introduction to Econometrics, Second Edition*, New York: Macmillian Publishing Company, Inc.

Parks, R.W. (1967), "Efficient Estimation of a System of Regression Equations when Disturbances are both Serially and Contemporaneously Correlated," *Journal of the American Statistical Association*, 62, 500—509.

U.S. Department of Energy, Energy Information Administration (1991), *State Energy Data Report: Consumption Estimates, 1960—1989*, Washington, D.C.: U.S. Government Printing Office.

U.S. Department of Energy, Energy Information Administration (1985), *State Energy Price and Expenditure Report, 1970—1982*, Washington, D.C.: U.S. Government Printing Office.

U.S. Department of Energy, Energy Information Administration (1990), *State Energy Price and Expenditure Report, 1988*, Washington, D.C.: U.S. Government Printing Office.

Part 2
Simulation

Chapter 9 Introduction to Simulation

Introduction

Simulation is an integral part of developing accurate models that capture the behavior of historical data. Simulation involves first finding a suitable model of how the endogenous (dependent) variable changes as a function of one or more exogenous (independent) variables, where suitability is determined by goodness-of-fit criteria. Once an appropriate model is found, you then use the model equation to simulate, or predict, values of the endogenous variable for specific values of the exogenous variables. By changing the values of the exogenous variables, you gain insight into how alternative situations affect the endogenous variable.

Economists use simulation to assess how well the model follows the actual values of the endogenous variables. Ideally, an appropriate simulation model follows the historical data very closely, or at least captures the overall trends. Simulated values can be plotted for visual assessment, and goodness-of-fit statistics can be calculated for a more rigorous assessment.

Simulation is also used for what-if and goal-seeking analyses. *What-if analysis* involves simulating endogenous variable values for different sets of exogenous variable values. For example, with a simple consumption function, you would determine how consumption expenditures would change for hypothetical levels of disposable income. *Goal-seeking analysis* involves determining the value of an exogenous variable, given a desired value of the endogenous variable. For example, with a simple consumption function, what would the level of disposable income have to be to generate a particular level of consumption expenditures?

In this chapter, you use the MODEL procedure in SAS/ETS software to fit and compare single-equation linear models, to simulate models with the actual data, to simulate models with hypothetical sets of data, and to perform what-if and goal-seeking simulations.

Simulating a Single-Equation Model

Suppose you are a budget analyst for the state of North Carolina. Your job entails developing a model of general fund revenues for simulation and policy analysis. In particular, you need to show how alternative legislative proposals affect revenues. This is important because decision makers need to know the level of general fund revenues available, as well as how they change as a function of policy.

A macroeconomic model of general fund revenues relates the level of revenues to U.S. gross national product (GNP) and the population of North Carolina. You expect that N.C. general fund revenues increase as U.S. GNP and N.C. population increase. This model is of the following form:

$$\text{GFUND}_t = d + f\,\text{GNP}_t + h\,\text{POP}_t + \varepsilon_t$$

where

GFUND_t	is the current-period general fund revenues.
d	is the intercept.
f	is the slope parameter associated with GNP.
GNP_t	is the current-period U.S. GNP.
h	is the slope parameter associated with POP.
POP_t	is the current-period North Carolina population.
ε_t	is the current-period random error.

The following section introduces and plots the BUDGET data set.

Introducing the BUDGET Data Set

The BUDGET data set consists of annual observations over the period 1973 through 1989 for the following variables:

GFUNDN   is the nominal N.C. general fund revenues in millions of dollars.*

GNPN   is the nominal U.S. GNP in billions of dollars.**

FED_REVN   is the nominal U.S. tax revenues collected by the Internal Revenue Service in billions of dollars.**

POP   is the N.C. population in thousands.**

CPI   is the U.S. consumer price index (CPI).***

The following statements create the BUDGET data set, create and label variables, title the example, and print the first ten observations. Note that general funds, U.S. GNP, and IRS collections are deflated by the CPI to account for the effect of inflation. Output 9.1 shows the results.

```
data budget;
    input year gfundn gnpn fed_revn pop cpi ;
            gfund = gfundn / cpi;
            gnp = gnpn / cpi;
            fed_rev = fed_revn / cpi;
    label gfund = 'Real General Fund in Millions'
          gnp = 'Real US GNP in Billions'
          fed_rev = 'Real Federal IRS Collections in Billions'
          pop = 'NC Population in Thousands'
          cpi = 'US CPI 82-84 = 100';
    cards;
73 1214.0  1359.3  237.8  5382  .444
74 1358.0  1472.8  269.0  5461  .493
75 1451.0  1598.4  293.8  5535  .538
76 1572.0  1782.8  302.5  5593  .569
77 1870.0  1990.5  358.1  5668  .606
78 2060.0  2249.7  399.8  5739  .652
79 2337.0  2508.2  460.4  5802  .726
80 2639.0  2732.0  519.4  5882  .824
81 2846.0  3052.6  606.8  5957  .909
82 3078.0  3166.0  632.2  6018  .965
83 3279.0  3405.7  627.2  6078  .996
```

---

*   N.C. Office of State Budget and Management, "Overview of the N.C. State Budget" (October 1990)

** U.S. Department of Commerce, *Statistical Abstracts of the U.S.* (Washington, D.C.: U.S. Government Printing Office)

*** Council of Economic Advisers, Economic Report of the President (Washington, D.C.: U.S. Government Printing Office, February 1991)

```
84 3814.0  3772.2  680.5  6167 1.039
85 4337.0  4010.3  742.9  6258 1.076
86 4695.0  4235.0  782.3  6327 1.096
87 5181.0  4524.3  886.3  6409 1.136
88 5552.0  4880.6  935.1  6489 1.183
89 5928.5  5200.8 1013.5  6571 1.240
;

proc print data=budget (obs=10) label;
   var year gfund gnp fed_rev pop;
   title 'General Fund Revenues Example';
   title2 'First Ten Observations BUDGET Data';
run;
```

Output 9.1
First Ten
Observations of
the BUDGET Data
Set

```
                    General Fund Revenues Example
                    First Ten Observations BUDGET Data

                                              Real Federal      NC
                      Real General   Real US      IRS       Population
                        Fund in      GNP in    Collections      in
       OBS   YEAR      Millions      Billions  in Billions   Thousands

        1     73        2734.23      3061.49     535.586       5382
        2     74        2754.56      2987.42     545.639       5461
        3     75        2697.03      2971.00     546.097       5535
        4     76        2762.74      3133.22     531.634       5593
        5     77        3085.81      3284.65     590.924       5668
        6     78        3159.51      3450.46     613.190       5739
        7     79        3219.01      3454.82     634.160       5802
        8     80        3202.67      3315.53     630.340       5882
        9     81        3130.91      3358.20     667.547       5957
       10     82        3189.64      3280.83     655.130       6018
```

Plotting the BUDGET Data Set

By plotting GFUND versus YEAR, you can look for trends and turning points in the data. Models used for simulation should generate predicted values that follow the trends in the data and exhibit the same turning points.

The following PLOT procedure statements produce Output 9.2.

```
proc plot data=budget vpct=60;
   plot gfund*year;
   title2 'General Fund Revenues versus YEAR';
run;
```

Output 9.2
Plot of GFUND
versus YEAR

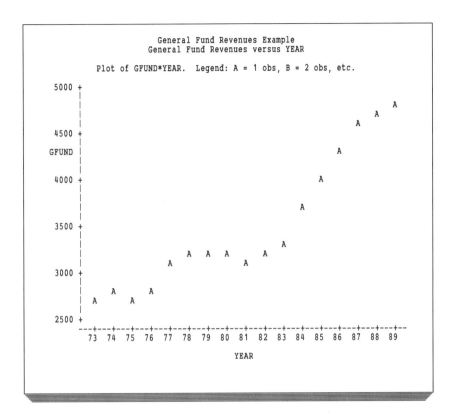

Interpretation of output

In Output 9.2, the plot of GFUND versus YEAR shows a general upward trend, with some cyclical variation corresponding to recessionary periods. Alternatively, you may view the series as consisting of a period of slow growth (1973 through 1983) and a period of rapid growth (1984 through 1989), or you may view the series as consisting of two periods of little growth (1973 through 1976 and 1977 through 1983) followed by a period of rapid growth.

If you want to analyze the component parts of the GFUND series, you can use the ARIMA procedure in SAS/ETS software. For details, see the *SAS/ETS User's Guide, Version 6, First Edition* and *SAS/ETS Software: Applications Guide 1, Version 6, First Edition.*

However you classify the trends of the data, a turning point occurs whenever there is a shift from one trend to another. Optimally, a model used for simulation produces values that are equivalent in magnitude and variability to the actual data while also displaying the same turning points.

Fitting the General Fund Model

You can fit the general fund model with PROC MODEL. In PROC MODEL, you write out the model, complete with arithmetic operators. The following SAS statements fit an ordinary least-squares model to the BUDGET data set. The following is an interpretation of the statements:

PROC MODEL
     invokes the MODEL procedure. The DATA= option specifies the BUDGET data set be used as input.

PARAMETERS

PARMS

specifies the parameters to be estimated. For this example, the parameters are *d*, *f*, and *h*.

ENDOGENOUS

ENDO

specifies the endogenous (dependent) variables. For this example, GFUND is the endogenous variable.

EXOGENOUS

EXO

specifies the exogenous (independent) variables. For this example, GNP and POP are the exogenous variables.

FIT

specifies the equation to be fit. The program statement beginning with GFUND= defines the equation to be fit. The default method of fitting a model to the data is ordinary least squares. The DW option requests the printing of the Durbin-Watson *d* statistic.

Only the final model generated by the following example code is displayed in Output 9.3.

```
proc model data=budget;
   parms d f h;
   endo gfund;
   exo gnp pop;
   gfund = d + f*gnp + h*pop;
   fit gfund / dw;
run;
```

Output 9.3
Fitting the General Fund Model with Ordinary Least Squares

```
                        General Fund Revenues Example

                              MODEL Procedure
                              OLS Estimation

                  Nonlinear OLS Summary of Residual Errors

              DF   DF                                              Durbin
   Equation Model Error     SSE      MSE  Root MSE R-Square Adj R-Sq Watson

   GFUND       3    14    236640  16902.88   130.01   0.9710   0.9669  1.086


                  Nonlinear OLS Parameter Estimates

                                     Approx.    'T'    Approx.
              Parameter   Estimate   Std Err   Ratio  Prob>|T|

                 D       -3808.14  799.89317   -4.76   0.0003
                 F        1.550531   0.26130    5.93   0.0001
                 H        0.317080   0.26893    1.18   0.2580


              Number of Observations       Statistics for System
              Used              17         Objective        13920
              Missing            0         Objective*N     236640
```

Interpretation of output

Output 9.3 displays the OLS fitted model. Be aware that the nonlinear methods of PROC MODEL reduce to OLS for linear models.

The Durbin-Watson d statistic (1.086) is statistically significant at the .05 level, and indicates the model should be refitted, correcting for autocorrelation. Subsequent examples assume the autocorrelation follows a first-order autoregressive process, AR(1).

Refitting the General Fund Model

You can refit the general fund model using PROC MODEL and the %AR macro to correct for first-order autoregression. In the following example, you use the OUTMODEL= option. This option creates a file, containing the fitted model, that can be recalled and used in subsequent invocations of PROC MODEL.

The following SAS example code refits the general fund model, correcting for first-order autoregression; creates an output data file containing the fitted model; and creates an output data set containing the predicted values. Options and statements not previously defined are interpreted as follows.

PROC MODEL
   invokes the MODEL procedure. The OUTMODEL= option creates an output data file, named BUD_MOD1, containing the fitted model. This file can be used only as input to a subsequent PROC MODEL statement.

%AR (*name, nlag, endolist*)
   specifies the %AR macro. In this example, the three arguments of the %AR macro are:

   name   specifies a prefix to the autoregressive parameter. For this example, the prefix AR_GF is specified. Note that PROC MODEL names the autoregressive parameter, AR_GF_L1.

   nlag   specifies the order of the AR(n) correction, or lists the subset of autoregressive parameters to be fitted. For this example, a first-order correction, AR(1), is specified.

   endolist specifies the list of equations to which the AR process is to be applied.

ID
   specifies the variables to be included in the output data set.

The final model, generated by the following example code, is displayed in Output 9.4.

```
proc model data=budget outmodel=bud_mod1;
   parms d1 f1 h1;
   gfund = d1 + f1*gnp + h1*pop;
   %ar(ar_gf, 1, gfund);
   endo gfund;
   exo gnp pop;
   id year;
   fit gfund / dw;
run;
```

Output 9.4

Fitting the General Fund Model and Correcting for First-Order Autoregression

```
                        General Fund Revenues Example

                            MODEL Procedure
                            OLS Estimation

                   Nonlinear OLS Summary of Residual Errors

                 DF   DF                                              Durbin
     Equation Model Error      SSE       MSE   Root MSE R-Square Adj R-Sq Watson

     GFUND      4    13     162441   12495.49    111.78   0.9801   0.9755  1.992



                       Nonlinear OLS Parameter Estimates

                            Approx.     'T'  Approx.
       Parameter  Estimate  Std Err   Ratio  Prob>|T|  Label

       D1        -4565.506  1205.13   -3.79   0.0023
       F1         0.943283  0.30636    3.08   0.0088
       H1         0.810401  0.34134    2.37   0.0337
       AR_GF_L1   0.789966  0.19372    4.08   0.0013  AR(AR_GF) GFUND LAG1 PARAMETER



                  Number of Observations      Statistics for System
                  Used            17          Objective         9555
                  Missing          0          Objective*N     162441
```

Interpretation of output

Output 9.4 contains information on autocorrelation, estimated parameters, and associated statistics. Notice the following:

□ The SSE, MSE, and Root MSE are lower for the refitted model while the R^2 (R-Square) and adjusted R^2 (Adj R-Sq) are higher.

□ The Durbin-Watson statistic for the AR(1) corrected model is 1.992, which is not significant at the .05 level; it is not shown on this output.

□ The structural portion of the AR(1) corrected model is

$$GFUND_t = -4565.506 + .943283 \ GNP_t + .810401 \ POP_t \ .$$

□ The t statistics for the individual parameters of the AR(1) corrected model indicate they are all different from zero at the .05 level.

□ The R-Square and Adj R-Sq statistics are .9801 and .9755, respectively. These statistics indicate the model explains a high proportion of the observed variation in the general fund revenues.

Based on the Durbin-Watson d statistic, the t statistics, and the R^2 statistics, the AR(1) corrected model provides a good fit to the BUDGET data. Comparing the models of Output 9.3 and Output 9.4, the refitted model of Output 9.4 is the model of choice.

Simulating the General Fund Model

You can simulate the general fund model using a SOLVE statement in PROC MODEL. The MODEL= option recalls the model file, BUD_MOD1, created previously. The following example code simulates the model, creates an output data set containing the simulated values, merges the simulated values with the original data set, and prints the resulting data set.

The simulated values are printed using PROC PRINT. You can print the
simulated values by submitting the following statements. Output 9.5 shows the
results.

```
    /* Simulating the Model */
proc model data=budget model=bud_mod1 noprint;
    solve gfund / simulate out=bud_out(rename=(gfund=s_gfund1));
run;

    /* Merging Data Sets */
data bud_outp;
    merge budget bud_out;
    by year;
run;

    /* Printing the Simulation Values */
proc print data=bud_outp;
    var year gfund s_gfund1;
    title2 'GFUND Simulations';
    title3 'GFUND Model with POP';
run;
```

Output 9.5
Actual and
Simulation Values
of the General
Fund Model

```
                   General Fund Revenues Example
                          GFUND Simulations
                        GFUND Model with POP

         OBS    YEAR     GFUND     S_GFUND1

          1      73     2734.23     2683.92
          2      74     2754.56     2678.08
          3      75     2697.03     2722.56
          4      76     2762.74     2922.58
          5      77     3085.81     3126.21
          6      78     3159.51     3340.15
          7      79     3219.01     3395.32
          8      80     3202.67     3328.76
          9      81     3130.91     3429.78
         10      82     3189.64     3406.24
         11      83     3292.17     3585.55
         12      84     3670.84     3856.93
         13      85     4030.67     4021.64
         14      86     4283.76     4206.80
         15      87     4560.74     4385.13
         16      88     4693.15     4584.81
         17      89     4781.05     4715.95
```

Plotting the Simulated Values

You can plot the simulated values with the GPLOT procedure in SAS/GRAPH
software to visually assess the fit of the model. In particular, look for the model's
ability to capture trends, movements, and variability in GFUND. Output 9.6 shows
the results.

```
goptions reset=symbol;

proc gplot data=bud_outp;
    plot gfund*year=1
         s_gfund1*year=2 / overlay haxis=axis1
                           vaxis=axis2 legend=legend1;
```

```
            symbol1 i=join l=1 color=black;
            symbol2 v=P font=swissb color=blue;
            axis1 offset=(2,2)pct order=(73 to 89 by 1) label=none;
            axis2 order=(2000 to 5000 by 500) minor=(number=1)
                  label=(a=-90 r=90 'GENERAL FUND');
            legend1 label=none value=('Actual GFUND' 'Simulated GFUND');
            title 'General Fund Revenues';
            title2 'Actual and Simulated, 1973-1989';
      run;
      quit;
```

Output 9.6
Plot of Actual and Simulated Values of the General Fund Model

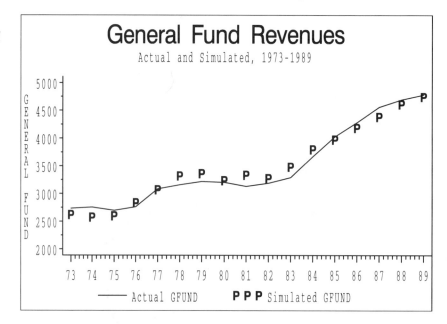

Interpretation of output

Output 9.6 displays the plot of general fund revenues for 1973 through 1989. The actual values are connected by the solid line, and the symbol P represents the simulated values. The plot shows that the simulated model captures much of the historical movements of GFUND. The simulated values appear to follow the actual values reasonably well. The degree to which they do not follow actual values can be assessed by examining the goodness-of-fit statistics.

Goodness-of-Fit Statistics

Several goodness-of-fit statistics are available to assess a model's ability to simulate.

Summary Statistics of Fit

If Y_t and Y_t^s are the actual and simulated values of the general fund revenues for period t (with T total periods), then you can define the goodness-of-fit statistics as follows:

□ Mean Error is defined as

$$\frac{1}{T} \sum_{t=1}^{T} (Y_t^s - Y_t)$$

□ Mean % Error is the mean percentage error and is defined as

$$\frac{1}{T} \sum_{t=1}^{T} \left(\frac{Y_t^s - Y_t}{Y_t} \times 100 \right)$$

□ Mean Abs Error is the mean absolute error and is defined as

$$\frac{1}{T} \sum_{t=1}^{T} | Y_t^s - Y_t |$$

□ Mean Abs % Error is the mean absolute percentage error and is defined as

$$\frac{1}{T} \sum_{t=1}^{T} \left| \frac{Y_t^s - Y_t}{Y_t} \right| \times 100$$

□ Mean Square Error or MSE is defined as

$$\frac{1}{T} \sum_{t=1}^{T} (Y_t^s - Y_t)^2$$

and the root mean square error, or RMS Error, is the positive square root of the MSE,

$$\sqrt{\frac{1}{T} \sum_{t=1}^{T} (Y_t^s - Y_t)^2}$$

□ RMS % Error is the root mean square percent error and is defined as

$$\sqrt{\frac{1}{T} \sum_{t=1}^{T} \left(\frac{Y_t^s - Y_t}{Y_t} \times 100 \right)^2}$$

The closer these summary statistics are to zero, the closer the simulated model follows the actual values.

Theil Forecast Error Statistics

In addition to the previous goodness-of-fit statistics, you can use the Theil U statistic (Theil 1971) and related statistics of fit. The Theil U statistic, also known as Theil's Inequality, is defined as the square root of the following equation:

$$U^2 = \frac{\displaystyle\sum_{t=1}^{T} (Y_t^s - Y_t)^2 / T}{\displaystyle\sum_{t=1}^{T} Y_t^2 / T}$$

The Theil U statistic is always between 0 and 1. If U is equal to zero, then the model simulates history perfectly. If U is equal to one, then the simulation performance of the model is said to be as poor as possible. Granger and Newbold suggested a slight improvement to the U statistic, the U1 statistic (1986).

The U statistic can be decomposed into bias, variance, and covariance components that sum to one. You can consider these components percentages of the U statistic value.

the bias portion
   indicates systematic error; you want this value to be zero.

the variance portion
   indicates the model's ability to replicate the variability of the dependent variable. You also want this value to be zero, indicating the model has exactly replicated the variability of the dependent variable.

the covariance portion
   measures random error. You want this value to be one, indicating that simulation errors are due to random fluctuations.

Theil also regresses the actual values on the simulated values. Statistics can be generated that decompose into bias, regression, and disturbance components that sum to one. If the intercept of this regression is zero, then the bias is zero. If the slope parameter is one, then the regression component is zero. Optimally, the bias and regression components are zero, and the disturbance component is one. Pindyck and Rubinfeld suggest that a bias component greater than .2 indicates the presence of systematic bias, and the model requires revision (1991).

Theil Relative Change Forecast Error Statistics

The relative change forecast error statistics are obtained by replacing Y_t with $(Y_t - Y_{t-1}) / Y_t$ and Y_t^s with $(Y_t^s - Y_{t-1}) / Y_{t-1}$ in the regression of Y_t on Y_t^s. These statistics indicate the relative change of error statistics in simulating the next value in the sequence.

Calculating Goodness-of-Fit Statistics

The following SAS example code simulates the AR(1) corrected general fund model shown in Output 9.4 and prints the Theil statistics, including the decompositions. The statements are interpreted as follows:

PROC MODEL

invokes the MODEL procedure. The MODEL= option reads the model created and stored in a previous PROC MODEL step. In this example, the model created in Output 9.4 is read.

SOLVE

specifies that the model be simulated or forecast for input data values. The following options of the SOLVE statement are specified:

SIMULATE	specifies that the solution of the model is a simulation.
THEIL	prints the Theil inequality coefficients.
STATS	prints the goodness-of-fit statistics.
OUT=	creates an output data set, BUD_OUT1.
RENAME	renames the simulated values, S_GFUND1.

```
proc model data=budget model=bud_mod1;
    solve gfund / simulate theil stats
                    out=bud_out1(rename=(gfund=s_gfund1));
run;
```

Output 9.7 shows only the goodness-of-fit statistics generated by this example code.

Output 9.7
The Statistics of Fit for the General Fund Model

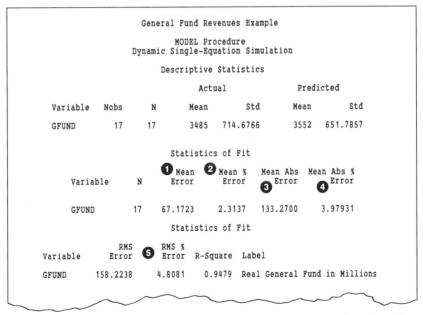

```
                    General Fund Revenues Example

                          MODEL Procedure
                  Dynamic Single-Equation Simulation

                        Descriptive Statistics

                               Actual              Predicted

   Variable   Nobs    N     Mean      Std       Mean      Std

   GFUND       17    17     3485    714.6766     3552    651.7857


                         Statistics of Fit

                       ❶ Mean   ❷ Mean %   Mean Abs   Mean Abs %
            Variable    N   Error     Error    ❸ Error    ❹ Error

            GFUND      17   67.1723   2.3137   133.2700   3.97931

                         Statistics of Fit

                  RMS   ❺ RMS %
     Variable     Error     Error   R-Square   Label

     GFUND      158.2238   4.8081    0.9479   Real General Fund in Millions
```

(continued)

Output 9.7
(continued)

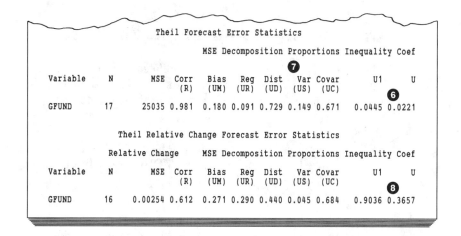

Variable	N	MSE	Corr (R)	Bias (UM)	Reg (UR)	Dist (UD)	Var (US)	Covar (UC)	U1	U
GFUND	17	25035	0.981	0.180	0.091	0.729	0.149	0.671	0.0445	0.0221

Theil Relative Change Forecast Error Statistics

Relative Change MSE Decomposition Proportions Inequality Coef

Variable	N	MSE	Corr (R)	Bias (UM)	Reg (UR)	Dist (UD)	Var (US)	Covar (UC)	U1	U
GFUND	16	0.00254	0.612	0.271	0.290	0.440	0.045	0.684	0.9036	0.3657

Interpretation of output

In Output 9.7, the goodness-of-fit statistics are displayed. Notice the following:

❶ The Mean Error is 67.1723. This indicates an overall upward bias in the simulated values. (Recall that the simulation errors are the simulated values minus the actual values.) In other words, on average the model overestimates the actual value of general fund revenues by $67.17 million.

❷ The Mean % Error is 2.3137. This relates the magnitude of the average (mean) error to the magnitude of GFUND. In other words, on average the model overestimates the actual value by about 2.31%.

❸ The Mean Abs Error is 133.2700. This is almost twice the Mean Error, indicating some of the errors are relatively large, some are positive, and some are negative.

❹ The Mean Abs % Error is 3.97931. This relates the magnitude of the simulation absolute error to the magnitude of GFUND.

❺ The RMS Error and the RMS % Error are 158.2238 and 4.8081%, respectively. These can be compared with other simulation models.

❻ The Theil U1 and U statistics are .0445 and .0221, respectively. These statistics are close to the ideal value of zero and indicate that the model simulates the actual data reasonably well.

❼ The Dist and Covar components are .729 and .671, respectively, while the Bias, Reg, and Var components are .180, .091, and .149, respectively. You conclude that there is some systematic bias in the model.

❽ The Theil U1 and U Relative Change Forecast Statistics are .9036 and .3657, respectively. The decomposition of the Relative Change Forecast Statistics indicates possible problems with the Bias and Reg proportion components.

These goodness-of-fit statistics indicate this simulation model has an upward bias and some errors are relatively large.

Comparing Models

Suppose in your work as an economist for the state of North Carolina, you consider another model of general revenue. The previous model for general fund revenues is one of many you could fit. An alternative model relates general fund revenues to U.S. GNP and IRS revenues (FED_REV).

In this section, you fit this new model of N.C. general funds, assess how well it fits the data, and compare it to the first model using goodness-of-fit statistics.

Fitting the New Model

You can fit a new model with a FIT statement in PROC MODEL. Use the %AR macro to correct for first-order autoregression. The following statements fit the new GFUND model and create an output file, BUD_MOD2, containing the fitted model. Note that the output file, BUD_MOD2, is different from an output data set created with the OUT= option.

```
proc model data=budget outmodel=bud_mod2;
    parms d2 f2 h2;
    gfund = d2 + f2*gnp + h2*fed_rev;
    %ar(ar_gf, 1, gfund);
    endo gfund;
    exo gnp fed_rev;
    id year;
    fit gfund / dw;
run;
```

Part of the output generated by the previous example code is displayed in Output 9.8. Only the final model is shown.

Output 9.8
Fitting the New
General Fund
Model

```
                        General Fund Revenues Example

                             MODEL Procedure
                             OLS Estimation

                   Nonlinear OLS Summary of Residual Errors

                   DF    DF                                        Durbin
       Equation Model Error     SSE      MSE   Root MSE R-Square Adj R-Sq Watson

        GFUND      4    13    154022  11847.84   108.85   0.9812   0.9768  2.080



                        Nonlinear OLS Parameter Estimates

                             Approx.    'T'  Approx.
       Parameter  Estimate   Std Err   Ratio Prob>|T| Label

       D2        -1966.635    557.12   -3.53  0.0037
       F2          1.017472   0.28110   3.62  0.0031
       H2          2.956075   1.10891   2.67  0.0194
       AR_GF_L1    0.722667   0.21489   3.36  0.0051 AR(AR_GF) GFUND LAG1 PARAMETER



                   Number of Observations      Statistics for System
                   Used              17         Objective         9060
                   Missing            0         Objective*N     154022
```

Interpretation of output

In Output 9.8, the structural portion of the fitted model, corrected for AR(1), is as follows:

$$\text{GFUND}_t = -1966.635 + 1.017472\ \text{GNP}_t + 2.956075\ \text{FED\_REV}_t\quad .$$

The Durbin-Watson statistic (2.080) is not significant at the .05 level. The individual *t*-tests of this model show the parameters are different from zero at the .05 level.

The models in Output 9.4 and Output 9.8 can be compared on the basis of their summary statistics, as shown in the following table.

Table 9.1

Comparison of General Fund Models by Summary Statistics

Summary Statistics	Model 1 (Output 9.4)	Model 2 (Output 9.8)
SSE	162441	154022
MSE	12495.49	11847.84
Root MSE	111.78	108.85
R-Square	.9801	.9812
Adj R-Sq	.9755	.9768

The SSE, MSE, and Root MSE are smaller for the model of Output 9.8, while the R-Square and Adjusted R-Sq are higher. Compared with Output 9.4, the model shown in Output 9.8 is superior.

You can assess the simulation performance of a model by examining its goodness-of-fit statistics for simulation. The next section shows you how to generate goodness-of-fit statistics.

Assessing the Simulation Performance

You can generate goodness-of-fit statistics with the STATS and THEIL options of the SOLVE statement in PROC MODEL. You use goodness-of-fit statistics to further compare the two models of Output 9.4 and Output 9.8. The model with goodness-of-fit statistics closer to zero is the better simulation model.

The following SAS example code simulates the second general fund model and prints the Theil statistics, including the decompositions. The output data set is named BUD_OUT2, and the simulated values are named S_GFUND2. Output 9.9 shows the results.

```
proc model data=budget model=bud_mod2;
   solve gfund / simulate theil stats
              out=bud_out2(rename=(gfund=s_gfund2));
run;
```

Output 9.9
Simulating the
New General Fund
Model

```
                      General Fund Revenues Example

                            MODEL Procedure
                 Dynamic Single-Equation Simulation

                         Descriptive Statistics

                            Actual              Predicted

    Variable   Nobs    N     Mean      Std      Mean      Std

    GFUND       17    17     3485    714.6766   3496    643.6930


                          Statistics of Fit

                            Mean     Mean %   Mean Abs  Mean Abs %
            Variable    N   Error     Error    Error      Error

            GFUND      17  11.2881   0.7104   109.6984   3.11433

                          Statistics of Fit

                    RMS      RMS %
     Variable      Error     Error   R-Square   Label

     GFUND        136.8003   3.9391   0.9611    Real General Fund in Millions


                    Theil Forecast Error Statistics

                              MSE Decomposition Proportions  Inequality Coef

   Variable    N      MSE   Corr   Bias   Reg   Dist   Var  Covar    U1     U
                             (R)   (UM)   (UR)  (UD)   (US) (UC)

   GFUND      17    18714  0.984  0.007  0.178 0.815  0.253 0.740   0.0385 0.0193


               Theil Relative Change Forecast Error Statistics

                  Relative Change   MSE Decomposition Proportions  Inequality Coef

   Variable    N      MSE   Corr   Bias   Reg   Dist   Var  Covar    U1     U
                             (R)   (UM)   (UR)  (UD)   (US) (UC)

   GFUND      16   0.00171 0.560  0.030  0.253 0.717  0.003 0.967   0.7414 0.3503
```

Interpretation of output

In Output 9.9 the goodness-of-fit statistics indicate the following:

□ The actual and predicted means are 3485 and 3496, respectively. The Mean Error and Mean % Error are 11.2881 and .7104%, respectively. The Mean Abs Error and the Mean Abs % Error are 109.6984 and 3.11433%, respectively, indicating positive and negative errors. There is some upward bias in the simulated values of this model.

□ The standard deviations (Std) of the actual and predicted means are 714.6766 and 643.6930, respectively. This indicates that the simulated values have less variability than the actual values.

□ The actual and simulated values have a correlation of 0.984. The regression of the actual values on the simulated values has a mean square error (MSE) of 18714, an RMS Error of 136.8003, an RMS % Error of 3.9391, and an R-Square of .9611. The R-Square is close to the ideal value of 1.0. You conclude that the simulated values are highly correlated with the actual values and provide a good fit.

□ The Theil Forecast Error Statistics U1 and U are .0385 and .0193, respectively. These statistics are close to the ideal value of zero, and indicate that the model simulates the actual data quite well. The areas of concern are revealed in decompositions of the Theil Statistics.

□ The Dist and Covar components are .815 and .740, respectively, while the Bias, Reg, and Var components are .007, .178, and .253, respectively. You conclude that the bias is not a serious problem; however, the variance of the simulated values is different from the variance of the actual values and may be of some concern.

□ The Theil Relative Change Forecast Statistics U1 and U are .7414 and .3503, respectively. The decomposition of these statistics indicates a possible problem with the Reg proportion component.

The following table compares the goodness-of-fit statistics of the general fund model with the original model in Output 9.7.

Table 9.2
Comparison of General Fund Models by Goodness-of-Fit Statistics

Goodness-of-Fit Statistics	Model 1 (Output 9.7)	Model 2 (Output 9.9)
Mean Error	67.1723	11.2881
Mean % Error	2.3137	0.7104
Theil U1	0.0445	0.0385
Theil U	0.0221	0.0193

The new model shown in Output 9.9 has goodness-of-fit error statistics closer to zero than the original model of Output 9.7. Based on these criteria, the new model is the better simulation model.

Using the Fitted Model

You can use the simulation model for what-if simulation and for goal-seeking simulation. What-if and goal-seeking simulations enable you to better understand the mathematical properties of your model, to perform simulations on the endogenous and exogenous variables, and perhaps, to find areas where further refinement of the model is required.

What-if simulation covers a broad range of questions. You provide what-if data and simulate the model to assess its behavior and to examine the effect on the endogenous variable. You perform goal seeking when you want to calculate the value of an exogenous variable, given the values of the remaining variables.

What-if Simulation

You can simulate the fitted model for different sets of values for the exogenous variables. If the history of one or more exogenous variables had been different, what would have been the level of the endogenous variable? This type of simulation is often called *what-if simulation*. Comparing one or more sets of what-if simulated values to the original predicted values is called policy experimentation.

The following sections examine the GFUND values that would have occurred if the exogenous variable FED_REV had not decreased in 1982 and 1983 but, instead, had continued increasing.

To perform this what-if simulation, you first need to create a data set with values of FED_REV under your proposed conditions. You may want to print and plot the what-if and actual values for FED_REV. Then, you can simulate the model using the what-if values.

There are several approaches to modifying one or more exogenous variables to create what-if data sets. These approaches include

□ choosing individual values

□ choosing specific growth rates and extrapolating

□ using the growth rate of a historical period and extrapolating

□ selecting a range of growth rates and performing multiple simulations

□ fitting a polynomial model of time to the exogenous variable, and then extrapolating

□ fitting a time series model to the exogenous variable, and then extrapolating.

The following sections illustrate the approach of using the historically observed growth rate and rates above and below that rate for the variable FED_REV, and then performing several simulations.

Creating, Printing, and Plotting What-if Data

Between 1973 and 1981, federal revenues grew at an annually compounded growth rate of about 2.5%. You can use the DATA step to create data sets in which FED_REV grows at rates of 1.00%, 2.50%, and 4.00%, for low, mid, and high growth rates, respectively.

The following SAS example code creates a what-if data set, prints it, and then plots FED_REV. Output 9.10 shows the results.

```
    /* Creating EXTRAP Data Set for What-If Simulation */
data extrap;
   set budget;
      if year >= 82 then do;
      fed_revl=667.547*(1+.010)**(year-81);
      fed_revm=667.547*(1+.025)**(year-81);
      fed_revh=667.547*(1+.040)**(year-81);
      gfund=.;
   end;
run;

    /* Printing Data */
proc print data=extrap (firstobs=7);
   var year fed_rev fed_revl fed_revm fed_revh;
   title2 'EXTRAP Data Set for What-If Simulations';
run;
```

```
goptions reset=symbol;

    /* Plotting Data */
proc gplot data=extrap;
   plot fed_rev*year=1
        fed_revl*year=2
        fed_revm*year=3
        fed_revh*year=4 / overlay haxis=axis1
                                  vaxis=axis2 legend=legend1;
      symbol1 i=join l=1 color=black;
      symbol2 i=join v=L font=swissb l=3 color=blue;
      symbol3 v=M font=swissb color=green;
      symbol4 i=join v=H font=swissb l=3 color=red;
      axis1 offset=(2,2)pct order=(73 to 89 by 1) label=none;
      axis2 order=(500 to 900 by 100) minor=(number=1)
            label=(a=-90 r=90 'FEDERAL REVENUE');
      legend1 label=none value=('Actual FED_REV' 'Low FED_REV'
                    'Mid FED_REV' 'High FED_REV');
      title 'Actual and What-If Federal Revenue';
      title2 '1973-1989';
   run;
quit;
```

Output 9.10

Printing and Plotting of Actual and What-If Values of Federal IRS Revenue

```
                       General Fund Revenues Example
                  EXTRAP Data Set for What-If Simulations

      OBS    YEAR    FED_REV    FED_REVL    FED_REVM    FED_REVH

       7      79     634.160        .           .           .
       8      80     630.340        .           .           .
       9      81     667.547        .           .           .
      10      82     655.130     674.222     684.236     694.249
      11      83     629.719     680.965     701.342     722.019
      12      84     654.957     687.774     718.875     750.900
      13      85     690.428     694.652     736.847     780.936
      14      86     713.777     701.599     755.268     812.173
      15      87     780.194     708.615     774.150     844.660
      16      88     790.448     715.701     793.504     878.446
      17      89     817.339     722.858     813.341     913.584
```

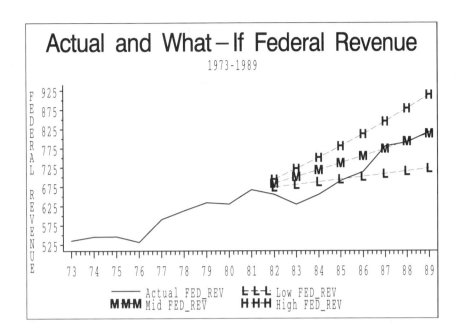

Interpretation of output

In Output 9.10, the actual, low, mid, and high values of FED_REV are plotted versus YEAR. The solid line represents the actual values while the symbols L, M, and H represent the low, mid, and high values of FED_REV. Notice the actual values decrease in 1982 and 1983, then increase. Initially, the low and mid values of FED_REV are greater than the actual values; however, by 1989, they are less than the actual values. The high values remain greater than the actual values throughout the 1982 through 1989 period.

Creating Data Sets

Before performing the simulations, you must create separate data sets for each what-if growth rate. The following code creates the three data sets:

```
data bud_lo(drop=fed_rev fed_revm fed_revh
          rename=(fed_revl=fed_rev))
    bud_mid(drop=fed_rev fed_revl fed_revh
          rename=(fed_revm=fed_rev))
    bud_hi(drop=fed_rev fed_revl fed_revm
          rename=(fed_revh=fed_rev));
  set extrap;
  if fed_revl=. then fed_revl=fed_rev;
  if fed_revm=. then fed_revm=fed_rev;
  if fed_revh=. then fed_revh=fed_rev;
run;

  /* Printing an Updated Data Set */
proc print data=bud_lo;
  var year fed_rev;
  title2 'FED_REV from BUD_LO Data Set';
run;
```

The output generated by the previous example code is displayed in Output 9.11.

Output 9.11

Printing the BUD_LO Data Set FED_REV Values Prior to Use in Simulation of the General Fund Model

```
                 General Fund Revenues Example
                 FED_REV from BUD_LO Data Set

            OBS     YEAR     FED_REV

             1       73      535.586
             2       74      545.639
             3       75      546.097
             4       76      531.634
             5       77      590.924
             6       78      613.190
             7       79      634.160
             8       80      630.340
             9       81      667.547
            10       82      674.222
            11       83      680.965
            12       84      687.774
            13       85      694.652
            14       86      701.599
            15       87      708.615
            16       88      715.701
            17       89      722.858
```

Performing the What-if Simulation

You are now ready to perform the what-if simulations of the general fund model. Use SOLVE statements in PROC MODEL to perform separate simulations with each what-if data set. The following statements perform the simulations, merge the output data sets, and print and plot the simulated values. Output 9.12 shows the results.

```
    /* Performing the What-If Simulation */
proc model model=bud_mod2 noprint;

    /* Predicted Values */
solve gfund / simulate start=10 data=budget
          out=out_p(drop=_type_ _mode_ _errors_
                    rename=(gfund=p_gfund));

    /* Low What-If FED_REV Simulation */
solve gfund / simulate start=10 data=bud_lo
          out=out_lo(drop=_type_ _mode_ _errors_
                    rename=(gfund=gfund_l));

    /* Mid What-If FED_REV Simulation */
solve gfund / simulate start=10 data=bud_mid
          out=out_mid(drop=_type_ _mode_ _errors_
                    rename=(gfund=gfund_m));

    /* High What-If FED_REV Simulation */
solve gfund / simulate start=10 data=bud_hi
          out=out_hi(drop=_type_ _mode_ _errors_
                    rename=(gfund=gfund_h));
run;
```

```
   /* Merging the What-If Simulations */
data what_if;
   merge budget out_p out_lo out_mid out_hi;
   by year;
run;

   /* Printing the What-If Simulations */
proc print data=what_if;
   var year gfund p_gfund gfund_l gfund_m gfund_h;
   title2 'What-If Simulations';
run;

goptions reset=symbol;

   /* Plotting the What-If Simulations */
proc gplot data=what_if;
   where year > 80;
   plot gfund*year=1
        p_gfund*year=2
        gfund_l*year=3
        gfund_m*year=4
        gfund_h*year=5 / overlay haxis=axis1
                         vaxis=axis2 legend=legend1;
   symbol1 i=join l=1 color=black;
   symbol2 v=* font=swissb color=blue;
   symbol3 i=join v=L font=swissb l=33 color=green;
   symbol4 i=join v=M font=swissb l=33 color=red;
   symbol5 i=join v=H font=swissb l=33 color=gray;
   axis1 offset=(2,2)pct order=(81 to 89 by 1) label=none;
   axis2 order=(3000 to 5100 by 300) minor=(number=1)
         label=(a=-90 r=90 'GENERAL FUND');
   legend1 label=none value=('Actual GFUND' 'Predicted GFUND'
           'Low GFUND' 'Mid GFUND' 'High GFUND');
   title 'General Fund';
   title2 'Actual, What-If, and Predicted Values';
run;
quit;
```

Output 9.12

*Printing and
Plotting the
What-if Simulated
Values of General
Fund Revenues
Given Low,
Medium, and High
Values of IRS
Revenue*

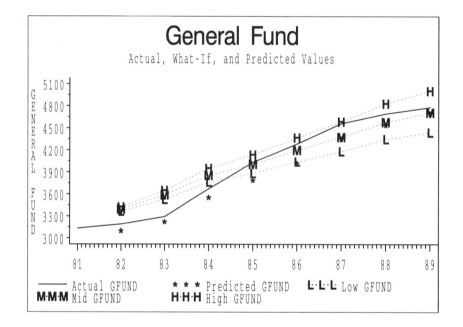

```
                        General Fund Revenues Example
                             What-If Simulations

    OBS    YEAR     GFUND     P_GFUND    GFUND_L    GFUND_M    GFUND_H

     1      73      2734.23      .          .          .          .
     2      74      2754.56      .          .          .          .
     3      75      2697.03      .          .          .          .
     4      76      2762.74      .          .          .          .
     5      77      3085.81      .          .          .          .
     6      78      3159.51      .          .          .          .
     7      79      3219.01      .          .          .          .
     8      80      3202.67      .          .          .          .
     9      81      3130.91      .          .          .          .
    10      82      3189.64    3096.65    3153.09    3182.69    3212.29
    11      83      3292.17    3221.15    3372.64    3432.87    3494.00
    12      84      3670.84    3553.06    3650.07    3742.01    3836.67
    13      85      4030.67    3786.67    3799.16    3923.89    4054.22
    14      86      4283.76    4017.23    3981.23    4139.88    4308.09
    15      87      4560.74    4350.24    4138.64    4332.37    4540.80
    16      88      4693.15    4537.56    4316.60    4546.59    4797.69
    17      89      4781.05    4695.18    4415.89    4683.37    4979.69
```

Interpretation of output

In Output 9.12, the actual GFUND values, predicted values from the structural model, and the low, mid, and high what-if simulations are printed and plotted for the period 1981 through 1989. In the plot, the actual values are represented by the solid line, the predicted values are represented by the asterisks, and the symbols L, M, and H represent the values of GFUND generated from FED_REV growing at low, mid, and high rates. Initially, all growth rates of FED_REV produce what-if GFUND values greater than the actual values. However, by 1985 actual GFUND values are greater than all the what-if values except those produced by the high FED_REV growth rate.

By comparison, the predicted values are less than the actual values from 1982 through 1989, and until 1986, the predicted values are less than the corresponding what-if values. From 1987 through 1989, the predicted values are very close to the mid what-if values.

Goal-Seeking Simulation

You can also use the general fund model and PROC MODEL to solve for an exogenous variable, given values for the other variables. This type of simulation is often called goal-seeking simulation. For example, if FED_REV is 750, what would GNP have to be for GFUND to be 5000? 5500? 6000?

To perform goal-seeking simulation, you create an input data set containing data necessary for goal-seeking simulation, and then use PROC MODEL with a SOLVE statement to solve for the values of GNP.

Solving the Model

The following statements perform goal-seeking simulation for GNP when GFUND values are 5000, 5500, and 6000, and FED_REV is 750. Because GNP is being solved for, it is endogenous in this goal-seeking example. Because the values of GFUND and FED_REV are given, they are exogenous values for this example. Note that the DATA= option, specifying the input data set, is used in the SOLVE statement because the input data are used to find solutions. Output 9.13 shows the results.

```
    /* Creating Goal-Seeking Data Set, GOAL*/
data goal;
   input year gfund fed_rev;
   cards;
1990 5000 750
1990 5500 750
1990 6000 750
;

    /* Goal-Seeking for GNP */
proc model model=bud_mod2 noprint;
   endogenous gnp;
   exogenous gfund fed_rev;
   solve gnp / data=goal out=goal_out;
run;

    /* Printing the Solution Values */
proc print data=goal_out;
   var gfund gnp fed_rev;
   title2 'Goal-Seeking Values of GNP';
run;
```

Output 9.13
The Goal-seeking Solutions for GNP Given GFUND and FED_REV Values

```
            General Fund Revenues Example
              Goal-Seeking Values of GNP

      OBS     GFUND      GNP      FED_REV

       1      5000     4668.12      750
       2      5500     5159.58      750
       3      6000     5651.03      750
```

Interpretation of output

Output 9.13 presents the goal-seeking solutions. These solutions are the GNP values that would generate the desired GFUND values, given that FED_REV is 750.

Chapter Summary

This chapter discussed simulation of models with actual data and with alternative sets of data for what-if simulation. Also discussed were goodness-of-fit and Theil statistics, which can be used to assess a model's ability to simulate, to reveal areas for refining the model, and to enable you to compare models. For visual comparisons, the PLOT and GPLOT procedures were used to plot the actual and simulated values. Lastly, this chapter presented an example of goal seeking simulation.

Learning More

□ For information on PROC MODEL and the %AR macro, see the *SAS/ETS User's Guide, Version 6, First Edition.*

□ For information on PROC GPLOT, see *SAS/GRAPH Software: Reference, Version 6, First Edition* and *SAS/GRAPH Software Usage: Version 6, First Edition.*

References

Council of Economic Advisers (1990), *Economic Report of the President,* Washington, D.C.: U.S. Government Printing Office.

Granger, C.W.J. and Newbold, P. (1986), *Forecasting Economic Time Series, Second Edition,* New York: Academic Press, Inc.

N.C. Office of State Budget and Management (1990), "Overview of the N.C. State Budget."

Pindyck, R.S. and Rubinfeld, D.L. (1991), *Econometric Models and Economic Forecasts, Third Edition,* New York: McGraw-Hill Book Company.

Theil, H. (1971), *Principles of Econometrics,* New York: John Wiley & Sons, Inc.

U.S. Department of Commerce, *Statistical Abstracts of the U.S.,* Washington, D.C.: U.S. Government Printing Office.

Chapter **10** Simulating Regression Models with Lagged Variables

Introduction

Contemporaneous models relate current values of the exogenous (independent) variables to the current value of the endogenous (dependent) variable. *Lag models* relate current and past values of the exogenous variables as well as past values of the endogenous variables to the current value of the endogenous variable. When economists simulate using lag models, they are interested in effects across time, that is, dynamics. Simulation with lag models enables you to examine the influence of these lagged values across time.

You can simulate models with lagged variables statically, dynamically, or a combination of the two. *Static simulation* uses the actual values of the lagged variables while dynamic simulation uses the solved values of the lagged variables. Your choice of static or dynamic simulation depends on whether it is appropriate to assume that past actual values or solved values are available for the simulation.

In this chapter, you use the MODEL procedure in SAS/ETS software and the HOMES data set to fit a model of new one-family home sales. The new home model is an example of a model with a lagged exogenous variable. You then simulate this model dynamically and statically with PROC MODEL. Also in this chapter, you use the AUTOREG procedure in SAS/ETS software and the MCON data set to fit a Koyck Infinite Lag Consumption Function. This model is an example of a model with a lagged endogenous variable. You simulate this model using the SIMLIN procedure. Finally, you compare models by goodness-of-fit and Theil statistics and by plotting the simulated and actual values.

Modeling with Lagged Independent Variables

This section introduces a model for new one-family home sales and the HOMES data set. After fitting the model, you simulate the model with dynamic and static simulation, and plot the actual and simulated values versus time.

Suppose you work for the United States Department of Housing and Urban Development. You are modeling U.S. annual sales of newly constructed one family homes over the period 1970 through 1990. You hypothesize that current sales depend on current income, last year's income, and current population. This model has the following form:

$$Q_t = a + bY_t + cY_{t-1} + dPOP_t + \varepsilon_t$$

where

a,b,c, and d	are parameters to be estimated.
Q_t	is new one-family home sales for year t.
Y_t	is real personal income for year t.
Y_{t-1}	is real personal income for year $t-1$.
POP_t	is the population for year t.
ε_t	is the random error term for year t.

To fit this model, you must first create the HOMES data set.

Introducing the HOMES Data Set

The HOMES data set consists of annual observations from 1970 through 1990 of the following variables:

YEAR	is the year for which data were collected.
Q	is the number of one-family houses sold (in thousands).*
POP	is U.S. population (in millions).*
YN	is nominal personal income (in billions of dollars).**
CPI	is the consumer price index (CPI).**

---

* U.S. Department of Commerce, *Statistical Abstracts of the U.S.* (Washington, D.C.: U.S. Government Printing Office, 1991)

** Council of Economic Advisers, *The Economic Report of the President* (Washington, D.C.: U.S. Government Printing Office, February 1991)

In this model, you need to deflate nominal personal income (YN) by the CPI to account for the effects of inflation. A new variable, Y, is created to reflect real personal income.

The following SAS example code creates the HOMES data set, prints the first five observations, and plots Q versus YEAR. Output 10.1 shows the results.

```
data homes;
    input year q pop yn cpi ƋƋ;
        y=yn/cpi;
    label q='New One-Family Houses Sold in Thousands'
        pop='U.S. Population in Millions'
        y='Real Personal Income in Billions'
        cpi='U.S. CPI 1982-1984 = 100';
    cards;
70 485 205.052  715.6  .388 71 656 207.661  776.8  .405
72 718 209.896  839.6  .418 73 634 211.909  949.8  .444
74 519 213.854 1038.4  .493 75 549 215.973 1142.8  .538
76 646 218.035 1252.6  .569 77 819 220.239 1379.3  .606
78 817 222.585 1551.2  .652 79 709 225.055 1729.3  .726
80 545 227.719 1918.0  .824 81 436 229.945 2127.6  .909
82 412 232.171 2261.4  .965 83 623 234.296 2428.1  .996
84 639 236.343 2668.6 1.039 85 688 238.466 2838.7 1.076
86 750 240.658 3013.3 1.096 87 671 242.820 3194.7 1.136
88 676 245.051 3479.2 1.183 89 650 247.350 3725.5 1.240
90 536 249.975 3945.8 1.307
;

proc print data=homes (obs=5) label;
    var year q y pop;
    title 'New Homes Example';
    title2 'First Five Observations HOMES Data';
run;
```

Output 10.1
The First Five Observations of the HOMES Data

```
                          New Homes Example
                  First Five Observations HOMES Data

                         New          Real        U.S.
                     One-Family     Personal    Population
                     Houses Sold    Income in      in
          OBS  YEAR  in Thousands   Billions    Millions
           1    70       485        1844.33     205.052
           2    71       656        1918.02     207.661
           3    72       718        2008.61     209.896
           4    73       634        2139.19     211.909
           5    74       519        2106.29     213.854
```

Plotting Home Sales

You can use the GPLOT procedure to plot new one-family home sales versus YEAR. The following SAS example code creates this plot. Output 10.2 shows the results.

```
goptions reset=symbol;

proc gplot data=homes;
    plot q*year=1 / hminor=1 vminor=1 haxis=axis1 vaxis=axis2;
    symbol1 i=join v=Q font=swissb l=1;
    axis1 offset=(2,2)pct order=70 to 90 by 2;
    axis2 label=(a=-90 r=90 'QUANTITY SOLD');
    title 'New One-Family Houses Sold in Thousands';
    title2 'in Thousands';
run;
quit;
```

Output 10.2
The Plot of
One-Family Home
Sales Versus YEAR

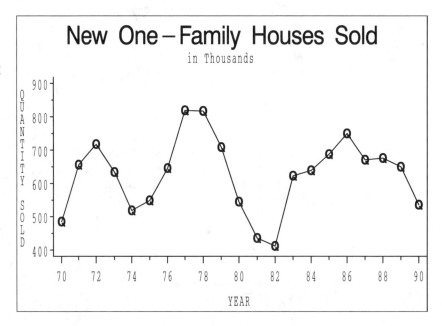

Interpretation of output

In Output 10.2, the plot of new one-family homes sold, Q, versus YEAR reflects the state of the U.S. economy. The recessionary periods of the mid-1970s, the early 1980s, and the early 1990s appear as three cycles in the number of new homes sold. Each extremum can be interpreted as a turning point.

If you want to analyze the component parts of this series, you can use the ARIMA procedure in SAS/ETS software. For details, see the *SAS/ETS User's Guide, Version 6, First Edition* and *SAS/ETS Software: Applications Guide 1, Version 6, First Edition*.

Fitting the Homes Model

You can fit the homes model with PROC MODEL using the lagging function to create one-period lagged values of Y and the %AR macro to correct for autoregression. The general form of the lagging function is LAGn(Y), which produces the nth lag of the variable Y. For example, LAG1(Y) produces the one-period lagged values of Y, LAG2(Y) produces the two-period lagged values of Y, and so on. The lag length of an equation is the longest lag length appearing in the equation. The lag length of a model is the lag length of the longest lagged equation. Also note that PROC MODEL keeps track of the use of lags and automatically determines the lag length of each equation, each instrumental variable (if any), and the model as a whole.

The following is an interpretation of the SAS statements used to fit the new homes model:

PROC MODEL

invokes the MODEL procedure. The following options of the PROC MODEL statement are specified:

DATA=	requests the HOMES data set.
OUTMODEL=	specifies an output model file to contain the estimated parameters. In this example, the model file is named HOME_MOD. The HOME_MOD data file is recalled for use in subsequent invocations of PROC MODEL.

PARAMETERS
PARMS

specifies the parameters to be estimated. For this example, the parameters to be estimated are A, B, C, and D.

%AR(*name,nlag,endolist*)

requests the %AR macro. The following is an interpretation of the three arguments of the %AR macro:

name	specifies a prefix to the autoregressive parameter. For this example, the prefix AR_Q is specified. Note that PROC MODEL names the autoregressive parameter AR_Q_L1.
nlag	specifies the order of the AR(n) process or lists the subset of autoregressive parameters to be fitted. For this example, a first-order process, AR(1), is specified.
endolist	specifies the list of equations to which the AR process is to be applied.

ENDOGENOUS
ENDO

specifies the endogenous variables. For this example, the endogenous variable is Q.

EXOGENOUS
EXO

specifies the exogenous variables. For this example, the exogenous variables are Y and POP.

ID

specifies the variables to be included in the output data set.

FIT

specifies the equation to be fitted. The equation Q= defines the equation to be fitted. In PROC MODEL, you must write out equations to be fitted or solved with all parameters, variables, and arithmetic operators. The following options of the FIT statement are specified:

DW	specifies the Durbin-Watson *d* statistic.

(FIT continued)

OUT=	creates an output data set named HOM_OUT.
OUTACTUAL	includes the actual values of the dependent variable used for estimation to the OUT= data set.

Part of the output generated by the following SAS example code is displayed in Output 10.3. The fitted model is shown; the model and estimation summaries are not.

```
proc model data=homes outmodel=home_mod;
   parms a b c d;
      q = a + b*y + c*lag(y) + d*pop;
   %ar(ar_q,1,q)
   endo q;
   exo y pop;
   id year;
   fit q / dw out=hom_out outactual;
run;
```

Output 10.3
The Fitted Homes
Model Corrected
for First-Order
Autoregression

```
                              New Homes Example

                             MODEL Procedure
                             OLS Estimation

                  Nonlinear OLS Summary of Residual Errors

                  DF    DF                                              Durbin
       Equation Model Error      SSE       MSE  Root MSE R-Square Adj R-Sq Watson

       Q           5    15      86388   5759.21  75.88949  0.6201   0.5188  1.741



                     Nonlinear OLS Parameter Estimates

                                 Approx.     'T'   Approx.
       Parameter   Estimate      Std Err    Ratio  Prob>|T|  Label

       A           2622.54       1196.5      2.19   0.0446
       B           1.216858      0.37226     3.27   0.0052
       C          -0.658095      0.36760    -1.79   0.0936
       D         -14.841801      8.64347    -1.72   0.1065
       AR_Q_L1     0.478075      0.24798     1.93   0.0730  AR(AR_Q) Q LAG1 PARAMETER



                    Number of Observations     Statistics for System
                    Used              20       Objective          4319
                    Missing            0       Objective*N       86388
```

Interpretation of output

In Output 10.3, the structural portion of the fitted model, corrected for first-order autoregression is as follows:

$$Q_t = 2622.54 + 1.2169\, Y_t - 0.6581\, Y_{t-1} - 14.8418\, POP_t \quad .$$

Note the following items:

□ The intercept (A) and the slope parameters for current income (B) have *p* values of .0446 and .0052, respectively, and are significant at the .05 level.

□ The slope parameter for income lagged one period (C) has a *p* value, Approx. Prob> | T | , of .0936, while the slope parameter for population (D) has a *p* value of .1065.

□ The R^2 (R-Square) is .6201, and the adjusted R^2 (Adj R-Sq) is .5188.

□ The Durbin-Watson *d* statistic is 1.741. Although it is not shown in Output 10.3, this *d* statistic is not significant at the .05 level. For the purpose of this example, assume no further correction for autocorrelation is required.

For the purposes of this example, the model is assumed to adequately fit the data.

Additional Functions in PROC MODEL

In addition to the LAG function, PROC MODEL also provides the following functions:

ZLAG*n*(Y)   creates the *n*th lag of Y with the lag length truncated to zero and missing values set to zero.

DIF*n*(Y)   creates the difference of Y at lag *n*.

ZDIF*n*(Y)   creates the difference of Y at lag *n* with the lag length truncated to zero and missing values set to zero.

The length of lagging and differencing are limited to values between zero and 9999. The ZLAG and the ZDIF functions are not counted in the determination of the model's lag length with the advantage that observations are not lost due to missing values. Note that the model's lag length is the longest lag in the model. In addition, the lagging and differencing functions may be combined to create new expressions.

For additional information about the LAG, ZLAG, DIF, and ZDIF functions, see *the SAS/ETS User's Guide*.

Dynamically Simulating the Model

You can use the SOLVE statement in PROC MODEL to simulate the homes model. The default simulation, dynamic, uses the solved values for the lagged variables. The output has a summary of the model, a summary of the simulation process, and a section of descriptive statistics, goodness-of-fit statistics, and Theil Statistics. These statistics are described in Chapter 9, "Introduction to Simulation."

The following statements dynamically simulate the homes model. The MODEL= option of the PROC MODEL statement specifies the model file containing the estimated model. In this example, the model file is named HOME_MOD and was created in Output 10.3. The following is an interpretation of the SOLVE statement and options.

SOLVE

specifies the solution to the equations with the listed variables. The following options of the SOLVE statement are specified:

SIMULATE   specifies that the solutions are functions of the input variables, even when actual data for some or all of the solution variables are available in the input data set.

(SOLVE continued)

DYNAMIC   specifies that the solved values of the lagged variables be used in the simulation. Dynamic simulation is the default.

STATS   requests goodness-of-fit statistics.

THEIL   requests THEIL U and U1, goodness-of-fit statistics, and the relative change statistics.

OUT=   specifies the creation of an output data set, HOM_SIM1, containing the solution values. You use this data set later to print and plot the solution values.

Part of the output generated by the following example code is displayed in Output 10.4. The model and solution summaries are not shown.

```
proc model data=hom_out model=home_mod;
   solve q / simulate dynamic stats theil
             out=hom_sim1(rename=(q=q_sim_d));
   run;
```

Output 10.4
The Dynamically Simulated Homes Model and Goodness-of-Fit Statistics

```
                           New Homes Example

                            MODEL Procedure
                   Dynamic Single-Equation Simulation
                         Descriptive Statistics

                              Actual            Predicted

      Variable   Nobs    N    Mean      Std     Mean      Std
      Q            19   19  633.5263 112.2756  629.3182  71.6724


                           Statistics of Fit

                           Mean    Mean %  Mean Abs Mean Abs %
                Variable  N  Error   Error   Error     Error
                Q        19 -4.2081  1.0398  66.9705  10.86879

                           Statistics of Fit

                RMS      RMS %
      Variable  Error    Error  R-Square Label
      Q        76.2574  12.3804  0.5131 New One-Family Houses Sold in Thousands


                     Theil Forecast Error Statistics

                          MSE Decomposition Proportions Inequality Coef

      Variable   N    MSE  Corr  Bias  Reg  Dist  Var  Covar    U1      U
                          (R)   (UM)  (UR) (UD)  (US)  (UC)
      Q         19   5815 0.722 0.003 0.014 0.983 0.269 0.728  0.1186 0.0598


              Theil Relative Change Forecast Error Statistics

              Relative Change   MSE Decomposition Proportions Inequality Coef

      Variable   N    MSE  Corr  Bias  Reg  Dist  Var  Covar    U1      U
                          (R)   (UM)  (UR) (UD)  (US)  (UC)
      Q         19 0.01463 0.741 0.000 0.034 0.966 0.038 0.962  0.6828 0.3657
```

Interpretation of output

In Output 10.4, there are four sets of statistics that measure how well the model simulates: Descriptive Statistics, Statistics of Fit, Theil Forecast Error Statistics, and Theil Relative Change Forecast Error Statistics. Note the following items:

□ The means of actual and simulated values are 633.5263 and 629.3182, respectively. The Mean Error and Mean % Error are −4.2081 and 1.0398%, respectively. Therefore, the model simulates the historical values with a slight downward bias. (Recall that the simulation residuals are defined as the simulated values minus the actual values.)

□ The standard deviation (Std) of the actual values, 112.2756, is larger than the Std of the simulated values, 71.6724. Therefore, the model simulates with a smaller variation than the actual data.

□ The Theil U1 and U statistics are .1186 and .0598, respectively. These values are reasonably close to the optimal value of zero.

□ The first decomposition of the Theil forecast error statistics shows the BIAS and REG proportions are small, .003 and .014, respectively, and the DIST proportion is large, .983. Recall that the sum of BIAS, REG, and DIST equals one, and optimally, the BIAS and REG components are zero and the DIST component equals unity.

□ The second decomposition of the Theil forecast error statistics shows the VAR component is relatively large and the COVAR component is relatively small. Recall that the sum of BIAS, VAR, and COVAR equals one, and optimally, the BIAS and VAR components are zero and the COVAR component is unity. This result indicates a possible problem with the model's ability to simulate the variability of Q, one-family homes sold in thousands.

□ The Theil Relative Change Forecast Error Statistics U1 and U are .6828 and .3657, respectively. These values are relatively large; however, the decompositions are close to the optimal distributions.

You conclude that this model dynamically simulates the historical data reasonably well. However, there is less variability in the simulated values than in the actual data. While this is of little concern if you are interested in the trends of the data, it is a problem if you are interested in the distributions of the simulated values.

Statically Simulating the Model

You can also perform static simulation by requesting the STATIC option of the SOLVE statement. For example, you can modify the SAS example code producing Output 10.4 as follows:

```
proc model data=hom_out model=home_mod;
   solve q / simulate static stats theil outlags
            out=hom_sim2(drop=_type_ _mode_ _lag_ _errors_
                         rename=(q=q_sim_s));
run;
```

The previous example code generates Output 10.5. Only the simulation statistics are shown. The model and solution summaries are not shown.

Output 10.5
*The Statically
Simulated Homes
Model and
Goodness-of-Fit
Statistics*

```
                              New Homes Example

                              MODEL Procedure
                     Static Single-Equation Simulation
                           Descriptive Statistics

                               Actual                  Predicted

     Variable   Nobs    N    Mean       Std       Mean       Std
     Q            19    19   633.5263  112.2756  633.1712   87.6181


                              Statistics of Fit

                          Mean     Mean %  Mean Abs Mean Abs %
              Variable    N    Error    Error     Error     Error
              Q          19   -0.3552   1.1723   51.6140   8.32386

                              Statistics of Fit

              RMS      RMS %
     Variable  Error    Error R-Square Label
     Q        67.3688  10.8783  0.6200 New One-Family Houses Sold in Thousands


                        Theil Forecast Error Statistics

                            MSE Decomposition Proportions Inequality Coef

     Variable    N      MSE  Corr  Bias  Reg  Dist  Var Covar    U1      U
                             (R)   (UM)  (UR) (UD)  (US) (UC)
     Q          19     4539 0.787 0.000 0.000 1.000 0.127 0.873  0.1048 0.0526


                   Theil Relative Change Forecast Error Statistics

              Relative Change   MSE Decomposition Proportions Inequality Coef

     Variable    N      MSE  Corr  Bias  Reg  Dist  Var Covar    U1      U
                             (R)   (UM)  (UR) (UD)  (US) (UC)
     Q          19   0.01252 0.783 0.000 0.030 0.970 0.266 0.734  0.6317 0.3773
```

Interpretation of output

In Output 10.5, the goodness-of-fit statistics are listed and can be compared with those of the simulated model in Output 10.4. Note the following items:

□ The actual and simulated mean values, 633.5263 and 633.1712, are very close in magnitude. The Mean Error and Mean % Error, −.3552 and 1.1723%, are close to zero. The model simulates the historical data with little bias.

□ The actual and simulated standard deviations (Std), 112.2756 and 87.6181, indicate the simulated values display less variability than the actual data. Even so, the variability of the statically simulated values is closer to the variability of the actual data than that of the dynamically simulated values.

□ The Theil U1 and U statistics are .1048 and .0526, respectively, which are smaller than the Theil Statistics in Output 10.4.

□ The decomposition of the U and U1 statistics shows there is no problem with the BIAS or REG; both are zero. The VAR proportion is .127, and is smaller than the VAR proportion of the dynamically simulated model.

Recall that static simulation uses the actual values of the lagged variables. Assuming the lagged values are accurately known provides additional information for the simulation. Your choice of simulating statically or dynamically depends on the appropriateness of this assumption. For some models, the impact of the lagged variables may continue for several periods, and the previous values cannot be known. For other models, the impact of the lagged variables may coincide with the frequency of observations, and hence, may be accurately known in subsequent periods.

Additional Simulation

You may want to simulate a model statically for several periods and then dynamically for the other periods. This type of simulation can be combined with what-if simulation to evaluate proposed policy changes. For example, in the model of new home sales, what if a proposed policy change is expected to affect income? Suppose a change in the personal income tax structure takes effect in 1976, but the full effect will not be known for several years. The first year, 1970, is used to start the lag process. You assume that income is known for each year over the next six years, 1971 through 1976, and static simulation is used. From 1977 onward, when income is unknown for the purposes of this example, dynamic simulation is used.

The following SAS example code uses the START= option of the SOLVE statement to begin dynamic simulation in 1977, the sixth observation. The statements were interpreted in previous examples. Output 10.6 shows the results.

```
    /* Simulating the Model */
proc model data=hom_out model=home_mod noprint;
   solve q / simulate start=6 outlags
            out=hom_sim3(rename=(q=q_sim_sd));
run;


    /* Printing Simulated Values */
proc print data=hom_sim3;
   var year q_sim_sd;
   title2 'Mixed Static and Dynamic Simulation';
run;
```

Output 10.6
Mixed Static and Dynamic Simulation of the Homes Model and Goodness-of-Fit Statistics

```
                        New Homes Example
                 Mixed Static and Dynamic Simulation

                 OBS    YEAR    Q_SIM_SD

                   1     71      656.000
                   2     72      689.246
                   3     73      772.425
                   4     74      544.273
                   5     75      575.154
                   6     76      635.409
                   7     77      664.484
                   8     78      711.285
                   9     79      612.845
                  10     80      506.592
                  11     81      525.483
                  12     82      487.630
                  13     83      569.202
                  14     84      635.655
                  15     85      603.217
                  16     86      660.051
                  17     87      631.383
                  18     88      713.560
                  19     89      671.974
                  20     90      608.975
```

Comparing the Simulations

You can directly compare the actual and simulated values by merging the data sets (by the variable YEAR) in a DATA step, and then printing the merged data set. The following SAS example code accomplishes this, and PROC PRINT prints the observations for YEAR, Q, Q_SIM_D, Q_SIM_S, and Q_SIM_SD. Output 10.7 shows the results.

```
data homes_p;
   merge homes hom_sim1 hom_sim2 hom_sim3;
   by year;
run;

proc print data=homes_p;
   var year q q_sim_d q_sim_s q_sim_sd;
   title2 'Actual Values';
   title3 'Dynamic and Static Simulation Values';
   title4 'and Mixed Simulation Values';
run;
```

Output 10.7
Actual and
Simulated
One-Family Home
Sales (in
Thousands)

```
                         New Homes Example
                           Actual Values
                 Dynamic and Static Simulation Values
                       and Mixed Simulation Values

   OBS    YEAR    Q     Q_SIM_D    Q_SIM_S    Q_SIM_SD

     1     70    485        .          .          .
     2     71    656    656.000    656.000    656.000
     3     72    718    689.246    689.246    689.246
     4     73    634    758.661    772.425    772.425
     5     74    519    603.947    544.273    544.273
     6     75    549    615.817    575.154    575.154
     7     76    646    667.394    635.409    635.409
     8     77    819    674.725    664.484    664.484
     9     78    817    716.188    785.251    711.285
    10     79    709    615.192    663.450    612.845
    11     80    545    507.715    552.620    506.592
    12     81    436    526.021    543.869    525.483
    13     82    412    487.887    444.795    487.630
    14     83    623    569.326    532.999    569.202
    15     84    639    635.714    661.407    635.655
    16     85    688    603.245    604.818    603.217
    17     86    750    660.065    700.636    660.051
    18     87    671    631.389    674.440    631.383
    19     88    676    713.563    732.525    713.560
    20     89    650    671.976    653.995    671.974
    21     90    536    608.975    598.456    608.975
```

Interpretation of output

In Output 10.7, the actual values for new one-family home sales, Q, and the simulated values, Q_SIM_D, Q_SIM_S, and Q_SIM_SD, are printed. Notice that for 1971 and 1972, the simulations match; they have the same information. After 1972, the Q_SIM_D and Q_SIM_S values differ. The Q_SIM_SD values match the static simulation values, Q_SIM_S, until 1977, not 1976, because the actual lagged value from 1976 is available in 1977. After 1977, Q_SIM_S and Q_SIM_SD differ because the solved values of the lagged variable are used in the Q_SIM_SD simulated values.

Plotting the Simulations

You visually assess a model's ability to simulate by plotting the actual data and the simulated values. The following SAS example code uses PROC GPLOT to plot Q, Q_SIM_D, and Q_SIM_S versus YEAR. Output 10.8 shows the results.

```
goptions reset=symbol;

proc gplot data=homes_p;
   plot q*year=1
        q_sim_d*year=2
        q_sim_s*year=3 / overlay hminor=1 vminor=1
                         haxis=axis1 vaxis=axis2 legend=legend1;
   symbol1 i=join l=1 color=black;
   symbol2 v=D font=swissb color=blue;
   symbol3 v=S font=swissb color=green;
   axis1 offset=(2,2)pct order=70 to 90 by 2;
   axis2 order=400 to 900 by 100 label=(a=-90 r=90 'QUANTITY SOLD');
   legend1 label=none value=('New One-Family Homes'
           'Dynamic Simulation' 'Static Simulation');
   title 'Dynamic and Static Simulation';
   title2 'New One-Family Homes Sold in Thousands';
run;
quit;
```

Output 10.8
Plot of Actual Values and Dynamically and Statically Simulated Values

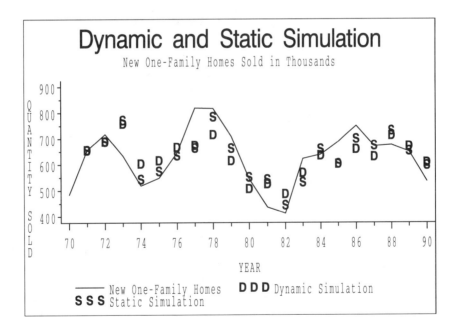

Interpretation of output

Output 10.8 contains the plot of actual values and the dynamically and statically simulated values versus YEAR. The solid line represents the actual values while the symbols D and S refer to the dynamically simulated and statically simulated values. In most years, the static simulation follows the actual values more closely than the dynamic simulation. Recall that closeness is measured by vertical distance.

Modeling Consumer Expenditures

Koyck modeled consumption expenditures as habit persistence with an infinite lag, where all previous values of disposable income affect current period consumption (1954). The Koyck lag model can be expressed

$$C_t = b_0 + wC_{t-1} + b_1DI_t$$

where

C_t is current period consumption expenditures, the endogenous variable.

b_0 is the (transformed) intercept.

w is the slope parameter associated with the lagged endogenous variable, C_{t-1}.

C_{t-1} is the previous-period consumption expenditures.

b_1 is the slope parameter associated with exogenous variable DI_t.

DI_t is current-period disposable income.

Note that consumption and disposable income are deflated to real terms with the consumer price index to account for the effects of inflation.

Models with lagged endogenous variables may be more difficult to fit, and it is often more difficult to assess their simulation performance. Including a lagged endogenous variable on the right-hand side of the equation implies that the previous period's simulation error affects this period's simulation.

In this section, you fit a model using PROC AUTOREG and then simulate the model using PROC SIMLIN and a lagging function. For more information about fitting models with lagged endogenous variables, see Chapter 5, "Fitting Regression Models with Lagged Variables."

Fitting the Model

The infinite (Koyck) lag consumption function is an example of a model with a lagged endogenous variable. Originally fit in Chapter 5 and interpreted following Output 5.2, the following SAS example code refits the model, correcting for first-order autoregression, and creates an output data set containing the estimated parameters. The following is an interpretation of the statements:

PROC AUTOREG
 invokes the AUTOREG procedure. The following options of the PROC AUTOREG statement are specified:

 DATA= specifies MCON as the input data set (introduced in Chapter 5).

OUTEST=   specifies the creation of an output data set, MCN_EST, containing the parameter estimates. This data set is used as input to PROC SIMLIN in the next section.

MODEL
    specifies the model to be fitted. The following options of the MODEL statement are specified:

METHOD=   specifies the estimation method. For this example, the Yule-Walker method, YW, is specified.

NLAG=   specifies the order of the autoregressive process.

LAGDEP=   identifies the lagged dependent variable and prints the Durbin h statistic.

The following SAS example code performs these steps:

```
proc autoreg data=mcon outest=mcn_est;
   model c=c_1 di / method=yw nlag=1 lagdep=c_1;
run;
```

Part of the output generated by the previous example code is displayed in Output 10.9. Only the final model is presented.

Output 10.9
The Koyck Lag Consumption Function Model Corrected for First-Order Autoregression

```
                    Monthly Consumption Function Example
                            Autoreg Procedure
Dependent Variable = C        Real Consumption in Billions of 1982$
                        Estimates of Autocorrelations
   Lag  Covariance  Correlation -1 9 8 7 6 5 4 3 2 1 0 1 2 3 4 5 6 7 8 9 1
    0    261.2849    1.000000  |                  |*******************|
    1    -78.9091   -0.302004  |            ******|                   |

                        Preliminary MSE =  237.454
                    Estimates of the Autoregressive Parameters
            Lag   Coefficient     Std Error      t Ratio
             1     0.30200417     0.10105030     2.988652

                          Yule-Walker Estimates
            SSE        21336.1    DFE              89
            MSE        239.7314   Root MSE    15.48326
            SBC        787.6553   AIC         777.5249
            Reg Rsq      0.9969   Total Rsq     0.9949

        Variable    DF    B Value    Std Error   t Ratio Approx Prob
        Intercept    1  26.3007406    18.291      1.438    0.1540
        C_1          1   0.9115481     0.040     22.773    0.0001
        DI           1   0.0773139     0.041      1.868    0.0650
```

Interpretation of output

In Output 10.9, the structural portion of the fitted model corrected for first-order autoregression is as follows:

$$C = 26.30074 + .91155\ C\_1 + .077314\ DI \quad .$$

You conclude that the final model fits the data reasonably well because all of the estimated parameters are significant at the .20 level, and the model explains almost all of the observed variation in consumption (Reg Rsq=.9969).

Simulating the Model

You can use the SIMLIN procedure to simulate the model, print the reduced form, and compute interim and total multipliers. The reduced form is a transformation of the model into equations with endogenous variables on the left-hand side and exogenous variables on the right-hand side.

An *interim multiplier* measures the change over one period in the endogenous variable as an exogenous variable is changed. For example, in the consumption model, disposable income may change to a permanently higher level. As disposable income changes in the current period, the current level of consumption is affected. This change in consumption is measured by the first interim (or impact) multiplier. In the next period, not only is disposable income at the higher level, but so is the previous period's consumption expenditures; both affect this period's level of consumption. Because the estimated parameter of lagged consumption is less than unity, the impact of each subsequent period is less than that of the previous period.

A *total multiplier* measures the full effect on the endogenous variable of a change in an exogenous variable. A total multiplier is equal to the sum of all of the interim multipliers. Thus, the total multiplier gives you the total effect, over all periods, of a one-unit change in an exogenous variable.

For more information on structural and reduced forms, and impact, interim, and total multipliers, see the *SAS/ETS User's Guide*.

The following statements compute the reduced form model and calculate the first two interim multipliers, the total multipliers, and the simulation goodness-of-fit statistics. The following is an interpretation of the statements:

PROC SIMLIN
> invokes the SIMLIN procedure. The following options of the PROC SIMLIM statement are specified:

EST=
> specifies the data set containing the structural coefficients of the model.

DATA=
> specifies MCON as the data set containing the input data for the simulation.

TYPE=
> specifies the type of estimates to be read from the EST= data set.

INTERIM=
> specifies that the interim multipliers be computed for interim periods one through the specified integer. For this example, the first two interim multipliers are requested.

TOTAL   specifies that total multipliers be computed.

ENDOGENOUS
   lists the endogenous (dependent) variables.

EXOGENOUS
   lists exogenous (independent) variables.

LAGGED *name, variable, degree*
   creates lagged variables. For each lagged variable created, you specify the following:

   name   names the lagged variable.

   variable   specifies the variable to be lagged.

   degree   specifies the degree of the lag.

   For this example, the variable C is lagged one period, and the lagged variable is named C_1.

OUTPUT
   creates an output data set containing the following predicted values:

   OUT=   names the output data set.

   PREDICTED=   names the simulated (or predicted) values.

   Output 10.10 shows the results of the following SAS example code:

```
proc simlin est=mcn_est data=mcon type=ols interim=2 total;
   endogenous c;
   exogenous di;
   lagged c_1 c 1;
   output out=mcn_out predicted=c_pred;
run;
```

Output 10.10
The Reduced Form and Multipliers of the Koyck Lag Consumption Function Model

```
                    Monthly Consumption Function Example

                            SIMLIN Procedure

            Inverse Coefficient Matrix for Endogenous Variables
                                    C
                    C         1.0000

            Reduced Form for Lagged Endogenous Variables
                                   C_1
                    C         0.9115

            Reduced Form for Exogenous Variables
                              DI        INTERCEP
                    C       0.0773      26.3007
```

(continued)

Output 10.10
(continued)

```
                    Interim Multipliers for Interim 1
                              DI          INTERCEP
                 C        0.0704753       23.97439

                    Interim Multipliers for Interim 2
                              DI          INTERCEP
                 C        0.0642417       21.85381

                         Total Multipliers
                              DI          INTERCEP
                 C        0.8740786       297.3452
```

```
                  Monthly Consumption Function Example

                          SIMLIN Procedure

                          Statistics of Fit

                             Mean     Mean %   Mean Abs   Mean Abs
             Variable    N   Error    Error    Error      % Error
                C       93   3.3999   0.0988   21.0681    0.79585

                          Statistics of Fit

                     RMS      RMS %
             Variable Error   Error  Label
                C     26.2318 0.9883  Real Consumption in Billions of 1982$
```

Interpretation of output

Output 10.10 contains the following information:

□ The Reduced Form coefficients are listed for the lagged endogenous variable (C_1), .9115, for the exogenous variable (DI), 0.0773, and for the intercept, 26.3007.

□ The first two interim multipliers, 0.070475 and 0.064242, show the impact of a one-unit change in DI on C for the first and second months. The total multiplier, 0.874079, is the total effect of the one-unit change of DI on C.

□ The Statistics of Fit are listed for comparison with other models.

Plotting the Simulated Values

You can print and plot the simulated and actual values using PROC PRINT and PROC GPLOT. The following SAS example code prints the first 12 values of the simulated and actual values of the endogenous variable, C, and plots them versus the variable DATE. Output 10.11 shows the results.

```
    /* Printing Simulated Values */
proc print data=mcn_out (obs=12) label;
   var date c_pred c c_1 di;
   title2 'First Twelve Simulation Values';
run;
```

```
goptions reset=symbol;

    /* Plotting Actual and Simulated Values */
proc gplot data=mcn_out;
    plot c*date=1
        c_pred*date=2 / overlay hminor=1 vminor=1
                        haxis=axis1 vaxis=axis2 legend=legend1;
    symbol1 v=none i=join l=1 color=black;
    symbol2 v=none i=join l=3 color=blue;
    axis1 label=none offset=(0,2)pct minor=(n=3)
        order=('01JAN82'd to '01JAN91'd by year);
    axis2 label=(a=-90 r=90 'CONSUMPTION');
    legend1 label=none value=('Actual Consumption'
                              'Simulated Consumption');
    title 'Actual and Simulated Consumption';
run;
quit;
```

Output 10.11
The First 12
Simulation Values
and a Plot of the
Actual and
Simulated Values
Versus Time

Monthly Consumption Function Example
First Twelve Simulation Values

OBS	DATE	Predicted Value for C	Real Consumption in Billions of 1982$	1 Month Lagged Real C in Billions 1982$	Real Disposable Income in Billions 1982$
1	SEP82	.	2186.01	.	2332.18
2	OCT82	2200.02	2197.45	2186.01	2341.96
3	NOV82	2214.88	2223.16	2200.02	2369.08
4	DEC82	2230.06	2241.91	2214.88	2390.06
5	JAN83	2244.43	2246.32	2230.06	2397.03
6	FEB83	2256.94	2249.64	2244.43	2389.38
7	MAR83	2269.49	2266.91	2256.94	2404.19
8	APR83	2281.82	2281.85	2269.49	2415.82
9	MAY83	2293.14	2295.26	2281.82	2416.73
10	JUN83	2303.63	2307.84	2293.14	2418.99
11	JUL83	2314.90	2320.42	2303.63	2441.04
12	AUG83	2324.19	2325.15	2314.90	2428.34

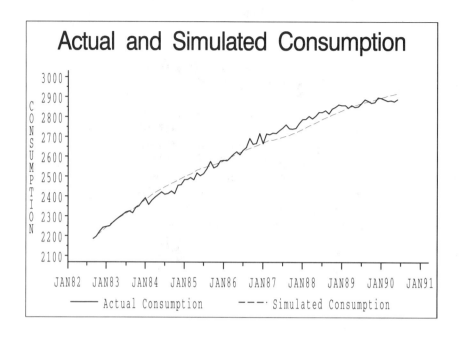

Interpretation of output

Output 10.11 shows the first 12 observations of the simulated structural model. In the plot, the solid and dashed lines represent the actual and simulated values, respectively. From this plot, you see that the actual data have a greater variance. The simulated values are biased upward in 1984 and 1985, and biased downward in 1987 through 1989. Overall, the simulated values are quite close to the actual data.

Changing the Simulation Period

You can further assess a lag model's ability to simulate by changing the starting period of the simulation. A model should simulate equally well, no matter when you start the simulation. By changing the starting period, you provide different solved values for lagged variables, which in turn affect the current period solution, which affects the next period solution, and so on. If changing the starting period of the simulation results in the model simulating poorly, then you may want to further refine the model through additional analysis.

The following statements drop the first six observations prior to MAR83 in a DATA step, simulate the model, and print the first eight observations. Output 10.12 shows the results.

```
    /* Dropping First Six Observations */
data mcon1;
set mcon;
    if date < '01mar83'd then delete;
run;
```

```
    /* Simulating the Model */
proc simlin est=mcn_est data=mcon1 type=ols;
    endogenous c;
    exogenous di;
    lagged c_1 c 1;
    output out=mcn_out1 predicted=c_pred1;
run;

    /* Printing Simulated Values */
proc print data=mcn_out1 (obs=8) label;
    var date c_pred1 c c_1 di;
    title 'Monthly Consumption Function Example';
    title2 'Simulation Starting March 1983';
    title3 'First Eight Simulation Values';
run;
```

Output 10.12
The First Eight
Observations of a
Simulation Starting
in MAR83

```
                          Monthly Consumption Function Example
                             Simulation Starting March 1983
                              First Eight Simulation Values

                                                       1 Month         Real
                                           Real       Lagged Real    Disposable
                            Predicted   Consumption     C in         Income in
                              Value      in Billions   Billions       Billions
          OBS    DATE        for C       of 1982$      1982$          1982$

            1    MAR83       2262.84      2266.91      2249.64        2404.19
            2    APR83       2275.76      2281.85      2262.84        2415.82
            3    MAY83       2287.61      2295.26      2275.76        2416.73
            4    JUN83       2298.59      2307.84      2287.61        2418.99
            5    JUL83       2310.30      2320.42      2298.59        2441.04
            6    AUG83       2320.00      2325.15      2310.30        2428.34
            7    SEP83       2329.79      2316.19      2320.00        2440.62
            8    OCT83       2341.31      2342.77      2329.79        2474.36
```

Interpretation of output

Output 10.12 prints the first eight observations of the simulation starting in
MAR83. You may want to compare these simulated values with those obtained in
Output 10.11 when the simulation started in SEP82. If desired, you can further
assess the model's ability to simulate by printing and comparing the Theil statistics
over the two periods.

Chapter Summary

This chapter presented examples of simulating models with lagged variables.
Lagged variables appear on the right-hand side of single-equation models and can
be endogenous or exogenous variables. If you create the model's lagged variables
with the lagging function of PROC MODEL, you can simulate the model
dynamically or statically. Dynamic simulation uses the solved values for the lagged
variables. Static simulation uses the actual values for the lagged variables. You can
further assess the stability of the lagged simulation model by varying the starting
period of the simulation. Also, this chapter discussed goodness-of-fit statistics and
plotting simulated values as methods of comparing simulation models.

Learning More

□ For full reference information on the AUTOREG, MODEL, and SIMLIN procedures, the %AR and %PDL macros and the LAG, ZLAG, DIF, and ZDIF functions, see the *SAS/ETS User's Guide, Version 6, First Edition.*

□ For full reference information on PROC GPLOT, see *SAS/GRAPH Software: Reference, Version 6, First Edition, Volume 1* and *Volume 2* and *SAS/GRAPH Software: Usage, Version 6, First Edition.*

References

Council of Economic Advisers (1991), *Economic Report of the President,* Washington, D.C.: U.S. Government Printing Office.

Koyck, L. (1954), *Distributed Lags and Investment Analysis,* Amsterdam, Netherlands: North-Holland.

U.S. Department of Commerce (1991), *Statistical Abstracts of the U.S.* Washington, D.C.: U.S. Government Printing Office.

U.S. Bureau of Economic Analysis, *Survey of Current Business,* Washington, D.C.: U.S. Government Printing Office.

Chapter # 11 Simulating Systems of Linear Equations

Introduction

You may often be interested in simulating and solving systems of equations. Simulation with historical data enables you to calibrate a model's consistency with the actual data: Do the simulated values follow the trends and turning points of the actual data? Additionally, you may want to examine the model's solutions as an exogenous (independent) variable is changed: Do the endogenous (dependent) variables change in the expected directions? After you are satisfied with your model's accuracy in simulating historical data, you can use it for what-if, policy experimentation, and goal-seeking simulations. Finally, simulations may reveal shortcomings and suggest areas for further refinement.

In this chapter, you use the MODEL procedure in SAS/ETS software and the Klein Model 1 of the U.S. economy for simulation. (See Chapter 6, "Fitting Systems of Linear Equations," for more information on the Klein Model 1.) First, you use historical data and examine the goodness-of-fit statistics to determine how well the model simulates history. Next, you print and plot the simulated values. Then, you use the model for what-if and goal-seeking simulations by replaying history with new data. These examples consider what would have happened if the Great Depression had not reduced private sector incomes and profits. The what-if simulations investigate what would happen to the endogenous variables while the goal-seeking analysis investigates what would happen to the exogenous variables.

This chapter also shows you how to use simulation to solve known systems of equations for left- and right-hand variables. A supply-and-demand model and a profit model are introduced, solved, and used for goal-seeking simulation. Supply and demand models are useful tools to analyze markets. Before accepting a long-term commitment to buy or sell in a market, it is worthwhile to analyze market characteristics. Basic analysis includes examining the supply-and-demand schedules over the relevant ranges of prices and quantities. The profit model helps you answer crucial business questions. For example, should you produce a new product, how much is the profit-maximizing quantity, and what are expected profits?

Simulating a System of Linear Equations

The Klein Model 1 has three equations and four identities. The consumption, investment, and private wages equations are as follows:

$$C = a_1 + a_2P + a_3P\_1 + a_4WT$$
$$I = b_1 + b_2P + b_3P\_1 + b_4K\_1$$
$$WP = c_1 + c_2X + c_3X\_1 + c_4TIME$$

where the variables are defined as follows:

C   is consumer expenditures.

P   is profits.

P_1   is profits lagged one period.

WT   is the total wage bill (the sum of private and government wages).

I   is investment expenditures.

K_1   is the capital stock lagged one period.

WP   is the private wage bill.

X   is total output of private industry.

X_1   is total output of private industry lagged one period.

TIME   is a linear time trend.

The four identities of the Klein Model 1 are production, profit, capital, and total wages, as follows:

$$\text{product } X = C + I + G$$
$$\text{profit } P = X - WP - T$$
$$\text{capital } K = K\_1 + I$$
$$\text{wage } WT = WP + WG$$

where the remaining variables are defined as follows:

G   is government expenditures.

T   is taxes.

WG   is the Government Wage Bill.

K   is the capital stock.

The following statements print the first five observations of the KLEIN data set, created in Chapter 6. Output 11.1 shows the results.

```
proc print data=klein (obs=5) label;
   var year c p wp i k x wg g t;
   title 'KLEIN Model 1 Example';
   title2 'First Five Observations KLEIN Data';
run;
```

Output 11.1
First Five
Observations of
the KLEIN Data
Set

```
                                     KLEIN Model 1 Example
                              First Five Observations KLEIN Data

                                               Private
                       Consumer                  Wage      Investment     Capital
        OBS    YEAR   Expenditures   Profits      Bill     Expenditures     Stock

         1     1919        .            .          .            .           180.1
         2     1920       39.8         12.7        28.8         2.7          182.8
         3     1921       41.9         12.4        25.5        -0.2          182.6
         4     1922       45.0         16.9        29.3         1.9          184.5
         5     1923       49.2         18.4        34.1         5.2          189.7

               Total Output
                of Private    Government   Government
        OBS     Industry      Wage Bill    Expenditures    Taxes

         1          .             .            .              .
         2        44.9           2.2          2.4            3.4
         3        45.6           2.7          3.9            7.7
         4        50.1           2.9          3.2            3.9
         5        57.2           2.9          2.8            4.7
```

Performing the Simulation

To simulate the Klein Model 1, you need to fit the model and then compute the simulated values using the fitted model. You can do both of these steps using PROC MODEL. For ease in fitting and simulating models, you can create and recall the fitted model with the OUTMODEL= and MODEL= options of the PROC MODEL statement. The following statements fit the Klein Model 1:

PROC MODEL
   invokes the MODEL procedure. The following options of the PROC MODEL statement are specified:

OUTMODEL=   creates an output file, KL_MOD, containing the fitted model.

NOPRINT   suppresses the printing of the fitted model.

ID
   specifies the variables to be included in the output data set.

FIT
>   specifies the model to be fitted. The 3SLS option specifies the estimation method of three-stage least squares.

The remaining statements and options have been interpreted in previous chapters.

```
    /* Invoking PROC MODEL */
proc model data=klein outmodel=kl_mod noprint;
    parms a1-a4 b1-b4 c1-c4;

       /* Model Equations */
    c=a1+a2*p+a3*lag(p)+a4*wt;
    i=b1+b2*p+b3*lag(p)+b4*lag(k);
    wp=c1+c2*x+c3*lag(x)+c4*time;

       /* Identities */
    x=c+i+g;
    p=x-wp-t;
    k=lag(k)+i;
    wt=wp+wg;

       /* Endogenous and Exogenous Variables */
    endo c i wp x p wt k;
    exo p_1 k_1 x_1 time t g wg;

       /* Variable Included in Output Data Set */
    id year;

       /* Estimating the Model */
    fit c i wp / 3sls;
run;
```

The following statements compute the simulated values using the fitted Klein Model 1:

PROC MODEL
>   invokes the MODEL procedure. The following option is specified:

>   MODEL=   recalls the KL_MOD data file.

SOLVE
>   solves (or simulates) the specified equations. The following options of the SOLVE statement are specified:

>   START=   specifies the observation when the simulation is to commence. For this example, simulation begins with the second observation. Note that for PROC MODEL to solve the model for an observation, values are required for all exogenous variables, including lagged variables.

>   STATS   prints the goodness-of-fit statistics.

>   THEIL   prints the Theil inequality coefficients.

OUT=   creates an output data set, KL_OUT1, containing the simulated values.

RENAME=   renames the listed variables. For this example, the simulated values are renamed SIM_C1, SIM_I1, and SIM_WP1.

Part of the output generated by this example code is displayed in Output 11.2. Only the goodness-of-fit and Theil statistics are shown. The model and simulation summaries are not displayed.

```
      /* Simulating the Model */
proc model data=klein model=kl_mod;
   solve c i wp / simulate start=2 stats theil
                out=kl_out1(rename=(c=sim_c1 i=sim_i1
                                    wp=sim_wp1));
run;
```

Output 11.2
Goodness-of-Fit and Theil Statistics from Simulation of the Klein Model 1

```
                        KLEIN Model 1 Example

                          MODEL Procedure
                  START=2 Simultaneous Simulation
                       Descriptive Statistics

                            Actual              Predicted

    Variable   Nobs    N    Mean       Std        Mean       Std

    C           21    21   53.9952    6.8609     53.9952    6.7429
    I           21    21    1.2667    3.5519      1.2667    3.3001
    WP          21    21   36.3619    6.3044     36.3619    6.2146


                        Statistics of Fit

                          Mean      Mean %   Mean Abs   Mean Abs %
    Variable      N      Error      Error      Error      Error

    C            21        0       0.0548     0.7535     1.36718
    I            21        0     -65.0117     1.1085    89.91228
    WP           21        0       0.0610     0.5945     1.64736

                        Statistics of Fit

                   RMS      RMS %
    Variable      Error     Error   R-Square  Label

    C            0.9434    1.6736     0.9801   Consumer Expenditures
    I            1.4257  243.3682     0.8308   Investment Expenditures
    WP           0.7213    2.0389     0.9863   Private Wage Bill


                    Theil Forecast Error Statistics

                           MSE Decomposition Proportions  Inequality Coef

  Variable   N     MSE   Corr   Bias  Reg  Dist  Var  Covar      U1      U
                         (R)    (UM)  (UR) (UD)  (US) (UC)

  C         21  0.88997  0.990  0.000 0.003 0.997 0.015 0.985  0.0173  0.0087
  I         21  2.03274  0.912  0.000 0.002 0.998 0.030 0.970  0.3863  0.1994
  WP        21  0.52022  0.993  0.000 0.004 0.996 0.015 0.985  0.0196  0.0098


               Theil Relative Change Forecast Error Statistics

               Relative Change   MSE Decomposition Proportions  Inequality Coef

  Variable   N     MSE   Corr   Bias  Reg  Dist  Var  Covar      U1      U
                         (R)    (UM)  (UR) (UD)  (US) (UC)

  C         20  0.0003264 0.944  0.000 0.028 0.972 0.000 1.000  0.2979  0.1490
  I         20  0.42497   0.976  0.101 0.138 0.761 0.218 0.680  0.2366  0.1264
  WP        20  0.0003865 0.977  0.016 0.062 0.922 0.124 0.859  0.2019  0.1049
```

Interpretation of output

In Output 11.2, the statistics of fit indicate that the means of the simulated and actual values are equal. Differences between the means of the actual and simulated values are the simulation biases. Although the magnitude of the mean error is zero for the investment expenditure equation (I), the percentage mean error is large, -65.0117%, and the Mean Abs % Error is 89.91228%. The Mean % Error, Mean Abs Error, and Mean Abs % Error are all small for the consumption expenditure and private wages equations.

Examining the Theil Forecast Error Statistics indicates that overall, the Theil statistics are low in magnitude (about .02 or less), except for the investment expenditure equation (I). The decompositions of the Theil statistics indicate that the Bias components are zero, and the Reg and Var components are near zero for all three equations.

The statistics of fit, Theil Statistics, and associated decompositions indicate the consumption expenditures and private wages equations simulate the actual data quite well while the investment expenditures equation does not simulate as well.

Printing and Plotting the Simulated Consumption Values

You can print and plot the simulated and actual values to assess how well the model simulates the historical data. The following SAS example code creates the KLEIN_P data set in a DATA step, then uses the PRINT and GPLOT procedures to print and plot the actual and simulated values. The printed values and the GPLOT plot are shown in Output 11.3.

```
   /* Merging Data */
data klein_p;
   merge klein kl_out1;
   by year;
      label sim_c1 = 'Simulated C'
            sim_i1 = 'Simulated I'
            sim_wp1 = 'Simulated WP';
run;

   /* Printing Simulated Values */
proc print data=klein_p label;
   var year c sim_c1 i sim_i1 wp sim_wp1;
   title 'KLEIN Model 1 Example';
   title2 'Actual and Simulated Values';
run;

goptions reset=symbol;

   /* Plotting Simulated and Actual Values */
proc gplot data=klein_p;
   plot c*year=1
        sim_c1*year=2 / overlay hminor=1 vminor=1
                        haxis=axis1 vaxis=axis2 legend=legend1;
   symbol1 i=join l=1 color=black;
   symbol1 v=C font=swissb color=blue;
   axis1 label=none offset=(2,2)pct order=1921 to 1941 by 2;
   axis2 label=(a=-90 r=90 'CONSUMPTION');
```

```
legend1 label=none value=('Actual Consumption'
                          'Simulated Consumption');
    title 'Actual and Simulated Consumption';
  run;
  quit;
```

Output 11.3

Printing the Actual and Simulated Values of the Klein Model 1 and Plotting the Actual and Simulated Values of the Consumption Equation

```
                              KLEIN Model 1 Example
                            Actual and Simulated Values

                                                          Private
                 Consumer    Simulated   Investment   Simulated   Wage    Simulated
  OBS   YEAR   Expenditures      C      Expenditures      I        Bill       WP

   1    1919        .            .            .           .          .          .
   2    1920       39.8          .           2.7          .        28.8         .
   3    1921       41.9       42.3345       -0.2        1.96106    25.5      26.7021
   4    1922       45.0       46.0160        1.9        1.74646    29.3      28.7809
   5    1923       49.2       50.7280        5.2        4.74644    34.1      32.5895
   6    1924       50.6       51.0969        3.0        4.85753    33.9      33.9858
   7    1925       52.6       52.6119        5.1        5.02190    35.4      35.6794
   8    1926       55.1       54.3222        5.6        4.56127    37.4      37.7374
   9    1927       56.2       54.8990        4.2        3.09849    37.9      38.5911
  10    1928       57.3       56.2021        3.0        2.42583    39.2      38.8535
  11    1929       57.8       58.3855        5.1        2.81602    41.3      40.0227
  12    1930       55.0       55.1831        1.0        2.31541    37.9      38.3029
  13    1931       50.9       51.4527       -3.4       -2.43118    34.5      34.2783
  14    1932       45.6       46.2653       -6.2       -4.89684    29.0      29.3708
  15    1933       46.5       45.9252       -5.1       -7.02343    28.5      28.1922
  16    1934       48.7       48.7199       -3.0       -2.88839    30.6      30.3293
  17    1935       51.3       51.2469       -1.3       -1.49144    33.2      33.1948
  18    1936       57.7       55.8499        2.1        0.15003    36.8      37.5202
  19    1937       58.7       59.1614        2.0        2.31113    41.0      40.0951
  20    1938       57.5       57.4375       -1.9        1.71054    38.2      39.0198
  21    1939       61.6       60.3477        1.3        0.55460    41.6      41.8709
  22    1940       65.0       64.0573        3.3        3.06668    45.0      46.0619
  23    1941       69.7       71.6568        4.9        3.98792    53.3      52.4212
```

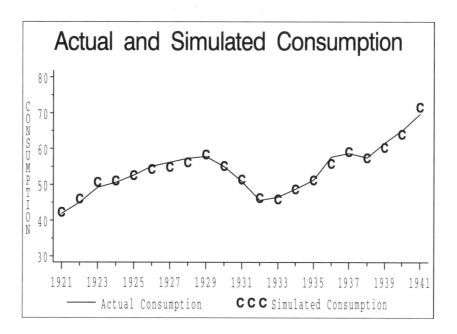

Interpretation of output

In Output 11.3, the actual and simulated values are listed for comparison. In the plot, the solid line represents the actual values, and the symbol C represents simulated values of consumption expenditures. The model simulates actual consumption expenditures very closely.

Printing and Plotting the Investment and Private Wages Simulated Values

You can also plot the simulated and actual values of the investment and private wages equations to assess how well the model simulates the actual data. The SAS statements to create these PROC GPLOT plots are very similar to those used to plot the consumption data and therefore are not shown. Output 11.4 shows the plots.

Output 11.4
Plotting the Actual and Simulated Values of the Investment and Private Wages Equations of the Klein Model 1

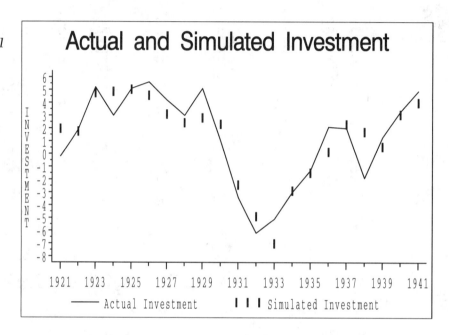

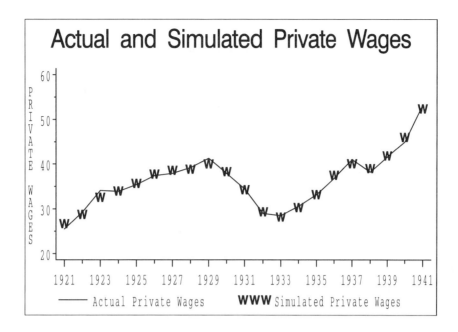

Interpretation of output

In the two plots of Output 11.4, the solid line represents the actual values, and the symbols I and W represent simulated values of investment expenditures and private wages. The model simulates the private wage values very closely; however, actual investment values are not simulated as well.

Using the Klein Model 1 for What-if Simulation

You can use the Klein Model 1 for what-if simulation (or policy experimentation). For example, by 1930 the Great Depression had reduced economic activity, specifically, consumption, investment, and private sector wages. You can create a what-if data set containing hypothetical values for private sector income, X, and profit, P. A simple approach is to let private sector income and profit grow at a rate similar to the 1920-through-1929 rate. What would have happened if private sector income and profit had continued to grow at a rate similar to the 1920-through-1929 rate?

To perform what-if simulation, you first create a what-if data set containing hypothetical values of private sector income and profit. Next, you merge the what-if data set with the KLEIN data set and plot the actual and simulated values. Finally, you simulate the model using PROC MODEL and the what-if data set.

Creating and Plotting What-if Data

This section shows you how to create a what-if data set, KL_SIM, and merge it with the original data for printing and plotting. The variables SIM_X and SIM_P are the what-if values of X and P. These variables are set to missing for observations prior to 1929. The following SAS example code performs these tasks. Output 11.5 shows the results.

```
data kl_sim;
   input year sim_x sim_p @@;
   cards;
1929 67.0 21.7 1930 69.1 24.6 1931 72.0 26.1 1932 74.9 27.7
1933 77.9 29.3 1934 81.1 31.1 1935 84.3 32.9 1936 87.7 34.9
1937 91.3 36.9 1938 94.9 39.1 1939 98.7 41.5 1940 102.7 44.0
1941 106.8 46.6
;

data klein_p1;
   merge klein kl_sim;
   by year;
run;

proc print data=klein_p1 (firstobs=10 obs=15);
   var year x sim_x p sim_p;
   title2 'Tenth-Fifteenth Observations';
   title3 'of KLEIN_P1 Data';
run;

proc plot data=klein_p1 vpct=60;
   plot x*year='A'
        sim_x*year='H' / overlay;
   title2 'Actual and What-If Simulation Values';
   title3 'Total Output of Private Industry';
run;

proc plot data=klein_p1 vpct=60;
   plot p*year='A'
        sim_p*year='H' / overlay;
   title2 'Actual and What-If Simulation Values';
   title3 'Profits';
run;
```

Output 11.5
Plotting the Actual and Hypothetical Values for What-if Simulation of the Klein Model 1

```
                   KLEIN Model 1 Example
                 Tenth-Fifteenth Observations
                      of KLEIN_P1 Data

       OBS    YEAR     X      SIM_X     P      SIM_P

        10    1928    64.5      .      21.1      .
        11    1929    67.0     67.0    21.7     21.7
        12    1930    61.2     69.1    15.6     24.6
        13    1931    53.4     72.0    11.4     26.1
        14    1932    44.3     74.9     7.0     27.7
        15    1933    45.1     77.9    11.2     29.3
```

(continued)

Output 11.5
(continued)

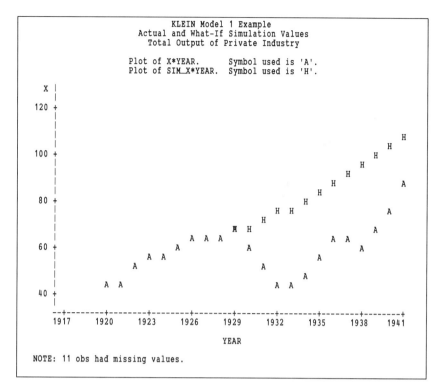

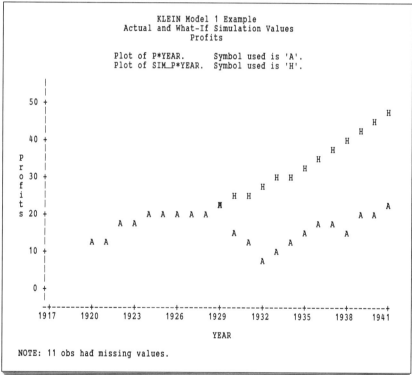

Interpretation of output

In the plots of Output 11.5, the symbol A represents the actual values, and the symbol H represents the hypothetical what-if values to be used in the what-if simulation. The growth rate of the actual values decreases. The what-if values grow throughout the period.

You may be concerned about future economic conditions and interested in predicting the future values of the endogenous variables using the hypothetical values of the exogenous variables. The next section shows you how to perform the what-if simulation.

Performing the What-if Simulation

You use PROC MODEL to perform what-if simulation of the Klein Model 1. Then, you can print and plot the simulated values. To perform the what-if simulation, follow these steps:

1. Update the KLEIN data set with the KL_SIM data set.
2. Perform the what-if simulation.
3. Merge the output data set, KL_OUT2, with the KLEIN data set.
4. Print the actual and simulated values of C, I, and WP.
5. Plot the actual and simulated values of C, I, and WP.

Only the SAS example code and output for the first of the three plots, actual and simulated values of consumption, is shown. The actual and simulated values of consumption, investment, and private wages are printed; the consumption values are plotted in Output 11.6. The model and solution summaries are not displayed. The investment and private wages plots are shown separately in Output 11.7.

```
    /* Updating the KLEIN Data Set */
data klein1;
    update klein kl_sim(rename=(sim_x=x sim_p=p));
    by year;
run;

    /* Performing the What-If Simulation */
proc model data=klein1 model=kl_mod noprint;
    solve c i wp / simulate start=2
                    out=kl_out2(rename=(c=sim_c2 i=sim_i2
                                        wp=sim_wp2));
run;

    /* Merging Data */
data klein_p2;
    merge klein kl_out2;
    by year;
    label sim_c2 = 'What-If Simulated C'
          sim_i2 = 'What-If Simulated I'
          sim_wp2 = 'What-If Simulated WP';
run;

    /* Printing Simulated Values */
proc print data=klein_p2 (firstobs=10) label;
    var year c sim_c2 i sim_i2 wp sim_wp2;
    title 'KLEIN Model 1 Example';
```

```
        title2 'What-If Simulated Values';
        title3;
    run;

    goptions reset=symbol;

        /* Plotting Simulated Values */
    proc gplot data=klein_p2;
        plot c*year=1
                sim_c2*year=2 / overlay hminor=1 vminor=1
                                haxis=axis1 vaxis=axis2 legend=legend1;
        symbol1 i=join l=1 color=black;
        symbol1 v=C font=swissb color=blue;
        axis1 label=none offset=(2,2)pct order=1921 to 1941 by 2;
        axis2 label=(a=-90 r=90 'CONSUMPTION');
        legend1 label=none value=('Actual Consumption'
                                  'What-If Consumption');
        title 'Actual and What-If Consumption';
    run;
    quit;
```

Output 11.6

Printing the Actual and What-if Simulated Values of the Klein Model 1, and Plotting the Actual and What-if Simulated Values for the Consumption Equation

OBS	YEAR	Consumer Expenditures	What-If Simulated C	Investment Expenditures	What-If Simulated I	Private Wage Bill	What-If Simulated WP
		KLEIN Model 1 Example					
		What-If Simulated Values					
10	1928	57.3	56.2021	3.0	2.4258	39.2	38.8535
11	1929	57.8	58.3855	5.1	2.8160	41.3	40.0227
12	1930	55.0	56.3187	1.0	2.2590	37.9	41.4666
13	1931	50.9	54.7636	-3.4	4.2325	34.5	43.1584
14	1932	45.6	51.2554	-6.2	6.0080	29.0	44.9951
15	1933	46.5	51.5580	-5.1	8.4015	28.5	46.8719
16	1934	48.7	54.0204	-3.0	10.5805	30.6	48.8469
17	1935	51.3	56.6732	-1.3	12.5023	33.2	50.8581
18	1936	57.7	61.0905	2.1	14.2288	36.8	52.9494
19	1937	58.7	64.4334	2.0	15.1745	41.0	55.1571
20	1938	57.5	63.6116	-1.9	16.2741	38.2	57.4010
21	1939	61.6	67.0373	1.3	18.2790	41.6	59.7249
22	1940	65.0	70.5870	3.3	19.8127	45.0	62.1652
23	1941	69.7	78.2764	4.9	21.0330	53.3	64.6818

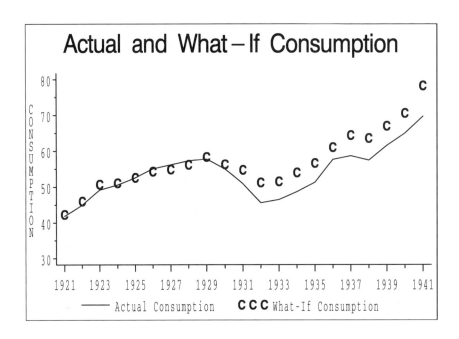

Interpretation of output

In the plot in Output 11.6, the solid line represents the actual values; the symbol C represents the what-if simulated values for consumption expenditures.

The what-if simulated values of the Klein Model 1 differ from the actual values beginning in 1930. You may want to compare these simulation values and this plot with Output 11.3.

Output 11.7

Plotting the Actual and What-if Simulated Values of the Investment and Private Wages Equations of the Klein Model 1

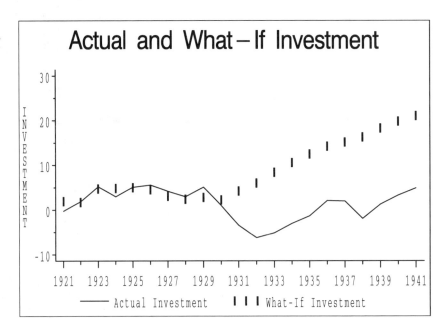

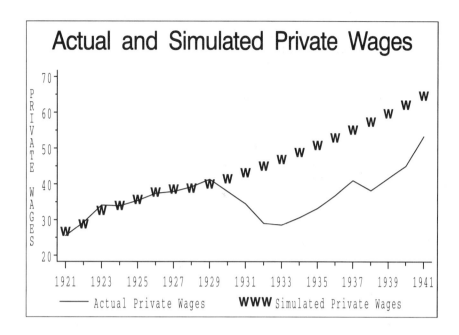

Interpretation of output

In the two plots in Output 11.7, the solid line represents the actual values; the symbols I and W represent the what-if simulated values for investment and private wages.

The what-if simulated values of the Klein Model 1 display a marked difference from the actual values beginning in 1930. You may want to compare these simulation values and plots with those of Output 11.4.

Using the Klein Model 1 for Goal Seeking

The Klein Model 1 can be used for goal seeking, that is, solving for values of a right-hand side variable given values of the remaining variables. For example, given the updated values of P and X in the KL_SIM data, what are the values of G that satisfy the product identity?

You use the KLEIN1 data set (created by updating the KLEIN data set with the KL_SIM data set) and a SOLVE statement in PROC MODEL to perform the goal-seeking simulation. The SATISFY= option of the SOLVE statement specifies that in the solution the X equation be satisfied. The following SAS statements generate Output 11.8. Only part of the output is shown. The model and solution summaries are not displayed.

```
    /* Performing Goal Seeking */
proc model data=klein1 model=kl_mod;
   solve g satisfy=x / simulate start=2
                    out=kl_out3(rename=(g=sim_g));
run;
```

```
                    /* Merging Data */
             data klein_p3;
                merge klein kl_out3;
                by year;
                label sim_g = 'Goal-Seeking G';
             run;

                    /* Printing Goal Seeking Values */
             proc print data=klein_p3 (firstobs=10) label;
                var year g sim_g;
                title2 'Actual and Goal-Seeking Values';
             run;
```

Output 11.8
Printing the Actual
and Goal-seeking
Values of the
Klein Model 1

```
                     KLEIN Model 1 Example
                  Actual and Goal-Seeking Values

                                             Goal
                                 Government  Seeking
             OBS    YEAR        Expenditures    G

             10     1928            4.2         4.2
             11     1929            4.1         4.1
             12     1930            5.2        13.1
             13     1931            5.9        24.5
             14     1932            4.9        35.5
             15     1933            3.7        36.5
             16     1934            4.0        35.4
             17     1935            4.4        34.3
             18     1936            2.9        27.9
             19     1937            4.3        30.6
             20     1938            5.3        39.3
             21     1939            6.6        35.8
             22     1940            7.4        34.4
             23     1941           13.8        32.2
```

Interpretation of output

In Output 11.8, the actual and goal-seeking values of G are listed. The goal-seeking values are the solved values of G, given the fitted model and the values of the remaining variables. In general, you can use goal seeking to solve for any right-hand side variables of interest.

For details on solution methods, see the *SAS/ETS User's Guide, Version 6, First Edition.*

Solving Simultaneous Equation Models

You may want to solve systems of linear equations. Models of the economy, supply and demand models, consumer behavior models, and input usage models are typical examples of such systems. These models may be deterministic models, derived from accounting techniques, or they may be models estimated and validated in previous studies.

In this section, you use the SOLVE statement in PROC MODEL to solve two simultaneous equation models: a supply-and-demand model and a profit model.

Solving a Supply-and-Demand Model

Suppose you have estimated supply and demand equations of the following form:

demand $\quad$ Q = 10000 − 11 P $\quad$ + 10 X

supply $\quad$ P = 40 $\quad$ + 0.07 Q − 0.5 Y

The demand equation is solved for quantity, Q, and the supply equation is solved for price, P. The variable X is a demand shifter, and the variable Y is a supply shifter.

Suppose you want to simulate this model for different values of X and Y. Changes in X reveal supply, while changes in Y reveal demand. By using relevant ranges of X and Y, you can solve the model for combinations of P and Q along the supply and demand schedules. You can also use the equations to solve for the equilibrium levels of P and Q, given the values of X and Y.

You can simulate this model by using the SOLVE statement of PROC MODEL and following these steps:

1. Create the SD data set.

2. Simulate the supply and demand schedules.

3. Print the simulated values of P and Q.

Part of the output generated by the following example code is displayed in Output 11.9. Only the solution values are displayed. The model and solution summaries are not displayed.

```
    /* Creating Values for X and Y */
data sd;
   q = .;
   p = .;
   do y=50 to 160 by 10;
      x = 100;
      id='D';
      output;
   end;
   do x=60 to 120 by 10;
      y = 125;
      id='S';
      output;
   end;
run;

    /* Simulating the Model */
proc model data=sd noprint;
      q = 10000 - 11*p + 10*x;
      p = 40 + 0.07*q - .5*y;
   endo q p;
   exo x y;
   solve q p / simulate out=sd_sim;
   id id;
run;
```

```
                    /* Printing the Simulated Values */
                proc print data=sd_sim;
                    var q p x y;
                    title 'General Supply and Demand Model Example';
                run;
```

Output 11.9
Simulating a
Supply-and-Demand
Model

```
                  General Supply and Demand Model Example

              OBS        Q         P        X       Y

                1      6121.47   443.503    100      50
                2      6152.54   440.678    100      60
                3      6183.62   437.853    100      70
                4      6214.69   435.028    100      80
                5      6245.76   432.203    100      90
                6      6276.84   429.379    100     100
                7      6307.91   426.554    100     110
                8      6338.98   423.729    100     120
                9      6370.06   420.904    100     130
               10      6401.13   418.079    100     140
               11      6432.20   415.254    100     150
               12      6463.28   412.429    100     160
               13      6128.53   406.497     60     125
               14      6185.03   410.452     70     125
               15      6241.53   414.407     80     125
               16      6298.02   418.362     90     125
               17      6354.52   422.316    100     125
               18      6411.02   426.271    110     125
               19      6467.51   430.226    120     125
```

Interpretation of output

In Output 11.9, the levels of price, P, and quantity, Q, are printed for the values of X and Y. The combinations of P and Q determine the demand and supply schedules. The points on the downward-sloping demand schedule are revealed as Y varies and X equals 100, as shown in observations 1 through 12. The points on the upward-sloping supply schedule are revealed as X varies and Y equals 125, as shown in observations 13 through 19.

Plotting the Supply and Demand Model

By plotting the simulated price and quantity points, the form of the supply and demand schedules can be more easily seen. The output generated by the following example code is displayed in Output 11.10:

```
proc plot data=sd_sim vpct=60;
    plot p*q=id;
    title2 'Plotting Supply and Demand Schedules';
run;
```

Output 11.10
Plotting the
Simulated Supply
and Demand
Model

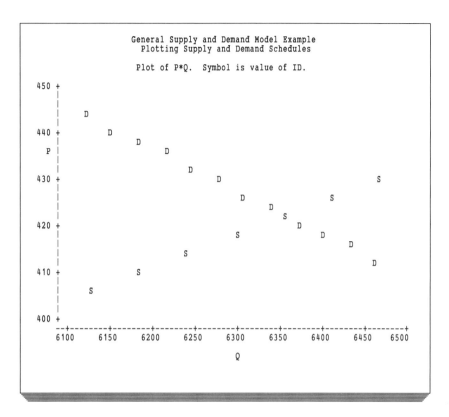

Interpretation of output

In Output 11.10, the values of price and quantity are plotted to show the form of the supply and demand schedules. The symbols D and S refer to points on the demand and supply schedules, respectively. As in Output 11.9, the demand schedule slopes downward, and the supply schedule slopes upward.

Introducing a Profit Model

Suppose you are the president of a firm that is planning to expand its operation into a new product line. If you decide to produce the new product, you have to hire additional employees and acquire new machines. In your decision-making process, you want to answer the following questions:

□   Is the new product line expected to be profitable?

□   What is the profit-maximizing quantity to produce?

□   What are profits expected to be?

□   How many workers, supervisors, and managers should be employed to maximize profit?

□   How many machines should be used to maximize profits?

You have studied the market and know the annual demand schedule is

PRICE = 550 − .0075 QUANTITY   .

You know that REVENUE is PRICE times QUANTITY:

$$\text{REVENUE} = 550\ \text{QUANTITY} - .0075\ \text{QUANTITY}^2 \ .$$

A \$100,000 permit is required to begin operation, and there is a \$100 tax for each unit sold. Thus, the tax schedule is

$$\text{TAX} = 100000 + 100\ \text{QUANTITY} \ .$$

REVENUE minus TAX equals net revenue, NET_REV:

$$\text{NET\_REV} = \text{REVENUE} - \text{TAX} \ .$$

Table 11.1 summarizes input requirements and their costs for different quantities of annual production.

Table 11.1
Input Requirements and Costs

| Inputs | Annual Production Quantity | | | Costs per |
	< 2,000	2,000–9,999	≥10,000	
Worker	Q/100	Q/100	Q/100	\$18,000
Supervisor	0	1/20 Workers	1/20 Workers	\$35,000
Manager	0	0	1/5 Supervisors	\$50,000
Machine 1	Q/500	Q/500	Q/500	\$12,000
Machine 2	0	0	Q/10,000	\$75,000
Fixed Costs	150,000	200,000	250,000	N/A

As shown in Table 11.1, production costs of labor and machines are step functions of QUANTITY. For example, you need one worker for every 100 units produced. As annual production reaches 2,000, you hire a supervisor for every 20 workers; as production reaches 10,000, you hire a manager for every 5 supervisors. The column labeled "Costs per" indicates that workers, supervisors, and managers have salaries of \$18,000, \$35,000, and \$50,000, respectively.

Note that the profit-maximizing quantity may imply hiring fractional numbers of workers, supervisors, and managers. Part-time employees could be hired for fractional units, or perhaps additional projects could be assigned. The profit-maximizing quantity may imply acquiring a fractional number of new machines. Perhaps machines can be leased for fractions of the year.

If quantity produced is less than 2,000 units, then your annual fixed costs of production are \$150,000. Fixed costs rise to \$200,000 if production is between 2,000 and 10,000 units, and they rise to \$250,000 if production is greater than 10,000 units.

Finally, profit is net revenues minus production costs, COST, or

$$\text{PROFIT} = \text{NET\_REV} - \text{COST} \ .$$

Creating the COST Data Set

You use a DATA step to create the COST data set and an iterative DO loop to create levels of quantity for analysis. The following statements create thousand-unit levels of quantity ranging from zero to 28,000.

```
data cost;
   cost = .;
   revenue = .;
   profit = .;
   do quantity=0 to 28000 by 1000;
      output;
   end;
run;
```

The remaining functions (REVENUE, TAX, NET_REV, COST, and PROFIT) can be defined with programming statements in PROC MODEL.

Solving the Profit Model

In PROC MODEL, you can define the REVENUE, TAX, NET_REV, and PROFIT functions with assignment statements. You can define the step function costs with IF-THEN/ELSE programming statements.

Part of the output generated by the following example code is displayed in Output 11.11. Only the solution values are shown. The model and solution summaries are not displayed.

```
proc model data=cost noprint;

   /* Defining the cost function */
   worker = quantity/100;
   if worker lt 20 then supervis = 0; else supervis = worker/20;
   if supervis lt 5 then manager = 0; else manager = supervis/5;
      machine1 = quantity/500;
   if machine1 lt 20 then machine2=0; else machine2 = quantity/10000;
   if quantity lt 2000
      then cost = 150000 + 18000*worker + 35000*supervis
                         + 50000*manager + 12000*machine1;
   if 2000 le quantity lt 10000
      then cost = 200000 + 18000*worker + 35000*supervis
                         + 50000*manager + 12000*machine1;
   if quantity ge 10000
      then cost = 250000 + 18000*worker + 35000*supervis
                 + 50000*manager + 12000*machine1 + 75000*machine2;

   /* Defining REVENUE, TAX, NET_REV, and PROFIT */
   revenue = 550*quantity - .0075*quantity**2;
   tax = 100000 + 100*quantity;
   net_rev = revenue - tax;
   profit = net_rev - cost;
```

```
                /* Solving the Model */
            endo cost revenue tax net_rev profit;
            exo quantity;
            solve revenue tax net_rev cost profit / simulate out=cst_sim;
         run;

                /* Printing Solution Values */
         proc print data=cst_sim;
            var quantity revenue tax net_rev cost profit;
            title 'Profit Model Example';
            title2 'Cost, Revenue, and Profit Simulation';
         run;
```

Output 11.11

Solving the Cost Model for Revenue, Tax, Net Revenue, Cost, and Profit

```
                              Profit Model Example
                        Cost, Revenue, and Profit Simulation

   OBS   QUANTITY    REVENUE      TAX      NET_REV      COST      PROFIT

    1         0           0     100000     -100000     150000    -250000
    2      1000      542500     200000      342500     354000     -11500
    3      2000     1070000     300000      770000     643000     127000
    4      3000     1582500     400000     1182500     864500     318000
    5      4000     2080000     500000     1580000    1086000     494000
    6      5000     2562500     600000     1962500    1307500     655000
    7      6000     3030000     700000     2330000    1529000     801000
    8      7000     3482500     800000     2682500    1750500     932000
    9      8000     3920000     900000     3020000    1972000    1048000
   10      9000     4342500    1000000     3342500    2193500    1149000
   11     10000     4750000    1100000     3650000    2590000    1060000
   12     11000     5142500    1200000     3942500    2824000    1118500
   13     12000     5520000    1300000     4220000    3058000    1162000
   14     13000     5882500    1400000     4482500    3292000    1190500
   15     14000     6230000    1500000     4730000    3526000    1204000
   16     15000     6562500    1600000     4962500    3760000    1202500
   17     16000     6880000    1700000     5180000    3994000    1186000
   18     17000     7182500    1800000     5382500    4228000    1154500
   19     18000     7470000    1900000     5570000    4462000    1108000
   20     19000     7742500    2000000     5742500    4696000    1046500
   21     20000     8000000    2100000     5900000    4930000     970000
   22     21000     8242500    2200000     6042500    5164000     878500
   23     22000     8470000    2300000     6170000    5398000     772000
   24     23000     8682500    2400000     6282500    5632000     650500
   25     24000     8880000    2500000     6380000    5866000     514000
   26     25000     9062500    2600000     6462500    6100000     362500
   27     26000     9230000    2700000     6530000    6334000     196000
   28     27000     9382500    2800000     6582500    6568000      14500
   29     28000     9520000    2900000     6620000    6802000    -182000
```

Interpretation of output

In Output 11.11, scan the listed variables and notice the following:

□ Profit is positive for quantities between 2,000 and 27,000 units.

□ Profit is maximized around 14,000 units.

□ Profit is $1,204,000 at 14,000 units.

You can conclude that the new product should be produced and that annual production should be set at 14,000 units.

Plotting the Net Revenue, Cost, and Profit Functions

As you examine the listing of net revenues and costs in Output 11.11, you see that both rise as quantity rises, but the rates of increase are difficult to assess. By plotting the net revenues and costs versus quantity, you see their levels and rates of change. By plotting the profit function, you see where it is positive in sign and where it is maximized.

For continuous functions, these points are found with differential calculus. For step functions, plotting the functions visually reveals their extrema and rates of change. You use PROC PLOT to create these plots. Output 11.12 shows the results.

```
proc plot data=cst_sim vpct=60;
   plot cost*quantity = 'c'
        net_rev*quantity = 'r' / overlay;
   title2 'Cost and Net Revenue versus Quantity';
run;

proc plot data=cst_sim vpct=60;
   plot profit*quantity = '*';
   title2 'Profit versus Quantity';
run;
```

Output 11.12
Plotting Cost and Net Revenue Versus Quantity and Profit Versus Quantity

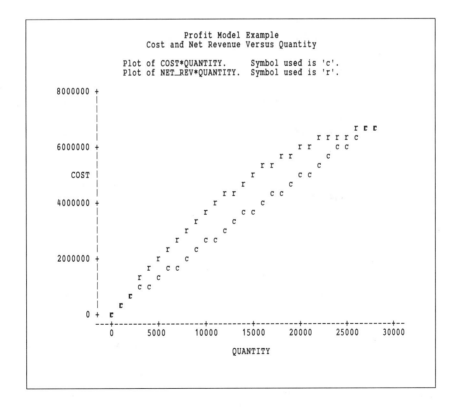

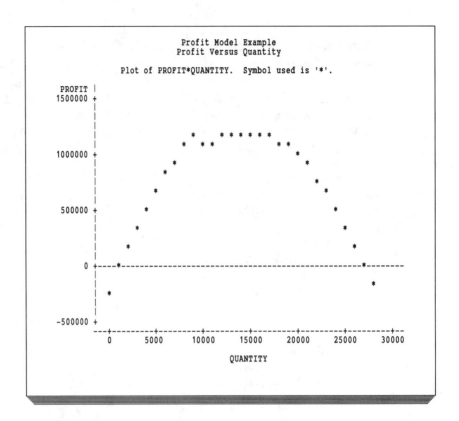

Interpretation of output

In Output 11.12, there are two plots. The first plot plots COST (represented by the symbol C) and NET_REV (represented by the symbol R) versus QUANTITY. As QUANTITY increases, both functions rise but at different rates. Profit is zero where cost equals net revenue and is positive where cost is less than net revenue. Profit is maximized where the positive difference between net revenue and cost is maximized.

The second plot plots PROFIT versus QUANTITY. In general, as QUANTITY increases PROFIT rises, peaks, and then declines.

Solving for the Input Usage Levels

You can solve for the input usage at all production levels using the SOLVE statement of PROC MODEL. The following SOLVE statement can replace the SOLVE statement in the SAS example code producing Output 11.11:

```
solve cost worker supervis manager machine1 machine2
      / simulate out=cst_sim1;
```

PROC PRINT lists the output data set, CST_SIM1. Output 11.13 shows the results.

```
proc print data=cst_sim1;
   var quantity worker supervis manager machine1 machine2;
   title2 'Input Usage Simulation';
run;
```

Output 11.13
Printing the Input
Usage

```
                        Profit Model Example
                        Input Usage Simulation

  OBS    QUANTITY    WORKER    SUPERVIS    MANAGER -   MACHINE1    MACHINE2

   1         0          0        0.0         0.0          0         0.0
   2       1000         10       0.0         0.0          2         0.0
   3       2000         20       1.0         0.0          4         0.0
   4       3000         30       1.5         0.0          6         0.0
   5       4000         40       2.0         0.0          8         0.0
   6       5000         50       2.5         0.0         10         0.0
   7       6000         60       3.0         0.0         12         0.0
   8       7000         70       3.5         0.0         14         0.0
   9       8000         80       4.0         0.0         16         0.0
  10       9000         90       4.5         0.0         18         0.0
  11      10000        100       5.0         1.0         20         1.0
  12      11000        110       5.5         1.1         22         1.1
  13      12000        120       6.0         1.2         24         1.2
  14      13000        130       6.5         1.3         26         1.3
  15      14000        140       7.0         1.4         28         1.4
  16      15000        150       7.5         1.5         30         1.5
  17      16000        160       8.0         1.6         32         1.6
  18      17000        170       8.5         1.7         34         1.7
  19      18000        180       9.0         1.8         36         1.8
  20      19000        190       9.5         1.9         38         1.9
  21      20000        200      10.0         2.0         40         2.0
  22      21000        210      10.5         2.1         42         2.1
  23      22000        220      11.0         2.2         44         2.2
  24      23000        230      11.5         2.3         46         2.3
  25      24000        240      12.0         2.4         48         2.4
  26      25000        250      12.5         2.5         50         2.5
  27      26000        260      13.0         2.6         52         2.6
  28      27000        270      13.5         2.7         54         2.7
  29      28000        280      14.0         2.8         56         2.8
```

Interpretation of output

In Output 11.13, the input usage for the range of quantities is printed. Workers
are hired at the rate of 1 per 100 quantity produced. One supervisor is hired
when there are at least 20 workers; thereafter, supervisors are hired at a rate of
1 per 20 workers. At the profit-maximizing quantity of 14,000 units, 7
supervisors are hired. Similarly, 1 manager is hired when there are 5
supervisors; thereafter, managers are hired at a rate of 1 per 5 supervisors. At
the profit-maximizing quantity, 1.4 managers are hired. A part-time manager
could be hired for the required fraction, or perhaps additional projects could be
assigned.

At the profit-maximizing level of production, 28 MACHINE1's and 1.4
MACHINE2's should be acquired.

Chapter Summary

This chapter discussed simulation of linear simultaneous equation models. You can
simulate and solve for any variable of interest on the left-hand or right-hand sides
of model equations. The models were simulated with actual data and with an
alternative data set for what-if and goal-seeking simulations. For comparison, the
actual and simulated values were listed and plotted. Plots were also used to show
the form of the simulated equations.

This chapter also presented an example of a profit model. This example
showed you how to use simulation techniques to help solve important business
problems and make profit-maximizing decisions.

Learning More

□ For full reference information on PROC MODEL, see the *SAS/ETS User's Guide, Version 6, First Edition.*

□ For full reference information on PROC GPLOT, see *SAS/GRAPH Software, Reference, Version 6, First Edition, Volume 1* and *Volume 2* and *SAS/GRAPH Software, Usage, Version 6, First Edition.*

□ For full reference information on PROC PLOT, see the *SAS Procedures Guide, Version 6, Third Edition.*

References

Klein, L.R. (1950), *Economic Fluctuations in the United States 1921—41*, New York: John Wiley & Sons, Inc.

Maddala, G.S. (1977), *Econometrics*, New York: McGraw-Hill, Inc.

Chapter **12** Simulating Nonlinear Equations

Introduction

This chapter discusses simulation of nonlinear equations. Once you have estimated a model, you can perform simulations with historical and what-if data and use them for goal-seeking simulations. Additionally, you can perform Monte Carlo simulations to generate distributions for predictions and simulations.

In this chapter, you use the MODEL procedure in SAS/ETS software to simulate (or solve) nonlinear models, perform historical and what-if simulations, and perform goal-seeking and Monte Carlo simulations.

Simulating a Nonlinear Equation

You may want to simulate fitted nonlinear models to better understand their properties. By simulating with historical data, you can benchmark the model's simulation properties. If the model is then used for what-if simulation and goal-seeking simulation, you will understand its simulation accuracy better.

In this section, a model of personal computers (PC) dispersion is used for historical simulation, goal-seeking simulation, and Monte Carlo simulation. The PC dispersion model is developed in Chapter 7, "Fitting Nonlinear Models."

The growth of PC use in U.S. elementary schools is modeled as a logistic curve. The fitted model is of the form

$$\text{PERCENT} = \frac{a}{1 + e^{b+c\text{YR}}} + \varepsilon$$

where e is the base of natural logarithms and the variables are as follows:

YR   is time in years (since 1980).

PERCENT   is the percentage of U.S. elementary schools with PCs.

The variables PERCENT and YR are contained in the PC data set introduced in Chapter 7. The following statements print the PC data set and produce Output 12.1:

```
proc print data=pc label;
   var yr percent;
   title 'Logistic Curve Example';
   title2 'PC Data';
run;
```

Output 12.1
Values of
PERCENT and YR
in the PC Data Set

```
                     Logistic Curve Example
                            PC Data

                              Percent of
                              Elementary
                                Schools
            OBS    YR         with PCs

             1     81          11.1
             2     82          20.2
             3     83          62.4
             4     84          82.2
             5     85          91.0
             6     86          94.9
             7     87          96.0
             8     88          96.8
```

Performing the Historical Simulation

A first step is to simulate with historical data. Goodness-of-fit and Theil statistics, which you can produce with PROC MODEL, measure how well the model simulates.

You can perform historical simulation of the PC dispersion model with the SOLVE statement of PROC MODEL. The following statements produce Output 12.2:

PROC MODEL
          invokes the MODEL procedure. The following options of the PROC MODEL statement are specified:

DATA=   requests that the PC data set be used as input.

MODEL=   specifies the model file, PC_MOD, containing the fitted model. Note that the PC_MOD file was created in Output 7.7.

SOLVE

specifies that the model be simulated or forecast for input data values. The following options of the SOLVE statement are specified:

SIMULATE   specifies that the solution of the model is a simulation.

STATS   prints the goodness-of-fit statistics.

THEIL   prints the Theil inequality coefficients.

OUT=   creates an output data set, PC_SIM1.

RENAME   renames the simulated values, SIM_P1.

```
proc model data=pc model=pc_mod;
   solve percent / simulate stats theil
                 out=pc_sim1(rename=(percent=sim_p1));
run;
```

Output 12.2 displays part of the output generated by the previous example code. The model and solution summaries are not shown. Only the goodness-of-fit and Theil statistics are displayed.

Output 12.2
Goodness-of-Fit and Theil Statistics of the Historical Simulation of the PC Dispersion Model

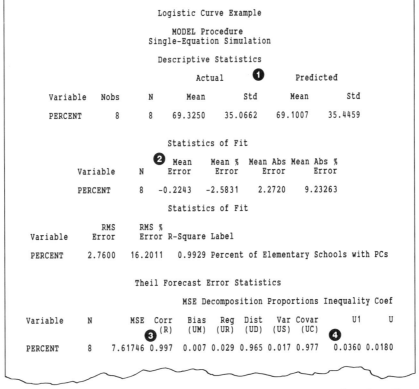

```
                           Logistic Curve Example

                             MODEL Procedure
                        Single-Equation Simulation

                           Descriptive Statistics

                            Actual      ❶        Predicted

        Variable   Nobs   N    Mean       Std      Mean      Std

        PERCENT     8     8   69.3250   35.0662   69.1007   35.4459


                            Statistics of Fit

                         ❷ Mean    Mean %  Mean Abs Mean Abs %
             Variable    N  Error    Error    Error     Error

             PERCENT     8  -0.2243  -2.5831  2.2720    9.23263

                            Statistics of Fit

                    RMS    RMS %
        Variable    Error  Error  R-Square Label

        PERCENT    2.7600  16.2011  0.9929  Percent of Elementary Schools with PCs


                      Theil Forecast Error Statistics

                           MSE Decomposition Proportions   Inequality Coef

        Variable   N    MSE  Corr  Bias  Reg  Dist  Var  Covar   U1     U
                             ❸(R)   (UM)  (UR) (UD)  (US) (UC)   ❹

        PERCENT    8  7.61746 0.997 0.007 0.029 0.965 0.017 0.977  0.0360 0.0180
```

(continued)

Output 12.2
(continued)

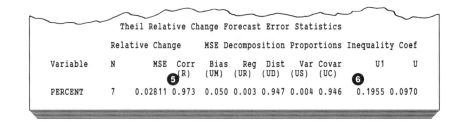

		Theil Relative Change Forecast Error Statistics								
		Relative Change		MSE Decomposition Proportions					Inequality Coef	
Variable	N	MSE	Corr (R) ❺	Bias (UM)	Reg (UR)	Dist (UD)	Var (US)	Covar (UC)	U1 ❻	U
PERCENT	7	0.02811	0.973	0.050	0.003	0.947	0.004	0.946	0.1955	0.0970

Interpretation of output

In Output 12.2, the goodness-of-fit and Theil statistics indicate that the model simulates well. Note the following:

❶ The predicted mean and standard deviation are very close in magnitude to the corresponding actual values.

❷ The mean error, −.2243, and mean percent error, −2.5831, are close to zero. The negative sign indicates that, on average, the model tends to underestimate the actual values. On the other hand, the mean absolute error, 2.2720, and the mean absolute percent error, 9.23263, are larger.

❸ The regression of the actual values on the simulated values has a mean square error (MSE) of 7.61746, which can be compared with the historical simulations of other models. The correlation, R, of .997 is close to the ideal value of 1.0.

❹ The Theil U1 and U statistics are close to the ideal value of zero. Their decompositions have DIST and COVAR components near the ideal value of one, and the BIAS, REG, and VAR components are close to the ideal value of zero.

❺ The regression of the percentage change of the actual values on the percentage change of the previous actual value to the next simulated value produces the Relative Change Forecast Statistics. The regression has an MSE of 0.02811. The correlation, R, of .973 is close to the ideal value of 1.0.

❻ The Theil Relative Change Forecast Error Statistics, U1 and U, are .1955 and .0970. Their decompositions have DIST and COVAR components near the ideal value of one, and the BIAS, REG, and VAR components are close to zero.

Based on these statistics, you conclude that the fitted model closely simulates the actual data.

Printing and Plotting the Simulated Values

You can compare the actual and simulated values when you print and plot them. Printing enables you to make a direct comparison. Plotting the simulated and actual values enables you to make a visual assessment of the model's ability to simulate the historical data.

Before printing and plotting the actual and simulated values, you must merge the output data set, PC_SIM1, which contains the simulated values, and the PC data set, which contains the actual values. You can then use the GPLOT procedure in SAS/GRAPH software to plot the actual and simulated values versus YEAR.

The PROC GPLOT statements have been interpreted in previous chapters; for example, see the SAS example code that produces Output 7.2.

```
    /* Merging Data */
data pc_p;
   merge pc pc_sim1;
   by yr;
   label sim_p1 = 'Simulated PERCENT';
run;

    /* Printing Actual and Simulated Values */
proc print data=pc_p label;
   var yr percent sim_p1;
   title 'Logistic Curve Example';
   title2 'PC_SIM1 Data';
run;

goptions reset=symbol;

    /* Plotting Actual and Simulated Values */
proc gplot data=pc_p;
   plot percent*yr=1
        sim_p1*yr=2 / overlay hminor=0 vminor=3 haxis=axis1
                      vaxis=axis2;
   symbol1 v=A font=swissb color=black;
   symbol2 i=join font=swissb l=3 color=blue;
   axis1 offset=(3) order=(81 to 88 by 1);
   axis2 label=(angle=90 'Percent of Schools')
         order=(0 to 100 by 10);
   title 'Personal Computer Use';
   title2 'Actual and Simulated';
run;
quit;
```

Output 12.3 displays the output generated by the above example code.

Output 12.3
Printing and Plotting the Actual and Simulated Values

```
                        Logistic Curve Example
                       Actual and Simulated Values

                              Percent of
                              Elementary
                                Schools        Simulated
              OBS    YR        with PCs         PERCENT

               1     81          11.1           6.7184
               2     82          20.2          24.7097
               3     83          62.4          58.8996
               4     84          82.2          84.1340
               5     85          91.0          92.7473
               6     86          94.9          94.8522
               7     87          96.0          95.3212
               8     88          96.8          95.4234
```

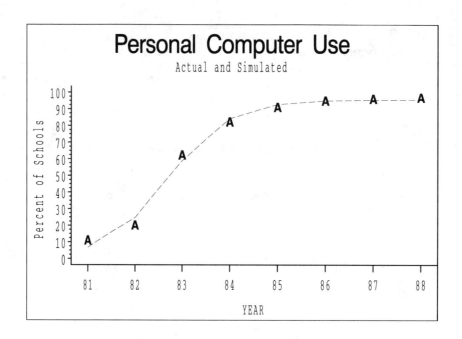

Interpretation of output

In Output 12.3, the printed and plotted values can be compared directly and
visually. In the plot, the actual values are represented by the symbol A. The
simulated values are connected by a dashed line. The simulated values have a
more rapid growth than the actual values from 1981 to 1982 and slower growth
from 1982 to 1983. Otherwise, the simulated values are close to the actual values.
The plot confirms the conclusions drawn from the goodness-of-fit and Theil
statistics of Output 12.2.

Performing Monte Carlo Simulations

Monte Carlo simulations are repeated simulations with random perturbations of
the endogenous variable solutions. Monte Carlo simulations generate distributions
of the simulated values. You can use these distributions to assess normality and to
determine the means, standard deviations, and percentiles.

The OUTS= option of the FIT statement outputs the errors covariance matrix
to a data set for later use. The following FIT statement outputs a covariance of
equation errors to the data set PC_S.

```
fit percent / outs=pc_s;
```

You can then use the OUTS= data set for random perturbations in a SOLVE
statement with the SDATA= option. The following SOLVE statement recalls the
covariance matrix of equation errors:

```
solve percent / sdata=pc_s;
```

You can use the following options to perform Monte Carlo simulation on the PC dispersion model:

SDATA=   specifies a data set that contains the covariance matrix of the equation errors.

RANDOM=   repeats the solution a specified number of times. For this example, the model is simulated 100 times. The default value is zero, which the random-number generators return as zero, or no perturbation.

SEED=   specifies a seed to use in generating pseudo-random numbers to perturb the model. Note the SEED= option is only valid if the RANDOM= option is also specified. The default is SEED=0. The six-digit seed used in this example was found in a random number table. Specifying a seed greater than zero enables you to replicate the Monte Carlo simulation exactly.

The following SAS example code performs these steps:

```
    /* Fitting the Model */
proc model data=pc outmodel=pc_mod;
    parms a b c;
        percent = a/(1 + exp(b + c*year));
    fit percent start=(a=100 b=100 10 c=-.5 -1 -1.5) /
            converge=.0001 method=marquardt outs=pc_s noprint;
    id yr;
run;

    /* Performing Monte Carlo Simulations */
proc model data=pc model=pc_mod noprint;
    solve percent / sdata=pc_s random=100 seed=174596
                    out=pc_sim2(drop=_type_ _mode_ _errors_
                    rename=(percent=sim_p2));
run;

    /* Printing Simulated Values */
proc print data=pc_sim2 (obs=24) label;
    var _rep_ yr sim_p2;
    title2 'Monte Carlo Simulations, Partial Listing';
run;
```

Output 12.4 displays part of the output generated by the above example code. The model and solution summaries are not shown. Only the first three replications are shown.

Output 12.4
Printing the Monte Carlo Simulated Values

```
                    Logistic Curve Example
            Monte Carlo Simulations, Partial Listing

                                            Percent of
                                            Elementary
                         Replication          Schools
              OBS          Number      YR    with PCs

               1             0         81       6.718
               2             0         82      24.710
```

(continued)

Output 12.4
(continued)

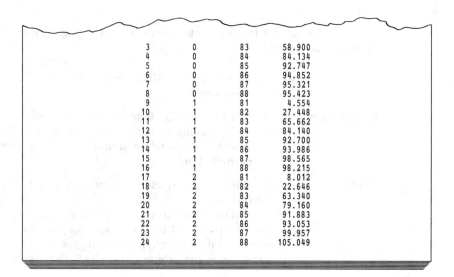

3	0	83	58.900
4	0	84	84.134
5	0	85	92.747
6	0	86	94.852
7	0	87	95.321
8	0	88	95.423
9	1	81	4.554
10	1	82	27.448
11	1	83	65.662
12	1	84	84.140
13	1	85	92.700
14	1	86	93.986
15	1	87	98.565
16	1	88	98.215
17	2	81	8.012
18	2	82	22.646
19	2	83	63.340
20	2	84	79.160
21	2	85	91.883
22	2	86	93.053
23	2	87	99.957
24	2	88	105.049

Interpretation of output

In Output 12.4, the observations with the Replication Number of zero are the
deterministic solutions. The observations with a Replication Number greater than
zero are those from perturbed solutions.

The deterministic solution for 1981 is 6.718. The two perturbed solutions are
4.554 and 8.012. A larger number of replications creates a distribution of values
from which a mean, a standard deviation, and percentiles can be calculated.

Printing Summary Statistics

You may be interested in calculating summary statistics for the distributions of the
Monte Carlo simulations for each year. For example, you might want to compare
the mean of the distribution of the Monte Carlo simulations with the historical
(deterministic) simulations. If they are equivalent, then the mean of the Monte
Carlo simulations has converged to the mean of the historical simulations. You
may also want the standard deviation of the distribution and the standard error of
the mean of the distribution.

After using the SORT procedure to sort the observations by YR, you can use
the MEANS procedure to calculate summary statistics for the distributions of the
Monte Carlo simulations for each year. An OUTPUT statement places these
statistics in an output data set, PC_SIM4. The following statements print the
actual and deterministic simulation values, the mean (MEAN), the standard
deviation (STD), and the standard error of the mean, STDERR.

```
    /* Sorting Data */
proc sort data=pc_sim2 out=pc_sim3;
   by yr;
run;

    /* Calculating Summary Statistics */
proc means data=pc_sim3 noprint;
   var sim_p2;
   by yr;
   output out=pc_sim4 mean=mean std=std stderr=stderr;
run;
```

```
    /* Merging Data */
data pc2;
    merge pc pc_sim1 pc_sim4;
    by yr;
run;

    /* Printing Summary Statistics */
proc print data=pc2;
    var yr percent sim_p1 mean std stderr;
    title2 'Summary Statistics';
    title3 'of Monte Carlo Simulations';
run;
```

Output 12.5 displays the output generated by the above example code.

Output 12.5
Printing Summary
Statistics of the
Monte Carlo
Simulated Values

```
                        Logistic Curve Example
                          Summary Statistics
                       of Monte Carlo Simulations

        OBS   YR   PERCENT   SIM_P1    MEAN      STD      STDERR

         1    81    11.1     6.7184    6.1507   3.25365   0.32375
         2    82    20.2    24.7097   24.0251   3.35286   0.33362
         3    83    62.4    58.8996   58.8070   3.61088   0.35930
         4    84    82.2    84.1340   83.9859   3.70704   0.36886
         5    85    91.0    92.7473   92.4791   3.53728   0.35197
         6    86    94.9    94.8522   94.7071   3.59112   0.35733
         7    87    96.0    95.3212   95.0743   3.42921   0.34122
         8    88    96.8    95.4234   94.4434   3.48084   0.34636
```

Interpretation of output

Output 12.5 lists the year, the actual and simulated values, the mean, the standard deviation, and the standard error of the Monte Carlo simulations. Note how closely the mean of the Monte Carlo simulations, MEAN, approximates the simulated values, SIM_P1.

Testing for Normality of Monte Carlo Simulations

You may want to test whether the simulation distributions are normally distributed. You can use the UNIVARIATE procedure to test for normality and to calculate percentiles of the distribution. The statements used in this example are interpreted as follows:

PROC UNIVARIATE
    invokes the UNIVARIATE procedure with the following options:

DATA=   specifies PC_SIM3 as the input data set.

NORMAL   tests whether the sample distribution follows a normal distribution. If the sample size is less than or equal to 2000, this is the Shapiro-Wilk statistic; otherwise, it is the Kolmogorov statistic.

VAR

> specifies the variables by which to perform separate analyses. In this example, the variable SIM_P2 is specified.

BY

> specifies separate analyses on observations in groups defined by the BY variable or variables. In this example, the BY variable is YR.

OUTPUT

> saves summary statistics in a new data set. The following options are included:

> OUT=
>> specifies the name of the output data set. In this example, the output data set is PC_SIM5.

> P5=
>> specifies that the fifth percentile be included in the output data set. In this example, the fifth percentile is P5.

> MEAN=
>> specifies that the mean be included in the output data set. In this example, the mean is MEAN.

> P95=
>> specifies that the ninety-fifth percentile be included in the output data set. In this example, the ninety-fifth percentile is P95.

The fifth and ninety-fifth percentiles and mean values are used in a later example.

```
proc univariate data=pc_sim3 normal;
   var sim_p2;
   by yr;
   output out=pc_sim5 p5=p5 mean=mean p95=p95;
   title 'Logistic Curve Example';
   title2 'Testing for Normality';
   title3;
run;
```

Output 12.6 displays part of the output generated by the above example code. Only the years 1982 and 1983 are shown.

Output 12.6
Testing the Distribution of Monte Carlo Simulations for Normality

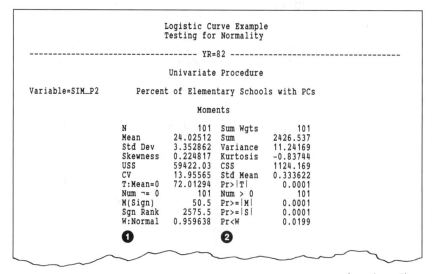

```
                          Logistic Curve Example
                          Testing for Normality
-------------------------------- YR=82 --------------------------------
                            Univariate Procedure

Variable=SIM_P2       Percent of Elementary Schools with PCs

                              Moments

               N              101   Sum Wgts         101
               Mean       24.02512  Sum          2426.537
               Std Dev    3.352862  Variance     11.24169
               Skewness   0.224817  Kurtosis     -0.83744
               USS        59422.03  CSS          1124.169
               CV         13.95565  Std Mean     0.333622
               T:Mean=0   72.01294  Pr>|T|         0.0001
               Num ¬= 0        101  Num > 0          101
               M(Sign)        50.5  Pr>=|M|        0.0001
               Sgn Rank     2575.5  Pr>=|S|        0.0001
               W:Normal   0.959638  Pr<W           0.0199
               ❶                    ❷
```

(continued)

Output 12.6
(continued)

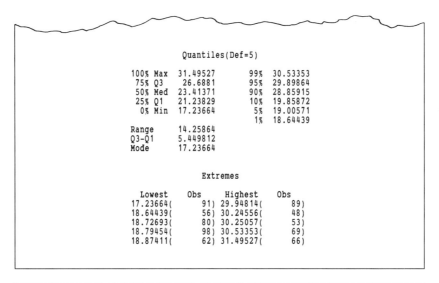

```
                        Quantiles(Def=5)

            100% Max   31.49527      99%  30.53353
             75% Q3    26.6881       95%  29.89864
             50% Med   23.41371      90%  28.85915
             25% Q1    21.23829      10%  19.85872
              0% Min   17.23664       5%  19.00571
                                      1%  18.64439
            Range      14.25864
            Q3-Q1       5.449812
            Mode       17.23664


                           Extremes

            Lowest     Obs     Highest     Obs
            17.23664(   91)    29.94814(    89)
            18.64439(   56)    30.24556(    48)
            18.72693(   80)    30.25057(    53)
            18.79454(   98)    30.53353(    69)
            18.87411(   62)    31.49527(    66)
```

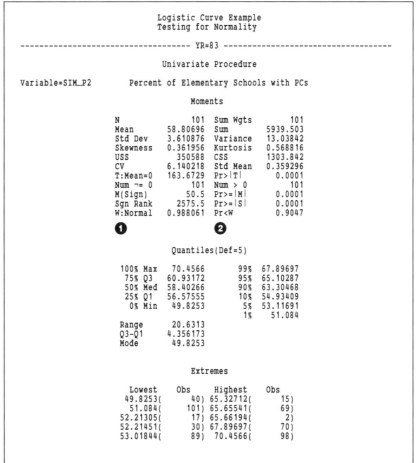

```
                     Logistic Curve Example
                      Testing for Normality

------------------------------ YR=83 ------------------------------

                       Univariate Procedure

Variable=SIM_P2     Percent of Elementary Schools with PCs

                           Moments

       N              101   Sum Wgts          101
       Mean      58.80696   Sum          5939.503
       Std Dev   3.610876   Variance     13.03842
       Skewness  0.361956   Kurtosis     0.568816
       USS         350588   CSS          1303.842
       CV        6.140218   Std Mean     0.359296
       T:Mean=0  163.6729   Pr>|T|         0.0001
       Num ¬= 0       101   Num > 0           101
       M(Sign)       50.5   Pr>=|M|        0.0001
       Sgn Rank    2575.5   Pr>=|S|        0.0001
       W:Normal  0.988061   Pr<W           0.9047
          ❶                     ❷

                        Quantiles(Def=5)

            100% Max   70.4566       99%  67.89697
             75% Q3    60.93172      95%  65.10287
             50% Med   58.40266      90%  63.30468
             25% Q1    56.57555      10%  54.93409
              0% Min   49.8253        5%  53.11691
                                      1%   51.084
            Range      20.6313
            Q3-Q1       4.356173
            Mode       49.8253


                           Extremes

            Lowest     Obs     Highest     Obs
            49.8253(    40)    65.32712(    15)
            51.084(    101)    65.65541(    69)
            52.21305(   17)    65.66194(     2)
            52.21451(   30)    67.89697(    70)
            53.01844(   89)    70.4566(     98)
```

Interpretation of output

Output 12.6 shows the results of PROC UNIVARIATE analyses for 1982 and 1983. The items of interest are ❶ the Shapiro-Wilk test statistic, W: NORMAL,

and ❷ its *p* value, PR<W. These items are numbered and listed last in the
columns of the section labeled Moments.

For 1982, the Shapiro-Wilk test statistic is .959638, and it has an associated *p*
value of .0199. The null hypothesis for the Shapiro-Wilk test is that the input data
are a random sample from a normal distribution. At the .05 level of significance,
you reject the null hypothesis and conclude that the 1982 simulations are not a
random sample from a normal distribution. For 1983, the test statistic is
.988061, and it has an associated *p* value of .9047. At levels of significance below
.9047, you retain the null hypothesis and conclude that this is a random sample
from a normal distribution at the .05 level of significance.

For a complete description of the statistics produced by PROC UNIVARIATE
and the Shapiro-Wilk test, see Chapter 42, "The UNIVARIATE Procedure," in the
SAS Procedures Guide, Version 6, Third Edition.

Finally, you may want to increase the number of Monte Carlo simulations.
More simulations may result in distributions that are closer to normal
distributions.

Printing and Plotting the Distribution Percentiles

Printing the percentiles of the Monte Carlo simulations and the actual values
enables you to compare them directly. Plotting the percentiles of the Monte Carlo
simulations and the actual values gives a nonparametric confidence interval. You
use PROC GPLOT to plot the fifth and ninety-fifth confidence intervals of the
simulations and the actual values versus YR.

To print and plot these values, first merge the sorted OUTPUT data set,
PC_SIM5, with the PC data set. Then, print the values with PROC PRINT and
plot them with PROC GPLOT.

```
    /* Merging Data */
data pc3;
   merge pc_sim5 pc;
   by yr;
run;

    /* Printing Data */
proc print data=pc3;
   var yr p5 mean percent p95;
   title 'Logistic Curve Example';
   title2 'Actual Values, Mean, and Percentiles';
run;

goptions reset=symbol;

    /* Plotting Data */
proc gplot data=pc3;
   plot p5*year=1
        percent*year=2
        p95*year=3 / overlay haxis=axis1 hminor=1
                     vaxis=axis2 vminor=1 legend=legend1;
   symbol1 v=L font=swissb color=black;
   symbol2 i=join l=1 color=blue;
   symbol3 v=H font=swissb color=green;
```

```
axis1 label=('YEAR in 1980s') offset=(2,2)pct order=1 to 8;
axis2 label=(a=-90 r=90 'PERCENT');
legend1 label=none value=('Fifth Percentile'
                          'Actual PC Dispersion'
                          'Ninety-Fifth Percentile');
title 'PC Dispersion with Percentiles 5 and 95;
run;
```

Output 12.7 displays the output generated by the above example code.

Output 12.7
Plotting the Actual Values, and the Fifth and Ninety-Fifth Percentiles versus YEAR

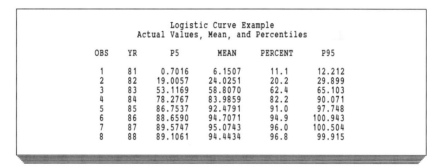

```
                      Logistic Curve Example
                 Actual Values, Mean, and Percentiles

    OBS    YR      P5        MEAN     PERCENT      P95

     1     81     0.7016    6.1507     11.1      12.212
     2     82    19.0057   24.0251     20.2      29.899
     3     83    53.1169   58.8070     62.4      65.103
     4     84    78.2767   83.9859     82.2      90.071
     5     85    86.7537   92.4791     91.0      97.748
     6     86    88.6590   94.7071     94.9     100.943
     7     87    89.5747   95.0743     96.0     100.504
     8     88    89.1061   94.4434     96.8      99.915
```

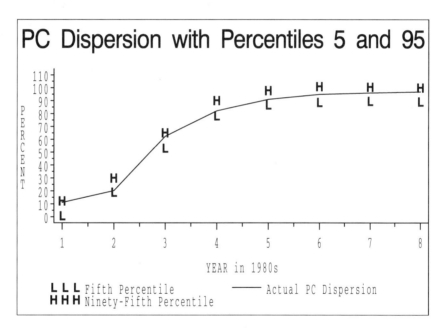

Interpretation of output

In Output 12.7, the fifth and ninety-fifth percentiles of the Monte Carlo simulated values and the actual values are printed and plotted versus YR. The symbols, L and H, represent the fifth and ninety-fifth percentiles, respectively. The solid line represents the actual values.

The printed values and the plot corroborate the findings of the normality tests in Output 12.5. For example, in 1982 the percentiles are not symmetric about the actual value; they are biased upwards. In 1986, the percentiles are more nearly symmetric about the actual value.

Performing Goal-seeking Simulation

Goal-seeking simulation is solving for an exogenous variable given the fitted model and values of the remaining variables. You can find goal-seeking solutions for linear equations in most cases. Goal-seeking solutions for nonlinear equations are not guaranteed to be successful. The solution algorithms may experience difficulties from the convergence criteria, the number of iterations, and given the starting values, discontinuities in the derivatives of the model.

The following section takes you through a goal-seeking example with the nonlinear PC dispersion model.

Goal-seeking Simulation Example

Perhaps you want to use the PC dispersion model to find the time at which exactly 50% of the U.S. elementary schools had PCs. The PC dispersion model has been shown to fit the actual data quite well (with an R^2 of .9929) and to simulate the historical data well (see Output 12.1); thus, you might expect little difficulty in performing a goal-seeking simulation.

To perform this goal-seeking example, first create an input data set, SIM_PC, and then use PROC MODEL and the fitted model to solve for the year. If you do not provide a starting value for YEAR, then PROC MODEL uses a default starting value of .0001, which may cause problems. A good starting guess for the year in which PERCENT equaled 50 is found in the PC data set, mid-year in 1982, or 82.5.

You can also change the convergence criteria with the CONVERGE= option. This starting guess should be very close to the actual value; thus, a convergence criteria of 1E−12 is specified.

This goal-seeking simulation example includes 82.5 as the starting value in the SIM_PC data set and uses the CONVERGE= option in the SOLVE statement.

```
    /* Creating the Input Data Set, PC_GOAL */
data pc_goal;
   input yr percent @@;
   year=yr-80;
   cards;
82.5 50
;

    /* Performing Goal-Seeking Simulation */
proc model data=sim_pc model=pc_mod noprint;
   solve year satisfy=percent / converge=1E-12
                              out=pc_goal1(rename=
                                         (percent=pc_gs));
run;

    /* Printing Solution Values */
proc print data=pc_goal1;
   var yr pc_gs;
   title 'Logistic Curve Example';
   title2 'Goal-Seeking Solutions';
run;
```

Output 12.8 displays the output generated by the above example code.

Output 12.8
Printing the
Goal-seeking
Simulation

```
                        Logistic Curve Example
                        Goal-seeking Solution

                   OBS        YR        PC_GS

                    1      82.7503       50
```

Interpretation of output

In Output 12.8, convergence is achieved, and the goal-seeking solution is
YR=82.7503. This solution suggests that 50% of the U.S. elementary schools had
PCs by October 1982.

Solving Nonlinear Equations

Economists frequently work with cost functions, present value models (PV
models), and growth models. When these models are expressed as polynomial
equations, the roots of the equation yield internal rates of return for PV models
and growth rates for growth models.

In this section, three models are introduced and used for simulation. The
models are a cubic cost function, a present value model, and an income growth
rate model.

A Cubic Cost Function

Suppose you are an industrial engineer or a cost analyst for a large manufacturing
firm. You are asked to find the maximum quantity that can be produced from a
given budget. Using historical data, you estimate a cost function as a cubic
equation in terms of quantity, Q. The function is as follows:

$$COST = 10000 + 20Q - .35Q^2 + .0025Q^3$$

The following code produces a plot of the cost curve. The DATA step creates a
range of values for Q and COST. The PLOT procedure is used to plot COST
versus Q.

```
    /* Creating the CUBIC Data Set */
data cubic;
   do q=0 to 100 by 2;
   cost=10000 + 20*q - .35*q**2 + .0025*q**3;
   output;
   end;
run;

    /* Plotting the Cost Function */
proc plot data=cubic vpct=60;
   plot cost*q;
   title 'Cubic Cost Function Example';
   title2 'Cost versus Quantity';
run;
```

Output 12.9 displays the output generated by the previous example code.

Output 12.9
Plotting the Cubic
Cost Function

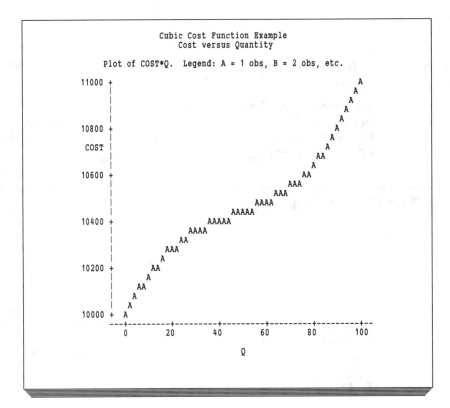

Interpretation of output

In Output 12.9, the cubic cost function is a curve with one inflection point and two bends. Initially, costs rise quickly as Q increases (from 0 to 40), then slowly (from 40 to 80), and finally, quickly again (from 80 onward). The economic justification for the cubic form of cost function is that there is an efficient range of production for a given production process. The efficient range of production is where costs are rising more slowly.

Simulating the Cost Cubic Function

Suppose you are asked, "Given our current production process and input costs, what are the maximum quantities, Q, that can be produced for costs of \$10,250, \$10,500, \$10,750, and \$11,000?" This is a goal-seeking problem that you can solve using a DATA step and the SOLVE statement of PROC MODEL.

You can provide PROC MODEL initial values that may decrease the number of iterations, the processing time, and the cost of finding solutions. For example, based on the plot in Output 12.9, reasonable starting values are 20, 60, 90, and 100.

```
    /* Creating the CUB_COST Data Set */
data cub_cost;
   input q cost @@;
   cards;
20 10250 60 10500 90 10750 100 11000
;
```

```
    /* Performing Goal-Seeking */
proc model data=cub_cost;
    cost = 10000 + 20*q - .35*q**2 + .0025*q**3;
    endo q;
    exo cost;
    solve q satisfy=cost / simulate out=cub_out noprint;
run;

    /* Listing Solution Values */
proc print data=cub_out;
    var cost q;
    title 'Cubic Cost Function Example';
    title2 'Simulations of Quantity Given Cost';
run;
```

Output 12.10 displays part of the output generated by the above example code. The model and solution summaries are not shown. Only the printed solution is displayed.

Output 12.10
Goal-seeking
Solutions of the
Cubic Cost
Function

```
                    Cubic Cost Function Example
                 Simulations of Quantity Given Cost

            OBS       COST        Q

             1       10250      16.890
             2       10500      63.701
             3       10750      87.800
             4       11000     100.000
```

Interpretation of output

Output 12.10 lists the solution quantities for the cost levels. They are interpreted as the quantities that can be produced given the cost level.

Often polynomial equations have more than one solution (root), and different starting values may produce different solutions. For this cost function, costs rise (monotonically) as Q rises, and so this cost function has a unique Q for every cost. Beware, for not all polynomial equations have this property.

In general, you want to check the robustness of goal-seeking solutions for polynomial functions by providing additional starting values. If small changes in the starting values produce different solutions, then you want to carefully explore the function and resulting solutions before making decisions based on any particular solution value.

A Present Value Model

Present value models compare streams of dollar amounts received over time. Future dollar values are discounted to present values by accounting for the time value of money. Discrete present value models are polynominal in terms of the interest rate. They are of the following form:

$$PV = -X + \frac{R}{1+I} + \frac{R}{(1+I)^2} + \ldots + \frac{R}{(1+I)^k} + \frac{S}{(1+I)^k}$$

where

PV   is the present value.

X   is the initial outlay.

R   is the return for each period.

I   is the interest rate used for discounting.

S   is the salvage value.

K   is the number of periods.

Simulating the Present Value Model

You may be considering an investment and want to calculate the present value (PV) or a range of values. Investments with positive PVs are to be considered, and the set of conditions yielding the highest PV is the best investment opportunity. The PV model can be used to calculate the PVs and investigate the sensitivity of the present value to changes in market conditions, that is, changes in X, R, I, S, and K.

Suppose, you are considering an investment opportunity yielding a return over four years. You expect the initial outlay (X) to be between $150,000 and $175,000, the return (R) each year of the four years to be between $35,000 and $37,500, the interest rate (I) to be between 5% and 6%, and finally, the salvage value (S) to be between $50,000 and $75,000. Under what conditions is it worthwhile to invest? What are the present values generated by each set of conditions? How much change occurs in the present value as market conditions change?

You can use DO loops in a DATA step to create a data set and then use PROC MODEL to solve for the PVs.

```
    /* Creating the PV Data Set */
data pv;
   do x=150000,175000;
      do r=35000,37500;
         do i=.05,.06;
            do s=50000,75000;
   pv=.;
   output;
            end;
         end;
      end;
   end;
   label pv='Present Value'
         x='Current Period Cost'
         r='Annual Return'
         i='Interest Rate'
         s='Salvage Value';
run;

    /* Performing the Simulation */
proc model data=pv;
   pv = -x + r*(1/(1+i) + 1/((1+i)**2) + 1/((1+i)**3)
        + 1/((1+i)**4)) + s*1/((1+i)**4);
```

```
        endo pv;
        exo x r i s;
        solve pv / simulate out=pv_out noprint;
run;

        /* Listing Solution Values */
proc print data=pv_out label;
        var pv x r i s;
        title 'Present Value Example';
        title2 'Solution Values';
run;
```

Output 12.11 displays part of the output generated by the above example code. The model and solution summaries are not shown. Only the printed solutions are displayed.

Output 12.11
Simulating the
Present Value
Model

```
                           Present Value Example
                              Solution Values

                        Current
                Present  Period   Annual   Interest  Salvage
        OBS      Value    Cost    Return     Rate     Value

         1     15243.39  150000   35000     0.05     50000
         2     35810.95  150000   35000     0.05     75000
         3     24108.27  150000   37500     0.05     50000
         4     44675.83  150000   37500     0.05     75000
         5     -9756.61  175000   35000     0.05     50000
         6     10810.95  175000   35000     0.05     75000
         7      -891.73  175000   37500     0.05     50000
         8     19675.83  175000   37500     0.05     75000
         9     10883.38  150000   35000     0.06     50000
        10     30685.72  150000   35000     0.06     75000
        11     19546.14  150000   37500     0.06     50000
        12     39348.49  150000   37500     0.06     75000
        13    -14116.62  175000   35000     0.06     50000
        14      5685.72  175000   35000     0.06     75000
        15     -5453.86  175000   37500     0.06     50000
        16     14348.49  175000   37500     0.06     75000
```

Interpretation of output

In Output 12.11, the PV solution values are positive in 12 of 16 cases. PVs range from a low of −$14,116.62 to a high of $44,675.83. The four negative PVs all occur when the current-period cost (X) is $175,000 and the salvage value (S) is $50,000. Do not invest under these circumstances. The worst circumstances for investing are found in observation 13 where the interest rate is 6%, the initial outlay is $175,000, and the salvage value is $50,000.

The four highest PVs (all above $30,000) occur when the current-period cost (X) is $150,000 and the salvage value (S) is $75,000. The best circumstances are in observation 4 where the interest rate is 5%, the initial outlay is $150,000, the annual return is $37,500, and the salvage value is $75,000.

The remaining observations produce PVs between those found in observations 4 and 13. They can be used to assess the effect on present value as the magnitude of the other variables change. For example, observations 1 and 2 can be used to assess the effect on the present value as the salvage value changes from $50,000 to $75,000, given a current period cost of $150,000, an annual return of $35,000, and an interest rate of 5%. In this case, present value rises from $15,243.39 to $35.810.95.

Using the Present Value Model for Goal-seeking Solutions

You can also use the present value model to calculate the interest rate required to generate a particular present value, given values for the remaining variables. These interest rates are interpreted as internal rates of return. For a given present value, the higher the internal rate of return, the better the investment opportunity. You may also be interested in the sensitivity of the internal rate of return to changes in market conditions.

Suppose you want to compare investment opportunities with a present value of $125,000. You expect a range of outlay between $45,000 and $50,000, four annual returns of between $40,000 and $50,000 each, and a salvage value between $35,000 and $40,000. Each combination of values yields a different internal rate of return.

To find the internal rates of return, create a data set with a DATA step and then use the SOLVE statement of PROC MODEL. The solved values are printed with PROC PRINT.

```
    /* Creating the IRR Data Set */
data irr;
   input pv i x r s;
   label pv='Present Value'
         i='Interest Rate'
         x='Current Period Cost'
         r='Annual Return'
         s='Salvage Value';
   cards;
125000  .  45000 40000 35000
125000  .  45000 40000 40000
125000  .  45000 50000 35000
125000  .  45000 50000 40000
125000  .  50000 40000 35000
125000  .  50000 40000 40000
125000  .  50000 50000 35000
125000  .  50000 50000 40000
;

    /* Solving the Model */
proc model;
   pv = -x + r*(1/(1+i) + 1/((1+i)**2) + 1/((1+i)**3)
         + 1/((1+i)**4)) + s*1/((1+i)**4);
   endo i;
   exo pv x r s;
   solve i satisfy=pv / simulate data=irr out=irr_out noprint;
run;

    /* Printing the Solutions */
proc print data=irr_out label;
   var pv x r i s;
   title 'Internal Rates of Return Example';
   title2 'Solution Values';
run;
```

Output 12.12 displays part of the output generated by the previous example code. The model and solution summaries are not shown. Only the printed solution is displayed.

Output 12.12
Goal-seeking
Solutions for the
Internal Rate of
Return of the
Present Value
Model

```
                     Internal Rates of Return Example
                            Solution Values

                          Current
                Present    Period   Annual   Interest   Salvage
         OBS     Value      Cost    Return     Rate      Value
          1     125000     45000    40000    0.05144    35000
          2     125000     45000    40000    0.06066    40000
          3     125000     45000    50000    0.13049    35000
          4     125000     45000    50000    0.13835    40000
          5     125000     50000    40000    0.04025    35000
          6     125000     50000    40000    0.04944    40000
          7     125000     50000    50000    0.11778    35000
          8     125000     50000    50000    0.12563    40000
```

Interpretation of output

In Output 12.12, the present values indicate that all combinations of conditions produce positive internal rates of return. Observation 4 produces the highest internal rate of return, .13835, or 13.835%, whereas observation 5 produces the lowest internal rate of return, .04025, or 4.025%.

The remaining observations produce internal rates of return between these values, and they can be used to assess the effect on the internal rate of return as each variable changes. For example, the first two observations can be used to assess the effect of the salvage value increasing from $35,000 to $40,000, given a current period cost of $45,000 and annual returns of $40,000. In this case, the internal rate of return rises from 5.144% to 6.066%.

An Income Growth Model

A nonlinear model is often the most appropriate approach to modeling growth rates. In the following example, suppose you are a sales manager of a new product with a growing market. You have monthly fixed costs, variable operating costs are proportional to sales, and year-end income is yearly sales minus annual costs.

Given the first-month sales, the income growth model has the following form for the remainder of a twelve-month period:

$$YS = S \times (1 + \sum_{I=1}^{11} (1 + G)^I)$$
$$C = V \times YS + F \times M$$
$$Y = YS - C$$

where

YS   is yearly sales.

S   is monthly sales.

I   is the monthly index number.

G is the growth rate of sales.

C is annual costs.

V is variable costs proportion.

F is monthly fixed costs.

M is months.

Y is year-end income.

Solving for Year-end Income

With data on S, G, F, and V, you can solve this model for year-end income. Your files indicate monthly fixed costs are $35,000 and variable operating costs are 40% of sales. In January, sales were $150,000. Suppose you expect sales to grow at 5% per month. You can solve the income growth model for the expected end-of-year income.

In this example, solve for Y. First, create an input data set, and then use PROC MODEL to solve for the year-end income. Note that a value is provided for Y; this value is used in a later example.

```
    /* Creating the GROW Data Set */
data grow;
    input y s f g v m;
    label y=Yearly Income
          s=Monthly Sales
          f=Fixed Costs
          g=Growth Rate
          v=Variable Cost Percentage
          m=Months;
    cards;
1200000 150000 35000 .05 .40 12
;

    /* Solving the Model */
proc model data=grow;
    var y s f g v m;
        ys=s*(1+(1+g)**1 + (1+g)**2 + (1+g)**3
                +(1+g)**4 + (1+g)**5 + (1+g)**6
                +(1+g)**7 + (1+g)**8 + (1+g)**9
                +(1+g)**10 + (1+g)**11);
        c=v*ys+f*m;
        y=ys-c;

    solve y satisfy=y / out=grw_out;
run;

    /* Printing the Output Data Set */
proc print data=grw_out label;
    var y s f g v m;
    title 'Income Growth Model Example';
    title2 'Yearly Income Simulation';
run;
```

Output 12.13 displays part of the output generated by the previous example code. The model and solution summaries are not shown. Only the printed solution is displayed.

Output 12.13
End-of-Year
Income for the
Income Growth
Model

```
                           Income Growth Model Example
                             Yearly Income Simulation

                                                       Variable
                       Yearly     Monthly   Fixed   Growth     Cost
             OBS       Income       Sales   Costs     Rate   Percentage   Months
              1      1012541.39    150000   35000     0.05       0.4        12
```

Interpretation of output

In Output 12.13, year-end income, given a 5% monthly growth in sales, is $1,012,541.39.

Solving for a Growth Rate

You can also use the income growth model for goal-seeking solutions. For example, you may want to solve the model for a growth rate. Perhaps, your goal for this year is to generate $1.2 million in income. What monthly growth rate is required?

In this example, you solve for G and satisfy the Y equation. The statements that produce Output 12.14 are similar to those producing Output 12.13. Only the SOLVE statement and the PROC PRINT step to print the output data set, GRW_OUT1, are shown.

```
    /* Solving the Model */
    .
    .
    .
    solve g satisfy=y / out=grw_out1;
run;

    /* Printing the Output Data Set */
proc print data=grw_out1 label;
    var y s f g v m;
    title 'Income Growth Model Example';
    title2 'Growth Rate Simulation';
run;
```

Output 12.14 displays part of the output generated by the above example code. The model and solution summaries are not shown. Only the printed solution is displayed.

Output 12.14
Goal-seeking
Solutions for the
Growth Rate of the
Income Growth
Model

```
                           Income Growth Model Example
                              Growth Rate Simulation

                                                       Variable
                       Yearly     Monthly   Fixed   Growth     Cost
             OBS       Income       Sales   Costs     Rate   Percentage   Months
              1       1200000      150000   35000   0.071056    0.4        12
```

Interpretation of output

In Output 12.14, the monthly growth rate in sales required to generate a year-end income of $1.2 million is .071056, or about 7.1%.

Chapter Summary

This chapter discussed simulation of nonlinear models. The models were simulated with historical data. Actual and simulated values were printed and plotted. Monte Carlo simulation was performed on the PC dispersion model. The actual values and the fifth and ninety-fifth percentiles were plotted versus time in years. Three nonlinear models were introduced, simulated, and used for what-if and goal-seeking simulations. These models were a cubic cost function, a present value model, and an income growth model.

Learning More

- For reference information on the MODEL procedure in SAS/ETS software, see the *SAS/ETS User's Guide, Version 6, First Edition*.

- For reference information on the MEANS, SORT, and UNIVARIATE procedures, see the *SAS Procedures Guide, Version 6, Third Edition*.

- For reference information on the GPLOT procedure, see *SAS/GRAPH Software: Reference, Version 6, First Edition* and *SAS/GRAPH Software: Usage, Version 6, First Edition*.

References

Pindyck, R.S. and Rubinfeld, D.L. (1991), *Econometric Models and Economic Forecasts, Third Edition*, New York: McGraw-Hill Book Company.

Part 3
Forecasting

Chapter **13** Introduction to Forecasting

Introduction

Economic forecasting is useful in making all types of economic decisions. Forecasting reduces the range of uncertainty surrounding a decision, enables more accurate predictions of the future to be made, and improves the efficiency of the decision-making process.

Forecasting sales is a good example of how a firm can use forecasting to make microeconomic decisions that may affect how the firm hires more workers, contracts for additional raw materials, and produces or stores output at new levels. Planning fiscal policy is a good example of the use of macroeconomic forecasting. If a forecast indicates an impending recession, then expansionary fiscal policy should be considered. On the other hand, if the forecast indicates a boom period, then expansionary policy may not be necessary.

Forecasting involves combining knowledge of the past with realistic expectations about the future. The following steps are generally used to generate forecasts. First, fit a model to the historical data, as discussed in Part 1, "Estimation." Next, determine how well the model fits the past data and validate the model through simulation, as discussed in Part 2, "Simulation." When you are satisfied that the model is realistic and reliable, it can be used to forecast into the future. To forecast, you must generate values for the exogenous variables in the model that reflect your expectations about what is likely to occur. Forecasts are the expected values of the endogenous (dependent) variable, determined by evaluating the model at the new values of exogenous (independent) variables.

Forecasting can involve generating a point estimate and confidence limits for the most likely scenario of the future, or it can involve comparing forecasts generated by different expectations of the future. This chapter describes three scenarios of low, baseline, and high future input values, which generate low, baseline, and high forecast values, respectively. Scenario forecasting can be viewed as an extension of what-if simulation analysis. In contrast to the typical use of forecasting for exploration of the unknown, what-if simulation is typically used to explore the known range of data. See Chapters 9 through 12 for discussion and examples of what-if simulation.

This chapter uses the AUTOREG procedure in SAS/ETS software and the general fund model to develop examples of point forecasting, calculation of confidence intervals, and scenario forecasting. The general fund model is introduced, fitted, and simulated in Chapter 9, "Introduction to Simulation."

Forecasting the General Fund Model

You can use the general fund model to forecast future values of the North Carolina general fund and to calculate confidence intervals for the forecasts. The GFUND model is a macroeconomic model relating the GFUND level to real U.S. GNP and the population of North Carolina. As U.S. GNP and N.C. population rise, so does the level of GFUND. The model is as follows:

$$GFUND_t = d + f\, GNP_t + h\, POP_t + \varepsilon_t$$

where

GFUND	is annual real North Carolina general fund revenues, which has been deflated by the consumer price index (CPI).
d, f, and h	are the model parameters.
GNP	is annual real U.S. gross national product (GNP), which has been deflated by the CPI.
POP	is annual North Carolina population.
ε	is a random error term.

Before you fit the model and compute predicted values and confidence limits, you must first create the BUDGET data set and variables to fit the model. The following SAS example code performs these required tasks:

DATA
  creates the BUDGET data set.

INPUT
  describes the arrangement of values in an input record (an observation) and assigns input values to corresponding SAS variables. The next three statements create new variables. For example, the first statement (GFUND=GFUNDN/CPI;) deflates nominal general revenues to real values with the CPI.

LABEL
  assigns labels to the variables.

TITLE
  titles the printed output.

CARDS
  indicates that data lines follow the statement. Always place the CARDS statement on the line before the first data line. In this example, the next 17 lines are the data.

```
data budget;
   input year gfundn gnpn fed_revn pop cpi aa;
```

```
     gfund = gfundn / cpi;
     gnp = gnpn / cpi;
     fed_rev = fed_revn / cpi;
  label gfund = 'Real General Fund in Millions'
        gnp = 'Real US GNP in Billions'
        fed_rev = 'Real Federal IRS Collections in Billions'
        pop = 'NC Population in Thousands'
        cpi = 'US CPI 82-84 = 100';
  title 'General Fund Revenues Example';
  cards;
73 1214.0  1359.3  237.8  5382  .444
74 1358.0  1472.8  269.0  5461  .493
75 1451.0  1598.4  293.8  5535  .538
76 1572.0  1782.8  302.5  5593  .569
77 1870.0  1990.5  358.1  5668  .606
78 2060.0  2249.7  399.8  5739  .652
79 2337.0  2508.2  460.4  5802  .726
80 2639.0  2732.0  519.4  5882  .824
81 2846.0  3052.6  606.8  5957  .909
82 3078.0  3166.0  632.2  6018  .965
83 3279.0  3405.7  627.2  6078  .996
84 3814.0  3772.2  680.5  6167 1.039
85 4337.0  4010.3  742.9  6258 1.076
86 4695.0  4235.0  782.3  6327 1.096
87 5181.0  4524.3  886.3  6409 1.136
88 5552.0  4880.6  935.1  6489 1.183
89 5928.5  5200.8 1013.5  6571 1.240
;
```

You now use PROC AUTOREG to fit the model and compute predicted values with confidence limits. The following SAS example code fits the model and creates predicted values and confidence limits:

PROC AUTOREG
    invokes the AUTOREG procedure. The following options of the PROC AUTOREG statement are specified:

DATA=*SAS-data-set*   specifies the data set to be used in the analysis. In this example, the BUDGET data set is specified.

NOPRINT   suppresses the printed output.

MODEL
    specifies the model to be fitted. For this example, the left-hand side variable, also known as the endogenous variable, is GFUND, and the two right-hand side variables, also known as exogenous variables, are GNP and POP. The following options of the MODEL statement are specified:

NLAG=*n*   specifies the order of the autoregressive process to be fitted or subset of lags to be fitted. For example, NLAG=2 specifies a second-order autoregressive process (both the first and second autoregressive parameters are estimated); NLAG=(2) specifies an autoregressive process in which only the second-order autoregressive parameter is estimated.

In this example, a first-order autoregressive process is specified. If the NLAG= option is not specified, then PROC AUTOREG does not fit an autoregressive model; instead, it fits an OLS model.

METHOD=   specifies the type of estimates to be computed. PROC AUTOREG enables you to fit models using maximum-likelihood (ML) estimation, the unconditional least-squares (ULS) method, or the Yule-Walker (YW) method. Typically, the methods produce different parameter estimates and generate different residuals, predicted values, and confidence limits. For this example, the method of maximum likelihood is specified.

OUTPUT

creates the output data set containing the selected, predicted, and residual values, and confidence limits.

PROC AUTOREG calculates two types of confidence limits, predicted values, and residuals. The first type is calculated from only the structural part of the model and is useful for values within the observed time period. This type of lower and upper confidence limits, predicted values, and residuals are calculated by specifying the LCLM=, UCLM=, PM=, and RM= options of the OUTPUT statement.

The second type is values calculated from the structural part and the error process of the model. This type is useful for values beyond the observed time period, for example, forecasts into the future. The second type is calculated by specifying the LCL=, UCL=, P=, and R= options.

The following options of the OUTPUT statement are specified:

OUT=   creates and names the output data set. In this example, the output data set is named BUD_F.

ALPHACLI=   specifies the confidence limits for the predictions, and the resulting confidence interval has $1 - number$ confidence.

     The ALPHACLI= option is used with the P, R, LCL, and UCL options. The default is ALPHACLI=.05, corresponding to a 95% confidence interval. Recall that as α decreases, the required confidence increases; thus, the confidence bands must be wider to reflect the higher level of confidence. For this example, the 95% confidence intervals are specified.

P=   outputs the predicted values (created from the structural part and the error process of the model) to the output data set under the name given. In this example, the predicted values are named P.

LCL=   outputs the lower confidence limits (created from the structural part and the error process of the model) to the output data set under the name given. In this example, the lower confidence limits are named L.

UCL=   outputs the upper confidence limits (created from the structural part and the error process of the model) to the output data set under the name given. In this example, the upper confidence limits are named U.

The following SAS example code performs these tasks:

```
/* Fitting the Model */
proc autoreg data=budget noprint;
   model gfund = gnp pop / nlag=1 method=ml;
   output out=bud_f alphacli=.05 p=p lcl=l ucl=u;
run;
```

Output 9.4 displays the estimated equation. The predicted values, P, are the forecasted values that are produced by substituting the actual values of GNP and population into the estimated model.

You use a DATA step to create a new data set, BUD_FP, and create a new variable, WIDTH (the width of the confidence interval). Finally, you use PROC PRINT to print the actual and predicted values, the confidence limits, and the width of the confidence intervals. The following SAS example code performs these tasks:

```
/* Calculating Confidence Interval Width */
data bud_fp;
   set bud_f;
   width=u-l;
run;
```

```
/* Printing Confidence Limits */
proc print data=bud_fp;
   var year l gfund p u width;
   title2 'Actual and Predicted Values';
   title3 'with 95% Confidence Limits';
run;
```

Output 13.1 is produced from the previous SAS example code, including the DATA steps, PROC AUTOREG, and PROC PRINT.

Output 13.1
Actual and
Predicted Values
and 95%
Confidence Limits
and Intervals for
Historical Values
of the General
Fund Model

```
                     General Fund Revenues Example
                      Actual and Predicted Values
                       with 95% Confidence Limits

    OBS   YEAR      L        GFUND        P         U        WIDTH

     1     73     2169.61    2734.23    2609.26    3048.91    879.294
     2     74     2338.78    2754.56    2687.31    3035.85    697.069
     3     75     2408.81    2697.03    2752.20    3095.59    686.779
     4     76     2567.12    2762.74    2891.08    3215.03    647.917
     5     77     2688.74    3085.81    3004.07    3319.39    630.656
     6     78     2983.01    3159.51    3304.63    3626.25    643.236
     7     79     2950.71    3219.01    3256.42    3562.13    611.414
     8     80     2879.77    3202.67    3185.52    3491.26    611.493
     9     81     3018.47    3130.91    3329.45    3640.44    621.977
    10     82     2826.24    3189.64    3180.07    3533.90    707.662
    11     83     3097.70    3292.17    3427.47    3757.24    659.545
    12     84     3342.76    3670.84    3652.59    3962.41    619.648
    13     85     3569.84    4030.67    3889.49    4209.13    639.286
    14     86     3889.36    4283.76    4214.17    4538.98    649.623
    15     87     4102.27    4560.74    4441.51    4780.74    678.471
    16     88     4354.15    4693.15    4713.42    5072.69    718.540
    17     89     4420.23    4781.05    4796.52    5172.82    752.585
```

Interpretation of output

In Output 13.1, the actual (GFUND) and predicted (P) values and the lower (L) and upper (U) 95% confidence limits for the general fund model are printed for the period 1973 through 1989.

By calculating confidence limits, you can assess the expected range of the endogenous variable, GFUND, for a given level of significance. The variable WIDTH contains the width of the confidence interval, that is, the upper minus the lower confidence limit. For mathematical details on the calculation of confidence intervals, see Pindyck and Rubinfeld (1991).

Plotting Confidence Intervals

You can assess the relationship between the actual and predicted values by plotting them with PROC GPLOT. You can also overlay the confidence intervals.

Note that preceding the PROC GPLOT code, the GOPTIONS statement with the RESET= option resets the graphics options. For this example, the graphics symbols used to plot the data are reset. When you end your interactive GPLOT session with the QUIT statement, the graphics options return to their default values.

The following SAS example code produces Output 13.2.

```
goptions reset=symbol;

proc gplot data=bud_fp;
   plot gfund*year=1
        p*year=2
        l*year=3
        u*year=4 / overlay hminor=1 vminor=1
                    haxis=axis1 vaxis=axis2 legend=legend1;
   symbol1 v=A font=swissb color=black;
   symbol2 i=join font=swissb l=1 color=blue;
   symbol3 i=join font=swissb l=20 color=green;
   symbol4 i=join font=swissb l=20 color=red;
   axis1 offset=(2,2)pct order=73 to 89 by 2;
   axis2 order=2000 to 5500 by 500
        label=(a=-90 r=90 'GENERAL FUND');
   legend1 label=none value=('Actual General Fund'
           'Predicted General Fund' 'Lower 95% Confidence Limit'
                              'Upper 95% Confidence Limit');
   title 'General Fund Revenues';
   title2 'Actual, Predicted, and 95% CI';
run;
quit;
```

Output 13.2
Plot of Actual and
Predicted Values,
and 95%
Confidence Limits
for Historical
Values of the
General Fund
Model

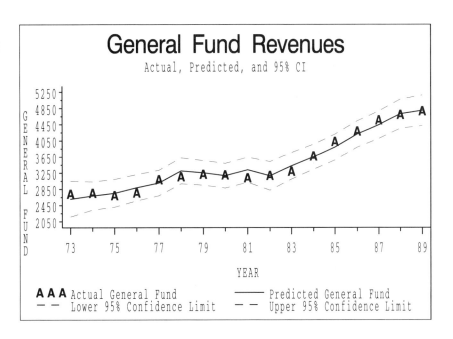

Interpretation of output

In Output 13.2, the symbol A represents the actual values. The solid line represents the predicted values, and the dashed lines represent the upper and lower 95% confidence limits. Notice that the confidence limits follow the fluctuations in the GFUND values.

Scenario Forecasting

The general fund model can be used to explore different scenarios of the future. Suppose in the 1990 session of the North Carolina General Assembly, legislation is being considered that would affect population growth in North Carolina, and you have been asked to analyze how this legislation would affect general fund revenues. For this example, you use population as a proxy variable for the effects of the proposed legislation.

One scenario assumes that legislation is not passed and recent trends are expected to continue. Alternatively, one proposed package of legislation encourages population growth (through lower licensing fees, reimbursement of moving expenses, and increased services), while another discourages growth (through higher licensing fees and reduced services). What are the expected general fund levels over the period 1990 through 1995 for each of these scenarios?

The forecasting strategy is to extrapolate the past growth rate of U.S. GNP and the alternative growth rates of population and use the resulting levels as input values for the general fund model. The following sections show you how to create the input data set, concatenate it to the BUDGET data set, calculate, print, and plot the forecasted values.

Extrapolating Input Variables

Prior to forecasting future values of the endogenous variable, GFUND, you must acquire or generate future values of exogenous variables, POP and GNP. With the future values of POP and GNP, you can use the estimated model to generate GFUND forecasts.

There are many approaches to generating future values of input (exogenous) variables for use in forecasting. These approaches include

□ choosing individual values

□ choosing specific growth rates and extrapolating

□ using the growth rate of a historical period and then extrapolating

□ selecting a range of growth rates, extrapolating multiple input variable values, and then performing multiple forecasts

□ fitting a low-order polynomial of time to the input variable and then extrapolating

□ fitting a time series model to the input variable and then extrapolating

□ combining the input variable extrapolation and the endogenous variable forecasting by fitting a transfer function to the data, as shown in Chapter 16, "Combining Forecasting Methods."

This example extrapolates the input variables using the historical growth rate for U.S. GNP and high and low rates about the historical growth rate for N.C. population.

Over the period 1973 through 1989, N.C. population grew at an annually compounded rate of about 1.2% and U.S. GNP grew at a rate of about 1.9%. A base scenario occurs if legislation is not passed and these trends continue. A growth case scenario occurs if population growth is encouraged; you expect a maximum annual growth rate of 1.8%. A low growth rate scenario occurs if population growth is discouraged; you expect a minimum annual growth rate of .6%. For all scenarios, you assume the U.S. GNP grows at 1.9% annually.

Before forecasting GFUND values for the different population growth scenarios, you create the POP data set containing the three different sets of extrapolated values for N.C. population. Next, you create three separate input data sets, BUDGETB, BUDGETL, and BUDGETG, for the baseline, low, and growth population scenarios, respectively. Create the data sets by concatenating the appropriate extrapolated population values of the POP data set to the actual N.C. population values in the BUDGET data set. Thus, each input data set contains the actual population values from 1973 through 1989 and the appropriate extrapolated population values from 1990 through 1995.

Note: In the following SAS example code, only the DATA step creating the data set BUDGETB is shown. You need to use similar SAS statements to create the BUDGETL and BUDGETG data sets.

To print and plot the population values for the different scenarios, you create the BUD_P1 data set by merging the BUDGET and POP data sets. The FIRSTOBS= option in the PROC PRINT statement enables you to begin printing at the specified observation. This example begins with the 15th observation; thus, the values for the period 1987 through 1995 are printed. Lastly, the BUD_P data set and PROC GPLOT are used to plot the actual and scenario values of POP versus YEAR for the period 1987 through 1995. Output 13.3 shows the results.

```
/* Creating POP Values for Forecasting */
data pop;
   do year=90 to 95;
```

```
      pop_base=6571*(1+.012)**(year-89);
      pop_low =6571*(1+.006)**(year-89);
      pop_grow=6571*(1+.018)**(year-89);
      gnp=(5200.8/1.240)*(1+.019)**(year-89);
      output;
   end;
run;

   /* Creating BUDGETB Data Set    */
   /* for Base Scenario Forecasting */
data budgetb;
   set budget pop(rename=(pop_base=pop));
   drop pop_low pop_grow;
run;

   /* Creating BUD_P Data Set for Plotting */
data bud_p;
   set budget pop;
run;

   /* Printing Observations */
proc print data=bud_p (firstobs=15) label;
   var year gnp pop pop_low pop_base pop_grow;
   title2 'Input Values for Forecasting';
   title3 'GNP and Population';
run;

goptions reset=symbol;

   /* Plotting Scenario Values */
proc gplot data=bud_p;
   where year > 86;
   plot pop*year=1
        pop_base*year=2
        pop_low*year=3
        pop_grow*year=4 / overlay hminor=1 vminor=0 haxis=axis1
                          vaxis=axis2 legend=legend1;
   symbol1 i=join v=A font=swissb l=1 color=black;
   symbol2 i=join v=B font=swissb l=3 color=blue;
   symbol3 i=join v=L font=swissb l=3 color=green;
   symbol4 i=join v=G font=swissb l=3 color=red;
   axis1 offset=(2,2)pct order=87 to 95 label=none;
   axis2 order=6300 to 7400 by 100
        label=(a=-90 r=90 'NC POPULATION');
   legend1 label=none value=('Actual Population'
        'Base Scenario Population' 'Low Scenario Population'
                          'Growth Scenario Population');
   title 'N.C. Population 1987-1995';
   title2 'Actual, Base, Low, and Growth';
run;
quit;
```

Output 13.3

Extrapolated Input Values for Forecasting the General Fund Model

General Fund Revenues Example
Input Values for Forecasting
GNP and Population

OBS	YEAR	Real US GNP in Billions	NC Population in Thousands	POP_LOW	POP_BASE	POP_GROW
15	87	3982.66	6409	.	.	.
16	88	4125.61	6489	.	.	.
17	89	4194.19	6571	.	.	.
18	90	4273.88	.	6610.43	6649.85	6689.28
19	91	4355.09	.	6650.09	6729.65	6809.69
20	92	4437.83	.	6689.99	6810.41	6932.26
21	93	4522.15	.	6730.13	6892.13	7057.04
22	94	4608.07	.	6770.51	6974.84	7184.07
23	95	4695.63	.	6811.13	7058.53	7313.38

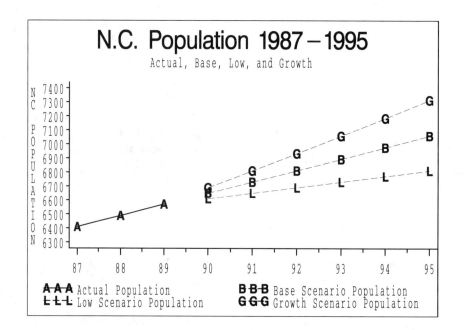

Interpretation of output

Output 13.3 prints and plots the actual and scenario values of population. The printed values enable you to make a direct comparison, while the plot enables you to make a visual comparison.

In the plot, the symbols A, L, B, and G represent the actual, low, base, and growth scenario values of population. The base values continue the previous trend, while the low and growth scenarios reflect the expected effects of the proposed legislation.

Forecasting the Baseline Scenario

First, consider the base scenario, where past trends are assumed to continue. It provides a baseline for measuring the effects of the legislative packages. You can use confidence intervals to assess the most likely range of future GFUND values in the base scenario.

The following SAS example code uses PROC AUTOREG and the BUDGETB data set to forecast GFUND for the base scenario and calculate and print 95% confidence limits; it uses PROC GPLOT to plot the actual and forecasted values with confidence limits versus YEAR. Output 13.4 shows the results.

```
    /* Predicting Base Scenario GFUND Values */
proc autoreg data=budgetb noprint;
   model gfund = gnp pop / nlag=1 method=ml;
   output out=budb_out alphacli=.05 p=f lcl=l ucl=u;
run;

    /* Deleting Unneeded Values */
data budgetbp;
   set budb_out;
   if year<90 then l=.;
   if year<90 then u=.;
   if year<90 then f=.;
   width=u-l;
run;

    /* Printing Actual and Scenario Values of GFUND */
proc print data=budgetbp (firstobs=15) label;
   var year l gfund f u width;
   title2 'GFUND Forecast and Confidence Limits';
   title3;
run;

goptions reset=symbol;

    /* Plotting the Values */
proc gplot data=budgetbp;
   where year > 86;
   plot gfund*year=1
        f*year=2
        l*year=3
        u*year=4 / overlay hminor=1 vminor=1
                   haxis=axis1 vaxis=axis2 legend=legend1;
   symbol1 i=join v=A font=swissb l=1 color=black;
   symbol2 i=join v=F font=swissb l=3 color=blue;
   symbol3 i=join v=L font=swissb l=3 color=green;
   symbol4 i=join v=U font=swissb l=3 color=red;
   axis1 offset=(2,2)pct order=87 to 95 label=none;
   axis2 order=4200 to 6300 by 300
        label=(a=-90 r=90 'General Fund');
   legend1 label=none value=('Actual GFUND'
         'Forecast GFUND' 'Lower 95% Confidence Limit'
         'Upper 95% Confidence Limit');
   title 'N.C. General Fund 1987-1995';
   title2 'Base Scenario';
run;
quit;
```

Output 13.4
Printing and
Plotting Actual
and Forecasted
GFUND Values
with Confidence
Limits

```
                    General Fund Revenues Example
                 GFUND Forecast and Confidence Limits

                               Real General
                                  Fund in
       OBS   YEAR     L          Millions        F         U        WIDTH

        15    87       .          4560.74          .         .          .
        16    88       .          4693.15          .         .          .
        17    89       .          4781.05          .         .          .
        18    90    4512.24          .          4907.65   5303.07    790.83
        19    91    4594.02          .          5042.07   5490.11    896.09
        20    92    4700.00          .          5182.64   5665.28    965.28
        21    93    4817.95          .          5328.25   5838.55   1020.60
        22    94    4942.59          .          5478.11   6013.64   1071.05
        23    95    5071.46          .          5631.71   6191.96   1120.50
```

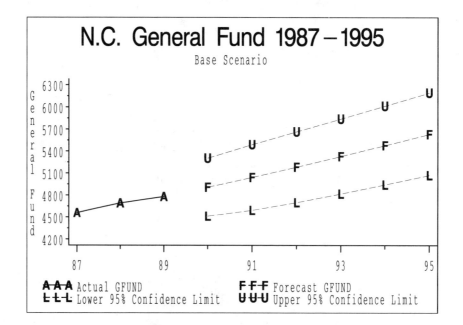

Interpretation of output

In Output 13.4, the actual and forecasted values of GFUND are printed and plotted. The symbols A, F, U, and L represent the actual and forecasted values and the upper and lower 95% confidence limits, respectively. The forecasts appear to continue the previous trend, establishing a baseline for comparing the proposed legislation.

As you examine the printed values, you notice that the width of the confidence interval, WIDTH, increases the farther into the future you forecast. This reflects future uncertainties and statistical properties of confidence intervals.

Forecasting Alternative Scenarios

You can use PROC AUTOREG and the data sets BUDGETL and BUDGETG (created in Output 13.3) to forecast for the low and high population growth scenarios. Because you use two data sets, you use PROC AUTOREG two times. The predicted values of GFUND for the low and growth scenarios are named GL and GG, respectively.

You use a DATA step to merge the actual and predicted values and delete unneeded values. You use PROC PRINT to print the actual and forecasted GFUND values. The FIRSTOBS= option enables you to begin printing at the specified observation. This example begins with the 15th observation; thus, the values for the period 1987 through 1995 are printed. Output 13.5 shows the results.

```
    /* Predicting GFUND Values */
proc autoreg data=budget1 noprint;
    model gfund = gnp pop / nlag=1 method=ml;
    output out=bud1_out p=gl;
run;

proc autoreg data=budgetg noprint;
    model gfund = gnp pop / nlag=1 method=ml;
    output out=budg_out p=gg;
run;

    /* Merging Data Sets */
data budgetp;
    merge budget bud1_out budgetbp budg_out;
    by year;
    if year<90 then gl=.;
    if year<90 then f=.;
    if year<90 then gg=.;
run;

    /* Printing Actual and Scenario Values of GFUND */
proc print data=budgetp (firstobs=15) label;
    var year gfund gl f gg;
    title2 'GFUND Forecasts';
    title3 'Low, Base, and Growth POP Scenarios';
run;
```

Output 13.5
Actual and Predicted Values of General Fund Revenues for Low, Base, and Growth Scenarios of the General Fund Model for 1987 through 1995

```
                  General Fund Revenues Example
                         GFUND Forecasts
                Low, Base, and Growth POP Scenarios

                      Real General
                        Fund in
      OBS    YEAR       Millions        GL         F         GG

       15     87        4560.74          .         .          .
       16     88        4693.15          .         .          .
       17     89        4781.05          .         .          .
       18     90            .         4875.12   4907.65    4940.19
       19     91            .         4976.40   5042.07    5108.12
       20     92            .         5083.26   5182.64    5283.21
       21     93            .         5194.55   5328.25    5464.35
       22     94            .         5309.48   5478.11    5650.79
       23     95            .         5427.53   5631.71    5842.04
```

Interpretation of output

In Output 13.5, the actual and predicted values of the GFUND for the low (GL), baseline (F), and growth (GG) scenarios are printed for the period 1987 through 1995. The differing forecasts of GFUND reflect the scenario growth rates for POP. Comparing Output 13.4 and Output 13.5, you notice that the low and rapid population growth scenario forecasts are within the 95% confidence intervals of the base scenario forecasts.

For further analysis of the scenarios, you can use the LCL and UCL options in the OUTPUT statement of PROC AUTOREG to generate the lower and upper confidence limits. In this example, the 95% confidence limits (if printed or plotted) would overlap for the different scenarios. Still, they provide additional information for evaluating each scenario and making comparisons among the scenarios.

Plotting Forecasts

You can visually assess the relationships of the scenario forecasts by plotting them versus YEAR. The following SAS example code uses PROC GPLOT to plot the forecasts. Output 13.6 shows the results.

```
goptions reset=symbol;

proc gplot data=budgetp;
   where year > 86;
   plot gfund*year=1
        gl*year=2
        f*year=3
        gg*year=4 / overlay hminor=1 vminor=1
                    haxis=axis1 vaxis=axis2 legend=legend1;
   symbol1 i=join v=A font=swissb l=1 color=black;
   symbol2 i=join v=L font=swissb l=3 color=blue;
   symbol3 i=join v=B font=swissb l=3 color=green;
   symbol4 i=join v=G font=swissb l=3 color=red;
   axis1 offset=(2,2)pct order=87 to 95 by 2 label=none;
   axis2 order=4500 to 6000 by 300
        label=(a=-90 r=90 'General Fund');
   legend1 label=none value=('Actual GFUND'
        'Low POP Scenario GFUND' 'Base POP Scenario GFUND'
        'Growth POP Scenario GFUND');
   title 'N.C. General Fund 1987-1995';
   title2 'Actual, Base, Low, and Growth';
run;
quit;
```

Output 13.6
GFUND Forecasts for the Low, Baseline, and Growth POP Scenarios

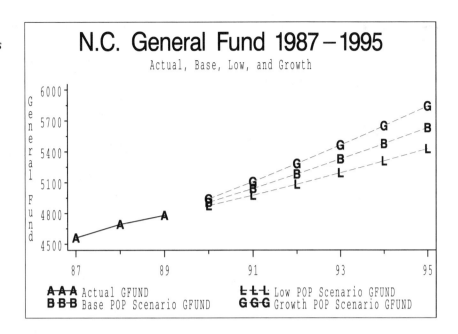

Interpretation of output

Output 13.6 plots the actual and forecasted GFUND values. The symbols A, L, B, and G represent the actual, low, base, and growth scenario values of GFUND, respectively. The values of the base scenario continue the previous GFUND trend, while the low and growth scenarios reflect the expected effects of the proposed legislation.

Chapter Summary

This chapter introduced forecasting with a single linear equation. The GFUND model was used to generate predicted values and confidence limits, and also for scenario forecasting. The forecasted values of the endogenous variable were used to reflect the different growth rates of the exogenous variable. The forecasted values were printed for direct comparison and plotted for visual assessment.

Learning More

□   For full reference information on the AUTOREG procedure in SAS/ETS software, see the *SAS/ETS User's Guide, Version 6, First Edition.*

□   For full reference information on the GPLOT procedure in SAS/GRAPH software, see *SAS/GRAPH Software: Reference, Version 6, First Edition, Volume 1* and *Volume 2.*

References

Council of Economic Advisers, *Economic Report of the President*, U.S. Government Printing Office.

N.C. Office of State Budget and Management, "Overview of the North Carolina State Budget."

Pindyck, R. and Rubinfeld, D. (1991), *Econometric Models and Economic Forecasts, Third Edition*, New York: McGraw-Hill, Inc.

U.S. Department of Commerce (1991), *Statistical Abstracts of the U.S.*, Washington, D.C.: U.S. Government Printing Office.

Introduction

In some models, Y_t (the value of the endogenous variable at time t) and X_t (the value of the exogenous variable at time t) are related contemporaneously; that is, if X_t is changed, the full effect on Y occurs in time period t. However, there are also situations where the full effect of a change in X occurs over more than one period; that is, Y_t is correlated not only with X_t, but also with X_{t-1}, X_{t-2}, and so on. A model for Y based on current and past values of X is referred to as a lagged model with a lagged exogenous variable. More complex models include additional exogenous variables, their lagged values, and even lagged values of the endogenous variable.

Keynes modeled consumption expenditures contemporaneously (1936). In this simple Keynesian consumption function, only current-period disposable income affects current-period consumption expenditures. Koyck modeled consumption as habit persistence with an infinite lag, where all previous values of disposable income affect current-period consumption expenditures (1954). In between these extremes are finite lag models. Almon modeled capital expenditures as a polynominal function of past values of capital appropriations (1965). Some past values of capital appropriations affect current capital expenditures for a finite amount of time only.

When economists forecast using lagged models, they are often interested in dynamics, that is, effects across time. The dynamics of a Keynesian consumption function are very different from those of the Koyck lag model. If disposable income is increased for one period, only current-period consumption is affected in the Keynesian model, whereas in the Koyck lag model, consumption is affected in the current period and every period thereafter.

To examine the forecasting dynamics of a model, you first generate new values for the exogenous variables to use in the forecast. Typically, you create a baseline scenario by extrapolating the observed past growth rate. You also create a hypothetical scenario either by perturbing specific values or by generating hypothetical growth rates. Next, you use the new observations in the fitted model to forecast the endogenous variable, the forecasts being conditional on the exogenous variable values. Comparing the baseline and perturbed scenarios reveals the model's forecast dynamics.

In this chapter, you use the AUTOREG, MODEL, and PDLREG procedures in SAS/ETS software to examine the forecast dynamics of lagged models. The Koyck lag consumption function is used to illustrate forecasting a model with a lagged endogenous variable. In this example, you investigate how a one-time shock in disposable income affects consumption over time by comparing it to a model hypothesizing a constant growth rate. You also use the Almon polynomial distributed lag (PDL) model to forecast a model with a lagged exogenous variable. In this example, you analyze the response in capital expenditures to a one-time shock in capital appropriations. These models are introduced and fitted in Chapter 5, "Fitting Regression Models with Lagged Variables," and then simulated in Chapter 10, "Simulating Regression Models with Lagged Variables."

Lagging Endogenous Variables: The Koyck Lag Model

Consumption functions model the expenditures of consumers. The Koyck lag consumption function is based on habit persistence of consumers and assumes that past levels of disposable income affect current consumption expenditures. In particular, the more recent a period, the more impact it has on current consumption. The Koyck lag model can be expressed in estimable form as follows:

$$C_t = b_0 + w\, C_{t-1} + b_1\, DI_t$$

where

C_t	is current-period consumption expenditures, the endogenous variable.
b_0	is the (transformed) intercept.
w	is the slope parameter associated with the lagged endogenous variable, C_{t-1}.
C_{t-1}	is the previous-period consumption expenditures. In this example, C_{t-1} is the lagged endogenous variable.
b_1	is the slope parameter associated with the exogenous variable, DI_t.
DI_t	is current-period disposable income.

Note that consumption and disposable income are deflated to real terms with the consumer price index to account for the effects of inflation.

In Chapter 5, the Koyck lag consumption function is fitted with PROC AUTOREG using the MCON data set. The following example code shows you how to use PROC MODEL to estimate this equation. The OUTMODEL= option of the

PROC MODEL statement stores the fitted model in a file named MC_MOD. The %AR macro is used to correct for first-order autoregression. The START= option of the FIT statement enables you to specify starting values for parameters to be estimated. In this example, the starting values −.5 and .5 are specified for the autoregressive parameter AR_C_L1. Part of the output generated by the following example code is displayed in Output 14.1. The model summary and model solution are not shown.

```
proc model data=mcon outmodel=mc_mod;
   parms b0 w b1;
      c = b0 + w*lag(c) + b1*di;
   %ar(ar_c,1,c)
   endo c;
   exo di;
   fit c start=(ar_c_l1 -.5 .5);
   id date;
run;
```

*Output 14.1
he Final Fitted
Model of the
oyck Lag
onsumption
unction*

```
              Monthly Consumption Function Example

                        MODEL Procedure
                        OLS Estimation

             Nonlinear OLS Summary of Residual Errors

              DF    DF
   Equation  Model Error      SSE        MSE     Root MSE  R-Square  Adj R-Sq

   C           4    89      21150    237.63551   15.41543   0.9949    0.9947



                   Nonlinear OLS Parameter Estimates

                         Approx.      'T'    Approx.
   Parameter   Estimate  Std Err     Ratio   Prob>|T|  Label

   B0         28.777846  17.22618     1.67    0.0983
   W           0.923441   0.03920    23.56    0.0001
   B1          0.065095   0.04052     1.61    0.1117
   AR_C_L1    -0.393219   0.10129    -3.88    0.0002   AR(AR_C) C LAG1 PARAMETER



             Number of Observations      Statistics for System
             Used              93        Objective    227.4146
             Missing            0        Objective*N    21150
```

Interpretation of output

Output 14.1 prints the final fitted parameters and statistics of fit for the model. The model is interpreted in Chapter 5. For this linear model, if disposable income grows at a constant rate, then consumption grows at a constant rate. However, if disposable income is unexpectedly large in one period, then consumption is also greater for that period. The larger the parameter b_1, the larger the effect on consumption. In future periods, the large disposable income value still affects consumption expenditures. In the next section, you explore the impact of the one-period shock in disposable income across time.

Examining the Model Dynamics

To examine the dynamics of an unexpected change in disposable income, you consider two possible scenarios. First, forecast consumption assuming that disposable income continues growing at 1%, the simple annual rate over the 12-month period July 1989 through June 1990. Next, forecast consumption assuming disposable income is unexpectedly large for the first forecast period, JUL90, and then grows at the historically observed rate of 1%. For example, this unexpectedly large disposable income value might occur because Congress offered a one-time personal income tax rebate that added $200 billion to disposable income.

Across subsequent periods, the predicted values of the perturbed growth rate case are expected to be higher than the baseline case, reflecting the effects of the shock to disposable income. Because the Koyck lag model contains an infinite lag, the forecasts for the perturbed case are never exactly equal to the baseline case. However, at some point the difference between the two forecasts becomes trivial for policy decisions.

The next several sections contain the steps required to create, print, and plot new disposable income values for each case and then forecast, print, and plot the corresponding consumption expenditures.

Extrapolating Exogenous Variables

In this section, you create a data set containing the hypothetical values for disposable income. One new variable, DI_BASE, contains values for disposable income under the assumption of constant growth of approximately 1% per year, the observed growth rate from JUL89 through JUN90. Note that the JUL89 and JUN90 real disposable income values are 3006.51 and 3037.49, respectively, and the annual growth rate is given by the equation $(3037.49/3006.51)-1$. A second new variable, DI_PER, contains values for disposable income under the assumption of a one-time shock of an additional $200 billion for JUL90, with disposable income returning to constant growth values after JUL90. *The two sets of disposable income values differ only in the first observation, in JUL90.*

In the DATA step, you first calculate the historical growth rate and assign the value to the variable DIG. Next, you use a DO loop to calculate the 12 new values of DI_BASE and DI_PER for the period JUL90 through JUN91. Note that you use the RETAIN and FORMAT statements with the INTNX function to create the future values for the variable DATE.

After creating the extrapolated values of disposable income, they can be printed using the PRINT procedure and plotted using the GPLOT procedure. Output 14.2 shows the results.

```
data mc_grow;

    /* Growth Rate of Disposable Income */
    dig= (3037.49/3006.51)-1;

    /* DO Loop */
    do i=1 to 12;
        retain date '01jun90'd;
        date=intnx('month',date,1);
        format date monyy.;
```

```
                    /* Constant Growth Rate DI Values */
            di_base= 3037.49*(((dig/12)*i)+1);

                    /* Perturbed Growth Rate DI Values */
            if i=1 then di_per=(3037.49*(((dig/12)*i)+1))+200;
            else di_per=di_base;

            output;
        end;
    run;

    data mcon2;
        set mcon mc_grow;
    run;

        /* Partial Listing of MCON2 Data Set */
    proc print data=mcon2 (firstobs=82);
        var date c di di_base di_per;
        title2 'Actual and Extrapolated Values';
    run;

    goptions reset=symbol;

        /* Plotting Constant DI Growth Case */
    proc gplot data=mcon2;
        where date ge '01FEB89'd;
        plot di*date=1
            di_base*date=2 / overlay hminor=2 vminor=1 haxis=axis1
                             vaxis=axis2 legend=legend1;
        symbol1 i=join font=swissb l=1 color=black;
        symbol2 i=join font=swissb l=3 color=blue;
        axis1 label=none offset=(2,2)pct;
        axis2 order=2900 to 3300 by 100
            label=(a=-90 r=90 'DI $ Billions');
        legend1 label=none value=('Actual Disposable Income'
                                 'Extrapolated Disposable Income');
        title 'Disposable Income FEB89-JUN91';
        title2 'Base (or Constant Growth) Case';
    run;

        /* Create Plot of Perturbed DI Growth Case */
    proc gplot data=mcon2;
        where date ge '01FEB89'd;
        plot di*date=1
            di_per*date=2 / overlay hminor=2 vminor=1 haxis=axis1
                            vaxis=axis2 legend=legend1;
        symbol1 i=join font=swissb l=1 color=black;
        symbol2 i=join font=swissb l=3 color=blue;
        axis1 label=none offset=(2,2)pct;
        axis2 order=2900 to 3300 by 100
            label=(a=-90 r=90 'DI $ Billions');
        legend1 label=none value=('Actual Disposable Income'
                                 'Extrapolated Disposable Income');
```

```
        title 'Disposable Income FEB89-JUN91';
        title2 'Perturbed Case';
    run;
    quit;
```

Output 14.2

The Last 13 Actual
Values of
Disposable
Income, the
Extrapolated
Values, and Plots
of the Actual and
Extrapolated
Values versus
DATE

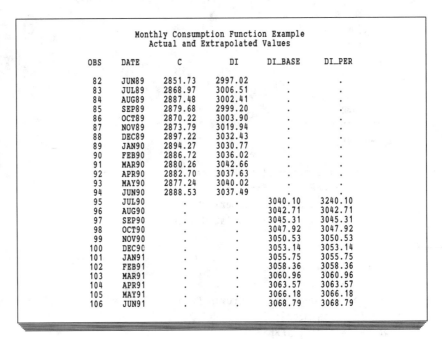

```
                Monthly Consumption Function Example
                    Actual and Extrapolated Values

    OBS     DATE        C        DI      DI_BASE     DI_PER

     82     JUN89    2851.73   2997.02      .          .
     83     JUL89    2868.97   3006.51      .          .
     84     AUG89    2887.48   3002.41      .          .
     85     SEP89    2879.68   2999.20      .          .
     86     OCT89    2870.22   3003.90      .          .
     87     NOV89    2873.79   3019.94      .          .
     88     DEC89    2897.22   3032.43      .          .
     89     JAN90    2894.27   3030.77      .          .
     90     FEB90    2886.72   3036.02      .          .
     91     MAR90    2880.26   3042.66      .          .
     92     APR90    2882.70   3037.63      .          .
     93     MAY90    2877.24   3040.02      .          .
     94     JUN90    2888.53   3037.49      .          .
     95     JUL90       .         .      3040.10    3240.10
     96     AUG90       .         .      3042.71    3042.71
     97     SEP90       .         .      3045.31    3045.31
     98     OCT90       .         .      3047.92    3047.92
     99     NOV90       .         .      3050.53    3050.53
    100     DEC90       .         .      3053.14    3053.14
    101     JAN91       .         .      3055.75    3055.75
    102     FEB91       .         .      3058.36    3058.36
    103     MAR91       .         .      3060.96    3060.96
    104     APR91       .         .      3063.57    3063.57
    105     MAY91       .         .      3066.18    3066.18
    106     JUN91       .         .      3068.79    3068.79
```

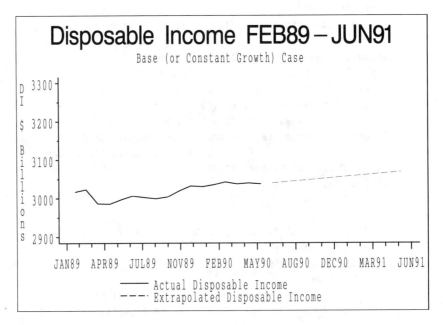

Disposable Income FEB89–JUN91

Base (or Constant Growth) Case

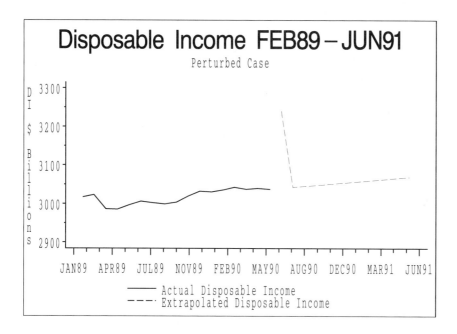

Interpretation of output

Output 14.2 prints the actual and extrapolated values of DI. The constant growth rate scenario hypothesizes that DI increases by about $2.61 billion each month. The perturbed growth rate scenario hypothesizes that in the first month DI grows by $202.61 billion, and in all other months DI grows by $2.61 billion.

In the plots, actual values are represented by a solid line and extrapolated values are represented by a dashed line. By direct and visual comparisons, you can check that DI_BASE values are extrapolations of the DI series. You can also observe the large increase in DI_PER in JUL90, after which the DI_PER series coincides with the DI_BASE series.

Forecasting the Koyck Consumption Function Model

Before you can use the new disposable income values created in Output 14.2 to forecast, you must create two new data sets, MC_BASE and MC_PER, that replace the missing values of DI with the appropriate hypothetical values of DI_BASE and DI_PER.

PROC MODEL uses these new data sets as input for forecasting. You also use the model file named MC_MOD containing the fitted model, and a SOLVE statement to generate output data sets containing the forecasts. The FORECAST option of the SOLVE statement specifies that the actual value of the solved variables be used *when available*; that is, PROC MODEL solves only for those variables that are missing in the input data set.

Forecasting starts with the second observation because a lagged value of C is required for each forecasted value. The START= option of the SOLVE statement enables you to specify the starting period for forecasting.

The OUT= option creates an output data set containing the predicted consumption expenditures. The output data sets are named BASE and PER for the

constant (baseline) growth and perturbed growth rate cases, respectively. The forecasted C values are renamed FORE_B and FORE_P.

```
      /* Constant Growth Case */
data mc_base;
   set mcon2;
   if di=. then di=di_base;
run;

      /* Perturbed Growth Case */
data mc_per;
   set mcon2;
   if di=. then di=di_per;
run;

      /* Forecasting C */
proc model model=mc_mod noprint;

      /* Forecasting Constant Growth Case */
   solve / forecast data=mc_base start=2
           out=mc_outb(drop=_type_ _mode_ _errors_
                       rename=(c=fore_b));

      /* Forecasting Perturbed Growth Case */
   solve / forecast data=mc_per start=2
           out=mc_outp(drop=_type_ _mode_ _errors_
                       rename=(c=fore_p));
run;
```

After forecasting consumption expenditures, you want to merge each set of input and output data sets for printing. The merged data sets are named MC_OUTB1 and MC_OUTP1.

```
      /* Merging Data Sets */
data mc_outb1;
   merge mc_base mc_outb;
   by date;
run;

data mc_outp1;
   merge mc_perb mc_outp;
   by date;
run;
```

The variables DATE, DI, and C and the forecasted values are printed for each merged data set starting with the 90th observation. Output 14.3 shows the results.

```
      /* Printing Constant Growth Rate Case */
proc print data=mc_outb1 (firstobs=90);
   var date di c fore_b;
   title2 'Base Case Forecasts';
run;
```

```
                    /* Printing Perturbed Growth Rate Case */
            proc print data=mc_outp1 (firstobs=90);
               var date di c fore_p;
               title2 'Perturbed Case Forecasts';
            run;
```

Output 14.3
The Actual and Forecasted Consumption Expenditures for the Constant Growth Rate (Base) Case and Perturbed Growth Rate Case of Real Disposable Income

```
                    Monthly Consumption Function Example
                              Base Case Forecasts

          OBS      DATE       DI         C        FORE_B

           90     FEB90    3036.02    2886.72    2886.72
           91     MAR90    3042.66    2880.26    2880.26
           92     APR90    3037.63    2882.70    2882.70
           93     MAY90    3040.02    2877.24    2877.24
           94     JUN90    3037.49    2888.53    2888.53
           95     JUL90    3040.10       .       2892.07
           96     AUG90    3042.71       .       2898.28
           97     SEP90    3045.31       .       2903.10
           98     OCT90    3047.92       .       2908.14
           99     NOV90    3050.53       .       2912.80
          100     DEC90    3053.14       .       2917.34
          101     JAN91    3055.75       .       2921.68
          102     FEB91    3058.36       .       2925.86
          103     MAR91    3060.96       .       2929.89
          104     APR91    3063.57       .       2933.78
          105     MAY91    3066.18       .       2937.54
          106     JUN91    3068.79       .       2941.19
```

```
                    Monthly Consumption Function Example
                            Perturbed Case Forecasts

          OBS      DATE       DI         C        FORE_P

           90     FEB90    3036.02    2886.72    2886.72
           91     MAR90    3042.66    2880.26    2880.26
           92     APR90    3037.63    2882.70    2882.70
           93     MAY90    3040.02    2877.24    2877.24
           94     JUN90    3037.49    2888.53    2888.53
           95     JUL90    3240.10       .       2905.09
           96     AUG90    3042.71       .       2910.30
           97     SEP90    3045.31       .       2914.20
           98     OCT90    3047.92       .       2918.39
           99     NOV90    3050.53       .       2922.27
          100     DEC90    3053.14       .       2926.08
          101     JAN91    3055.75       .       2929.75
          102     FEB91    3058.36       .       2933.31
          103     MAR91    3060.96       .       2936.77
          104     APR91    3063.57       .       2940.14
          105     MAY91    3066.18       .       2943.41
          106     JUN91    3068.79       .       2946.61
```

Interpretation of output

Output 14.3 prints DATE, DI, and the actual and forecasted values of C for constant growth of DI. Notice that when you use the FORECAST option and C is available, PROC MODEL uses the actual value as the predicted value. Thus, the values of C and the forecasted values match until JUL90; then PROC MODEL forecasts consumption expenditures.

The forecasts of the base case continue to grow from JUN90, but at a decreasing rate. The JUL90 value is $2,892.07 billion, or increased consumption of $3.54 billion from JUN90. The consumption forecast of the perturbed growth rate case has a higher value in JUL90 of $2,905.09 billion, showing increased consumption of $16.56 billion from JUN90. The additional $200 billion of disposable income produces a net increase in consumption of $13.02 billion.

It is interesting to note the strength of habit in forecasting consumption expenditures with this model. A $200 billion increase in DI resulted in only $13.02 billion of additional consumption over the base consumption forecast. This is a very different forecast than a contemporaneous Keynesian consumption function would yield.

Comparing Forecasts with and without One-Time Shock

By comparing the constant DI growth and perturbed DI growth cases, you can assess the dynamic impact of a one-period increase in DI on the forecasted levels of C. You can make comparisons visually by plotting the series versus DATE. PROC GPLOT is used to create these plots. The dynamic effects may be more easily assessed by comparing the changes and rates of change in each series, and the differences between the series. These new variables are created in a DATA step and printed with PROC PRINT.

The following SAS example code creates and prints the changes, rates of change, and differences, and with PROC GPLOT, plots the series versus DATE.

```
    /* Data for Comparison Variables */
data mc_comb;
   merge mc_outb1 mc_outp1;
   by date;

      /* Changes in Each Series */
   fore_bd=fore_b-lag(fore_b);
   fore_pd=fore_p-lag(fore_p);

      /* Rates of Changes in Each Series */
   fore_bd2=fore_bd-lag(fore_bd);
   fore_pd2=fore_pd-lag(fore_pd);

      /* Differences between the Series */
   dif_pb=fore_p-fore_b;
run;

    /* Printing the Comparison Variables */
proc print data=mc_comb (firstobs=92);
   var date fore_bd fore_pd fore_bd2 fore_pd2 dif_pb;
   title2 'Differences in Forecasts';
run;

    /* Creating COMBINE1 Data Set for Plotting */
data mc_comb1;
   merge mc_outb1 mc_outp1;
   if date le '01JUN90'd then fore_b=.;
   if date le '01JUN90'd then fore_p=.;
run;
```

```
goptions reset=symbol;

   /* Plotting the Series */
proc gplot data=mc_comb1;
   where date ge '01FEB89'd;
   plot c*date=1
        fore_b*date=2
        fore_p*date=3 / overlay hminor=2 vminor=1 haxis=axis1
                        vaxis=axis2 legend=legend1;
   symbol1 i=join font=swissb l=1 color=black;
   symbol2 v=B i=join font=swissb l=3 color=blue;
   symbol3 v=P i=join font=swissb l=3 color=green;
   axis1 label=none offset=(2,2)pct;
   axis2 label=(a=-90 r=90 'CONSUMPTION');
   legend1 label=none value=('Actual Consumption'
           'Consumption from Constant DI Growth'
           'Consumption from Perturbed DI Growth');
   title 'Consumption Expenditures FEB89-JUL91';
run;
quit;
```

Output 14.4 displays the output generated by the previous example code. Recall that the variable FORE_BD is the first difference of the baseline scenario forecasts, while FORE_PD is the first difference of the perturbed scenario forecast. The variables FORE_B2 and FORE_P2 are the second differences. The variable DIF_PB is the contemporaneous difference between the perturbed and baseline scenario forecasts.

utput 14.4
he Differences in
e Forecasts and
tween Forecasts

		Monthly Consumption Function Example Differences in Forecasts				
OBS	DATE	FORE_BD	FORE_PD	FORE_BD2	FORE_PD2	DIF_PB
92	APR90	2.4356	2.4356	8.8902	8.8902	0.0000
93	MAY90	-5.4552	-5.4552	-7.8908	-7.8908	0.0000
94	JUN90	11.2851	11.2851	16.7402	16.7402	0.0000
95	JUL90	3.5399	16.5588	-7.7452	5.2738	13.0190
96	AUG90	6.2112	5.2145	2.6714	-11.3443	12.0223
97	SEP90	4.8153	3.8948	-1.3960	-1.3197	11.1018
98	OCT90	5.0451	4.1951	0.2298	0.3003	10.2519
99	NOV90	4.6601	3.8752	-0.3850	-0.3200	9.4670
100	DEC90	4.5394	3.8146	-0.1207	-0.0606	8.7422
101	JAN91	4.3355	3.6662	-0.2038	-0.1483	8.0729
102	FEB91	4.1837	3.5656	-0.1519	-0.1006	7.4549
103	MAR91	4.0291	3.4584	-0.1545	-0.1072	6.8841
104	APR91	3.8920	3.3650	-0.1371	-0.0934	6.3571
105	MAY91	3.7632	3.2765	-0.1288	-0.0885	5.8704
106	JUN91	3.6451	3.1957	-0.1181	-0.0808	5.4210

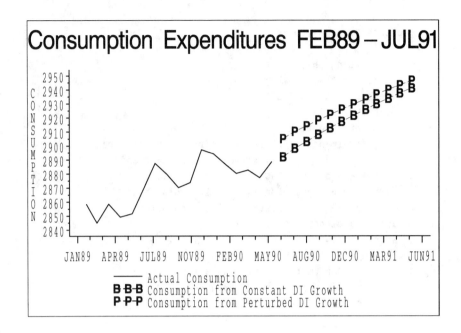

Interpretation of output

Output 14.4 prints DATE, the changes in the forecast series, their rates of change, the differences between them, and plots the actual values and the forecasted series versus DATE. The monthly differences in each series are equivalent through JUN90. Then, the JUL90 differences move in opposite directions, as shown by the second differences. Note that the difference between the series decreases steadily over time, as shown by the variable DIF_PB.

In the plot of the actual and forecasted values, the solid line represents actual C values, while the symbols B and P (which are connected by dashed lines) represent the base scenario (constant DI growth) and perturbed DI growth. The plot also shows the diminishing differences between the series.

Because the model has an infinite lag, the difference between the series will persist; however, at some point it will become trivial. If the two series were continued through the year 2000, the difference between them would be less than $.1 million, a trivial figure for national income accounting.

Comparing Forecasts of the Koyck Lag and Keynesian Consumption Function Models

You may want to compare the dynamic response of the Koyck lag consumption function with the contemporaneous response of the Keynesian consumption function. The Koyck lag consumption function is based on the habit persistence of consumers while the Keynesian consumption function relates current disposable income to current consumption expenditures. Keynesian consumption functions are introduced and fitted in Chapter 3, "Using Dummy Variables," and can be expressed as follows:

$$C_t = a + b\,DI_t \quad .$$

The following SAS example code uses PROC MODEL to fit the Keynesian consumption function with a correction for first-order autoregression. (The fitted model is not shown.) The fitted model is then used to forecast the base and perturbed scenarios. The forecasts are printed with PROC PRINT and plotted with PROC GPLOT.

```
/* Fitting the Keynesian Consumption Function */
proc model data=mcon outmodel=mcky_mod noprint;
   parms a b;
   c = a + b*di;
   %ar(ar_c,1,c)
   endo c;
   exo di;
   fit c start=(ar_c_l1 -.5 .5);
   id date;
run;


/* Forecasting C */
proc model model=mcky_mod noprint;

   /* Forecasting Constant Growth Case */
   solve / forecast data=mc_base start=2
          out=mc_outbk(drop=_type_ _mode_ _errors_
                       rename=(c=fore_b));

   /* Forecasting Perturbed Growth Case */
   solve / forecast data=mc_per start=2
          out=mc_outpk(drop=_type_ _mode_ _errors_
                       rename=(c=fore_p));
run;


/* Merging Data Sets */
data mc_combk;
   merge mc_base mc_outbk mc_outpk;
   by date;
   if date le '01JUN90'd then fore_b=.;
   if date le '01JUN90'd then fore_p=.;
run;


/* Printing Forecasts */
proc print data=mc_combk (firstobs=90);
   var date c fore_b fore_p;
   title2 'Keynesian Consumption Function Forecasts';
run;
```

```
        goptions reset=symbol;

            /* Plotting the Series */
        proc gplot data=mc_combk;
            where date ge '01FEB89'd;
            plot c*date=1
                  fore_b*date=2
                  fore_p*date=3 / overlay hminor=2 vminor=1 haxis=axis1
                                  vaxis=axis2 legend=legend1;
            symbol1 i=join font=swissb l=1 color=black;
            symbol2 v=B i=join font=swissb l=3 color=blue;
            symbol3 v=P i=join font=swissb l=3 color=green;
            axis1 label=none offset=(2,2)pct;
            axis2 label=(a=-90 r=90 'CONSUMPTION');
            legend1 label=none value=('Actual Consumption'
                     'Consumption from Constant DI Growth'
                     'Consumption from Perturbed DI Growth');
            title 'Keynesian Consumption Function';
            title2 'Consumption Expenditures FEB89-JUL91';
        run;
        quit;
```

Output 14.5 displays the output generated by the previous example code. Recall that the variables FORE_B and FORE_P are the forecasted values for the baseline and perturbed scenarios.

Output 14.5
The Actual and Forecasted Consumption Expenditures for the Keynesian Consumption Function

```
              Monthly Consumption Function Example
           Keynesian Consumption Function Forecasts

     OBS     DATE      C       FORE_B      FORE_P

      90     FEB90   2886.72      .           .
      91     MAR90   2880.26      .           .
      92     APR90   2882.70      .           .
      93     MAY90   2877.24      .           .
      94     JUN90   2888.53      .           .
      95     JUL90      .       2891.84     3081.10
      96     AUG90      .       2894.92     2894.92
      97     SEP90      .       2897.83     2897.83
      98     OCT90      .       2900.61     2900.61
      99     NOV90      .       2903.31     2903.31
     100     DEC90      .       2905.94     2905.94
     101     JAN91      .       2908.52     2908.52
     102     FEB91      .       2911.07     2911.07
     103     MAR91      .       2913.60     2913.60
     104     APR91      .       2916.11     2916.11
     105     MAY91      .       2918.61     2918.61
     106     JUN91      .       2921.10     2921.10
```

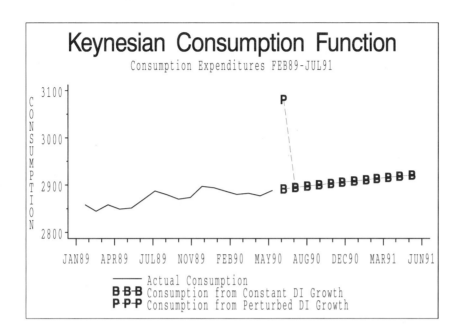

Interpretation of output

Output 14.5 prints and plots the actual and forecasted consumption values generated by the Keynesian consumption function. The one-time shock to disposable income generates a one-time spike in consumption for JUL90. All of the subsequent forecast values are equivalent. Without lagged disposable income in the model, only the current value of disposable income affects consumption. You may want to compare these forecasts with those of Output 14.3.

Lagging Exogenous Variables: The Almon PDL Model

The Almon polynomial distributed lag (PDL) model is an example of a model with lagged exogenous variables. The exogenous variables are current and lagged values of capital appropriations, APPRO. The endogenous variable is capital expenditures, CAP_EXP. The model assumes that all capital appropriations are not spent immediately, but are spent within a finite period of time.

The polynomial distributed lag model is of the following form:

$$CAP\_EXP_t = \alpha + w_0 \, APPRO_t + w_1 \, APPRO_{t-1} + \ldots + w_P \, APPRO_{t-P} + u_t$$

where

α is the intercept.

w_i are the lag parameters, where i runs from 0 to P.

P   is the length of the lag.

u_t is the random error term.

The w_i follow a polynomial form:

$$w_i = c_0 + c_1 i + c_2 i^2 + \ldots + c_D i^D$$

where

c   are polynomial coefficients for the lag parameters.

D   is the degree of the polynomial lag.

The final fitted model of Chapter 5 is corrected for second-order autoregression and is a seven-period quadratic lag model with the last endpoint restricted to zero. This model can be fitted with PROC PDLREG. You use PROC PRINT to print the actual and predicted values with 95% confidence limits. Only the final fitted model generated by the following example code is displayed in Output 14.6. The fitted model is interpreted in Chapter 5.

```
   /* Fitting the Model */
proc pdlreg data=almon;
   model cap_exp=appro(7,2,2,last) / nlag=2;
   output out=al_out alphaclm=.05 pm=p lclm=l uclm=u;
run;

   /* Printing Predicted Values */
proc print data=al_out (firstobs=48);
   var date cap_exp p l u;
   title2 'Actual and Predicted Values';
   title3 'with Confidence Limits';
run;
```

Output 14.6
The Final Fitted
Seven-Period,
Quadratic PDL
Model with the
Last Endpoint
Restricted to Zero,
Corrected for
Second-Order
Autoregression

```
                Almon Polynomial Distributed Lag Example

                          PDLREG Procedure

                     Estimates of Autocorrelations

   Lag  Covariance  Correlation -1 9 8 7 6 5 4 3 2 1 0 1 2 3 4 5 6 7 8 9 1

    0   15291.04     1.000000  |                    |********************|
    1   11468.45     0.750011  |                    |***************     |
    2    6563.232    0.429221  |                    |*********           |


                     Preliminary MSE = 6068.569

              Estimates of the Autoregressive Parameters

          Lag    Coefficient      Std Error       t Ratio
           1     -0.97852848      0.13747472     -7.117879
           2      0.30468610      0.13747472      2.216306


                       Yule-Walker Estimates

          SSE           307984.8   DFE               48
          MSE             6416.35   Root MSE    80.10212
          SBC           630.6588    AIC         620.8073
          Reg Rsq         0.9640    Total Rsq     0.9956
          Durbin-Watson   1.9195
```

(continued)

Output 14.6
(continued)

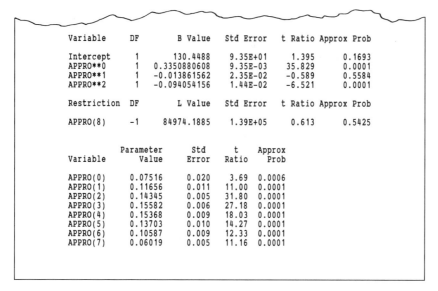

Variable	DF	B Value	Std Error	t Ratio	Approx Prob
Intercept	1	130.4488	9.35E+01	1.395	0.1693
APPRO**0	1	0.3350880608	9.35E-03	35.829	0.0001
APPRO**1	1	-0.013861562	2.35E-02	-0.589	0.5584
APPRO**2	1	-0.094054156	1.44E-02	-6.521	0.0001

Restriction	DF	L Value	Std Error	t Ratio	Approx Prob
APPRO(8)	-1	84974.1885	1.39E+05	0.613	0.5425

Variable	Parameter Value	Std Error	t Ratio	Approx Prob
APPRO(0)	0.07516	0.020	3.69	0.0006
APPRO(1)	0.11656	0.011	11.00	0.0001
APPRO(2)	0.14345	0.005	31.80	0.0001
APPRO(3)	0.15582	0.006	27.18	0.0001
APPRO(4)	0.15368	0.009	18.03	0.0001
APPRO(5)	0.13703	0.010	14.27	0.0001
APPRO(6)	0.10587	0.009	12.33	0.0001
APPRO(7)	0.06019	0.005	11.16	0.0001

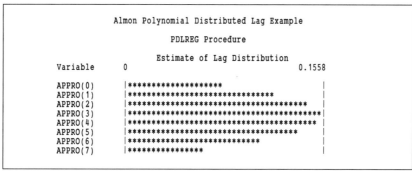

```
                 Almon Polynomial Distributed Lag Example

                          PDLREG Procedure

                     Estimate of Lag Distribution
Variable      0                                            0.1558

APPRO(0)   |********************                              |
APPRO(1)   |******************************                    |
APPRO(2)   |*************************************             |
APPRO(3)   |********************************************      |
APPRO(4)   |******************************************        |
APPRO(5)   |*************************************             |
APPRO(6)   |****************************                      |
APPRO(7)   |****************                                  |
```

```
                 Almon Polynomial Distributed Lag Example
                       Actual and Predicted Values
                         with Confidence Limits

        OBS   DATE   CAP_EXP      P         L         U

         48   64Q4    3815     3786.14   3701.99   3870.30
         49   65Q1    4093     4024.53   3936.04   4113.03
         50   65Q2    4262     4258.00   4157.39   4358.61
         51   65Q3    4531     4482.35   4373.31   4591.40
         52   65Q4    4825     4722.03   4598.35   4845.72
         53   66Q1    5160     4970.53   4834.84   5106.21
         54   66Q2    5319     5238.89   5087.56   5390.21
         55   66Q3    5574     5454.48   5309.20   5599.77
         56   66Q4    5749     5635.89   5486.53   5785.26
         57   67Q1    5715     5697.39   5539.22   5855.57
         58   67Q2    5637     5687.48   5524.38   5850.58
         59   67Q3    5383     5638.31   5477.25   5799.36
         60   67Q4    5467     5545.50   5391.01   5699.98
```

You can use PROC GPLOT to plot the actual values (CAP_EXP), the predicted values (P), and the 95% confidence limits (L and U) versus DATE for the period 65Q2 through 67Q4. Output 14.7 shows the results.

```
goptions reset=symbol;

proc gplot data=al_out;
   where date ge '01APR65'd;
   plot cap_exp*date=1
        p*date=2
        l*date=3
        u*date=4 / overlay hminor=2 vminor=1 haxis=axis1
                    vaxis=axis2;

   symbol1 v=A font=swissb color=black;
   symbol2 i=join font=swissb l=1 color=blue;
   symbol3 i=join font=swissb l=3 color=green;
   symbol4 i=join font=swissb l=3 color=red;
   axis1 label=none offset=(2,2)pct
         order='01apr65'd to '31dec67'd by qtr;
   axis2 label=(a=-90 r=90 'CAP_EXP')
         order=4000 to 6000 by 400;
   title 'Capital Expenditures';
   title2 'with 95% Confidence Intervals';
run;
quit;
```

Output 14.7
Plot of Actual and Predicted Capital Expenditures with 95% Confidence Limits

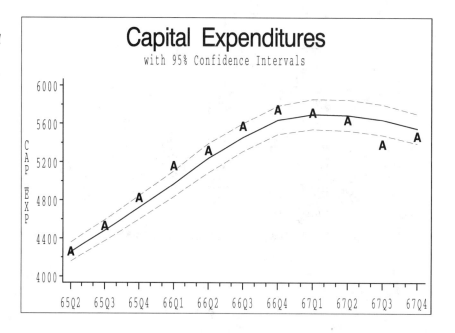

Interpretation of output

Output 14.7 plots CAP_EXP actual and predicted values versus DATE for the period 65Q2 through 67Q4. The solid line represents predicted CAP_EXP values, the symbol A represents the actual values, and the dashed lines represent the upper and lower 95% confidence limits.

Examining the Model Dynamics

The model appears to fit the data reasonably well but shows little of the dynamic properties of the PDL model. The following sections show you an approach for assessing the dynamic properties.

You might expect that any unexpectedly large or small quarterly APPRO value would affect the level of CAP_EXP over the length of the seven-quarter lag. Moreover, the effect should follow a quadratic polynomial, and because the last endpoint is restricted to zero, the effect after the seven lag periods should be zero.

To examine the dynamics, follow these steps.

1. Extrapolate the exogenous variable, APPRO, for a base case and a perturbed case.

2. Forecast capital expenditures for both cases.

3. Assess the dynamic properties of the model by comparing the forecasted series.

Extrapolating Exogenous Variables

There are several ways you can extrapolate the exogenous variable, APPRO. (For discussion of extrapolation methods, see Chapter 13, "Introduction to Forecasting.") You could fit a time series model or a low-order time polynomial model. This section shows you how to fit a quadratic time model to create new values.

You use a DATA step to create linear and quadratic time variables in a data set named AL_TIME.

```
data al_time;
   set almon;
   do t=_n_;
      t2=t*t;
   output;
   end;
run;
```

Next, you create a data set containing additional observations of the time variables with corresponding missing values for APPRO. Recall that the model is fitted with quarterly data over the period 53Q1 through 67Q4, or 60 observations in all. Additional observations are created for the period 68Q1 through 70Q4, or 12 additional observations.

```
                        /* Creating New Time Observations to Extrapolate APPRO */
                     data al_grow;
                        do t=61 to 72;
                           retain date '01oct67'd;
                           date=intnx('qtr',date,1);
                           format date yyq.;
                           t2=t*t;
                           appro=.;
                        output;
                        end;
                     run;
```

Finally, you combine these data sets in a DATA step to create the AL_GROW1 data set.

```
                     /* Combining Data Sets */
                     data al_grow1;
                        set al_time al_grow;
                     run;
```

You can fit the quadratic polynominal time model with the AL_GROW1 data set and create extrapolated values for APPRO in one invocation of PROC AUTOREG.

The following SAS example code uses PROC AUTOREG to create the extrapolated APPRO values, then creates the AL_GROW2 data set in a DATA step, and lastly uses PROC PLOT and the AL_GROW2 data set to plot the actual and extrapolated APPRO values. Output 14.8 shows the results.

```
                     /* Extrapolating APPRO */
                     proc autoreg data=al_grow1 noprint;
                        model appro=t t2;
                        output out=al_out1 pm=approp;
                     run;

                     /* Eliminating Unneeded Observations */
                     data al_grow2;
                        set al_out1;
                        if date < '01jan68'd then approp=.;
                     run;

                     /* Plotting APPRO */
                     proc plot data=al_grow2 vpct=60;
                        plot appro*date = 'A'
                             approp*date = 'F' / overlay
                                          haxis='01oct54'd to '31dec70'd by year
                                          href='01jan68'd;
                        title2 'Capital Appropriations 54Q4-70Q4';
                        title3 'Actual and Predicted';
                     run;
```

Output 14.8
Plotting the extrapolated appropriation values for Use in Forecasting Capital Expenditures

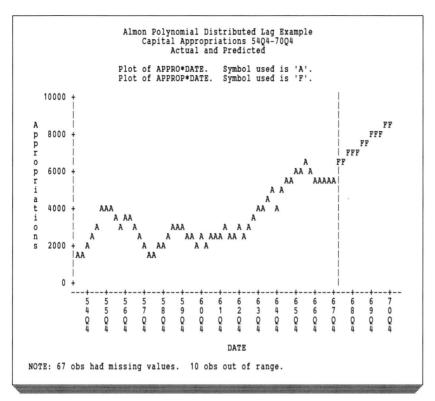

Output 14.8
Plotting the extrapolated appropriation values for Use in Forecasting Capital Expenditures

Interpretation of output

Output 14.8 plots the actual and forecasted values of APPRO that are used to forecast capital expenditures. The horizontal reference line at 68Q1 marks the first extrapolated value.

Forecasting the Almon PDL Model

The values of APPRO created in the previous example can be used as a baseline case for examining the dynamic properties of the PDL model. If you make the first value (68Q1) unusually large, then you create a set of perturbed APPRO values. By comparing the forecasts of CAP_EXP generated by these two cases, you can examine the PDL model dynamics.

To forecast these cases you create two data sets, BASE and PER, in DATA steps. The following SAS example code creates these data sets and prints the 56th through 65th observations. These are the last five observations used in fitting the PDL model and the first five observations of the forecast period.

```
data al_base;
   set al_grow2;
   if appro=. then appro=approp;
run;

proc print data=al_base (firstobs=56 obs=65);
   var date cap_exp appro approp;
   title2 'Base Scenario';
run;
```

```
data al_per;
   set al_grow2;
   if date='01jan68'd then appro=approp+2000;
   if date>'01jan68'd then appro=approp;
run;

proc print data=al_per (firstobs=56 obs=65);
   var date cap_exp appro approp;
   title2 'Perturbed Scenario';
run;
```

The output generated by the previous example code is displayed in Output 14.9. Notice that the AL_BASE and AL_PER data sets are equivalent except for the 68Q1 value of APPRO.

Output 14.9

Printing the 56th through 65th Observations of the Data Sets to be Used for Forecasting Capital Expenditures

```
           Almon Polynomial Distributed Lag Example
                        Base Scenario

      OBS    DATE    CAP_EXP     APPRO     APPROP

      56     66Q4     5749      5707.00       .
      57     67Q1     5715      5412.00       .
      58     67Q2     5637      5465.00       .
      59     67Q3     5383      5550.00       .
      60     67Q4     5467      5465.00       .
      61     68Q1       .       6401.11    6401.11
      62     68Q2       .       6584.98    6584.98
      63     68Q3       .       6772.86    6772.86
      64     68Q4       .       6964.75    6964.75
      65     69Q1       .       7160.64    7160.64
```

```
           Almon Polynomial Distributed Lag Example
                      Perturbed Scenario

      OBS    DATE    CAP_EXP     APPRO     APPROP

      56     66Q4     5749      5707.00       .
      57     67Q1     5715      5412.00       .
      58     67Q2     5637      5465.00       .
      59     67Q3     5383      5550.00       .
      60     67Q4     5467      5465.00       .
      61     68Q1       .       8401.11    6401.11
      62     68Q2       .       6584.98    6584.98
      63     68Q3       .       6772.86    6772.86
      64     68Q4       .       6964.75    6964.75
      65     69Q1       .       7160.64    7160.64
```

You can now use PROC PDLREG and the data sets AL_BASE and AL_PER to forecast CAP_EXP. The following SAS example code calculates the predicted values and the 95% lower and upper confidence limits for each case. These values are stored in output data sets, AL_OUTB and AL_OUTP, and are printed with PROC PRINT. Output 14.10 shows the results.

```
   /* Forecasting Base Case */
proc pdlreg data=al_base noprint;
   model cap_exp=appro(7,2,2,last) / nlag=2;
   output out=al_outb alphaclm=.05 pm=f_base
                      lclm=l_base uclm=u_base;
run;
```

```
        /* Forecasting Perturbed Case */
proc pdlreg data=al_per noprint;
    model cap_exp=appro(7,2,2,last) / nlag=2;
    output out=al_outp alphaclm=.05 pm=f_per
                       lclm=l_per uclm=u_per;
run;

        /* Printing Values */
proc print data=al_outb (firstobs=57);
    var date cap_exp l_base f_base u_base;
    title2 'Base Scenario';
run;

proc print data=al_outp (firstobs=57);
    var date cap_exp l_per f_per u_per;
    title2 'Perturbed Scenario';
run;
```

Output 14.10
Printing the Actual and Forecasted Capital Expenditures and 95% Confidence Limits Starting at the 57th Observations

```
                Almon Polynomial Distributed Lag Example
                            Base Scenario

        OBS    DATE    CAP_EXP     L_BASE     F_BASE     U_BASE

         57    67Q1     5715      5539.22    5697.39    5855.57
         58    67Q2     5637      5524.38    5687.48    5850.58
         59    67Q3     5383      5477.25    5638.31    5799.36
         60    67Q4     5467      5391.01    5545.50    5699.98
         61    68Q1        .      5372.93    5516.30    5659.67
         62    68Q2        .      5404.81    5554.18    5703.55
         63    68Q3        .      5533.49    5695.18    5856.86
         64    68Q4        .      5716.66    5890.18    6063.70
         65    69Q1        .      5943.27    6127.28    6311.29
         66    69Q2        .      6180.36    6374.59    6568.83
         67    69Q3        .      6414.55    6619.28    6824.02
         68    69Q4        .      6633.49    6848.93    7064.36
         69    70Q1        .      6811.36    7036.85    7262.34
         70    70Q2        .      6992.77    7228.57    7464.37
         71    70Q3        .      7177.74    7424.09    7670.45
         72    70Q4        .      7366.27    7623.42    7880.56
```

```
                Almon Polynomial Distributed Lag Example
                          Perturbed Scenario

        OBS    DATE    CAP_EXP     L_PER      F_PER      U_PER

         57    67Q1     5715      5539.22    5697.39    5855.57
         58    67Q2     5637      5524.38    5687.48    5850.58
         59    67Q3     5383      5477.25    5638.31    5799.36
         60    67Q4     5467      5391.01    5545.50    5699.98
         61    68Q1        .      5497.00    5666.62    5836.25
         62    68Q2        .      5613.11    5787.31    5961.51
         63    68Q3        .      5803.77    5982.07    6160.38
         64    68Q4        .      6017.54    6201.83    6386.11
         65    69Q1        .      6241.98    6434.65    6627.32
         66    69Q2        .      6446.26    6648.66    6851.06
         67    69Q3        .      6619.31    6831.02    7042.73
         68    69Q4        .      6749.93    6969.31    7188.68
         69    70Q1        .      6811.36    7036.85    7262.34
         70    70Q2        .      6992.77    7228.57    7464.37
         71    70Q3        .      7177.74    7424.09    7670.45
         72    70Q4        .      7366.27    7623.42    7880.56
```

Interpretation of output

Output 14.10 prints the actual and forecasted values of CAP_EXP with the lower and upper 95% confidence limits. The baseline and perturbed scenario forecasts are F_BASE and F_PER. The baseline scenario confidence limits are L_BASE and

U_BASE. The perturbed scenario confidence limits are L_PER and U_PER. You see that the 68Q1 forecasted values are different, but by 70Q1 the values are equivalent.

Comparing Forecasts of the PDL Model

You can combine the two output data sets, AL_OUTB and AL_OUTP, to compare the forecasts and observe the dynamics of the PDL model. The difference between the two CAP_EXP forecasts reveals the period-by-period impact of the perturbed APPRO value in 68Q1. You can examine these dynamics directly by printing the values, and visually by plotting them versus DATE.

Prior to printing or plotting, you want to merge the data sets in a DATA step and eliminate unneeded values. The following SAS example code creates the AL_COMB data set and the variable DIFF, the difference between the two forecasts. Then, the forecasts and DIFF are printed. Output 14.11 shows the results.

```
data al_comb;
   merge al_outb al_outp;
   by date;
   if date le '01DEC67'd then delete;
   diff=f_per-f_base;
run;

proc print data=al_comb;
   var date f_per f_base diff;
   title2 'Comparing Forecasts';
run;
```

Output 14.11
Printing the Forecasted Capital Expenditures and Their Differences

```
                  Almon Polynomial Distributed Lag Example
                            Comparing Forecasts

         OBS    DATE     F_PER      F_BASE        DIFF

          1     68Q1    5666.62    5516.30     150.325
          2     68Q2    5787.31    5554.18     233.125
          3     68Q3    5982.07    5695.18     286.898
          4     68Q4    6201.83    5890.18     311.646
          5     69Q1    6434.65    6127.28     307.369
          6     69Q2    6648.66    6374.59     274.065
          7     69Q3    6831.02    6619.28     211.736
          8     69Q4    6969.31    6848.93     120.381
          9     70Q1    7036.85    7036.85       0.000
         10     70Q2    7228.57    7228.57       0.000
         11     70Q3    7424.09    7424.09       0.000
         12     70Q4    7623.42    7623.42       0.000
```

Interpretation of output

Output 14.11 prints the two sets of forecasted values of CAP_EXP and the differences between them. The difference (DIFF) begins in the current period (68Q1), increases until reaching a peak in the 3rd lag period (68Q4), then decreases to zero in the 8th lag period (70Q1) and is zero in all subsequent periods. This pattern implies a quadratic lag structure of seven periods with the last endpoint restricted to zero.

Plotting Forecast Differences

The dynamics of the PDL model are more readily apparent through visual inspection. The variable DIFF is expected to follow a seven-period quadratic lag structure. The following SAS example code using PROC GPLOT plots the difference of the two forecasts versus DATE. Output 14.12 shows the results.

```
goptions reset=symbol;

proc gplot data=al_comb;
   where date ge '01DEC67'd;
   plot diff*date=1 / overlay hminor=2 vminor=1 haxis=axis1
                      vaxis=axis2;
   symbol1 v=D i=join font=swissb l=1;
   axis1 label=none offset=(2,2)pct
         order='01jan68'd to '01oct70'd by qtr;
   axis2 label=none order=-50 to 350 by 50;
   title 'Difference of Forecasts';
   title2 'Capital Expenditures';
run;
quit;
```

Output 14.12 Plotting the Differences of the Two Forecasts of Capital Expenditures

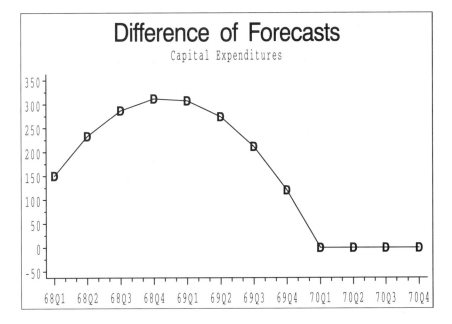

Interpretation of output

Output 14.12 plots DIFF, the difference of the two sets of forecasted CAP_EXP values. The symbol D represents the points. From the plot, it is clear that DIFF follows a quadratic polynomial. The time period 68Q1 is the period in which the change occurs; the impact effect of this period is the contemporaneous effect. The following seven periods, 68Q2 through 69Q4, represent the seven-period lag of the quadratic polynomial. The time period 70Q1 is the period immediately following the seven-period quadratic lag, and it is restricted to zero by the LAST argument of the PDL effect in the MODEL statement. All subsequent periods are also zero.

You conclude that perturbations of the trend in APPRO are reflected in the forecasts of CAP_EXP over the length of the modeled lag, and they reflect the polynomial structure of the lag. Thus, for the quadratic lag, you expect that over time, the impact of the perturbation grows, reaches a peak, and then declines to zero. You would not expect the initial impact or the first period lagged impact to reflect the largest change in CAP_EXP.

This conclusion can be applied in forecasting investment in a larger model, for example, a macroeconomic model of the economy. During the early periods of an economic recovery, increasing capital appropriations are made. If capital appropriations follow a quadratic PDL model, as in this chapter, then capital expenditures will follow appropriations (with a lag), and the resulting investment helps to sustain the recovery.

Chapter Summary

This chapter presented examples of forecasting with models containing lagged exogenous or lagged endogenous variables. The infinite lag Koyck consumption function was used as an example of a lagged endogenous model, and the Almon polynomial distributed lag model was used as an example of a lagged exogenous model. The dynamics of the infinite lag Koyck consumption function were examined, and for purposes of national income accounting, found to be much less than infinite. The dynamics of the Almon polynomial distributed lag model were examined and found to follow the degree of the polynomial. The length of the lag and the endpoint restriction also affected the forecasted values.

Learning More

□ For full reference information on the MODEL procedure in SAS/ETS software, see the *SAS/ETS User's Guide, Version 6, First Edition.*

□ For full reference information on the GPLOT procedure in SAS/GRAPH software, see *SAS/GRAPH Software: Reference, Version 6, First Edition, Volume 1* and *Volume 2.*

□ For full reference information on the PLOT procedure in base SAS software, see the *SAS/Procedures Guide, Version 6, Third Edition.*

□ For more information on DATA step processing and functions, see *SAS Language: Reference, Version 6, First Edition.*

References

Almon, S. (1965), "The Distributed Lag between Capital Appropriations and Expenditures," *Econometrica*, 33, 407—423.

Keynes, J. (1936), *The General Theory of Employment, Interest, and Money*, New York: Macmillan Publishing Company, Inc.

Klein, L.R. (1950), *Economic Fluctuations in the United States 1921—41*, New York: John Wiley & Sons, Inc.

Koyck, L. (1954), *Distributed Lags and Investment Analysis*, Amsterdam, Netherlands: North-Holland.

Maddala, G.S. (1977), *Econometrics*, New York: McGraw-Hill, Inc.

Pindyck, R. and Rubinfeld, D. (1991), *Econometric Models and Economic Forecasts, Third Edition*, New York: McGraw-Hill, Inc.

U.S. Bureau of Economic Analysis, *Survey of Current Business*, Washington, D.C.: U.S. Government Printing Office.

Chapter 15 Forecasting with Linear Systems

Introduction

While single equation models are a simple approach to modeling aggregate economic behavior, multiple equation models (referred to as *systems*) can capture several simultaneously determined components of the behavior. These systems consist of at least two equations. Typically, economists forecast with linear systems to predict the future behavior of several simultaneously determined variables.

Linear systems are typically fitted with time series data or cross-sectional data. For example, the Klein Model 1 is a small model of the U.S. national economy fitted with time series data (observations on one economic unit across multiple time periods). A supply-and-demand model of aggregate U.S. energy consumption, used to examine average energy prices and quantities, is fitted with cross-sectional data (observations on multiple economic units for one time period).

In this chapter, you use the MODEL procedure in SAS/ETS software and the Klein Model 1 to forecast scenarios of the future. The Klein Model 1 is introduced and fitted with time series data in Chapter 6, "Fitting Systems of Linear Equations," and then simulated in Chapter 11, "Simulating Systems of Linear Equations." To forecast the Klein Model 1, you first create hypothetical growth rates or extrapolate past growth rates for exogenous variables for each forecast scenario. Then, you use the extrapolated values to forecast endogenous variables. This model has historical interest and illustrates the complexities of predicting future behaviors of economic variables in a linear, simultaneous equation model. Forecasters still face the same issues when forecasting with more complex systems.

Also in this chapter, you use forecasting to validate a model. You use PROC MODEL to fit a simple cross-sectional model of U.S. energy supply and demand; then, you use the model to forecast price and quantity for additional economic units. The model of energy use is fitted with data for eastern states. The fitted model is used to forecast average price and quantity for western states. The forecasts are plotted, and goodness-of-fit statistics are generated to assess the quality of the forecasts.

Scenario Forecasting the Klein Model 1

In Chapter 6, the Klein Model 1 of the economy is fitted for the period 1920 through 1941. The Klein Model 1 consists of four identities and three fitted equations: consumption, investment, and private wages. The endogenous variables include consumption (C), investment (I), and private wages (WP). The exogenous variables are government expenditures on wages (WG), government expenditures on goods (G), tax receipts (T), and time (TIME). The predetermined variables are profits lagged one period (P_1), capital stock lagged one period (K_1), and output from the private sector lagged one period (X_1).

Suppose you were an economic forecaster for the Roosevelt administration in November 1941 and you had been asked to provide forecasts of the U.S. economy in two scenarios:

□   In the base scenario, the economy continues along the trend from 1937 through 1941. Tax receipts and government expenditures on goods and services grow at the annual compound rate observed over that five-year period.

□   In the war scenario, the U.S. enters World War II, and tax receipts and government expenditures on goods and wages rise.

The following SAS example code fits the Klein Model 1. The output from this code is displayed and interpreted in Chapter 6.

```
proc model data=klein outmodel=kl_mod;
   parms a1-a4 b1-b4 c1-c4;
   c=a1+a2*p+a3*lag(p)+a4*wt;
   i=b1+b2*p+b3*lag(p)+b4*lag(k);
   wp=c1+c2*x+c3*lag(x)+c4*time;
   x=c+i+g;
   p=x-wp-t;
   k=lag(k)+i;
   wt=wp+wg;
   endo c i wp x p wt k;
   exo p_1 k_1 x_1 time t g wg;
   id year;
   fit c i wp / 3sls;
   instruments p_1 k_1 x_1 time t g wg;
run;
```

The OUTMODEL= option creates a file, named KL_MOD containing the fitted model. The model file KL_MOD was created in Output 11.2 and is used in subsequent invocations of PROC MODEL to perform the forecasting. For details on the OUTMODEL= option, see the *SAS/ETS User's Guide, Version 6*, First Edition.

The following sections lead you through the tasks of calculating growth rates, extrapolating exogenous variables, concatenating the extrapolated values to the original data for printing and plotting, forecasting the endogenous variables for each scenario, and then printing and plotting the forecasted values.

Extrapolating the Exogenous Variables

Prior to using the Klein Model 1 for forecasting, you must acquire or generate future values of the exogenous variables. For discussion of different approaches, see Chapter 13, "Introduction to Forecasting."

In this example, the growth rates of the exogenous variables (except TIME) are used to extrapolate their future values. To extrapolate the exogenous variables for the base scenario, you must first calculate their growth rates. The following formula shows the annually compounded growth rate relationship:

$$r = (F / P)^{1/n}$$

where the variables are defined as follows:

r   is the annually compounded growth rate plus one.

F   is the final value (the 1941 value).

P   is the first value (the 1937 value).

n   is the number of years from the first to the final value, (in this example, five years).

You use the data in the KLEIN data set to calculate the base growth rates. For example, the base growth rate (plus one) for government wage expenditures is calculated as follows:

$$r = (8.5 / 6.7)^{(1/5)} = 1.04874$$

The wartime growth rates are speculative and reflect the expected wartime expenditures. The growth rates (plus one) are summarized in Table 15.1.

Table 15.1
Growth Rates for Exogenous Variables of the Klein Model 1

Variable	Base Growth Rate	Wartime Growth Rate
WG	1.04874	1.150
G	1.26265	1.400
T	1.11603	1.200

You use the growth rates in an iterative DO loop to create extrapolated values for the exogenous variables of the Klein Model 1.

The variable TIME is created as an instrumental variable to fit the Klein Model 1 to the KLEIN data set. Additional values of TIME are required to forecast the Klein Model 1. These tasks are performed in a DATA step. After the variables

YEAR, WG, G, and T are extrapolated, PROC PRINT is used to print the extrapolated values. Output 15.1 shows the results.

```
data kl_fore;

    /* Creating Extrapolated Input Values */
do year=1942 to 1946;
    time=year-1919;
    time1=year-1941;

        /* Base Scenario Growth Rates,        */
        /* Growth Rate Raised to Appropriate */
        /* Power Times 1941 Value            */
        wg_b= 8.5*(1.04874)**time1;
        g_b =13.8*(1.26265)**time1;
        t_b =11.6*(1.11603)**time1;

        /* War Scenario Growth Rates */
        wg_w= 8.5*(1.15)**time1;
        g_w =13.8*(1.40)**time1;
        t_w =11.6*(1.20)**time1;
    output;
end;
label wg_b = 'Government Wages Base Scenario'
      g_b = 'Government Goods Base Scenario'
      t_b = 'Government Taxes Base Scenario'
      wg_w = 'Government Wages War Scenario'
      g_w = 'Government Goods War Scenario'
      t_w = 'Government Taxes War Scenario';
run;

proc print data=kl_fore label;
    var year wg_b g_b t_b wg_w g_w t_w;
    title 'KLEIN Model 1 Example';
    title2 'Extrapolated Data for Forecasting';
run;
```

Output 15.1
Growth Rates and Extrapolated Values of Exogenous Variables for Scenario Forecasting

```
                              KLEIN Model 1 Example
                         Extrapolated Data for Forecasting

          Government Government Government Government Government Government
          Wages Base Goods Base Taxes Base Wages War  Goods War  Taxes War
OBS YEAR  Scenario   Scenario   Scenario   Scenario   Scenario   Scenario

 1  1942   8.9143    17.4246    12.9459     9.7750    19.3200    13.9200
 2  1943   9.3488    22.0011    14.4481    11.2413    27.0480    16.7040
 3  1944   9.8044    27.7797    16.1245    12.9274    37.8672    20.0448
 4  1945  10.2823    35.0761    17.9954    14.8666    53.0141    24.0538
 5  1946  10.7835    44.2888    20.0834    17.0965    74.2197    28.8645
```

Plotting Extrapolated Values

Plotting the actual and extrapolated values enables you to visually assess the historical trend of the data and the growth rate of the extrapolated values.

Before plotting with the GPLOT procedure in SAS/GRAPH software, you concatenate the extrapolated values to the KLEIN data set using a DATA step. In the following SAS example code, only the code for the plot of government wages, WG, versus YEAR is shown. Output 15.2 shows the results.

```
    /* Concatenating Data Sets */
data klein_p4;
    set klein kl_fore;
run;

goptions reset=symbol;

    /* Plotting Actual and Extrapolated Values */
proc gplot data=klein_p4;
    where year ge 1932;
    plot wg*year=1
        wg_b*year=2
        wg_w*year=3 / overlay hminor=1 vminor=1
                      haxis=axis1 vaxis=axis2 legend=legend1;
    symbol1 i=join font=swissb l=1 color=black;
    symbol2 v=B i=join font=swissb l=3 color=blue;
    symbol3 v=W i=join font=swissb l=3 color=green;
    axis1 label=none offset=(2,2)pct order=1932 to 1946 by 2;
    axis2 label=none order=4 to 18 by 2;
    legend1 label=none value=('Actual Government Wages'
            'Base Scenario Wages' 'War Scenario Wages');
    title 'Government Wages 1932-1946';
    title2 'Actual and Extrapolated';
run;
quit;
```

Output 15.2
Plot of Actual and Extrapolated Government Wages

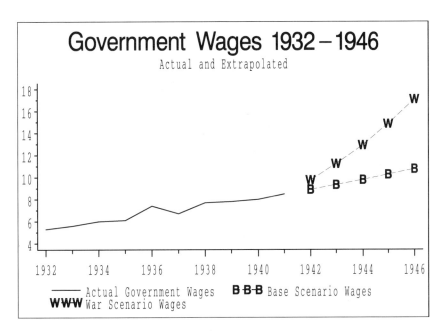

Interpretation of output

Output 15.2 plots the actual and extrapolated values of the exogenous variable, G, versus YEAR. In the plot, the solid line represents actual values, and the symbols B and W represent the extrapolations for the base and wartime scenarios.

With this plot, you can assess the rates of growth of the extrapolated values and compare them to your expectations of the future. You may want to assess several sets of growth rates for the wartime scenario. Expectations of the length and intensity of involvement may affect the growth rates you ultimately select.

Plotting Other Exogenous Variables

The two remaining plots (G versus YEAR and T versus YEAR) are produced using similar SAS example code. Output 15.3 shows these plots.

Output 15.3
Plots of Actual and Extrapolated Government Expenditures and Taxes

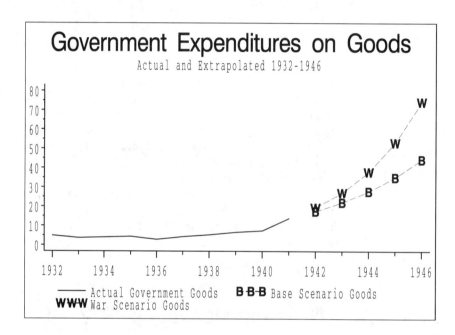

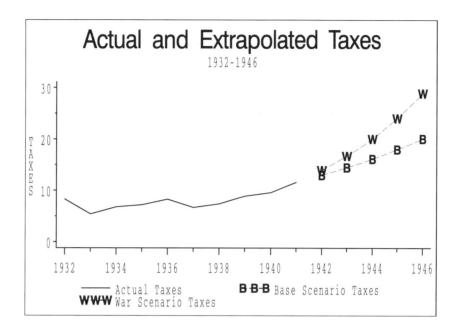

Interpretation of output

Output 15.3 plots the actual and extrapolated values of the exogenous variables, WG and T, versus YEAR. In each plot, the solid line represents actual values, and the symbols B and W represent the extrapolations for the base and wartime scenarios.

Creating New Data Sets

Before you can use PROC MODEL to forecast, you need to create separate data sets for the base and wartime scenarios. You use the KLEINP_4 data set, created in the previous example, to create new data sets, named BASE and WAR, in a DATA step. The DROP= option drops the listed variables. The IF-THEN statements set the missing values equal to the appropriate extrapolated values. The PRINT procedure prints the values of YEAR, WG, T, and G, starting with the 22nd observation. Output 15.4 shows the results.

```
data kl_base (drop=wg_b g_b t_b wg_w g_w t_w);
   set kleinp_4;
      if wg=. then wg=wg_b;
      if g=. then g=g_b;
      if t=. then t=t_b;
run;

proc print data=kl_base (firstobs=22);
   var year wg t g;
   title 'KLEIN Model 1 Example';
   title2 'Partial Listing of Base Case Data';
run;

data kl_war (drop=wg_b g_b t_b wg_w g_w t_w);
   set klein6;
```

```
            if wg=. then wg=wg_w;
            if g=. then g=g_w;
            if t=. then t=t_w;
        run;

        proc print data=kl_war (firstobs=22);
            var year wg t g;
            title 'KLEIN Model 1 Example';
            title2 'Partial Listing of Wartime Data';
        run;
```

Output 15.4
Actual and
Extrapolated Base
and Wartime
Values of the
Exogenous
Variables of the
Klein Model 1
from 1940 through
1946

```
                        KLEIN Model 1 Example
                   Partial Listing of Base Case Data

            OBS    YEAR      WG         T         G

            22     1940     8.0000     9.6000     7.4000
            23     1941     8.5000    11.6000    13.8000
            24     1942     8.9143    12.9460    17.4245
            25     1943     9.3488    14.4481    22.0010
            26     1944     9.8045    16.1246    27.7796
            27     1945    10.2824    17.9955    35.0758
            28     1946    10.7836    20.0836    44.2884
```

```
                        KLEIN Model 1 Example
                   Partial Listing of Wartime Data

            OBS    YEAR      WG         T         G

            22     1940     8.0000     9.6000     7.4000
            23     1941     8.5000    11.6000    13.8000
            24     1942     9.7750    13.9200    19.3200
            25     1943    11.2413    16.7040    27.0480
            26     1944    12.9274    20.0448    37.8672
            27     1945    14.8666    24.0538    53.0141
            28     1946    17.0965    28.8645    74.2197
```

Interpretation of output

In Output 15.4, the actual and extrapolated values of the exogenous variables are printed for the period 1940 through 1946. This output confirms that the data sets KL_BASE and KL_WAR contain the appropriate extrapolated values. The new data sets are used in the next section to forecast the endogenous variables of the Klein Model 1.

Forecasting the Klein Model 1

After fitting the Klein Model 1, you can forecast values of the endogenous variables, C, I, and WP, with PROC MODEL and the data sets KL_BASE and KL_WAR. You can then print the forecasts with PROC PRINT. The following is an interpretation of the PROC MODEL statements and options:

PROC MODEL

invokes the MODEL procedure. The following MODEL statement options are specified:

MODEL=   recalls the model file containing the fitted Klein Model 1.

NOPRINT   suppresses the printed output.

SOLVE

specifies the model be simulated or forecasted. The SOLVE statement is used twice, once with the BASE data set and once with the WAR data set. The following options of the SOLVE statement are specified:

FORECAST   specifies the model solution is to be a forecast and not a simulation. In FORECAST mode, PROC MODEL solves only for those variables that are missing in the input data set.

DATA=   specifies the data set to be used in the forecast.

START=   specifies the observation with which the solutions are to start. PROC MODEL requires values for all exogenous variables (even lagged variables) to solve the system. In this example, the solutions start with the third observation.

OUT=   creates an output data set containing the solution values. The forecasted values are contained in the output data sets, KL_OUTB and KL_OUTW.

RENAME=   renames the listed variables. For this example, the baseline forecasted values are renamed C_B, I_B, and WP_B while the wartime forecasted values are renamed C_W, I_W, and WP_W.

The following SAS example code forecasts the endogenous variables of the Klein Model 1 for the base and wartime scenarios. Output 15.5 shows the results.

```
    /* Invoking PROC MODEL */
proc model model=kl_mod noprint;

    /* Forecasting Base Scenario */
  solve / forecast data=kl_base start=3
          out=kl_outb(rename=(c=c_b i=i_b wp=wp_b));
run;

    /* Forecasting War Scenario */
  solve / forecast data=kl_war start=3
          out=kl_outw(rename=(c=c_w i=i_w wp=wp_w));
run;

    /* Printing Base Scenario Forecasted Values */
proc print data=kl_outb (firstobs=23) label;
   var year c_b i_b wp_b;
   label c_b='Consumption Base Scenario'
         i_b='Investment Base Scenario'
        wp_b='Private Wages Base Scenario';
   title2 'Base Case Scenario Forecasts';
run;
```

```
                    /* Printing Wartime Scenario Forecasted Values */
            proc print data=kl_outw (firstobs=23) label;
               var year c_w i_w wp_w;
               label c_w='Consumption Wartime Scenario'
                     i_w='Investment Wartime Scenario'
                    wp_w='Private Wages Wartime Scenario';
               title2 'Wartime Scenario Forecasts';
            run;
```

Output 15.5
Forecasted Values of the Endogenous Variables of the Klein Model 1 from 1942 through 1946 for the Base and Wartime Scenarios

```
                            KLEIN Model 1 Example
                          Base Case Scenario Forecasts

                         Consumption   Investment    Private
                            Base          Base      Wages Base
             OBS   YEAR    Scenario      Scenario    Scenario

             23    1942     77.820        4.8135      59.541
             24    1943     85.933        6.9041      67.722
             25    1944     95.934        9.3505      77.849
             26    1945    108.267       12.3065      90.346
             27    1946    123.654       16.0214     105.927
```

```
                            KLEIN Model 1 Example
                          Wartime Scenario Forecasts

                                                     Private
                         Consumption   Investment     Wages
                           Wartime       Wartime     Wartime
             OBS   YEAR    Scenario      Scenario    Scenario

             23    1942     79.955        4.8045      61.151
             24    1943     93.040        7.9535      73.738
             25    1944    111.833       12.7793      92.021
             26    1945    138.228       19.8027     117.860
             27    1946    175.061       29.8425     154.072
```

Interpretation of output

Output 15.5 prints the forecasted values of consumption, investment, and private wages (the endogenous variables) for the period 1942 through 1946.

Note the continued rapid rise in consumption expenditure forecasts during the wartime scenario. Given wartime conditions, you might expect wartime consumption expenditures to rise less rapidly after several years of wartime involvement.

From regression analysis of consumption functions in Chapter 3, "Using Dummy Variables," you know that during wartime there can be structural shifts in the economy. A priori, you expect consumers to consume less during wartime due to shortages and rationing. Also, by consuming less, consumers save more, and the increased savings encourages even greater investment. For the wartime scenario forecasts, you may want to adjust the levels of consumption and investment with one or more dummy variables. Given only the data available in late 1941, an analysis of U.S. consumption and investment during World War I (1917 through 1919) might be of assistance in finetuning the forecasts.

Plotting Forecasted Consumption Expenditures

Even though printing the forecasted values enables you to make direct comparisons, plotting them may be a more useful approach. You can use

PROC GPLOT to plot the forecasted values of consumption expenditures for the period 1936 through 1946.

Prior to plotting the values, you merge the output data sets, KL_OUTB and KL_OUTW, in a DATA step. The DATA step merging also enables you to eliminate unneeded values with ARRAY processing. Output 15.6 shows the results.

```
    /* Merging Data Sets */
data kleinp_5;
   merge klein kl_outb kl_outw;
   by year;
   array miss{6} c_b i_b wp_b c_w i_w wp_w;
   do j=1 to 6 while (year le 1941);
      miss{j}=.;
   end;
run;


goptions reset=symbol;

    /* Plotting Forecasts */
proc gplot data=kleinp_5;
   where year ge 1936;
   plot c*year=1
        c_b*year=2
        c_w*year=3 / overlay hminor=1 vminor=2
                     haxis=axis1 vaxis=axis2 legend=legend1;
   symbol1 i=join font=swissb l=1 color=black;
   symbol2 v=B i=join font=swissb l=3 color=blue;
   symbol3 v=W i=join font=swissb l=3 color=green;
   axis1 label=none offset=(2,2)pct order=1936 to 1946 by 2;
   axis2 label=(a=-90 r=90 'CONSUMPTION')
         order=45 to 180 by 15;
   legend1 label=none value=('Actual Consumption'
         'Base Scenario Consumption'
         'War Scenario Consumption');
   title 'Consumption 1936-1946';
   title2 'Actual and Forecasted';
run;
quit;
```

Output 15.6
Plot of Actual and
Forecasted
Consumption
Expenditures

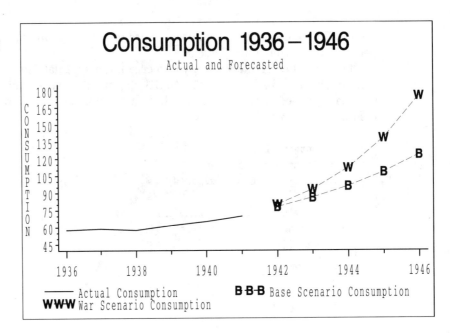

Interpretation of output

Output 15.6 displays the forecasts of consumption; the solid line represents actual values, and the symbols B and W represent the forecasts for the base and wartime scenarios. In both scenarios, the forecasts show increasing consumption expenditures.

You may want to expand the model to include the different mix of national product in the wartime scenario. For example, you may want to allow for decreased consumption, increased saving and investment, and higher wages through private sector overtime work and additional government employment. There are many scenarios you could explore based upon the expectations you have about the future in times of war or peace.

Plotting Other Forecasted Values

You can also use PROC GPLOT to plot the forecasted values of investment expenditures and private wages for the period 1936 through 1946. The SAS example code to generate these plots is similar to that generating Output 15.6 and is not shown.

Output 15.7
*Plots of Actual
and Forecasted
Investment
Expenditures and
Private Wages*

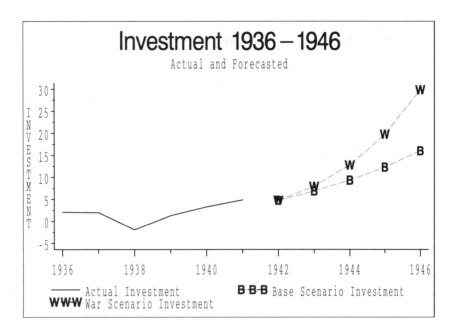

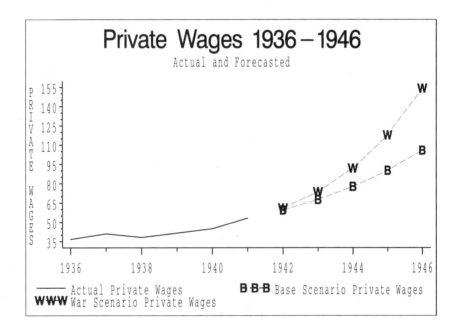

Interpretation of output

Output 15.7 displays the forecasts of investment and private wages. In each plot, the solid line represents actual values, and the symbols B and W represent the forecasts for the base and wartime scenarios. In both scenarios, the economy seems to function similarly. The forecasted values are higher each period in the wartime scenario. In both forecasts there is an upward trend in investment and private wages, reflecting the growth of government expenditures on goods and wages, and the growth in tax receipts.

Validating Models through Forecasting

Suppose you are a forecaster who needs to develop a general model of energy consumption for the eastern part of the U.S., that is, states east of the Mississippi River. You have a cross-sectional data set for the entire U.S. Each observation of the data set corresponds to the values for a state, the cross-sectional unit. You can view the data set as being composed of two parts, eastern and western. You might consider fitting the model to the data for the eastern part and discarding the data for the western part. Yet, the following is a superior approach because it uses both parts to develop the energy model:

1. Fit the energy model with data for the eastern states.

2. Use the fitted model to forecast average energy prices and quantities consumed for eastern and western states.

3. Compare the goodness-of-fit statistics generated from the forecasted and actual values for both parts of the country.

If the goodness-of-fit statistics are similar for the eastern and western parts of the U.S., then the model is validated in that it forecasts as well for the additional cross-sectional units as it does for those used for estimation.

Note the approach shown in this example is related to the use of dummy variables, as discussed in Chapter 3, "Using Dummy Variables." In Chapter 3, you created dummy variables to separate the data into parts based on suspected occurence of structural changes or qualitative differences. Then, you used a Chow F test to jointly test the dummy variables as a test of model stability. (You can also apply this methodology to the general model of energy consumption by creating dummy variables for the western states data and then fitting and testing the model.) Both approaches help you assess a model's goodness of fit to data that can be subset into parts. To be thorough, you may want to use both approaches to test the validity of the fitted model.

Fitting the U.S. Energy Model

A general model of total energy demand and supply is used to illustrate the steps involved in fitting and validating a simultaneous cross-sectional model. This model cannot be expected to perfectly match specific state energy consumption patterns.

The simple cross-sectional U.S. energy model is as follows:

$$\text{DEMAND:} \quad Q = d_0 + d_1 P + d_2 \text{ POP } + \varepsilon_D$$

$$\text{SUPPLY:} \quad Q = s_0 + s_1 P + s_2 \text{ ELEC} + \varepsilon_S$$

where

d_0, d_1, d_2	are the parameters of the demand equation.
s_0, s_1, s_2	are the parameters of the supply equation.
Q	is energy consumption (in millions of dollars).

P	is the average energy price (in dollars per million BTUs) calculated by dividing energy expenditures by energy consumed.
POP	is population (in thousands).
ELEC	is net electric energy generated (in billions of KWH). ELEC can be thought of as a proxy variable for input fuels used to generate electricity, for example, coal and gas.
ε_D	is the demand equation random error term.
ε_S	is the supply equation random error term.

The energy model is fitted using the 26 states (and the District of Columbia) east of the Mississippi River. The data include observations of Q, POP, ELEC, and the following variables:

EXP	is energy expenditures in millions of dollars.
PI	is per capita personal disposable income.
VAM	is value added in manufacturing in millions of dollars.
LAND	is land in square miles.
ID	is the U.S. Postal Service state abbreviations.

The data are from *Statistical Abstracts of the United States* for the year 1988, except for LAND, which is for the year 1980. Note that average energy price, P, is calculated by dividing energy expenditures, EXP, by energy consumption, Q.

The model is fitted in general equation form using PROC MODEL. Because price and quantity are simultaneously determined and hence correlated with the error term, the estimation method selected should account for this estimation problem. For this example, the estimation method of two-stage least squares is specified to mitigate simultaneous equation bias. The variable ELEC is used as a right-hand side variable. It is not used as an instrumental variable because it, too, is simultaneously determined and is therefore correlated with the error terms. The instrumental variables are PI, POP, VAM, and LAND.

The following SAS example code reads the ENERGY_E data set, prints the first five observations of the data set, and fits the energy model. The OUTMODEL= option creates an output data file named EN_MOD containing the fitted model. Only the final fitted model is shown in Output 15.8.

```
data energy_e;
   input exp q pi pop vam land elec id $ aa;

            /* Energy Expenditures / Energy Consumption = Price */
      p=exp/q;
   label exp='Energy Expenditures'
         q='Energy Consumption'
         p='Energy Price'
         pi='Personal Disposable Income'
         pop='Population'
         vam='Value Added in Manufacturing'
         land='Land Area in Square Miles'
         elec='Electricity Generation'
         id='State Name';
```

```
      cards;
   7284 1614 10993   4103 18652 50767   67.5 AL
   5475  757 19559   3232 22349  4872   36.4 CT
   1049  174 18397    613  1525    63    0.5 DC
   1223  230 14137    660  3866  1932    9.0 DE
  17750 2929 14144  12338 27574 54153  124.1 FL
  10911 2038 12925   6339 33708 58056   82.4 GA
  19665 3577 15103  11613 63350 55645  123.3 IL
  11052 2478 12638   5559 39279 35932   84.0 IN
   6674 1401 11088   3726 18092 39669   76.4 KY
   8915 1346 17690   5890 35770  7824   34.7 MA
   6941 1240 16491   4626 14020  9837   40.4 MD
   2204  372 13068   1206  5271 30995    9.5 ME
  15199 2753 13958   9240 60259 56954   88.9 MI
   4394  938  9560   2620 10503 47233   25.1 MS
  10841 1947 12212   6489 47007 48843   78.4 NC
   1687  243 17201   1085  8189  8993    7.0 NH
  13991 2286 18998   7718 42527  7468   40.2 NJ
  23422 3586 16269  17909 80033 47377  124.7 NY
  19047 3785 13261  10865 71707 41004  124.0 OH
  18889 3601 13881  11998 57605 44888  152.9 PA
   1436  216 14352    993  4788  1055    0.8 RI
   5825 1143 11098   3465 19112 30203   65.2 SC
   8558 1714 12228   4898 27050 41155   60.0 TN
   9763 1840 15010   6013 26857 39704   45.2 VA
    902  129 13126    558  2543  9273    5.0 VT
   7516 1392 13129   4832 31653 54426   45.0 WI
   3160  778 10279   1876  5404 24119   81.3 WV
   ;

proc print data=energy_e (obs=5);
   var id q exp p pi pop vam land elec;
   title 'ENERGY Model Example';
   title2 'ENERGY_E Data';
run;

proc model data=energy_e outmodel=en_mod;
   parms d0-d2 s0-s2;
   endo q p;
   exo pi pop vam land elec;
   eq.demand=d0+d1*p+d2*pop-q;
   eq.supply=s0+s1*p+s2*elec-q;
   id id;
   fit demand supply / 2sls;
   instruments pi pop vam land;
run;
```

Output 15.8
The First Five
Observations of
the ENERGY_E
data set and the
Fitted Energy
Model

```
                         ENERGY Model Example
                           ENERGY_E Data

OBS   ID     Q     EXP      P        PI      POP     VAM     LAND    ELEC

 1    AL    1614   7284   4.51301   10993    4103   18652   50767    67.5
 2    CT     757   5475   7.23250   19559    3232   22349    4872    36.4
 3    DC     174   1049   6.02874   18397     613    1525      63     0.5
 4    DE     230   1223   5.31739   14137     660    3866    1932     9.0
 5    FL    2929  17750   6.06009   14144   12338   27574   54153   124.1
```

```
                         ENERGY Model Example
                           ENERGY_E Data

                           MODEL Procedure
                           2SLS Estimation

              Nonlinear 2SLS Summary of Residual Errors

                  DF    DF
  Equation      Model  Error      SSE        MSE      Root MSE  R-Square  Adj R-Sq

  DEMAND          3     24      2263091    94295.5    307.07568
  SUPPLY          3     24      6297285   262386.9    512.23712


                  Nonlinear 2SLS Parameter Estimates

                                     Approx.     'T'    Approx.
           Parameter    Estimate     Std Err    Ratio   Prob>|T|

              D0         1980.48    545.50332    3.63    0.0013
              D1      -305.865865    95.45357   -3.20    0.0038
              D2         0.248413     0.01377   18.04    0.0001
              S0        -2259.08     1046.1     -2.16    0.0410
              S1       381.515590   172.41681    2.21    0.0367
              S2        29.227932     2.70942   10.79    0.0001


           Number of Observations        Statistics for System
           Used                27        Objective           68369
           Missing              0        Objective*N       1845958
```

Interpretation of output

Output 15.8 prints the first five observations of the ENERGY_E data set and
displays the fitted model, which is as follows:

Demand: $Q = 1980.48 - 305.866\,P + 0.2484\,POP$

Supply: $Q = -2259.08 + 381.516\,P + 29.2279\,ELEC$

The parameters d_1 and s_1 are the average price parameters of the demand and
supply equations. The signs of the estimated parameters indicate that the demand
equation slopes downward while the supply equation slopes upward.

   In general form, no R^2 or adjusted R^2 are printed. However, the *t*-tests for
each individual parameter indicate that all are different from zero at the .05 level.
For purposes of this example, the model is assumed to contain the important
exogenous variables. You may want to continue energy market research and add
additional variables and equations to the model.

Printing Goodness-of-Fit Statistics

You can further assess the fit of a model by examining the Theil and
goodness-of-fit statistics. You can print these statistics and the simulated values by
using the STATS and THEIL options in the SOLVE statement of PROC MODEL. In

its default mode of SIMULATE, the SOLVE statement solves the equations for P
and Q, even though the actual values of P and Q are available in the ENERGY_E
data set.

The following SAS example code solves the energy model for average price
and quantities of energy consumed by the eastern states and creates the OUT_EN
data set. The prices, quantities, and the goodness-of-fit statistics are displayed in
Output 15.9.

```
proc model model=en_mod;
    solve p q / data=energy_e stats theil
              out=en_oute(drop=_type_ _mode_ _errors_
              rename=(p=price_e q=quant_e));
run;
```

Output 15.9
Theil and
Goodness-of-Fit
Statistics for the
Eastern States

```
                        ENERGY Model Example
                          ENERGY_E Data

                          MODEL Procedure
                      Simultaneous Simulation

                        Descriptive Statistics

                         Actual              Predicted

        Variable  Nobs   N    Mean     Std     Mean     Std

          P        27    27  5.6117  0.8304   5.6117  0.9722
          Q        27    27   1648    1159     1648    1128


                        Statistics of Fit

                           Mean    Mean %  Mean Abs  Mean Abs %
        Variable    N      Error   Error    Error     Error

          P         27      0      0.2912   0.5973    10.71861
          Q         27      0      8.8057  221.5028   18.53170

                        Statistics of Fit

                      RMS      RMS %
        Variable     Error     Error   R-Square  Label

          P          0.7042   12.6517   0.2531   Energy Price
          Q        304.0251   27.7620   0.9286   Energy Consumption


                   Theil Forecast Error Statistics

                               MSE Decomposition Proportions  Inequality Coef

 Variable   N     MSE    Corr   Bias   Reg   Dist   Var  Covar    U1      U
                         (R)    (UM)   (UR)  (UD)   (US) (UC)

   P        27  0.49594 0.694  0.000  0.305 0.695  0.039 0.961  0.1242  0.0620
   Q        27   92431  0.964  0.000  0.001 0.999  0.010 0.990  0.1518  0.0762


               Theil Relative Change Forecast Error Statistics

         Relative Change      MSE Decomposition Proportions  Inequality Coef

 Variable   N     MSE    Corr   Bias   Reg   Dist   Var  Covar    U1      U
                         (R)    (UM)   (UR)  (UD)   (US) (UC)

   P        26  0.01798 0.789  0.005  0.031 0.964  0.026 0.969  0.6241  0.3290
   Q        26  0.51244 0.980  0.001  0.042 0.956  0.011 0.987  0.1895  0.0938
```

Interpretation of output

Output 15.9 prints the Theil and goodness-of-fit statistics. These statistics are
introduced and discussed in Chapter 9, "Introduction to Simulation."

The goodness-of-fit statistics indicate that, on average, the model fits very well. The Theil U and U1 statistics are acceptable; however, the REG proportion of the Theil statistics for P ❶ is .305 and is considerably larger than the optimal value of zero.

Overall, the goodness-of-fit statistics indicate a reasonable fit on average; yet, the statistics based on absolute size and percentage size of residuals ❷ indicate some large absolute errors and fairly large percentage errors. Given the general nature of the model, the fit is acceptable.

Plotting Predicted Values

Plotting the predicted values versus the actual values enables you to visually assess the goodness of fit. If the actual and predicted values coincide, then the plotted points lie on a 45-degree line from the origin. If a point deviates from the 45-degree line, then the deviation is a visual measure of the lack of fit. Both the predicted prices and quantities are plotted against their respective actual values.

The following SAS example code uses a DATA step to merge the ENERGY_E and OUT_EN data sets, and then uses PROC PLOT to create two plots, one for prices and one for quantities. Output 15.10 shows the results. Your output will not contain the 45-degree lines; the lines were added to Output 15.10 for ease in assessing the goodness of fit.

```
    /* Merging Data Sets for Plotting */
data en_outep;
   merge energy_e en_oute;
   by id;
   label price_e='Predicted Price'
         quant_e='Predicted Quantity';
run;

    /* Plotting Actual versus Predicted Values */
proc plot data=en_outep vpct=60;
   plot p*price_e='*';
   plot q*quant_e='*';
   title 'ENERGY Model Example';
   title2 'ENERGY_E Data';
   title3 'Actual and Predicted Values';
run;
```

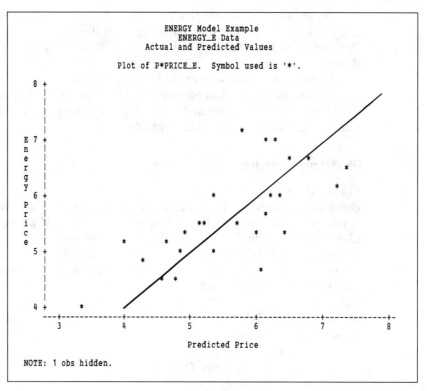

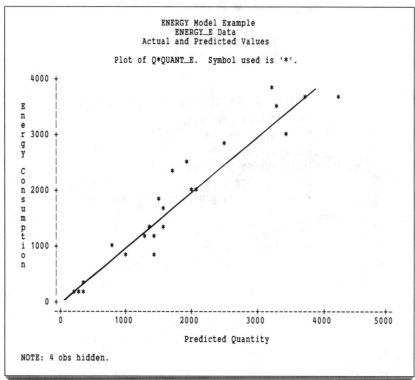

Interpretation of output

Output 15.10 plots the actual price and quantity values versus their predicted values. The plot of prices shows that few points lie on the 45-degree line. This corroborates the low R^2 (R-Square), .2531, as shown in Output 15.9. The plot of actual and predicted quantities have a much greater range and variability. Yet, most points lie close to a 45-degree line. This corroborates larger standard deviation of quantities and the higher R-Square, .9286.

The plots reveal that, in general, the simple energy model fits the eastern states data moderately well. The model can be validated by using it to predict prices and quantities for the western states. If western states follow similar supply-and-demand patterns for energy, then a valid model should produce similar goodness-of-fit statistics and similar plots of predicted and actual values.

Forecasting

After the energy model is fitted using the District of Columbia and states east of the Mississippi River, it can be used to forecast average prices and quantities for the states west of the Mississippi River.

The ENERGY_W data set contains the same variables as the ENERGY_E data set, but with values for the 24 western states. Prior to forecasting, a new data set named ENERGY is created in a DATA step that sets average prices and quantities to missing.

The following SAS example code uses the FORECAST option of the SOLVE statement in PROC MODEL, the model file, EN_MOD, and the ENERGY data set to forecast average prices and quantities. When you specify the FORECAST option of the SOLVE statement, PROC MODEL uses the actual values for forecasts, if available; thus, the ENERGY data set with average prices and quantities set to missing is used.

The forecasted values are stored in an output data set, EN_OUTW; then, renamed and merged with the ENERGY_W data set; and lastly, plotted for comparison.

```
data energy_w;
   input exp q pi pop vam land elec id $ @@;
      p=exp/q;
   label exp='Energy Expenditures'
         q='Energy Consumption'
         p='Energy Price'
         pi='Personal Disposable Income'
         pop='Population'
         vam='Value Added in Manufacturing'
         land='Land Area in Square Miles'
         elec='Electricity Generation'
         id='State Name';
   title 'ENERGY Model Example';
   title2 'ENERGY_W Data';
   title3;
   cards;
 1491  520 17089   525    834 570833   4.2 AK
 4014  790 10630  2396  10827  52078  33.8 AR
 5616  898 13008  3483  11299 113508  61.6 AZ
39553 6970 16059 28323 132638 156299 126.0 CA
 4594  902 14187  3300  12046 103595  30.9 CO
 1581  266 14294  1096   1405   6425   7.6 HI
 4820  942 12213  2830  14469  55965  27.7 IA
 1572  355 11177  1003   3057  82412   6.7 ID
```

```
 4826 1057 13425  2496  12909  81778  31.4 KS
11322 3450 10793  4407  16426  44521  56.8 LA
 6756 1315 13785  4308  23322  79548  40.3 MN
 8324 1511 13240  5140  25917  68945  59.7 MO
 1457  334 11371   805   1112 145388  24.8 MT
 1425  311 10844   667    979  69300  27.4 ND
 2732  536 12567  1603   5819  76644  20.6 NE
 2479  524 10672  1510   1653 121335  26.4 NM
 1899  355 15121  1054   1279 109894  20.3 NV
 5232 1280 10956  3234   9857  68655  44.0 OK
 4255  880 12687  2768  11610  96184  41.0 OR
 1115  203 11369   714   1476  75952   7.9 SD
36304 9583 12908 16834  63899 262017 221.2 TX
 2548  534 10650  1691   4883  82073  29.6 UT
 6929 1807 14347  4652  19016  66511  83.6 WA
 1323  377 11803   480    493  96989  39.1 WY
;

data energy;
   set energy_w;
   q=.;
   p=.;
run;


   /* Forecasting Average Price and Quantity */
proc model model=en_mod noprint;
   solve p q / forecast data=energy
            out=en_outw(drop=_type_ _mode_ _errors_
                        rename=(p=p_fore q=q_fore));
run;


   /* Merging Data Sets */
data energy_p;
   merge energy_w en_outw;
   by id;
   label p_fore='Forecasted Average Price'
         q_fore='Forecasted Quantity';
run;
```

Plotting the actual values versus the forecasted values may be more revealing than examining the listed values. The following SAS example code plots the actual price and quantity values versus the predicted values in separate plots. One set of plots contains unlabeled points to show their relative position, while the remaining plot contains labeled points. Output 15.11 shows the results. Your output will not include the 45-degree lines; the lines were added to illustrate the relationship among the actual and forecasted values.

```
    /* Plotting Forecasts */
proc plot data=energy_p vpct=60;
    plot p*p_fore='*';
    plot p*p_fore='*' $ id;
    plot q*q_fore='*';
    plot q*q_fore=' ' $ id;
    title 'ENERGY Model Example';
    title2 'Western States';
    title3 'Actual and Predicted Values';
run;
```

Output 15.11
Plotting the Actual and Forecasted Values of the Energy Model for the Western States

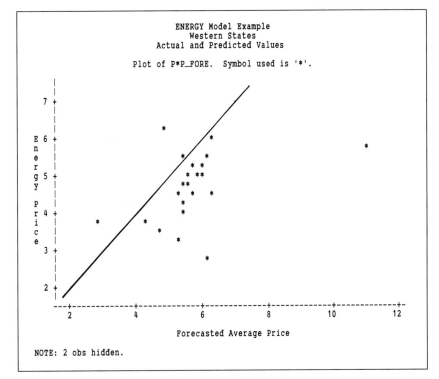

(continued)

Output 15.11
(continued)

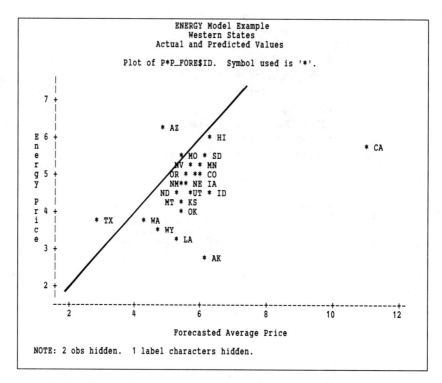

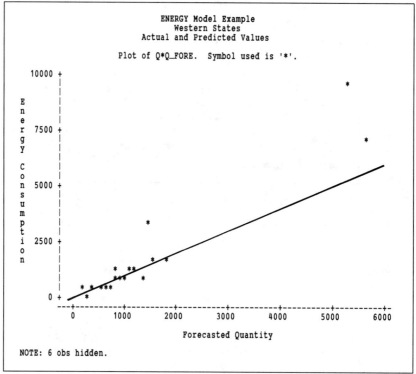

(continued)

Output 15.11
(continued)

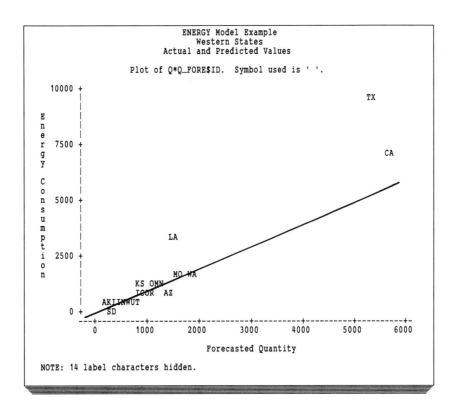

Interpretation of output

Output 15.11 plots the actual and forecasted values of average price and quantity versus their respective forecasted values. The labeled average price plot also contains the plotting symbol *, while the labeled quantity plot does not. You see a cluster of points and some outliers. In particular, CA and TX produce and consume much larger quantities of energy than eastern states. This additional range is well beyond that used for fitting the model. Overall, it appears that if CA and TX are excluded as anomalous observations, the energy model is adequate for forecasting.

You may want to try improving the energy model by adding dummy variables for large energy-producing states, or by including additional right-hand side variables to explicitly account for the differences in eastern- versus western-state energy production and consumption patterns.

Direct and visual comparisons between actual and predicted values enable you to make some assessment of the model's validity for forecasting. Examining the goodness-of-fit statistics enables you to make a further assessment. Unfortunately, using a data set with missing values, such as ENERGY, PROC MODEL cannot generate goodness-of-fit statistics for these data. However, the next section shows you how to generate them.

Assessing the Forecasts

After using the model fit with data from the eastern states to generate forecasts for the western states, you may want to assess the quality of the forecasts. You can calculate goodness-of-fit statistics using the DATA step and PROC SUMMARY. Statistics of interest are as follows:

MAD is the mean average deviation, also known as the mean error.

MPER is the mean percentage error.

MABS is the mean absolute value error.

MABSP is the mean absolute percentage error. This statistic is also known as the mean average percent error, MAPE.

MSE is the mean square error.

RMSE is the root mean square error.

MSEP is the mean square percent error.

RMSEP is the root mean square percent error.

The smaller these summary statistics are in absolute value, the closer the simulated model follows the actual values. Goodness-of-fit statistics are discussed in Chapter 9.

The following SAS example code calculates and prints the goodness-of-fit statistics for average prices and quantities of energy in western states. Output 15.12 shows the results.

```
data energy1;
  set energy_p;

    /* Forecast Errors, mean is mean error */
  e_p=p-p_fore;
  e_q=q-q_fore;

    /* Percent Error, mean is mean percent error */
  per_p=(e_p*100)/p;
  per_q=(e_q*100)/q;

    /* Absolute Error, mean is mean abs error */
  abs_p=abs(e_p);
  abs_q=abs(e_q);

    /* Absolute Percentage Error */
    /* mean is mean abs % error */
  absp_p=abs(e_p/p)*100;
  absp_q=abs(e_q/q)*100;

    /* Square Error, mean is mse  */
    /* sq root of mse is root mse */
  se_p=e_p**2;
  se_q=e_q**2;

    /* Square Percentage Error */
    /* sq root of mean is rms % error */
  sep_p=((e_p/p)*100)**2;
  sep_q=((e_q/q)*100)**2;
  run;
```

```
              /* Calculating Mean Values */
proc summary data=energy1 mean;
   var e_p e_q per_p per_q abs_p abs_q absp_p absp_q
       se_p se_q sep_p sep_q;
   output out=en_stat mean=mad_p mad_q mper_p mper_q mabs_p mabs_q
          mabsp_p mabsp_q mse_p mse_q msep_p msep_q;
run;

             /* Taking Square Roots */
data en_stat1;
   set en_stat;
   rmse_p=sqrt(mse_p);
   rmse_q=sqrt(mse_q);
   rmsep_p=sqrt(msep_p);
   rmsep_q=sqrt(msep_q);
run;

proc print data=en_stat1;
   var mad_p mad_q mper_p mper_q mabs_p mabs_q mabsp_p mabsp_q
       mse_p mse_q rmse_p rmse_q msep_p msep_q rmsep_p rmsep_q;
   title 'ENERGY Model Example';
   title2 'Goodness-of-Fit Statistics';
   title3 'Western States';
run;
```

Output 15.12
Printing the Goodness-of-Fit Statistics for Average Prices and Quantities of Energy in Western States

```
                        ENERGY Model Example
                     Goodness-of-Fit Statistics
                          Western States

OBS    MAD_P      MAD_Q     MPER_P    MPER_Q    MABS_P    MABS_Q   MABSP_P   MABSP_Q

 1    -0.97797   264.674   -23.1393  -9.93977  1.17893   447.534  27.1741   30.0130

OBS    MSE_P       MSE_Q      RMSE_P    RMSE_Q    MSEP_P    MSEP_Q   RMSEP_P   RMSEP_Q

 1    2.59444   1038729.64   1.61073   1019.18   1462.52   1431.43  38.2429   37.8343
```

Interpretation of output

Output 15.12 prints goodness-of-fit statistics for the average prices and quantities. Due to the presence of CA and TX, all of the goodness-of-fit statistics are larger in absolute value than those of the eastern states. You can compare the goodness-of-fit statistics for the eastern and western states with Output 15.9 and Output 15.12.

Recalculating the Goodness-of-Fit Statistics

You can recalculate the goodness-of-fit statistics excluding CA and TX. They are the only states with quantities greater than 6000, and they can be deleted with the following IF-THEN statement in a DATA step:

```
if q>6000 then delete;
```

You can modify the previous SAS example code to recalculate the goodness-of-fit statistics excluding CA and TX. The resulting statistics are shown in Output 15.13.

Output 15.13
Printing the
Goodness-of-Fit
Statistics for
Average Prices and
Quantities for the
Western States
Excluding CA and
TX

```
                        ENERGY Model Example
                      Goodness-of-Fit Statistics
                            Western States
                      California and Texas Omitted

OBS    MAD_P     MAD_Q     MPER_P     MPER_Q    MABS_P   MABS_Q  MABSP_P  MABSP_Q

 1    -0.86558  33.1261  -22.0717  -13.7476   0.99912  232.609  24.2114  29.8373

OBS    MSE_P     MSE_Q     RMSE_P    RMSE_Q    MSEP_P   MSEP_Q   RMSEP_P  RMSEP_Q

 1    1.47866  215479.98  1.21600  464.198   1160.15  1453.81  34.0610  38.1289
```

Interpretation of output

Output 15.13 prints goodness-of-fit statistics for the average price and quantities for the western half of the U.S. after CA and TX have been deleted.

As you compare Output 15.13 and Output 15.12, you notice that the MAD for Q is much closer to zero, as are the MABS, MABSP, MSE, and RMSE, while the MPER, MSEP, and RMSEP are slightly larger. The goodness-of-fit statistics for price are also improved; all are closer to zero.

As you compare Outputs 15.13, 15.12, and 15.9, you notice that by deleting CA and TX the goodness-of-fit statistics of the western states become closer to those of the eastern states. The model now forecasts reasonably well for the remaining western states.

You may want to continue fine-tuning the energy model and expand its forecasting applications. For example, the model could be fitted using all states for 1988, validated using input data for 1989, then used to forecast P and Q for 1990.

Chapter Summary

This chapter presented examples of forecasting with a linear system of simultaneous equations. The first example illustrated scenario forecasting using the Klein Model 1. Two scenarios were developed. Growth rates were created and calculated, and then used to extrapolate the endogenous variables. Separate data sets were created for each scenario and used for forecasting. The actual and forecasted values were plotted versus time in years.

The second example was an example of model validation through forecasting. A simple, cross-sectional model of energy supply and demand by states was fitted using the eastern half of the U.S. The model was judged to adequately fit the data. Then the model was used to forecast the average price and quantity for states in the western half of the U.S. The resulting goodness-of-fit statistics indicated that the forecasts for the western states were of approximately the same quality as the model's predictions for the eastern states.

Learning More

□ For full reference information on the MODEL procedure in SAS/ETS software, see the *SAS/ETS User's Guide, Version 6, First Edition.*

□ For full reference information on the GPLOT procedure in SAS/GRAPH software, see *SAS/GRAPH Software: Reference, Version 6*, First Edition, *Volume 1* and *Volume 2.*

□ For full reference information on the SAS/BASE PLOT and SUMMARY procedures, see the *SAS Procedures Guide, Version 6, Third Edition.*

References

Klein, L.R. (1950), *Economic Fluctuations in the United States 1921-41*, New York: John Wiley & Sons, Inc.

Maddala, G.S. (1977), *Econometrics*, New York: McGraw-Hill, Inc.

Pindyck, R. and Rubinfeld, D. (1991), *Econometric Models and Economic Forecasts, Third Edition*, New York: McGraw-Hill, Inc.

U.S. Department of Commerce, *Statistical Abstracts of the U.S.*, Washington, D.C.: U.S. Government Printing Office.

Chapter **16** Combining Forecasting Methods

Introduction

Chapter 1, "Background Topics," discusses the basic differences between regression models and time series models. By design, regression models forecast using information contained in exogenous variables, whereas time series models forecast using information in historical values of the endogenous variable. Bates and Granger first demonstrated that two forecasts can be combined to produce a new forecast that is more accurate than either of the original forecasts (1969). Makridakis et al. compared, contrasted, and combined forecasts in search of more accurate forecasts (1984). Thus, by combining forecasts from two different models, you may be able to obtain more accurate forecasts.

An alternative and more sophisticated approach is to fit a transfer function and utilize the time series information contained in exogenous and endogenous variables. The regression model captures the structural variation of the endogenous variable. Some of the remaining variation can be captured by fitting a time series process to each exogenous variable. By capturing more of the variation in the endogenous variable, transfer functions produce more accurate forecasts than either regression or time series models alone.

In this chapter, you use the ARIMA and AUTOREG procedures in SAS/ETS software and the GFUND model to fit a regression model and a time series model.

You generate additional exogenous values to forecast future GFUND values separately for each model, and you calculate goodness-of-fit statistics. You then form linear combinations of the two forecasts, select the weighting that minimizes the absolute magnitude of the goodness-of-fit statistics, and use the weights to combine the forecasts. Finally, you fit a transfer function, forecast GFUND values, and compare the four sets of forecasts.

Fitting Forecasting Models

The regression model of North Carolina general fund revenues, GFUND, was introduced in Chapter 9, "Introduction to Simulation." This model relates U.S. GNP and North Carolina population to GFUND. Alternatively, you could have fitted a time series model to the annual GFUND series or a transfer function model to the BUDGET data set. The models contain different information about GFUND and would provide different forecasts.

Recall that the BUDGET data set contains 17 observations from 1973 through 1989 of North Carolina general fund revenues (GFUND), U.S. GNP (GNP), and North Carolina population (POP).

The following sections show you how to create new values for the exogenous variables, fit a regression model and a time series model, and print the predicted values over the period 1973 through 1989.

The Regression Model

The regression model of GFUND has the following form:

$$\text{GFUND}_t = d + f\,\text{GNP}_t + h\,\text{POP}_t + \varepsilon_t$$

where

GFUND_t	is the current-period general fund revenues, deflated by the consumer price index (CPI).
d	is the intercept.
f	is the slope parameter associated with GNP.
GNP_t	is the current-period U.S. GNP, deflated by the CPI.
h	is the slope parameter associated with POP.
POP_t	is the current-period N.C. population.
ε_t	is the current-period random error.

The regression model can be fitted with PROC AUTOREG. The following SAS example code fits the regression GFUND model with a correction for first-order autoregression by the method of unconditional least squares. The BUDGET data set, introduced in Chapter 9, is not shown. Output 16.1 shows the results. For interpretation of the output, see the discussion following Output 9.3.

```
proc autoreg data=budget;
    model gfund = gnp pop / nlag=1 method=uls dw=1 dwprob;
run;
```

Output 16.1
The GFUND
Model Corrected
for First-Order
Autoregression

```
                      General Fund Revenues Example

                          Autoreg Procedure

Dependent Variable = GFUND      Real General Fund in Millions

                    Ordinary Least Squares Estimates

            SSE         236640.3    DFE              14
            MSE         16902.88    Root MSE    130.0111
            SBC          218.942    AIC         216.4423
            Reg Rsq       0.9710    Total Rsq     0.9710
            Durbin-Watson 1.0864    PROB<DW       0.0046


      Variable     DF     B Value    Std Error   t Ratio Approx Prob

      Intercept     1  -3808.13906      799.89    -4.761      0.0003
      GNP           1      1.55053        0.26     5.934      0.0001
      POP           1   0.317079837       0.27     1.179      0.2580


                   Estimates of Autocorrelations

   Lag  Covariance  Correlation -1 9 8 7 6 5 4 3 2 1 0 1 2 3 4 5 6 7 8 9 1

    0    13920.02    1.000000  |              |********************|
    1    6125.965    0.440083  |              |*********           |


                   Preliminary MSE = 11224.09

            Estimates of the Autoregressive Parameters

         Lag    Coefficient    Std Error     t Ratio
          1     -0.44008305   0.24904848   -1.767058


                Unconditional Least Squares Estimates

            SSE         158509.6    DFE              13
            MSE         12193.05    Root MSE    110.4221
            SBC         215.8161    AIC         212.4833
            Reg Rsq       0.8803    Total Rsq     0.9806
            Durbin-Watson 1.9028    PROB<DW       0.3099


      Variable     DF     B Value    Std Error   t Ratio Approx Prob

      Intercept     1  -4981.39375       1411.2    -3.530      0.0037
      GNP           1  0.9465574792     0.305064    3.103      0.0084
      POP           1  0.8725432268     0.366162    2.383      0.0331
      A(1)          1  -0.757615218     0.196505   -3.855      0.0020
```

```
                      General Fund Revenues Example

                          Autoreg Procedure

              Autoregressive parameters assumed given.


      Variable     DF     B Value    Std Error   t Ratio Approx Prob

      Intercept     1  -4981.39375       1326.6    -3.755      0.0024
      GNP           1  0.9465574792     0.294882    3.210      0.0068
      POP           1  0.8725432268     0.342964    2.544      0.0245
```

Interpretation of output

Output 16.1 displays the OLS fitted GFUND model corrected for first-order autoregression. The model is

$$\text{GFUND}_t = -4981.3938 + 0.9466\,\text{GNP}_t + 0.8725\,\text{POP}_t + v_t$$

where the error term v_t follows a first-order autoregressive process and is defined as

$$v_t = 0.7576\, v_{t-1} + \varepsilon_t$$

and ε_t conforms to the standard OLS error assumptions. For more information about the autoregressive error term structure used by PROC AUTOREG, see Chapter 4, "Violations of the OLS Error Assumptions," and the *SAS/ETS User's Guide, Version 6, First Edition.*

Extrapolating Exogenous Variables

Prior to using the regression model for forecasting, you need future values of the exogenous variables, GNP and POP. Several approaches to generating additional exogenous variable values are listed in Chapter 13, "Introduction to Forecasting."

In the following SAS example code, you create values for GNP and POP from 1990 through 1995 in a DATA step with an iterative DO loop and the annually compounded growth rates observed from 1985 through 1989.

```
data extrap1;

    /* Calculating Growth Rates */
    pop_g=(6571/6258)**(1/5);
    gnp_g=((5200.8/1.240)/(4010.0/1.076))**(1/5);
    gfund=.;

    /* Creating New Exogenous Values */
    do year=90 to 95;
        pop=6571*(pop_g)**(year-89);
        gnp=(5200.8/1.240)*(gnp_g)**(year-89);
        output;
    end;
run;
```

After their creation, the extrapolated values are concatenated to the BUDGET data set in a DATA step to create the BUDGET1 data set.

```
    /* Concatenating Data Sets */
data budget1;
    set budget extrap1;
run;
```

You can use the BUDGET1 data set and the GFUND model to forecast future general fund revenue values.

The Regression Model

In one invocation of PROC AUTOREG you can

□ fit the GFUND regression model

□ forecast GFUND values for 1990 through 1995

□ save the predicted values, named GFUND_R, and the residual values, named RES_R, in an output data set named BUD_OUTR.

The residual values are to be used later in model comparisons. The following SAS example code performs these steps. The output from this SAS example code is not shown.

```
    /* Fitting the Regression Model */
proc autoreg data=budget1;
    model gfund = gnp pop / nlag=1 method=uls dw=1 dwprob;
    output out=bud_outr p=gfund_r r=res_r;
run;
```

The Time Series Model

Prior to fitting a time series model, you can plot GFUND versus YEAR to visually assess trends in the data. The GNP and POP series are plotted versus YEAR for later use. The following SAS example code creates the plots.

```
proc plot data=budget vpct=60;
    plot (gfund gnp pop)*year;
run;
```

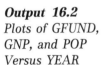

Output 16.2
Plots of GFUND, GNP, and POP Versus YEAR

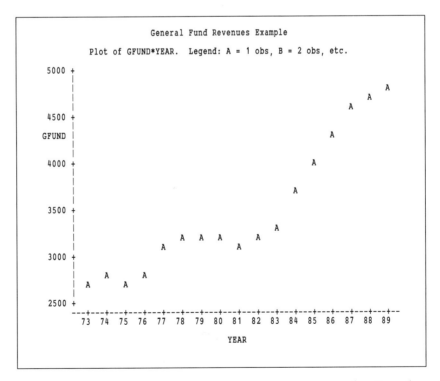

(continued)

Output 16.2
(continued)

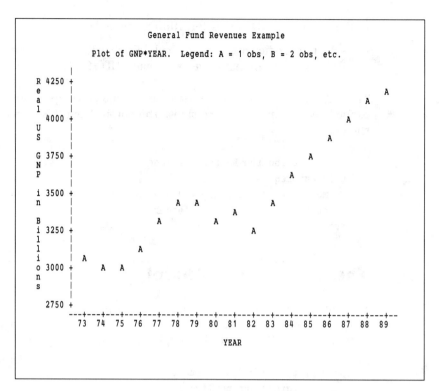

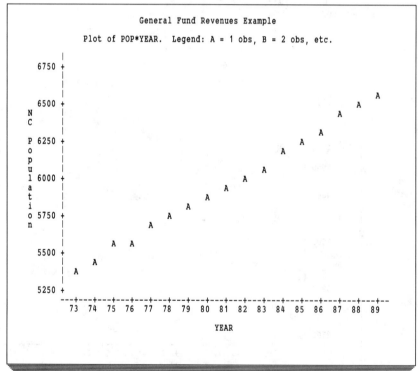

Interpretation of output

Output 16.2 plots general fund revenues, GNP, and population versus YEAR. As noted in Chapter 9, there are many ways to define and interpret perceived patterns in plots. Overall, in each plot there appears to be an increasing trend with some deviations. For purposes of fitting time series models to these series, it is assumed that a linear trend is an acceptable approximation.

In general, time series with trends are not stationary; that is, the mean or variance of the series changes over time. *Differencing* often transforms a nonstationary time series into stationary time series. Thus, you want to difference the GFUND series to remove the trend and create a stationary series. For details on formal statistical tests for stationarity, see Chapter 5, "Stationarity," in *SAS/ETS Software: Applications Guide 1, Version 6, First Edition* and Dickey and Fuller (1979).

Fitting the Time Series Model

A GFUND time series model can be fitted using the Box-Jenkins methodology of identifying and fitting the model and then using it for forecasting. A much more detailed explanation of this methodology is found in *SAS/ETS Software: Applications Guide 1*.

You identify a time series process by examining its autocorrelation function (ACF), inverse autocorrelation function (IACF), and partial autocorrelation function (PACF). The list below defines each function and its use.

ACF

lists the estimated autocorrelation coefficients at each lag of the series. This function measures the importance of progressively distant observations ($GFUND_{t-1}$, $GFUND_{t-2}$, . . .) to the current value ($GFUND_t$). A plot of the ACF shows the pattern of the autocorrelations.

IACF

is the autocorrelation function of the inverted model. For example, the IACF of an autocorrelated process is equivalent to the ACF for the same process modeled as a moving average model.

PACF

can be thought of as the autocorrelation function at lag p accounting for the effects of all intervening series observations. The partial autocorrelation at lag 1 is identical to the autocorrelation at lag 1, but the PACF and ACF are different at all higher lags.

If an autocorrelation coefficient is statistically significant, it is called a *spike*. If the first lag is statistically different from zero and all other autocorrelations are not, then the ACF is said to *drop* to zero after the first lag. If the ACF plot shows a steady exponential decline, then the plot is said to *decay* or *tail off*. Time series processes are described in the following list:

□   An autoregressive process (AR) follows a specific pattern. The ACF tails off exponentially while the IACF and PACF drop to zero after lag p, where p is the order of the AR process.

□   A moving average process (MA) follows a specific pattern. The IACF and PACF tail off exponentially while the ACF drops to zero after lag q, where q is the order of the MA process.

□   Mixed autoregressive and moving average models have more complex, yet discernable patterns. For more information, see *SAS/ETS Software: Applications Guide 1*.

In the following SAS example code, you use the ARIMA procedure in SAS/ETS software to identify the time series processes of the first differenced GFUND series. The statements are interpreted as follows.

PROC ARIMA

invokes the ARIMA procedure. The following option is specified:

DATA=   specifies BUDGET1 as the input data set.

IDENTIFY

computes statistics to help identify models to fit. The following option is specified:

VAR=   specifies the variable containing the time series. The optional parenthetical value specifies the order of differencing. In this case, the series is differenced once.

QUIT

specifies the end of an interactive PROC ARIMA session.

The following SAS example code produces Output 16.3.

```
proc arima data=budget1;
   identify var=gfund(1);
run;
quit;
```

Output 16.3
ACF, IACF, PACF
of the First
Differenced
GFUND Series

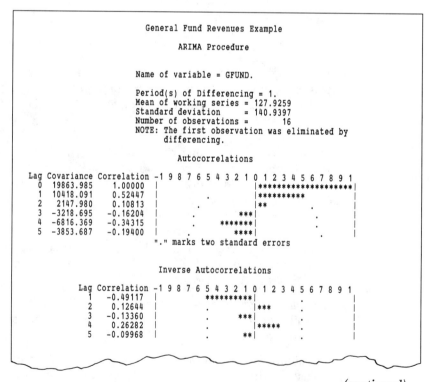

```
                    General Fund Revenues Example

                           ARIMA Procedure


             Name of variable = GFUND.

             Period(s) of Differencing = 1.
             Mean of working series = 127.9259
             Standard deviation     = 140.9397
             Number of observations =       16
             NOTE: The first observation was eliminated by
                   differencing.

                         Autocorrelations

Lag Covariance Correlation -1 9 8 7 6 5 4 3 2 1 0 1 2 3 4 5 6 7 8 9 1
  0 19863.985   1.00000   |                    |********************|
  1 10418.091   0.52447   |          .         |**********          |
  2  2147.980   0.10813   |          .         |**          .       |
  3 -3218.695  -0.16204   |          .      ***|            .       |
  4 -6816.369  -0.34315   |          .  *******|            .       |
  5 -3853.687  -0.19400   |          .     ****|            .       |
                    "." marks two standard errors


                     Inverse Autocorrelations

    Lag Correlation -1 9 8 7 6 5 4 3 2 1 0 1 2 3 4 5 6 7 8 9 1
      1  -0.49117   |        **********|         .          |
      2   0.12644   |         .        |***      .          |
      3  -0.13360   |         .      ***|         .          |
      4   0.26282   |         .        |*****    .          |
      5  -0.09968   |         .       **|         .          |
```

(continued)

Output 16.3
(continued)

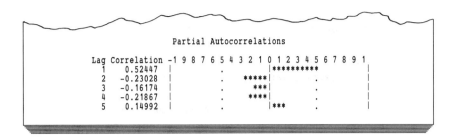

```
                          Partial Autocorrelations

    Lag Correlation -1 9 8 7 6 5 4 3 2 1 0 1 2 3 4 5 6 7 8 9 1
     1    0.52447   |                  .   |**********          |
     2   -0.23028   |                  . *****|                 |
     3   -0.16174   |                  .   ***|                 .   |
     4   -0.21867   |                  . ****|                 .   |
     5    0.14992   |                  .   |***               .   |
```

Interpretation of output

Output 16.3 displays the ACF, IACF, and PACF of the first differenced GFUND series. The ACF tails off exponentially while the IACF and PACF drop to zero after the first lag. These autocorrelation function patterns indicate a first-order autoregressive process, AR(1).

For more information on identifying and modeling autoregressive processes, see Chapter 3, "Autoregressive Models," in *SAS/ETS Software: Applications Guide 1.*

Estimating and Forecasting the Time Series Model

You can fit the AR(1) model to the first differenced GFUND series with the ESTIMATE statement of PROC ARIMA. The series is predicted for the period 1990 through 1995 with the FORECAST statement of PROC ARIMA. The FORECAST statement is also used to calculate the residual values, RES_T, for use later in comparisons of models. The following SAS example code performs these steps. The statements not previously interpreted are as follows:

IDENTIFY
　computes statistics to help identify models to fit. The NOPRINT option suppresses printing of the IDENTIFY phase output.

ESTIMATE
　specifies an estimate of the model for the variables specified in the previous IDENTIFY statement. The following option is specified:

　P=　　　specifies the degree of the autoregressive part of the model. In this example, P=1. The default value of zero means that no autoregressive parameters are to be fitted. Note that Q= specifies the degree of the moving average part of the model; again, zero is the default.

FORECAST
　generates forecasts for the model estimated by the previous ESTIMATE statement. The following options are specified:

　LEAD=　　specifies the number of forecasts to compute. For LEAD=6, PROC ARIMA forecasts for six periods after the end of the data set. The default is 24.

　OUT=　　creates and names the output data set to contain the forecasts.

　NOPRINT　suppresses printing of the FORECAST phase output.

The following SAS example code produces Output 16.4.

```
proc arima data=budget1;
   identify var=gfund(1) noprint;
   estimate p=1;
   forecast lead=6 id=year out=bud_outt(rename=
            (forecast=gfund_t residual=res_t)) noprint;
run;
quit;
```

Output 16.4
The First
Differenced,
First-Order
Autoregressive
GFUND Time
Series Model

```
                    General Fund Revenues Example

                          ARIMA Procedure


                 Conditional Least Squares Estimation

                                  Approx.
        Parameter   Estimate    Std Error    T Ratio  Lag
        MU          111.78237    62.76104      1.78    0
        AR1,1         0.53816     0.22697      2.37    1

        Constant Estimate = 51.6261106

        Variance  Estimate = 16349.9298
        Std Error Estimate = 127.866844
        AIC               = 202.501193*
        SBC               = 204.04637*
        Number of Residuals=      16
        * Does not include log determinant.

                    Correlations of the Estimates


            Parameter          MU          AR1,1

            MU              1.000         -0.112
            AR1,1          -0.112          1.000


                  Autocorrelation Check of Residuals

       To    Chi
      Lag  Square DF   Prob          Autocorrelations
       6    4.08   5  0.538   0.118 -0.055 -0.104 -0.353 -0.040 -0.130
      12    8.70  11  0.650   0.224  0.163 -0.156 -0.020 -0.075 -0.099



                    Model for variable GFUND

                    Estimated Mean = 111.782373
                    Period(s) of Differencing = 1.

                    Autoregressive Factors
                    Factor 1: 1 - 0.53816 B**(1)
```

Interpretation of output

Output 16.4 lists the first differenced AR(1) GFUND time series model, which is

$$\Delta\text{GFUND}_t - 111.78 = .54(\Delta\text{GFUND}_{t-1} - 111.78) + \varepsilon_t$$

where $\Delta\text{GFUND}_t = \text{GFUND}_t - \text{GFUND}_{t-1}$. In backshift notation, the model is

$$\varepsilon_t = (1 - 0.54 \text{ B})(1 - \text{B})(\text{GFUND}_t - 111.78)$$

where $\text{B}(\text{GFUND}_t) = \text{GFUND}_{t-1}$.

The AR(1) parameter has a T Ratio of 2.37, which is significant at the .05 level. The autocorrelation check for residuals performs Ljung and Box chi-square tests for the null hypothesis of random disturbances (white noise)(1978). The chi-square tests are also called *Q statistics*. For the AR(1) model, the Q statistics are not significant at the .05 level of significance. You conclude that the AR(1) time series model provides a reasonable fit to the first differenced GFUND series.

Combining Forecasts

The predicted and actual values for the regression and time series models can be compared directly by printing, and visually by plotting. Clearly, predicted values closer to the actual values indicate the better model. An absolutely superior model would have smaller residuals for all observations. However, these models produce smaller residuals for different observations. Because the two models utilize different information, perhaps a linear combination of the two sets of predicted values has smaller residuals and goodness-of-fit statistics still closer to zero.

In the next section, you compare and contrast the two sets of predicted values. Then, you create linear combinations and select the weighting that generates the goodness-of-fit statistics closest to zero. The weight can then be used to combine the two sets of forecasts and generate the final forecasted values.

Printing and Plotting Predicted Values

To print and plot the predicted values from the regression and time series models, you must first merge the two output data sets in a DATA step. The new data set is named BUD_OUT3. After merging, the actual and predicted values can be printed and plotted. The following SAS example code performs these steps. Output 16.5 shows the results.

```
    /* Merging Data Sets */
data bud_out3;
   merge budget1 bud_outr bud_outt;
   by year;
run;

    /* Printing Actual and Predicted Values */
proc print data=bud_out3;
   var year gfund gfund_t gfund_r res_t res_r;
   title2 'Actual and Predicted GFUND';
run;

    /* Plotting Actual and Predicted Values */
proc plot data=bud_out3 vpct=70;
   plot gfund*year='A'
        gfund_t*year='T'
        gfund_r*year='R' /overlay href=89;
   title2 'Actual and Predicted GFUND';
run;
```

Note that GFUND_T contains the time series model forecast, and GFUND_R contains the regression model forecasts.

Output 16.5

The Actual Values, Predicted Values, and Residuals of the GFUND Models and a Plot of Actual and Predicted Values versus YEAR

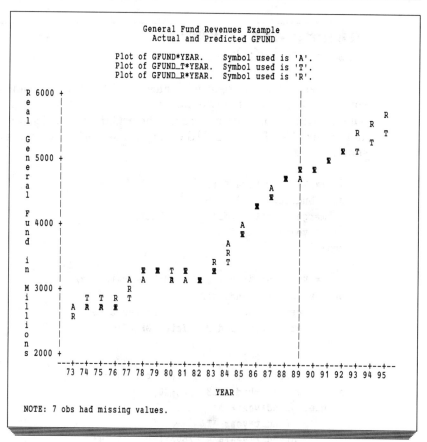

```
                          General Fund Revenues Example
                            Actual and Predicted GFUND

      OBS    YEAR    GFUND     GFUND_T     GFUND_R      RES_T       RES_R

       1      73    2734.23       .        2612.51        .        121.727
       2      74    2754.56    2846.02     2703.56     -91.453      51.008
       3      75    2697.03    2817.13     2768.87    -120.104     -71.846
       4      76    2762.74    2717.69     2892.29      45.054    -129.548
       5      77    3085.81    2849.73     2996.19     236.076      89.615
       6      78    3159.51    3311.29     3301.67    -151.786    -142.162
       7      79    3219.01    3250.80     3250.77     -31.789     -31.759
       8      80    3202.67    3302.65     3189.03     -99.984      13.639
       9      81    3130.91    3245.50     3329.48    -114.590    -198.565
      10      82    3189.64    3143.92     3174.93      45.714      14.703
      11      83    3292.17    3272.87     3418.08      19.303    -125.910
      12      84    3670.84    3398.97     3634.33     271.865      36.503
      13      85    4030.67    3926.25     3881.59     104.423     149.075
      14      86    4283.76    4275.94     4214.78       7.819      68.975
      15      87    4560.74    4471.59     4446.48      89.153     114.257
      16      88    4693.15    4761.42     4722.18     -68.271     -29.029
      17      89    4781.05    4816.04     4803.56     -34.990     -22.516
      18      90       .       4879.98     4917.94        .           .
      19      91       .       4984.84     5061.12        .           .
      20      92       .       5092.90     5209.81        .           .
      21      93       .       5202.68     5363.42        .           .
      22      94       .       5313.38     5521.54        .           .
      23      95       .       5424.58     5683.88        .           .
```

Interpretation of output

Output 16.5 prints the actual values and both sets of predicted and residual values, and plots the actual and predicted values versus time. For some years, the predicted values from the regression model produce smaller residuals, and for other observations the time series model produces smaller residual values. For example, examine the plotted points for the years 1975 and 1976. Neither model is absolutely superior; that is, neither has the smallest residuals for all observations.

The plot also shows the difference in the forecasts of the two models. The horizontal reference line at the year 1989 separates the years used to fit the model (to the left of the line and including the line) and the years used for forecasting (to the right of the line).

Given that neither model is absolutely superior and that both models contain different information, goodness-of-fit statistics enable further assessments. The next section shows you how to calculate goodness-of-fit statistics.

Calculating Goodness-of-Fit Statistics

Goodness-of-fit statistics assist in assessing the fit of a model. These statistics can be compared across competing models (fitted to the same data), and typically the model with goodness-of-fit statistics closest to zero provides the best fit. Goodness-of-fit statistics are introduced and discussed in Chapter 9.

The mean square error (MSE) and its positive square root (RMSE) are often used to evaluate the fit of models. The MSE minimizes the sum of the variance and the square of the bias. Other goodness-of-fit statistics can be generated; for details, see Chapter 15, "Forecasting with Linear Systems."

The following SAS example code uses a DATA step to delete unneeded observations, and the SUMMARY procedure in base SAS software and another DATA step to calculate the goodness-of-fit statistics. PROC PRINT prints the statistics. The printed goodness-of-fit statistics are as follows.

MAD is the mean average deviation, also known as the mean error.

MPER is the mean percentage error.

MSE is the mean square error.

RMSE is the root mean square error.

Output 16.6 shows the results.

```
data budget2;
   set bud_out3;
   if year > 89 then delete;

      /* Percent Error, mean is mean percent error */
   per_t=(res_t*100)/gfund;
   per_r=(res_r*100)/gfund;

      /* Square Error, mean is mse  */
      /* sq root of mse is root mse */
   se_t=res_t**2;
   se_r=res_r**2;
run;
```

```
                /* Calculating Mean Values */
proc summary data=budget2 mean;
   var res_t res_r per_t per_r se_t se_r;
   output out=bud_ave mean=mad_t mad_r mper_t mper_r mse_t mse_r;
run;

                /* Taking Square Roots */
data bud_st;
   set bud_ave;
   rmse_t=sqrt(mse_t);
   rmse_r=sqrt(mse_r);
run;

                /* Printing Statistics */
proc print data=bud_st;
   var mad_t mad_r mper_t mper_r mse_t mse_r rmse_t rmse_r;
   title2 'Goodness-of-Fit Statistics';
run;
```

Output 16.6
Goodness-of-Fit
Statistics for the
Regression and
Time Series
Models

```
                  General Fund Revenues Example
                    Goodness-of-Fit Statistics

OBS    MAD_T     MAD_R     MPER_T    MPER_R     MSE_T    MSE_R    RMSE_T    RMSE_R

 1    6.65237  -5.40205   0.056340  -0.30543  14306.19  9824.39  119.608   99.1181
```

Interpretation of output

Output 16.6 prints goodness-of-fit statistics for the regression and time series models. The suffixes T and R refer to the time series and regression models. Note that the mean average deviation (MAD) of the time series model is 6.65237 and is −5.40205 for the regression model. In other words, the time series model generates forecasts that are on average too low, while the regression model generates forecasts that are on average too high. (Recall that residuals are actual values minus predicted values.) A linear combination of the two should produce residuals on average closer to zero.

Calculating Weights

The easiest way to combine the forecasts is to average them, or weight each forecast by .5. However, a different weighting scheme will most likely generate smaller absolute residuals and goodness-of-fit statistics closer to zero.

You can calculate weights for a combination of the predicted values by using an iterative DO loop in a DATA step. The first year, 1973, is deleted because the first differencing for the time series model produced a missing value for that year.

The following SAS example code shows you how to perform these tasks. Output 16.7 shows the results.

```
data budget3;
   set budget2;
   if year=73 then delete;
   do weight=0 to 1 by .1;
```

```
        /* Combined GFUND Predictions */
     gfund_c=weight*gfund_r+(1-weight)*gfund_t;

        /* GFUND Residuals */
     res_c=gfund-gfund_c;

        /* Goodness of Fit Statistics */
     per_c=(res_c*100)/gfund;
     se_c=res_c**2;
     output;
   end;
run;

   /* Sorting Combined Forecasts */
proc sort data=budget3;
   by weight;
run;

   /* Calculating Mean Values */
proc summary data=budget3 mean;
   var res_c per_c se_c;
   by weight;
   output out=bud_ave1 mean=mad_c mper_c mse_c;
run;

   /* Taking Square Roots */
data bud_st1;
   set bud_ave1;
   rmse_c=sqrt(mse_c);
run;

   /* Printing the Statistics */
proc print data=bud_st1;
   var weight mad_c mper_c mse_c rmse_c;
   title2 'Goodness-of-Fit Statistics';
   title3 'from Weighted Averages';
run;
```

Output 16.7
Goodness-of-Fit
Statistics for
Finding the
Weights

```
                    General Fund Revenues Example
                     Goodness-of-Fit Statistics
                       from Weighted Averages

     OBS    WEIGHT     MAD_C       MPER_C       MSE_C      RMSE_C

      1      0.0       6.6524      0.05634     14306.19    119.608
      2      0.1       4.6524     -0.00957     12813.64    113.197
      3      0.2       2.6524     -0.07548     11546.23    107.453
      4      0.3       0.6524     -0.14139     10503.98    102.489
      5      0.4      -1.3476     -0.20730      9686.87     98.422
      6      0.5      -3.3476     -0.27321      9094.91     95.367
      7      0.6      -5.3476     -0.33912      8728.09     93.424
      8      0.7      -7.3476     -0.40503      8586.43     92.663
      9      0.8      -9.3476     -0.47095      8669.91     93.112
     10      0.9     -11.3476     -0.53686      8978.54     94.755
     11      1.0     -13.3476     -0.60277      9512.32     97.531
```

Interpretation of output
Output 16.7 prints goodness-of-fit statistics for the linear combinations of the regression and time series models. For our purposes, the weights are calculated to only one decimal place. You may want to use a smaller increment than .1 in the DO loop for increased accuracy. Weights of .3 and .1 yield the MAD and MPER statistics (respectively) closest to zero, while the weight of .7 yields the closest-to-zero values for the MSE and RMSE.

Following standard practices of using the MSE and RMSE as the goodness-of-fit statistics used for comparing models, the value of .7 is selected as the weight.

Calculating Combined Forecasts

The weighting scheme can be used to combine the forecasts of the period 1990 through 1995 to reflect the information contained in both the time series and regression models. The combining is performed in a DATA step, and the final forecasts are printed with PROC PRINT. Output 16.8 shows the results.

```
data bud_f1;
   set bud_out3;
   if year < 90 then delete;
   gfund_f=.7*gfund_r+(1-.7)*gfund_t;
run;

proc print data=bud_f1;
   var year gfund_f;
   title2 'Combined Forecasts';
run;
```

Output 16.8
The Combined
GFUND Forecasts

```
           General Fund Revenues Example
                 Combined Forecasts

         OBS     YEAR     GFUND_F

          1       90      4906.55
          2       91      5038.24
          3       92      5174.74
          4       93      5315.20
          5       94      5459.10
          6       95      5606.09
```

Interpretation of output
Output 16.8 prints the combined GFUND forecasts for the period 1990 through 1995. The forecasts reflect continued growth in U.S. GNP and N.C. population at the 1985-through-1989 rate.

Fitting a Simple Transfer Function

A more rigorous way to combine the information contained in the time series and regression models is to fit a transfer function to the BUDGET data. Transfer functions differ from regression models in that forecasted values of the exogenous variables are used to forecast the endogenous variable. Variability of the exogenous variables is included in the forecasts of the endogenous variable.

If you assume that POP and GNP are uncorrelated and that current values of POP and GNP affect only the current value of GFUND, then a simple transfer function can be fitted to the GFUND series. To fit a simple transfer function to the GFUND series and use it for forecasting, you follow these steps:

1. Identify the process underlying the exogenous variables.

2. Estimate a model for the exogenous variables.

3. Identify and estimate the transfer function for the endogenous variable using the exogenous variables and the appropriate error processes.

4. Forecast the endogenous variables.

The next section uses PROC ARIMA interactively to perform these steps.

For more information on fitting transfer functions and forecasting with them, see *SAS/ETS Software: Applications Guide 1* and *SAS System for Forecasting Time Series, 1986 Edition.*

Identifying the Exogenous Variables

Prior to forecasting additional values of the exogenous variables, GNP and POP, use the IDENTIFY statement of PROC ARIMA to identify the time series process that underlies them. Because these two series have an upward trend, use their first differences. The following SAS example code identifies the first differenced GNP and POP series. Output 16.9 shows the results.

```
proc arima data=budget;
   identify var=gnp(1);
   identify var=pop(1);
run;
```

Output 16.9
Identifying the
Underlying
Processes of the
Exogenous
Variables

```
                    General Fund Revenues Example

                          ARIMA Procedure


                    Name of variable = GNP.

                    Period(s) of Differencing = 1.
                    Mean of working series = 70.79419
                    Standard deviation     = 100.1938
                    Number of observations =       16
                    NOTE: The first observation was eliminated by
                          differencing.

                          Autocorrelations

Lag Covariance Correlation -1 9 8 7 6 5 4 3 2 1 0 1 2 3 4 5 6 7 8 9 1
 0  10038.795   1.00000   |                    |********************|
 1   3040.602   0.30289   |               .    |******   .          |
 2   -605.733  -0.06034   |               .   *|         .          |
 3  -2805.779  -0.27949   |               . ******|       .          |
 4  -4671.192  -0.46531   |               . ********|      .          |
                    "." marks two standard errors
```

(continued)

Output 16.9
(continued)

```
                              Inverse Autocorrelations

          Lag Correlation -1 9 8 7 6 5 4 3 2 1 0 1 2 3 4 5 6 7 8 9 1
           1    -0.16027  |                .      ***|          .          |
           2     0.10874  |                .         |**         .          |
           3     0.02716  |                .         |*          .          |
           4     0.30654  |                .         |******     .          |


                              Partial Autocorrelations

          Lag Correlation -1 9 8 7 6 5 4 3 2 1 0 1 2 3 4 5 6 7 8 9 1
           1     0.30289  |                .         |******     .          |
           2    -0.16744  |                .      ***|          .          |
           3    -0.23498  |                .    *****|          .          |
           4    -0.37336  |                .  *******|          .          |
```

```
                          General Fund Revenues Example

                                ARIMA Procedure


                         Name of variable = POP.

                         Period(s) of Differencing = 1.
                         Mean of working series =  74.3125
                         Standard deviation     = 9.732155
                         Number of observations =       16
                         NOTE: The first observation was eliminated by
                               differencing.

                              Autocorrelations

     Lag Covariance Correlation -1 9 8 7 6 5 4 3 2 1 0 1 2 3 4 5 6 7 8 9 1
      0   94.714844   1.00000   |                         |********************|
      1    8.837646   0.09331   |                .        |**          .          |
      2  -31.113770  -0.32850   |                .  *******|           .          |
      3   18.161377   0.19175   |                .        |****        .          |
      4   23.077148   0.24365   |                .        |*****       .          |
                      "." marks two standard errors


                              Inverse Autocorrelations

          Lag Correlation -1 9 8 7 6 5 4 3 2 1 0 1 2 3 4 5 6 7 8 9 1
           1    -0.29383  |                .  ******|          .          |
           2     0.31385  |                .        |******     .          |
           3    -0.21932  |                .     ****|          .          |
           4    -0.04762  |                .        *|          .          |


                              Partial Autocorrelations

          Lag Correlation -1 9 8 7 6 5 4 3 2 1 0 1 2 3 4 5 6 7 8 9 1
           1     0.09331  |                .        |**         .          |
           2    -0.34017  |                .  *******|          .          |
           3     0.30181  |                .        |******     .          |
           4     0.05984  |                .        |*          .          |
```

Interpretation of output

Output 16.9 shows the ACF, PACF, and IACF of the first differenced GNP and POP series. The ACF tails off for POP, and none of the lagged autocorrelations are significant for either GNP or POP. The PACF and IACF have no statistically significant correlations. You conclude that a good candidate model for both first differenced series is a purely random model, containing no autocorrelated or moving average processes.

Estimating the Exogenous Variables

After identifying the underlying processes of the exogenous variables, you use the processes to forecast additional values of the exogenous variables. The following

SAS example code uses ESTIMATE statements to fit an ARIMA model to each exogenous variable. Because the P= and Q= options are not specified, PROC ARIMA does not fit any autoregressive or moving average parameters. Note that when using PROC ARIMA interactively, the procedure remains invoked until you submit a QUIT statement. Output 16.10 shows the results.

```
    identify var=gnp(1) noprint;
    estimate;
    identify var=pop(1) noprint;
    estimate;
run;
```

Output 16.10
Fitting a Time Series Model to the First Differences of GNP and POP

```
                    General Fund Revenues Example

                          ARIMA Procedure


               Conditional Least Squares Estimation

                                   Approx.
          Parameter   Estimate   Std Error   T Ratio   Lag
          MU          70.79419   25.86992      2.74    0

          Constant Estimate  = 70.7941914

          Variance  Estimate = 10708.0477
          Std Error Estimate = 103.479697
          AIC                =  194.83343*
          SBC                = 195.606019*
          Number of Residuals=       16
          * Does not include log determinant.


               Autocorrelation Check of Residuals

     To   Chi                    Autocorrelations
    Lag  Square DF  Prob
      6   8.88  6  0.180   0.303 -0.060 -0.279 -0.465  0.005  0.064
     12  10.43 12  0.579   0.130  0.115 -0.088 -0.035  0.003 -0.046


                    Model for variable GNP

               Estimated Mean = 70.7941914
               Period(s) of Differencing = 1.
```

```
                    General Fund Revenues Example

                          ARIMA Procedure


               Conditional Least Squares Estimation

                                   Approx.
          Parameter   Estimate   Std Error   T Ratio   Lag
          MU          74.31250    2.51283     29.57    0

          Constant Estimate  =   74.3125

          Variance  Estimate = 101.029167
          Std Error Estimate = 10.0513266
          AIC                = 120.219965*
          SBC                = 120.992554*
          Number of Residuals=       16
          * Does not include log determinant.
```

(continued)

Output 16.10
(continued)

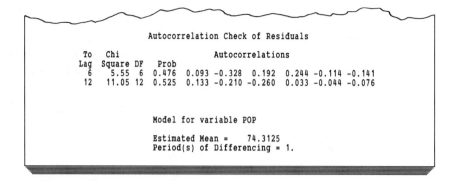

```
                    Autocorrelation Check of Residuals

    To   Chi                     Autocorrelations
   Lag Square DF  Prob
     6    5.55  6  0.476  0.093 -0.328  0.192  0.244 -0.114 -0.141
    12   11.05 12  0.525  0.133 -0.210 -0.260  0.033 -0.044 -0.076



                    Model for variable POP

                    Estimated Mean =    74.3125
                    Period(s) of Differencing = 1.
```

Interpretation of output

Output 16.10 contains the fitted time series models for the first differences of GNP and POP. Only a mean value was fitted to the series. The mean values, labeled MU, are 70.7942 and 74.3125 for the first differenced GNP and POP series. Both mean values are statistically significant at the .05 level. Additionally, none of the Q statistics are significant at the .05 level. You conclude that both first differenced series are purely random.

Estimating the Transfer Function

After identifying the underlying processes of GNP and POP and fitting models to them, you can use forecasted values of these variables to forecast GFUND. A good candidate time series model for the GFUND series is a first-order autoregressive model. Recall this model is used to fit a time series model to the GFUND series in Output 16.4.

The following SAS example code continues the use of PROC ARIMA interactively to fit a first-order autoregressive transfer function model to the BUDGET data and print the forecasted values. After submitting the previous statements, submit the following statements.

IDENTIFY
   computes statistics to help identify models to fit. The following options are specified:

   VAR=   specifies the variable containing the time series, the endogenous variable. The optional parenthetical value specifies the order of differencing. In this case, the series is differenced once.

   CROSSCOR=   specifies the variables crosscorrelated with the endogenous variable. The optional parenthetical value specifies the order of differencing. In this case, each series is differenced once.

   NOPRINT   suppresses the printed output.

ESTIMATE
   specifies an estimate of the model for the variables specified in the previous IDENTIFY statement. The following options are specified:

   P=   specifies the degree of the autoregressive part of the model.

INPUT specifies the input variables and the forms for the transfer function. The input series must be specified in the CROSSCOR= list in the previous IDENTITY statement.

Note that the *k*th crosscorrelation between the endogenous variable, Y, at time *t* and the exogenous variable, X, at time $t+k$ is defined as $\gamma_{YX}(k)=\text{cov}(Y_t, X_{t+k})$. For general transfer functions, the crosscorrelations assist you in determining the length of lag for changes in X to influence Y.

NOPRINT suppresses the printed output.

FORECAST

generates forecasts for the model estimated by the previous ESTIMATE statement. The following options are specified:

LEAD= specifies the number of forecasts to compute. For LEAD=6, PROC ARIMA forecasts for six periods after the end of the data set. The default is 24.

ID specifies a variable in the input data set that is used to identify the observations in the output data set. Note that the ID variable and the endogenous variable are the only variables copied from the input to the output data set.

OUT= creates and names the output data set to contain the forecasts.

The following SAS example code produces Output 16.11.

```
      /* Identifying, Fitting, and Forecasting GFUND */
   identify var=gfund(1) crosscor=(pop(1) gnp(1));
   estimate p=1 input=(pop gnp);
   forecast lead=6 id=year out=bud_trn;
run;
```

Output 16.11
Fitting a Transfer Function to the BUDGET Data with P=1

```
                    General Fund Revenues Example

                         ARIMA Procedure


              Name of variable = GFUND.

              Period(s) of Differencing = 1.
              Mean of working series = 127.9259
              Standard deviation     = 140.9397
              Number of observations =      16
              NOTE: The first observation was eliminated by
                    differencing.

                         Autocorrelations

Lag Covariance Correlation -1 9 8 7 6 5 4 3 2 1 0 1 2 3 4 5 6 7 8 9 1
 0  19863.985   1.00000   |                    |********************|
 1  10418.091   0.52447   |          .         |*********          |
 2   2147.980   0.10813   |          .         |**        .        |
 3  -3218.695  -0.16204   |          .      ***|          .        |
 4  -6816.369  -0.34315   |          .   *******|         .        |
                          "." marks two standard errors
```

(continued)

Output 16.11
(continued)

```
                          Inverse Autocorrelations

          Lag Correlation -1 9 8 7 6 5 4 3 2 1 0 1 2 3 4 5 6 7 8 9 1
           1    -0.46410  |         .*********|              .           |
           2     0.12179  |         .        |**             .           |
           3    -0.06887  |         .        *|              .           |
           4     0.15618  |         .        |***            .           |


                          Partial Autocorrelations

          Lag Correlation -1 9 8 7 6 5 4 3 2 1 0 1 2 3 4 5 6 7 8 9 1
           1     0.52447  |         .        |**********     .           |
           2    -0.23028  |         .    *****|              .           |
           3    -0.16174  |         .      ***|              .           |
           4    -0.21867  |         .     ****|              .           |



                         Correlation of GFUND and POP
                         Variable POP has been differenced.
                         Period(s) of Differencing = 1.
                         Both series have been prewhitened.
                         Variance of transformed series = 19863.99 and 94.71484
                         Number of observations =       16
                         NOTE: The first observation was eliminated by
                               differencing.

                              Crosscorrelations

    Lag Covariance Correlation -1 9 8 7 6 5 4 3 2 1 0 1 2 3 4 5 6 7 8 9 1
    -4    116.640   0.08504  |         .        |**             .           |
    -3    346.778   0.25282  |         .        |*****          .           |
    -2    307.343   0.22407  |         .        |****           .           |
    -1    660.459   0.48151  |         .        |**********     .           |
     0    608.413   0.44356  |         .        |*********.                 |
```

```
                         General Fund Revenues Example

                              ARIMA Procedure


    Lag Covariance Correlation -1 9 8 7 6 5 4 3 2 1 0 1 2 3 4 5 6 7 8 9 1
     1   -133.499  -0.09733  |         .       **|              .           |
     2    9.225500  0.00673  |         .        |              .           |
     3    63.692223 0.04643  |         .        |*             .           |
     4  -19.775790 -0.01442  |         .        |              .           |
                         "." marks two standard errors



                         Correlation of GFUND and GNP
                         Variable GNP has been differenced.
                         Period(s) of Differencing = 1.
                         Both series have been prewhitened.
                         Variance of transformed series = 19863.99 and 10038.79
                         Number of observations =       16
                         NOTE: The first observation was eliminated by
                               differencing.

                              Crosscorrelations

    Lag Covariance Correlation -1 9 8 7 6 5 4 3 2 1 0 1 2 3 4 5 6 7 8 9 1
    -4 -32.559745 -0.00231  |         .        |              .           |
    -3 -4020.251  -0.28469  |         .   ******|              .           |
    -2   219.827   0.01557  |         .        |              .           |
    -1  5489.679   0.38875  |         .        |********       .           |
     0  8915.516   0.63135  |         .        |*************  .           |
     1  9778.795   0.69249  |         .        |**************              |
     2  -332.911  -0.02358  |         .        |              .           |
     3 -4062.737  -0.28770  |         .   ******|              .           |
     4 -5524.923  -0.39125  |         . ********|              .           |
                         "." marks two standard errors
```

(continued)

Output 16.11
(continued)

```
                    General Fund Revenues Example

                         ARIMA Procedure


                 Conditional Least Squares Estimation

                              Approx.
     Parameter   Estimate    Std Error   T Ratio  Lag  Variable Shift
     MU          -376.73372  192.66658   -1.96     0   GFUND      0
     AR1,1         -0.29472    0.29313   -1.01     1   GFUND      0
     NUM1           5.82189    2.60506    2.23     0   POP        0
     NUM2           1.03200    0.23976    4.30     0   GNP        0


     Constant Estimate  = -487.76653

     Variance  Estimate = 11080.9019
     Std Error Estimate = 105.265863
     AIC                = 197.810774*
     SBC                = 200.901129*
     Number of Residuals=       16
     * Does not include log determinant.

                   Correlations of the Estimates


                               GFUND      GFUND       POP       GNP
     Variable    Parameter       MU       AR1,1      NUM1      NUM2

     GFUND       MU           1.000      0.180     -0.990     0.037
     GFUND       AR1,1        0.180      1.000     -0.169    -0.163
     POP         NUM1        -0.990     -0.169      1.000    -0.126
     GNP         NUM2         0.037     -0.163     -0.126     1.000


                  Autocorrelation Check of Residuals

     To   Chi                    Autocorrelations
     Lag  Square DF  Prob
      6    4.68   5  0.457  -0.050 -0.078  0.198 -0.377  0.055 -0.072
     12    6.98  11  0.801  -0.118  0.079 -0.133 -0.057 -0.094 -0.058


           Crosscorrelation Check of Residuals with Input POP

     To   Chi                    Crosscorrelations
     Lag  Square DF  Prob
      5    8.23   6  0.221   0.048 -0.162  0.309 -0.233 -0.566  0.128
     11    8.79  12  0.721   0.055 -0.081 -0.109 -0.107 -0.018 -0.034


           Crosscorrelation Check of Residuals with Input GNP

     To   Chi                    Crosscorrelations
     Lag  Square DF  Prob
      5    8.10   6  0.231  -0.118  0.401  0.024 -0.238 -0.145 -0.504
     11   11.90  12  0.453  -0.062  0.166  0.134  0.349  0.030 -0.256
```

```
                    General Fund Revenues Example

                         ARIMA Procedure


          Model for variable GFUND

          Estimated Intercept = -376.73372
          Period(s) of Differencing = 1.

          Autoregressive Factors
          Factor 1: 1 + 0.29472 B**(1)


          Input Number 1 is POP.
          Period(s) of Differencing = 1.
          Overall Regression Factor  = 5.821891

          Input Number 2 is GNP.
          Period(s) of Differencing = 1.
          Overall Regression Factor  = 1.032004
```

(continued)

Output 16.11
(continued)

```
                        General Fund Revenues Example

                            ARIMA Procedure


        Forecasts for variable GFUND

        Obs    Forecast Std Error   Lower 95%    Upper 95%
        18    4934.6356  160.9647   4619.1505   5250.1207
        19    5056.3444  215.0585   4634.8374   5477.8514
        20    5187.4486  260.8294   4676.2323   5698.6648
        21    5315.7837  298.9509   4729.8507   5901.7167
        22    5444.9349  332.9266   4792.4108   6097.4590
        23    5573.8456  363.6901   4861.0262   6286.6650
```

Interpretation of output

Output 16.11 contains the fitted transfer function, which is

$$\varepsilon_t = (1 + 0.2947\,B)\,\{[(1 - B)\text{GFUND}_t + 376.7337]$$
$$- 5.8219(1 - B)\text{POP}_t - 1.0320(1 - B)\text{GNP}_t\} \quad .$$

The ACF, IACF, and PACF indicate little autoregressive or moving average processes. Note that all estimated parameters are significant except the AR(1) parameter. The transfer function fitted as an AR(1) process is overparameterized and should be refitted without the AR(1) parameter.

Note that the crosscorrelation plot between GFUND and POP reveals a possible spike at lag -1 for POP. This may be problematic, indicating feedback, and you may want to pursue more in-depth analysis.

Forecasting the Endogenous Variable

With a slight modification of the SAS example code that produced Output 16.11, you can refit the transfer function without the autoregressive process. The ESTIMATE statement becomes

```
estimate input=(pop gnp) noprint;
```

By removing the P= option and renaming the OUT= data set, you can forecast the transfer function by submitting the following statements. Note that the QUIT statement ends the interactive PROC ARIMA session. Output 16.12 shows the results.

```
     /* Fitting and Forecasting GFUND */
   estimate input=(pop gnp);
   forecast lead=6 id=year out=bud_trn1;
run;
quit;
```

Output 16.12
Fitting a Transfer
Function to the
BUDGET Data
without P=1

```
                    General Fund Revenues Example

                          ARIMA Procedure


                 Conditional Least Squares Estimation

                            Approx.
Parameter    Estimate     Std Error    T Ratio  Lag  Variable Shift
MU          -366.36917    199.61230     -1.84    0   GFUND     0
NUM1           5.84146      2.66839      2.19    0   POP       0
NUM2           0.85038      0.25919      3.28    0   GNP       0


Constant Estimate  = -366.36917

Variance  Estimate = 10742.6826
Std Error Estimate = 103.646913
AIC                = 196.595485*
SBC                = 198.913251*
Number of Residuals=        16
* Does not include log determinant.

                     Correlations of the Estimates


                                    GFUND        POP        GNP
          Variable    Parameter       MU        NUM1       NUM2

          GFUND       MU           1.000      -0.987     -0.026
          POP         NUM1        -0.987       1.000     -0.066
          GNP         NUM2        -0.026      -0.066      1.000


                  Autocorrelation Check of Residuals

 To   Chi                       Autocorrelations
Lag  Square DF   Prob
  6    6.48  6  0.372  -0.139 -0.052  0.204 -0.446  0.093 -0.064
 12    8.96 12  0.706  -0.069  0.120 -0.072 -0.026 -0.118 -0.102


          Crosscorrelation Check of Residuals with Input POP

 To   Chi                       Crosscorrelations
Lag  Square DF   Prob
  5    6.51  6  0.368   0.000 -0.175  0.318 -0.290 -0.396  0.185
 11    6.98 12  0.859  -0.038 -0.066 -0.114 -0.099 -0.012 -0.022


          Crosscorrelation Check of Residuals with Input GNP

 To   Chi                       Crosscorrelations
Lag  Square DF   Prob
  5    9.53  6  0.146   0.000  0.507 -0.134 -0.259 -0.184 -0.468
 11   12.52 12  0.405   0.064  0.158  0.135  0.292 -0.035 -0.230
```

```
                    General Fund Revenues Example

                          ARIMA Procedure


              Model for variable GFUND

              Estimated Intercept = -366.36917
              Period(s) of Differencing = 1.

              Input Number 1 is POP.
              Period(s) of Differencing = 1.
              Overall Regression Factor  = 5.841459

              Input Number 2 is GNP.
              Period(s) of Differencing = 1.
              Overall Regression Factor  = 0.850375
```

(continued)

Output 16.12
(continued)

```
                    General Fund Revenues Example

                           ARIMA Procedure


       Forecasts for variable GFUND

       Obs    Forecast Std Error   Lower 95%   Upper 95%
        18   4908.9743  148.0995   4618.7046   5199.2440
        19   5036.9002  209.4443   4626.3968   5447.4035
        20   5164.8260  256.5159   4662.0642   5667.5879
        21   5292.7519  296.1990   4712.2126   5873.2913
        22   5420.6778  331.1605   4771.6151   6069.7406
        23   5548.6037  362.7682   4837.5911   6259.6163
```

Interpretation of output

Output 16.12 contains the transfer function model of random effects fitted to the first differenced series and its forecasts. The model is

$$(1 - B)\text{GFUND}_t = -366.3692 + 5.8415(1 - B)\text{POP}_t$$
$$+ 0.8504(1 - B)\text{GNP}_t + \varepsilon_t$$

The forecasted values and standard errors are smaller for this model as compared to the forecasts generated from the AR(1) transfer function of Output 16.11. Additionally, the width of the confidence intervals around the forecasts are also smaller for this model.

Moreover, as you compare Akaike's information criterion (AIC) and Schwarz's Bayesian criterion (SBC) of the models in Output 16.11 and Output 16.12, you notice that both are closer to zero for the model of Output 16.12, which indicates a better fit to the data.

You can compare the regression model, the time series model, and the transfer function model on the basis of the AIC and SBC. Table 16.1 summarizes the values.

Table 16.1
Comparing
GFUND Models

Model	AIC	SBC
Regression	212.483	215.816
Time Series	202.501	204.046
Transfer Function	196.595	198.913

On the criteria of the AIC and SBC closest to zero, the time series model is superior to the regression model while the transfer function model is superior to the time series model.

For more information about the AIC and the SBC, see Akaike (1974) and Schwarz (1978), respectively.

Comparing Forecasts with Reality

How good are the GFUND forecasts produced in the examples in this chapter? The following DATA step merges the forecasts and names them according to the method used to generate them. Output 16.13 shows the results.

```
data bud_comp;
   merge budget1 bud_f1 bud_trn1;
   by year;
   if year<90 then delete;
   label gfund_r='Regression Forecast'
         gfund_t='Time Series Forecast'
         gfund_f='Combined Forecast'
         forecast='Transfer Function Forecast';
run;

proc print data=bud_comp;
   var year gfund_r gfund_t gfund_f forecast;
   title2 'Forecasts by Different Methods';
run;
```

Output 16.13
GFUND Forecasts from Regression, Time Series, Combined Regression and Time Series, and Transfer Function Models

		Forecasts by Different Methods			
OBS	YEAR	Regression Forecast	Time Series Forecast	Combined Forecast	Transfer Function Forecast
1	90	4917.94	4879.98	4906.55	4908.97
2	91	5061.12	4984.84	5038.24	5036.90
3	92	5209.81	5092.90	5174.74	5164.83
4	93	5363.42	5202.68	5315.20	5292.75
5	94	5521.54	5313.38	5459.10	5420.68
6	95	5683.88	5424.58	5606.09	5548.60

Interpretation of output

Output 16.13 contains the forecasts generated from the regression, time series, combined regression and time series, and transfer function models.

In actuality, the recession of 1990 through 1991 produced a shift in the economy that the models could not foresee. The past trends were, in fact, not particularly good guides for the future. The recession is reflected in the actual values of GFUND for 1990 and 1991, 5020.20 and 4913.73. Thus, in 1990 the regression forecast was more accurate, while in 1991 the time series model was more accurate.

It is interesting to note that in 1990 the N.C. Office of Budget and Management (OBM) forecasted the 1991 value as 5401.90. The OBM shortfall was 488.20, or about a 10 percent error. North Carolina, like many other states, approved its budget based on a revenue forecast that proved to be too high and then had to work to reduce expenditures to balance the budget.

Scenario forecasting may help planners consider the range of possibilities for the future. Scenario forecasting is presented in Chapter 15, "Forecasting with Linear Systems." Alternatively, you could create a larger model and forecast U.S. GNP and N.C. POP. Forecasting these and other right-hand side variables in larger models is part of the forecasting approach used by the N.C. OBM.

Chapter Summary

This chapter presented an example of combining forecasts. A regression model and a time series model were fitted, and separate forecasts were produced. The forecasts were compared, and goodness-of-fit statistics were generated. Linear combinations of the two sets of forecasts were created. The weight that produced the goodness-of-fit statistics closest to zero was used to weight the two sets of forecasts for a combined final forecast. Then, a transfer function was fitted to the BUDGET data, and another set of forecasts was generated. Lastly, forecasts from the models were compared with the 1990-through-1991 actual values.

Learning More

□ For full reference information on the ARIMA and AUTOREG procedures in SAS/ETS software, see the *SAS/ETS User's Guide, Version 6, First Edition.*

□ For full reference information on the PLOT and SUMMARY procedures in base SAS software, see the *SAS Procedures Guide, Version 6, Third Edition.*

□ For more information on statistical tests for stationarity and fitting time series and transfer function models, see *SAS/ETS Software: Applications Guide 1* and *SAS System for Forecasting Time Series, 1986 Edition.*

References

Akaike, H. (1974), "A New Look at the Statistical Model Identification," *IEEE Transaction on Automatic Control*, AC-19, 716—723.

Bates, J.M. and Granger, C.W.J. (1969), "The Combination of Forecasts," *Operational Research Quarterly*, 20, 451—68.

Box, G.E.P. and Jenkins, G.M. (1970), *Time Series Analysis: Forecasting and Control*, San Francisco: Holden-Day.

Dickey, D.A. and Fuller, W.A. (1979), "Distribution of the Estimators for Autoregressive Time Series With a Unit Root," *Journal of the American Statistical Association*, 74, 427—431.

Holden, K., Peel, D.A., and Thompson, J.L. (1990), *Economic Forecasting: An Introduction*, New York: Cambridge University Press.

Ljung, G.M. and Box, G.E.P. (1978), "On a Measure of Lack of Fit in Times Series Models," *Biometrika*, 64, 517—522.

Makridakis, S., Andersen, A., Carbone, R., Fildes, R., Hibon, M., Lewandowski, R., Newton, S., Parzen, E., and Winkler, R. (1984), "The Accuracy of Extrapolation (Times Series) Methods: Results of a Forecasting Competition," *Journal of Forecasting*, 1, 111—153.

N.C. Office of State Budget and Management (1990), "Overview of the North Carolina State Budget."

Schwarz, G. (1978), "Estimating the Dimension of a Model," *Annals of Statistics*, 6, 461—464.

U.S. Department of Commerce, *Statistical Abstracts of the U.S.* (1991), Washington, D.C.: U.S. Government Printing Office.

Glossary

analysis of variance (ANOVA)
a statistical technique for determining whether differences exist across levels of a classification factor. ANOVA compares the observed differences among sample means so that inferences about differences in corresponding population means can be made.

ARIMA model
a general probabilistic model for stationary time series involving any combination of autoregressive (AR) and moving-average (MA) parameters. ARIMA models involve differenced time series variables.

autocorrelation
the internal correlation between observations in a time series. Autocorrelation coefficient values range from -1 to $+1$. When autocorrelation coefficient values are positive, deviations from the mean of one sign tend to be followed by deviations of the same sign. When they are negative, deviations of one sign tend to be followed by deviations of the opposite sign.

autocorrelation function (ACF) plot
the autocorrelation coefficients of order p plotted against p.

autoregressive (AR) model
one of two fundamental types of probabilistic models for stationary time series data in the Box-Jenkins approach. Autoregressive models involve parameter estimates associated with lagged time series values. See also moving-average (MA) model.

autoregressive process
a stochastic process underlying the generation of autoregressive time series observations.

backshift operator
an operator of the form B^l that calculates values of the specified variable lagged by the amount, l.

base SAS software
software that includes a programming language that manages your data, procedures for data analysis and reporting, procedures for managing SAS files, a macro facility, help menus, and a windowing environment for text editing and file management.

bias
a systematic effect that causes the mean or expected value of an estimator to differ from the true value. In contrast, the mean or expected value of an unbiased estimator is the true value.

Box-Jenkins approach
an approach to time series data analysis consisting of identification of candidate models, estimation of model parameters, and diagnostic checking. See also autoregressive (AR) model and moving-average (MA) model.

BY-group processing
the process of using the BY statement to process observations that are ordered, grouped, or indexed according to the values of one or more variables. Many SAS procedures and the DATA step support BY-group processing. For example, you can use BY-group processing with the PRINT procedure to print separate reports for different groups of observations in a single SAS data set.

collinearity
a condition in which two explanatory variables are strongly correlated.

conditional least-squares (CLS) method
a least-squares method of estimation that assumes the value of the infinite past of a time series is equal to the mean of the time series.

confidence limits
the upper and lower values of a confidence interval. There is a percentage of confidence (typically 95%) that the true value of the parameter being estimated lies within the interval.

contemporaneous correlation
correlation among variables within the same time period, often among cross-sectional units.

convergence criterion
a stopping criterion for iterated estimation methods.

correlation
the tendency for the values of a variable to become larger or smaller as the values of a variable increase or decrease.

covariance
the expected value of the product of two variables when both are measured as deviations about their means. For example, the sample covariance for n observations of the variables x and y is defined as

$$\text{Cov}(x,y) = \frac{1}{n-1}\sum (x_i - \bar{x})(y_i - \bar{y}) \quad .$$

crosscorrelation
the linear relationship between two time series variables.

cross-sectional data
observations on multiple units in one time period. Examples of cross-sectional units are individuals, firms, and geographic aggregations. See also panel data and time series.

DATA step
a group of statements in a SAS program that begins with a DATA statement and ends with either a RUN statement, another DATA statement, a PROC statement, the end of the job, or the semicolon that immediately follows instream data lines. The DATA step enables you to read raw data or other SAS data sets and use programming logic to create a SAS data set, write a report, or write to an external file.

dependent variable
a variable whose value is determined by the value of another variable or set of variables. The dependent variable is also known as an endogenous variable.

deterministic variable
a variable with values that are known with certainty. Deterministic variables can be used as predictor variables in time series regression models. The value of time is an example of a deterministic variable.

differencing
the process of subtracting a previous time series observation from a current observation, often used to achieve stationarity.

drop to 0
a pattern in a plot of autocorrelation coefficients (for example, ACF, IACF, PACF) where all values following a given lag are 0.

dummy variable
a variable used in a regression model to represent qualitative characteristics. For example, a variable may take on the value 0 or 1 to indicate a discrete change in a process.

Durbin *h* statistic
a statistic used to test the hypothesis of no first-order autocorrelation in models with lagged dependent variables used as predictors. The Durbin *h* statistic is distributed normally with unit variance, so test statistics can be compared to tables of the normal distribution.

Durbin-Watson statistic
a ratio with a range of 0 to 4 used to test the hypothesis of no autocorrelation in a time series. If there is no autocorrelation, the expected value of the Durbin-Watson statistic is 2. Values near 0 indicate positive autocorrelation, while values near 4 indicate negative autocorrelation.

endogenous variable
a variable whose values are explained by the model.

estimation
the process of calculating parameter values for a model from sample data.

exogenous variable
a variable whose values are determined outside of the model. See also explanatory variable.

explanatory variable
a variable included in a regression model to explain the variation in the dependent variable. Explanatory variables, also called independent, input, predictor, or regressor variables, can be deterministic or probabilistic.

extrapolation
the continuation of a series beyond known values.

feedback
an interrelationship between two or more time series, where past values of one or more series affect current values of one or more other series.

forecast
a numerical prediction of a future value for a time series.

forecast standard error
the standard error of a future-period forecast from a time series model, calculated from the variance of the original series and the estimated model parameters.

full information maximum-likelihood (FIML) method
a maximum-likelihood method for estimating the parameters of multiple equation models simultaneously. Information in cross-equation restrictions is utilized.

general form equations
a rewriting of the model equations with the error term on the left side and the endogenous (or dependent) variable and the explanatory variables on the right side. See also normalized equations.

generalized least-squares (GLS) method
a least-squares method for estimating the model parameters when the error terms are not independent but the error-covariance matrix is known. See also least-squares method.

general transfer function
a model for a time series process involving lagged values of explanatory time series and time series errors.

goal-seeking simulation
the process of solving for the value of an explanatory variable when values for the remaining model variables are given.

heteroskedasticity
in regression models, the condition in which the error terms do not have a constant variance.

homoskedasticity
in regression models, the condition in which the error terms have a constant variance.

hypothesis testing
the statistical process of making a decision from experimental results. By comparing the value of a test statistic with its critical value, you can conclude whether to reject the null hypothesis in favor of an alternative.

identification
(1) in ARIMA modeling, the process of determining the order of the ARIMA model that best approximates a given time series process.
(2) in a system of equations, a condition that occurs when one of the following is true:
(a) Only one set of numerical values can be obtained for the parameters of a structural equation. In this case, the equation is said to be just identified.
(b) Multiple sets of numerical values can be obtained for some of the parameters of the structural equation. In this case, the equation is said to be overidentified.
(c) No numerical values can be obtained for some of the parameters of the structural equation. In this case, the equation is said to underidentified.

independent variable
(1) a variable that does not depend on the value of another variable; in a two-dimensional plot, the independent variable is usually plotted on the x (horizontal) axis.
(2) See explanatory variable.

instrumental variable
a variable correlated with an explanatory variable and uncorrelated with the error term. In regression estimation, instrumental variables are used to replace an explanatory variable that is correlated with the error terms.

interpolation
the process of calculating values for missing data.

inverse autocorrelation function (IACF) plot
the inverse autocorrelation coefficients of order p plotted against p. The IACF coefficients are calculated as the autocorrelation coefficients of an autoregressive model remodeled as a moving-average model.

jointly determined variables
endogenous variables in a system of equations, such that solving for any one variable requires solving for the other variables.

lag
(1) a previous value for a variable or observation of a time series. For example, lag1 is the value from the previous period, while lag12 is the value from 12 periods ago.
(2) the number of time periods between two ordered values from the same time series.

lag model
a regression model in which current values of the endogenous variable depend on past values of the explanatory variables, past values of the endogenous variable, or both.

least-squares method
an estimation method in which the estimated parameters minimize a quadratic form of sums of squared errors.

limited information maximum-likelihood (LIML) method
a maximum-likelihood method for estimating the parameters of an identified or
overidentified equation in isolation from the other equations of a simultaneous
equations model. Information in cross-equation restrictions is not utilized.

maximum-likelihood (ML) method
an estimation method in which the estimated parameters maximize the likelihood
that a sample comes from the population represented by the model.

missing value
a value in the SAS System indicating that no data are stored for the variable in
the current observation. By default, the SAS System prints a missing numeric
value as a single period (.) and a missing character value as a blank space.

Monte Carlo simulation
in econometrics, a method of calculating distributions for predicted values,
particularly for nonlinear models.

moving-average (MA) model
one of two fundamental types of probabilistic models for stationary time series
data in the Box-Jenkins approach. Moving-average models involve parameter
estimates associated with lagged error terms. The other fundamental type of model
is known as an autoregressive (AR) model.

multicollinearity
a correlation of an explanatory variable with a linear combination of other
explanatory variables.

multiple linear regression
an analysis where a response (or endogenous) variable is modeled as a linear
combination of two or more explanatory variables. The variables can be
continuous, discrete, or a combination.

multivariate time series
a vector consisting of two or more single time series variables.

normalized equations
model equations that have been solved for an endogenous variable on the left side,
and the right side contains exogenous variables, predetermined variables, and
possibly other endogenous variables.

observation
a row in a SAS data set. An observation is a collection of data values associated
with a single entity, such as a customer or state. Each observation contains one
data value for each variable.

ordinary least-squares (OLS) method
See least-squares method.

panel data
observations on two or more cross-sectional units over two or more time periods.
See also cross-sectional data and time series.

parameter

in statistics, a quantity, usually unknown, that occurs in expressions defining frequency distributions (for example, the mean, μ, and the variance, σ, define the normal distribution) or in models describing stochastic situations (for example, regression parameters such as the intercept and slope).

partial autocorrelation function (PACF) plot

the partial autocorrelation coefficients of order p plotted against p. The PACF coefficients are similar to the autocorrelation coefficients between two lags with the effect of all intervening lags removed.

predetermined variable

an exogenous variable or lagged endogenous variable.

predicted value

in a regression model, the value of the dependent variable calculated by evaluating the estimated regression equation for a specified set of values of the explanatory variables.

present value

a calculation of the value of an asset or liability, taking into account the timing of payments and the interest that can be earned. For example, the present value of one dollar one year from now is worth less than the present value of one dollar today.

PROC step

a group of SAS statements that call and execute a procedure, usually with a SAS data set as input.

p-value

the observed significance level of a statistical test, representing the probability of observing a sample outcome more contradictory to the null hypothesis than the observed sample result. The smaller the p-value, the stronger the evidence for rejecting the null hypothesis. See also significance level.

reduced-form method

a method of estimating the parameters of a system of equations. In this method, the system has been solved for the endogenous variables in terms of the exogenous or predetermined variables.

residual

the difference between the observed data value, y_i, and the predicted value, $\hat{y}_i$. The residual, denoted as e_i, is defined as

$$e_i = y_i - \hat{y}_i \quad .$$

SAS data set

descriptor information and its related data values organized as a table of observations and variables that can be processed by the SAS System.

SAS date constant
a string in the form '*ddMMMyy*'d or '*ddMMMyyyy*'d representing a date in a SAS statement. The string should be enclosed in quotes and followed by the character d (for example '06JUL91'd).

SAS program
a group of SAS statements that guide the SAS System through a process or series of processes.

SAS statement
a string of SAS keywords, SAS names, and special characters and operators ending in a semicolon that instructs the SAS System to perform an operation or gives information to the SAS System.

scatter plot
a two- or three-dimensional plot showing the joint variation of two (or three) variables from a group of observations. The coordinates of each point in the plot correspond to the data values for a single observation.

seemingly unrelated regressions (SUR) method
a least-squares estimation method used for regression equations that are unrelated except for correlated error terms. This method provides parameter estimates with smaller variances than OLS estimates of each equation in isolation.

significance level
the probability of rejecting a true null hypothesis. See also *p*-value.

simulation
in econometrics, a process of solving a model for the value of the endogenous variable when specific values of the exogenous variables are given. What-if simulation is useful in exploring the range of solution values when hypothetical sets of exogenous variable values are given.

simultaneous-equation bias
a bias in OLS estimation that occurs when endogenous variables are also used as explanatory variables in simultaneous-equation models, due to the correlation of the error terms with the endogenous variables.

simultaneous-equations model
a multiple-equation model that represents a system of jointly determined variables.

spatial correlation
correlation among cross-sectional units that typically represent geographic locations. Spatial correlation can be contemporaneous or across time periods.

spike
a statistically significant autocorrelation coefficient.

stationarity
a property of time series data where the mean and variance are constant over time.

tailing off

a pattern in a plot of autocorrelation coefficients (for example, ACF, IACF, or PACF) where the values gradually decrease after a given lag. This is also known as dying out or tapering off.

three-stage least-squares (3SLS) method

a least-squares method of estimating the parameters of a system of simultaneously determined equations as a whole rather than as a set of single equations in isolation.

time series

any univariate or multivariate data collected over time and arranged in temporal order. Time series can consist of discrete or continuous values.

title

in the SAS System, a heading printed at the top of each page of SAS output or of the SAS log.

transfer function

a model for a time series process involving explanatory time series and time series errors. See also general transfer function.

trend

a long-term consistent change in time series values.

turning point

the point at which a time series shifts from one trend to another.

two-stage least-squares (2SLS) method

a least-squares method of estimating the parameters of any identifiable equation in isolation from the other equations in a simultaneous-equations model.

unconditional least-squares (ULS) method

a least-squares method of estimation using only the available time series observations. The ULS method makes no assumption about the infinite past of a time series.

variance

a statistical measure of dispersion of data values. This measure is an average of the total squared dispersion between each observation and the sample mean. The variance is defined as

$$\text{var}(y) = \frac{1}{n-1} \sum (y_i - \bar{y})^2$$

what-if simulation

See simulation.

Yule-Walker (YW) estimation

a least-squares method of estimating the parameters of autoregressive models based on solving the Yule-Walker equations, which relate the autoregressive coefficients and the autocorrelations of a time series generated by an autoregressive process.

Index

Your Turn

If you have comments or suggestions about *SAS/ETS Software: Applications Guide 2, Version 6, First Edition: Econometric Modeling, Simulation, and Forecasting,* or SAS/ETS software, please send them to us on a photocopy of this page.

Please return the photocopy to the Publications Division (for comments about this book) or the Technical Support Division (for suggestions about the software) at SAS Institute Inc., SAS Campus Drive, Cary, NC 27513.